A NEW IDEA OF INDIA

Celebrating 35 Years of
Penguin Random House India

'This book discusses many contentious subjects concerning modern India, none more so than the vexing issue of state capacity and the lack thereof. Rajeev and Harsh's data-backed analysis calls for re-architecting and reorganizing all arms of the Indian State, including the judiciary, as a precondition for creating the India of its founders' dreams. Over the last decade, the authors have emerged as new, authentic voices of India's intellectual and policy scene. One may disagree with them on the issues, but no one interested in the India story can afford to ignore them'—Reuben Abraham, CEO, Artha Global

'This is an impressive book, exhibiting deep scholarship, that supports a nuanced and well-reasoned narrative. It fully deserves to be an integral part of a consensus-building dialogue about how India's millennia-old civilizational ethos, captured in the word Dharma, can be built into developing a modern State and global power based on individual rights and economic freedom. A must-read'—Mukul G. Asher, professorial fellow (retired), Lee Kuan Yew School of Public Policy, National University of Singapore

'India suffers from political scientists who slavishly recommend that India follow in the footsteps of their counterparts in the United States, and frame its policies around ethnic groups rather than around individuals and their fundamental rights. Rajeev and Harsh, two brilliant young authors, confront these political scientists head-on with a fabulous book'—Jagdish Bhagwati, University Professor of Economics, Law and International Relations, Columbia University

'In a welcome departure, Harsh and Rajeev discuss important issues about State, governance, and political and economic freedoms—and refrain from being politically correct. They call it as they see it—that is, the world, and poor individuals, will be considerably better off without the pseudo-trappings of socialist doctrine. From Nehru to Modi, from intellectuals to ordinary folks, Harsh and Rajeev have ploughed a productive and enlightening journey. For a modern unapologetic rendition of what freedom should be all about, their just war is against an encroaching State. And their rightful battle, spread throughout the text, is that the new idea of India is an old idea—a State that sees all citizens as equal individuals'—Surjit S. Bhalla, economist and public intellectual

'This is a unique book. It deals head-on with contemporary issues and provides solutions, rooting the hypotheses at the intersection of the country's social, economic and political history. This is a refreshing effort because the two young and articulate authors use a combination of *viveka* (patient structuring), *vidya* (subject matter expertise) and *vishwas* (open and direct arguments) to bolster their work. They explain why the superficial division of India and Bharat in the popular commentary glosses over our interconnectedness as products of an ancient, rich and common civilization. The authors use pegs of history to explore India and Indians, without any sense of the otherwise routine guilt and insecurity. The book talks about a confident India, which takes pride in its civilizational roots and yet embraces, indeed leads, the world in all its modernity. It celebrates a civilization and its people who equally embody the virtues represented by Lakshmi, Saraswati and Durga. Harsh and Rajeev have produced a fabulous work on the philosophy of Indian political economy and philosophy'—Aashish Chandorkar, author and public policy commentator

'Harsh and Rajeev are amongst the young voices of reason coming in to prominence in recent years. They have written a new comprehensive book covering economics, politics, philosophy, history and governance. They have taken a well-researched view in contra distinction to the Nehruvian-Socialist vision which dominated India for decades in foreign policy, domestic policy and social debates. India needs to debate, discuss and evolve new directions in each of these areas based on new emerging realities and experiences gathered since Independence. May the debates proceed on all sides based on such rigour and wisdom'—Ashish Chauhan, CEO, National Stock Exchange of India

'Since 2014, the demise of the old order based loosely on the Nehruvian consensus has been widely acknowledged. There is, however, less clarity over the emerging alternatives. In this provocative book, Rajeev and Harsh identify the contours of an emerging civilizational order based on a blend of traditional values and Indian modernity. This book will contribute immeasurably to the ongoing debate on India's quest for an identity based on cultural self-confidence and economic prosperity'—Swapan Dasgupta, public intellectual and former MP

'A New Idea of India is a wonderful book that makes the reader think about Bharat, that is, India. Drawing on our legacy and history, post-Independence, we should have put in place a construct of a new India. Instead, we imported and implanted, devising a system of government and citizen rights that was alien. Rajeev and Harsh have deconstructed and suggested the building blocks for a true idea of India'—Bibek Debroy, chairman, Prime Minister's Economic Advisory Council

'The Indian nation is an ancient project, crafted over thousands of years by its civilizational ethos. India is not a Westphalian State of recent vintage. What Rabindranath Tagore called the 'idea of India' is inseparable from the diverse and plural strands of India's civilizational history. This book, authored by Rajeev and Harsh, two of the brightest conservative minds in 'Rising India', explores the many aspects of a civilizational republic, offers fresh perspectives and prescribes policies to shape the trajectory of India's future'—Kanchan Gupta, senior advisor, Ministry of Information and Broadcasting, Government of India

'One troubling part about 'the idea of India' floated by modern-day Nehruvians is not so much the 'idea' part, but their insistence on the 'the' part, write Rajeev and Harsh. No idea can hold a monopoly forever, least of all one that defines a nation as complex and diverse as India. The book is a passionate plea for a systems upgrade in the way we reimagine India today. It calls for a break from 'the deniers of India's heritage' who view it as merely 'an accident of history and a collection of communities'. Beyond philosophical foundational ideas, the book also argues for a new model of running the country by bolstering State capacity, cutting State flab and reforming administrative talent. It is a valuable and instructive book for anyone who wishes to understand the new Indian zeitgeist with an open mind'—Shekhar Gupta, founder and editor-in-chief, ThePrint

'I am delighted to write about this insightful book titled *A New Idea of India: Individual Rights in a Civilizational State*. This book, written by two young intellectuals Harsh Madhusudan and Rajeev Mantri, presents a unique perspective of India whose civilizational resurgence is being scripted. I hope that the book is widely read by people who wish to gain an in-depth understanding of India's cultural ethos and the transformational policies that are shaping the trajectory of India's future'—Piyush Goyal, Minister of Commerce and Industry, Government of India

'Nothing can be more tyrannical intellectually than to claim that there can be only one Idea of India, an idea patented by India's 'secular' Nehruvian elite after 1947. In this hard-hitting and wonderful counter-narrative, the authors expand on the concept of a civilizational State. The new idea of India is surely a work in progress, but there is little doubt that an ancient civilization is morphing into a modern nation within the framework of a democratic republic, while remaining rooted in its own heritage. A must-read for anyone who is open to questioning the narrow Nehruvian idea of India'—R. Jagannathan, editorial director, *Swarajya* magazine

'*A New Idea of India* presents a vision for a twenty-first-century India as a civilizational republic, assimilating and harnessing its historical inheritance. Harsh and Rajeev outline how a post-colonial society with a history of subjugation can transform itself into a forward-looking nation state. This book makes the case for India's emergence as one of the world's great powers while being rooted in its rich heritage, rather than as a pale imitation of its colonial overlord'—Razib Khan, geneticist and writer

'There are two kinds of intellectuals in India: those who believe we are a country created in 1947 and those who believe we are civilizational State, with 1947 being only one marker in a long history. Through this pathbreaking book, Harsh and Rajeev, who belong to the second school of thought, articulate a comprehensive view of the individual and a State with a civilizational history and heritage as ours. For the first time, we have an integrated vision that spans social, cultural, political and economic issues from the viewpoint of a Dharmic Liberal, someone who seeks individual liberties while being bounded by the collective. Such a philosophy, of balancing individual freedom and collective responsibility can only be found in our civilizational ethos. This unique framework predates Western models and was unfortunately lost to us due to centuries of colonization. Deftly weaving various strands into one tapestry of thought, this book is a manifesto of sorts for the Dharmics. The authors make a compelling case for revisiting our roots, re-imbibing our civilizational thought and using this indigenous framework for building a State with the individual at its very core'—Hari Kiran, founder, Indic Academy

'Thoughtful, provocative but never disagreeable, Rajeev and Harsh have produced a book that interrogates the many facets of today's India. A republic that is increasingly civilizational and at once more modern; a society that unselfconsciously marries religious impulses and secular imperatives; a nation still seeking that optimal balance between group rights and individual justice; a national narrative that represents the subtle interplay of state, community and citizen, whether in social habits or economic approaches. This book offers its many themes a fair, honest treatment. And it leaves its reader the richer'—Ashok Malik, writer and commentator

'How can India transform itself from a civilization to a nation through a sovereign and democratic state? This well-researched, scholarly book with new ideas and riveting writing makes this a must-read for all'—Raghunath A. Mashelkar, president, Pune International Centre

'A must-read for the open-minded. For far too long have we lived with a received wisdom. There is little doubt that we need to revisit and look afresh at Indian public policy, governance and politics. Governance for the twenty-first century requires widespread and radical reform across the board. Harsh and Rajeev have presented one interesting and intriguing possibility for us to look at'—Rajiv Mehrishi, former Home Secretary (2015–2017) and Finance Secretary (2014–2015) of India

'When two youngsters with a passion for scholarship, penchant for argument and skilled in writing take on the shibboleths of the tried and tired old warriors on the idea of India, the end result makes for a compelling reading'—V. Anantha Nageswaran, chief economic advisor, Ministry of Finance, Government of India

'Many vested interests, over time, have tried to impose on us their Idea of India, as the definitive Idea of India, which we should accept. But the people of India and our founding fathers have always believed India to be a continuing civilization with a rich heritage, which is now transforming into a republic, governed by the rule of law. India is different from the republics of the West. This book, with deep arguments, explains how India is the only democratic republic globally with a very rich continuing civilization'—T.V. Mohandas Pai, chairman, Aarin Capital Partners

'In this brilliant book, Rajeev and Harsh, two of India's leading young authors, make a case for building an India around its citizens as individuals rather than social or religious groups. In doing so, they tackle many fallacies in the realms of economics, politics and religion. Those who agree with them will still feel enlightened by them; those who disagree will have their work cut out for them'—Arvind Panagariya, Jagdish Bhagwati Professor of Indian Political Economy, Columbia University

'In recent years, India has emerged as an international geopolitical actor, after decades of mostly looking inwards. This shift is aided by India's identity as a "civilizational republic" as well as our clear trajectory to becoming the world's third-largest economy and growing strategic capabilities. I'm hopeful that this book can foster a conversation to re-energize the best aspects of India's ancient civilizational ethos'—Baijayant Panda, national vice-president, BJP

'Move over Sunil Khilnani's *The Idea of India* (1999); Harsh Madhusudhan and Rajeev Mantri's *A New Idea of India* is here'—Makarand Paranjape, professor, School of Language, Literature and Culture Studies, Jawaharlal Nehru University

'The book *A New Idea of India* gives a great understanding of India's challenges and potential opportunities. It is clear that the authors, Rajeev and Harsh, have done a lot of research to produce this book. *A New Idea of India* is an excellent read, offering solutions on how some of India's difficult problems can be addressed'—S. Ramadorai, former CEO, Tata Consultancy Services

'A crash course on our modern yet ancient republic, disentangling its million contradictions from socialism to secularism, freedom to free markets, by two of India's brightest minds on the subjects of the economy and finance, this is an enthralling book not to be missed by laymen and academics alike. As unputdownable as India itself'—Anand Ranganathan, scientist and author

'How can an ancient civilization build a modern nation state? How can individual rights be protected in a society with strong identity politics? What is the role of the State and market in economic strategy? Harsh and Rajeev have taken an ambitious relook at some of the core themes of the Indian nation-building and governance project, redefining them for the twenty-first century from an original perspective. The result is a book that is insightful, provocative and lucid' —Niranjan Rajadhyaksha, CEO and senior fellow, Artha India

'A cohesive and comprehensive articulation of a confident, prosperous Indian future—anchored in its rich dharmic traditions yet reinterpreted through the lens of individual rights, freedom and choice. This book sets a reform agenda for India, finally renouncing the vestiges of the Nehruvian ice age and achieving prosperity through competitive markets regulated by an effective state'—Alan Rosling, co-founder, ECube Investment Advisors

'We don't have to be Western to be modern. This book is a wonderful contribution to what has for too long been a one-sided battle of ideas'—Manish Sabharwal, vice chairman, TeamLease Services

'What exactly is the idea of India? Two young writers have very dispassionately discussed this question in this book. The book effectively deals with the entire gamut of issues that are both, honestly but recklessly argued and more often than not, wantonly misunderstood. Rich with references, this book also tells us as to how insightful is this 'thinking generation-next' about India's past. It also argues that the conventional Left–Right binary is no more relevant in India and if we talk about fundamentalism, since the basics of Hindu philosophy are all about *Sarve Santu Niramaya*, there cannot be any negative Hindu fundamentalism.

What adds to the intellectual bliss that one derives while reading this book is its fresh approach towards individual rights. As the title may help one understand, the essential message of the book is that in India, individualism and collectivism go hand in hand—and the beauty is, one need not sacrifice either for the other'— Vinay Sahasrabuddhe, president, Indian Council for Cultural Relations

'At a time when individual, community and national identities are being recast and reshaped, Rajeev and Harsh urge us to evaluate sustainable pathways for freedom and prosperity through a civilizational prism. Eschewing tropes and labels, embracing empiricism and first principles, and responding to critics and criticism, *A New Idea of India* is a diligent and attentive effort by the authors to engage with a debate that is as ancient as it is contemporary'—Samir Saran, president, Observer Research Foundation

'This well-researched and eminently readable volume crafts a stimulating perspective on modern India—tracing its roots from an ancient civilization to a democratic republic. The authors have done a commendable job in forging a coherent philosophy of governance suitable for India'—Prabhat P. Shukla, member, Advisory Council, Vivekananda International Foundation

'Twenty-first-century India is decisively different from the India of the twentieth century. It is a nation with renewed cultural confidence bolstered by economic growth and technological success. India is set to play its due role at the global level in the years ahead. Why did it take four generations after Independence for this new New India to be realized? Could this have been attained earlier? What will a culturally, economically and militarily empowered India offer to the world? *A New Idea of India* offers a refreshing take on several issues of the past as well as a positive and progressive vision of the future on many contemporary topics and debates'— Kanwal Sibal, former Foreign Secretary (2002–2003), Ministry of External Affairs, Government of India

'A clear look into India's political, social and economic history unobstructed by decades of agenda-driven narratives that sought to muddy the waters of our civilizational truths'—Nirmala Sitharaman, Minister of Finance and Corporate Affairs, Government of India

'*A New Idea of India* stands out both as a manifesto and manual, addressing contentious debates as well as offering policy solutions with rigour and insight. As a new India takes wings, this book will serve as an anchor for citizens and policymakers alike'—Vikram Sood, former Secretary (2000–2003), Research and Analysis Wing, Cabinet Secretariat, Government of India

'A must-read for Western observers and lovers of real India, *A New Idea of India* will disrupt all stereotypes and prejudices nurtured by the Nehruvian socialist ideology. The authors convincingly demonstrate that individualism, entrepreneurship and liberal values are fully part of the Indian civilization. This is a work of intellectual decolonization which explains why India is now a rising global power'—Guy Sorman, public intellectual and author

'*A New Idea of India* is a distinguished work on India given the range and depth of topics it covers, from philosophy, history and politics to practical aspects of policymaking, governance and political economy. Rajeev and Harsh have wonderfully contextualized the ongoing socio-economic transformation of India. This book is a must-read for all interested in India's evolution and its role in the world'—K.V. Subramanian, executive director, International Monetary Fund and former chief economic advisor (2018–2021), Ministry of Finance, Government of India

'It has become fashionable to suggest that the Indian right has no intellectuals. Rajeev and Harsh set about disproving this in their well-researched and fluently written book. Though there is much I disagree with in both their premises and their conclusions, it is a pleasure to engage with their ideas and find much common ground in the defence of free speech, economic freedom, government reform and individual liberty'—Shashi Tharoor, MP and author

'There is no country like India. A pre-bronze age culture that is still alive (China is not a bronze-age culture and is relatively recent). A civilization, whose continuous memories reach back to the very beginning of the human journey. The only civilizational democratic republic in the world. And yet, India is not as well understood, even by modern Indians. A major lacuna has been the tendency of Indian establishment historians and sociologists to attempt to understand India by force-fitting Western theories. That will not work. We need theories that are rooted in our Indian experience but which draw from the wisdom of other cultures as well. Harsh and Rajeev are uniquely placed to do this. Deeply rooted in the soil of Mother India, and yet blessed with a self-assured understanding of other cultural theories, especially of the most dominant culture of the last few centuries: the West. We need our own understanding to build a new idea of India. An idea of India that is actually connected to the real India. An idea of India that works. A good first step to build that is to read this wonderful book by these two young intellectuals'—Amish Tripathi, director, The Nehru Centre, London, and author

'Is India a continuous civilization of thousands of years or is it simply a modern nation state born seven decades ago? The answer to this question will determine India's position on the global high table of governance and how India negotiates with the rest of the world. Harsh and Rajeev, both perceptive thinkers and well-regarded public intellectuals, have written a thought-provoking and insightful analysis of India as a civilizational state and answer many questions that have plagued India since Independence. This book is a must-read for those who are interested in India and India's place in the world'—Sunanda Vashisht, writer and political commentator

'We truly live in extraordinary times. The pandemic has exposed pre-existing problems in the global order and so many old certainties have died. What is the path ahead for India in this uncertain world? This book makes the compelling case for India as a civilizational State in the form of a constitutional republic. It eloquently argues that we must examine the idea of India from first principles, drawing upon our own ancient civilizational ethos and our Dharma. It is an important contribution to our national discourse'—Sridhar Vembu, CEO, Zoho Corp.

'The idea of economic freedom in India is neither alien nor imported. It is very much a part of ancient Indian ethos and Kautilyan thinking. From the Mahabharata to the *Arthashastra*, we see economic ideas consistent with the notion of individual freedom be it with the prescription of low taxation rates or with advocacy free flow of foreign trade. The finest of examples of this ancient Indian ethic of economic freedom rooted in individual rights are to be found in the Mahabharata when Narada converses with Yudhishthira on keeping taxes low and encouraging foreign trade, as well as when Markandeya explains to Yudhishthira why Rama chose to build a bridge to Lanka rather than use boats to transport his large army to avoid adversely impacting maritime trade and commerce.

A *New Idea of India* by Rajeev and Harsh is a landmark contribution in making the case for individual rights from an Indic perspective'—Shashi Shekhar Vempati, former CEO (2017–2022), Prasar Bharati

'*A New Idea of India* brings together a range of ideas and theses into a coherent whole, offering a fresh lens from which to view the rise of India. It is a must-read for all interested in understanding India, its history and its prospects'—Arvind Virmani, chairman, EGROW Foundation and former chief economic advisor (2007–2009), Ministry of Finance, Government of India

A NEW IDEA OF INDIA

THE CIVILIZATIONAL REPUBLIC

HARSH MADHUSUDAN
RAJEEV MANTRI

PENGUIN
VIKING

An imprint of Penguin Random House

VIKING

USA | Canada | UK | Ireland | Australia
New Zealand | India | South Africa | China | Singapore

Viking is part of the Penguin Random House group of companies
whose addresses can be found at global.penguinrandomhouse.com

Published by Penguin Random House India Pvt. Ltd
4th Floor, Capital Tower 1, MG Road,
Gurugram 122 002, Haryana, India

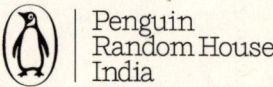
Penguin
Random House
India

First published by Westland Publications Pvt Ltd 2020
Published in Viking by Penguin Random House India 2023

Copyright © Harsh Madhusudan and Rajeev Mantri 2020

10 9 8 7 6 5 4 3 2

ISBN 9780670097876

Typeset in Adobe Garamond Pro by Manipal Technologies Limited, Manipal
Printed at Replika Press Pvt. Ltd, India

www.penguin.co.in

Harsh Madhusudan: To my brother, Dhruv

Rajeev Mantri: To Bauji and Maa

Contents

Abbreviations

BJP	Bharatiya Janata Party
CAA	Citizenship (Amendment) Act
CSIR	Council of Scientific and Industrial Research
CJI	Chief Justice of India
FDI	Foreign Direct Investment
GDP	Gross Domestic Product
GST	Goods and Services Tax
IAS	Indian Administrative Service
IBC	Insolvency and Bankruptcy Code
IFS	Indian Foreign Service
IIM	Indian Institute of Management
IIT	Indian Institute of Technology
IPS	Indian Police Service
IUML	Indian Union Muslim League
JAM	Jan Dhan–Aadhaar–Mobile
KCR	K. Chandrashekar Rao
LGBT	Lesbian, gay, bisexual, transgender
MP	Member of Parliament
MGNREGS	Mahatma Gandhi National Rural Employment Guarantee Scheme
NDA	National Democratic Alliance
OBC	Other Backward Classes
PIL	Public Interest Litigation
PMO	Prime Minister's Office
PPP	Public–Private Partnership

PSU	Public Sector Unit
RAW	Research & Analysis Wing
RSS	Rashtriya Swayamsevak Sangh
RTI	Right to Information
RTE	Right to Education
SC	Scheduled Caste
ST	Scheduled Tribe
TDP	Telugu Desam Party
TTD	Tirupati Tirumala Devasthanam
UIDAI	Unique Identification Authority of India
UPA	United Progressive Alliance
UPI	Unified Payment Interface
UPSC	Union Public Service Commission
WHO	World Health Organization
YSR	Y.S. Rajasekhara Reddy

Acknowledgements

This project has been an effort to contribute to India's political and policy debates. It is a collaborative work we were able to complete despite our respective professional responsibilities, our residing in different cities and time zones as well as personal and family commitments. Nonetheless, we could not have completed this without some friends and mentors. We would especially like to thank economist and writer Sanjeev Sanyal for his guidance and encouragement. We would also like to thank diplomat, author and director of the Nehru Centre, London, Amish Tripathi for many helpful discussions and encouragement. Also, a word of thanks to entrepreneur, writer and podcaster Kushal Mehra, who read an early draft and gave us valuable pointers and suggestions.

A special word of gratitude is due to the editors we have had over the years. We have jointly and individually published our articles in over a dozen Indian as well as international publications. Editors such as Niranjan Rajadhyaksha, R. Sukumar, Sundeep Khanna, R. Jagannathan, Dhirendra Tripathi, Sreemoy Talukdar, Aresh Shirali, Vandita Mishra, Prashant Jha, Pranav Sirohi, Lalita Panicker and Shekhar Gupta were very kind with their time and good offices.

Over the years, we have both had the good fortune of having friendships and interactions with eminent policy practitioners, researchers and analysts who have shared their wealth of knowledge and experience with us. Directly and indirectly, these individuals have somewhere shaped our thinking, though of course that does not mean that they align completely with our ideas. They include Dr Arvind Panagariya, Dr Raghunath A. Mashelkar, Dr V. Anantha Nageswaran,

Dr Samir Saran, Neelkanth Mishra, Shashi Shekhar Vempati, Dr Anand Ranganathan, Dr Ajit Ranade, Vijay Chada, Sunanda Vashisht, Prasanna Viswanathan, Amar Govindarajan, Smita Barooah, Akhilesh Mishra, Shefali Vaidya, Kartikeya Tanna, Anuj Gupta, Aashish Chandorkar, Rangesh Sridhar, Dr Aditya Kuvalekar, Rahul Bajoria, Utsav Mitra, Himanshu Sharma, Ankur Gulati, Rishav Kajaria, Chirag Jain, Abheek Bhattacharya, Abhinav Prakash, Karan Bhasin, Rahul Roushan and Swati Goel Sharma amongst others. We are grateful to Arihant Pawariya for providing us research and editorial support as we went about completing the manuscript.

Finally, we would like to thank our respective families for many weekends and weeknights which we spent away from them, working on producing this volume. Therefore, a big thank you (from Harsh) to Aankhi and (from Rajeev) to Sonam.

Rajeev Mantri, Kolkata   Harsh Madhusudan, Mumbai

10 October 2022

Preface to the Second Edition

The world has dramatically changed over the last two years and more since *A New Idea of India* was first published. A once-in-a-century pandemic which appears to have finally become endemic, followed by an ongoing war in Europe that has further exacerbated economic pressures throughout the world. The rise of communist China continues, but how it deals with the end of 'collective leadership' is an open question. Many stolid assumptions of economic and political orthodoxy now come attached with a question mark.

For India, this turbulence comes during an especially critical transition window from 'rule takers' in the global system to 'rule makers'. Such a change is never without hindrance or opposition, even by friends. The domestic opposition, having been overwhelmingly rejected by the voters twice in a row, has resorted to the final weapon—the street veto, as we saw during the protests against the Citizenship Amendment Act and the farm laws.

There have been death threats issued and even beheadings carried out against innocents for just saying something, or worse, supporting someone who has said something while conveniently painting the very victim as 'Nazi' or 'fascist'. The economy has managed to have lower inflation for almost a year now, as of the time of this writing, compared to some developed economies—an unprecedented achievement. The so-called West is throwing a bit of a fit as India refuses to blindly copy their Russia policy. While any invasion or aggression is wrong, the world cannot be completely oblivious to the energy and defence requirements of India and the Global South at large.

In this lightly updated edition, we try to capture the colour of these volatile times somewhat while still focusing on the big picture. For the first edition, we have received munificent feedback about the thesis and prescriptions presented. On the whole, the overwhelmingly positive response humbled us and we are very grateful for all the kind words. However, to dwell on that is not very useful beyond a point. It is better to discuss some of the more constructive criticism that came our way.

Let us start with the title and subtitle of the book itself because that in some ways encapsulates the criticism we received (and which benefited us) from across the political-ideological spectrum. While the 'A' in *A New Idea of India* was received well for its epistemic humility, the subtitle for the first edition *Individual Rights in a Civilisational State* was occasionally misunderstood. Some perceived it to be prioritizing rights over duties, but that was categorically not the intent. The juxtaposition was between *individual* and *group* rights and a core thesis of the book is our argument for the former as far as the default philosophy of State policy is concerned, both in social and economic spheres, with nuances and narrow exceptions being inevitable.

When it comes to society, duties need to be emphasized. Societal interaction is voluntary, while the State has coercive power and ideally, a monopoly on physical violence. At the level of family and community, most of us anyway focus on our rights, but we sometimes have to be reminded of duties. With respect to the State, if we do not discharge our duties, we are reminded of the penalties, but talking about rights in that context is a more thankless job.

Similarly, some found 'individual rights' to be an endorsement of 'individualism'. Again, this is a misreading for the same reason as above. While the individual, and not groups (especially religious groups), must remain the primary unit of State policy, it is obvious that the family is and should be the primary unit of societies—exceptions notwithstanding. The fragmentation of the family is directly correlated to adverse socio-economic outcomes in many parts of the world. However, that should not be seen as code to suppress individual dignity and choice when it comes to choosing a profession or life partner; it is by striking the correct balance that all societies including India can fulfil their potential.

Hence to be clearer and pithier, we have modified the subtitle from *Individual Rights in a Civilisational State* to *The Civilizational Republic*, while still fully agreeing with the earlier subtitle. We still insist that our idea of India is new and yet grounded in Dharma, and the phrase 'civilizational republic' also calls out the false binary between civilizational rootedness and republican modernity. India, that is Bharat, as our first chapter is titled—recognizes that India is an ancient civilization but also a young democratic republic where citizens are at least normatively treated by the State as free and equal individuals. The Indian civilizational republic is also the only such major entity in the world, hence the 'the' in the subtitle but not in the title.

The word 'civilization' can be used in different ways as we briefly discuss, but India is 'the' only meta-ethnic entity with a large population that is also a unified republic. China is not democratic and the so-called West consists of multiple states though a United States of Europe could be an interesting entity to analyse, if it fructifies, like the United States of America is today. While the idea of *ummah* inspires many within global Sunni Islam—there is no one State there either, assuming that one can create a modern mega-State based on the principles of proselytizing monotheism. African unity is still in its nascent stages and will have to overcome significant ethnic divides and meld ancient traditions. The same can broadly be said for Southeast Asia, which is smaller but further along the path of integration.

Additionally, the core ethos of a democracy or a democratic republic is not alien to India—indeed Prime Minister Narendra Modi himself has described Bharat as 'the mother of democracy', and that idea is as credible as (if not more) calling Ancient Greece the cradle of democracy. But it is true that while the Occident prioritized organization over theological flexibility, the Orient did the reverse—it under-invested in what we can today call a proto-modern State (the Chinese civilization being a partial and notable exception). State capacity and economic power constitute the exoskeleton that preserves and nurtures the soft power of Dharma which does not translate as 'religion', and where the State has under-invested in capacity—such as when it comes to providing important public goods, ensuring the security and defence of national territory and providing adequate welfare for those who need it—should make corrections.

On the policy and administrative side, the position we took on trade and industrial policy, in the context of a large and growing domestic market such as India—has perhaps been further proven right due to the severity of the pandemic, Chinese aggression against several countries including India, as well as the Russian invasion of Ukraine. Supply chains concentrated in one country, based solely on the principle of comparative economic advantage, are no longer seen as reliable no matter their durability thus far or their provenance. Similarly, the importance of digital public goods owned and operated by government or quasi-government institutions is now accepted as a better approach in contrast to network effect-driven private companies flourishing in areas like payments and online commerce. India is the global leader in this regard, by a significant distance. The recent proliferation of many such global-first public–private policy innovations (and at scale) is extremely encouraging, and represents a phase shift in the thinking of policy researchers and practitioners alike.

India remains around thirty times poorer than America in per capita income terms, and even after adjusting for the cost of living, the gap would be about an order of magnitude. We owe it to all Indians, and indeed all of humanity, to close this gap even as the economic–technological frontier itself moves ahead. This will and must happen in a holistic manner for politics, society, economics and, indeed, our natural environment are all intricately interconnected. A mind at relative peace about material issues will think more about social and spiritual ones, locally and globally. May Goddesses Lakshmi, Saraswati and Durga bless us and may Bharat rise as part of the larger rise of Dharma, leading the way in providing such a holistic model of governance, and setting an example for the rest of the world as regards the means and methods employed for achieving such success.

10 October 2022

Foreword to the First Edition

This book is an important step in India's intellectual evolution. For around six decades, our intellectual life has been dominated almost entirely by ideas and ideologies derived exclusively from various shades of the Left—the Nehruvian Left, the Marxist Left, the Lohiaist Left, the Lodhi Road Left and so on. Even those who were explicitly not from the Left, such as B.R. Ambedkar, were captured and deployed from a Left perspective. The dominance showed up in every aspect of life—political rhetoric, economic policy, geopolitical stance, literature, film plots, social policy, school and university curriculums, even urban master plans.

Till the mid-1950s, however, the country had enjoyed a much more genetically diverse intellectual landscape. The ideas of Veer Savarkar, B.R. Ambedkar, C. Rajagopalachari, S.P. Mookerjee, Sardar Patel and even M.K. Gandhi were alive in debate and discussion. The even older ideas of Swami Vivekananda, Sri Aurobindo, Rabindranath Tagore, Lala Lajpat Rai and Lokmanya Tilak were still part of the living milieu, and not merely as ritualistic quotes from past icons. All of this disappeared under the hegemonic dominance of the Left.

This complete dominance of the Left, backed by the patronage of a socialist State, meant that certain ideological assumptions became so hardwired into the economic, political, cultural and social discourse that it became India's default setting. This showed up, for instance, in a peculiar approach to secularism that perpetuated systematic biases against the country's Hindus. Similarly, the poor economic performance of the first three decades after Independence was dubbed by establishment economist Raj Krishna as the 'Hindu rate of growth'. The message was clear: it was not Nehruvian economic policies that had failed India, but it was India's cultural moorings that had failed Nehru.

Of course, this dominance did not go entirely unchallenged. A handful of writers like Sita Ram Goel and Arun Shourie did push back but their contributions, while important, were those of a critic. They did not really provide a clear alternative vision. Thus, when change came, it did not happen due to an endogenous change in the intellectual landscape within India but due to the turn of events: the fall of the Berlin Wall, the collapse of the USSR and a severe economic crisis in 1990–91. In other words, the process of economic liberalization that began in 1991 was due to the force of circumstances and not due to a change of mind. This explains why Indian reformers would remain apologetic about their policies over the next quarter century despite clear evidence that the changes were an improvement on socialist-era policies.

It is only in the last ten years that the intellectual landscape began to evolve with a revival of non-Left frameworks of thinking. It shows through, for instance, in the efforts by writers like Bibek Debroy and Swapan Dasgupta to reconnect with older traditions of Indian thought. The former undertook the mammoth task of translating India's ancient epics into English while the latter explored Indian thinkers of the late nineteenth and early twentieth centuries in his book *Awakening Bharat Mata*. It is in the context of this reawakening that we need to read this book by Rajeev and Harsh.

Through their regular newspaper columns, Harsh and Rajeev have already established a reputation as serious public intellectuals at a young age. However, this book takes their contribution to the next level. By combining a civilizational idea of India with a strong advocacy of individual rights, they present a coherent political and economic philosophy that has wide-ranging applications in policy and governance.

What I particularly liked is that it is fast paced and very readable for a book on such a heavy topic. It demolishes many of the assumptions and hypocrisies of the various shades of Left while systematically making its case for an alternative. Apart from drawing linkages to an older tradition of non-Left thinking in India, the book introduces the Indian reader to new strains of Western thought. This is not a small contribution because the long dominance of the Left has meant that Indians are only familiar with Western thinkers of a certain tilt—Karl Marx, Harold Laski, Noam Chomsky, Amartya Sen, J.K. Galbraith and so on. In contrast, Harsh and Rajeev introduce us to thinkers such as Karl Popper, Nassim Taleb and Thomas Sowell.

The Indian non-Left is made up of a wide range of ideas and world views: classical liberals, right-of-centre liberals, free marketeers, mercantilists, libertarians, Kautilyan realists, cultural traditionalists, Savarkarite modernizers, Ambedkarite constitutionalists, Swadeshi nativists and so on. So far, they had remained only on the fringes of Indian intellectual life, but writers like Rajeev and Harsh are bringing some of these ideas to the centre stage. However, in keeping with their liberal approach, they make no absolutist claims. The book is titled *A New Idea of India* and deliberately makes space for other formulations. Contrast this with claims of *the* idea of India made by an earlier generation of writers.

20 June 2020   Sanjeev Sanyal, economist and writer
New Delhi

Introduction

The Idea: The Civilizational Republic

Both of us have written dozens of columns over the last decade, many of them together, and we decided to publish them as a book. However, we soon realized that instead of an anthology, it would be better if we wrote a book with updated content and connected the issues. Once we decided to go down that path, it was back to burning the midnight oil, and much of the book became new content. At the same time, we modified and suitably referenced our own, pre-existing material.

The genesis of this book is traceable to a debate on political philosophy initiated in the *Mint* newspaper in 2013, triggered by a comment made by Brown University political scientist Ashutosh Varshney. Speaking to the *New York Times*, Varshney had observed that 'Modi's politics is against the idea of India . . . The idea of India has a clear place for minorities as minorities, not minorities simply as individuals'.[1] Responding to this formulation by Varshney, we wrote an op-ed in the *Mint* titled 'Let Us Debate the Idea of India'.[2]

This expanded into a multi-part debate carried out in the *Indian Express,* with both of us as well as now Finance Minister Nirmala Sitharaman on one side, and Ashutosh Varshney along with Javed Anand offering the counterview. Other writers and commentators, such as R. Jagannathan, then-editor of Firstpost, also joined in on this fundamental question of modern Indian political philosophy. This free and vigorous exchange of views and ideas stretching over two months was hailed by Newslaundry as 'the resurrection of the op-ed space'.[3]

The *manthan* continued for us, and we were invited to author the cover piece[4] for the inaugural issue of the relaunched *Swarajya* magazine, a journal founded by C. Rajagopalachari (fondly known as Rajaji), who had been hailed by Mahatma Gandhi[5] as 'the keeper of my conscience', and whose current editorial director is R. Jagannathan. We gave that piece the same title as of this book, and the relaunched *Swarajya's* first issue was released by Sri Sri Ravi Shankar. This book is, thus, the culmination of an intellectual journey and a friendship that has spanned over a decade.

A Note on Labels

In India, we routinely use terms such as Right and Left in our political discourse. As a convention and a shorthand, this is understandable. But the meaning ascribed to these terms in Western democracies is hardly transferable to India. In the West, the Right and Left have connotations of being 'conservative' and 'progressive' as far as social issues are concerned. On economic issues, Right and Left generally imply more support for liberal markets and intervention in the economy or redistribution, respectively.

In India, the label of the Right is primarily associated with the BJP, which in turn has its roots in the Sangh Parivar or the Hindutva movement. Just as 'Right' is loosely used for the BJP and its brand of politics, 'Left' is used for the politics that is oppositional to the BJP, principally led by the Congress party. The Left and 'centre-left' positions are roughly aligned with what is also described as 'Nehruvian'.

There are many shades of Hindutva, just like there are many shades of Zionism or Christian democrats or Islamism or even political Confucianism. The term 'Hindutva' itself was popularized around a century ago by Vinayak Damodar Savarkar, an independence movement leader and a prominent member of the Hindu Mahasabha. Savarkar's version need not be taken as gospel, but it is clear that his motivation was that of a modernizer and a builder of an incipient nation-state. In his writings, Savarkar identified seven shackles that were holding back Hindu society, and sought to break them to empower and transform Hindu society:[6] prohibition of touch (*sparshbandi*) of certain castes, prohibition of inter-dining (*rotibandi*) with certain castes, prohibition of inter-caste marriages (*betibandi*), prohibition of pursuing certain occupations (*vyavasayabandi*), prohibition of seafaring (*sindhubandi*), prohibition of rites sanctioned by the Vedas (*vedoktabandi*) and prohibition of reconversion (*shuddhibandi*) to the Hindu fold. Savarkar practised what he advocated when he was released from jail (though largely confined to Ratnagiri from 1924 to 1937), inviting the censure of conservative Hindus.[7]

By some accounts an atheist, Savarkar wanted to tame the centrifugal forces of region and language (and the stratifying forces of caste) with that of a unifying identity of Hindutva, which for him was more than Hinduism and included other Indic religions. In the process, he no doubt 'othered' the two proselytizing monotheistic faiths of Islam and Christianity. Given India's medieval as well as modern colonial history and the subsequent religion-based partition of the subcontinent, it cannot be said that there was no truth in his conceptualization. Moreover, Savarkar was explicit that all Indian citizens irrespective of religion were to be treated equally by the State.[8] This facet of history about Savarkar and 'the Right' is neither widely known nor appreciated, and is germane to our conceptualization of the new India as one with 'individual rights in a civilizational state'.

This book talks about civilization, nation, State and government too. The word 'State'—used in this book with a capitalized first letter to differentiate it from the sense of 'state' to indicate a province in the Indian system—encapsulates the collection of institutions tasked with exercising the will of the people of India and governing the Republic, with the Constitution of India as its lighthouse and charter. The executive, which is responsible for day-to-day governance and typically referred to as 'the government', is one organ of the State, with the others being the legislature and the judiciary.

In his 1882 lecture titled 'What Is a Nation?', French philosopher Ernest Renan had said that 'race, language, [community] interests, religious affinity, geography, military necessities' do not suffice to create the basis for a nation'. Renan observed:[9]

A nation is a soul, a spiritual principle. Two things which, properly speaking, are really one and the same constitute this soul, this spiritual principle. One is the past, the other is the present. One is the possession in common of a rich legacy of memories; the other is present consent, the desire to live together, the desire to continue to invest in the heritage that we have jointly received. *Messieurs*, man does not improvise. The nation, like the individual, is the outcome of a long past of efforts, sacrifices, and devotions.

A civilization is a broader entity than a nation. In fact, a civilization can be considered to be the broadest coherent human grouping short of all of humanity itself. The United States and France are clearly distinct nations, but they belong to the same civilization, namely, 'the West'. It is true that a civilization can be an amorphous entity and that its borders can be subjective. This of course excludes the universalist meaning of 'civilization' where it refers to all of humanity, or all of humanity minus the 'barbarians' however defined.[10]

For example, with the salience of Protestant–Catholic differences decreasing (the Irish island being one of the last holdouts), scholars such as Samuel Huntington ignored that fault line but counted Orthodox Russia, the successor State of the Soviet Union, as a distinctive civilization.[11] Similarly, can Nepal be counted as part of Indian or Hindu civilization despite occasional tensions, but would Buddhist Bhutan or Sri Lanka not be included despite the concept of Dharma including both Hinduism and Buddhism? There are no easy answers. Nonetheless, what is now India[12] has been seen as one civilization by many scholars and writers.[13]

And as we shall argue, India is a civilization which is transforming into a 'nation' through the instrumentality of a sovereign, democratic State.

The Sanskrit word 'Dharma' is difficult to translate into the English language—indeed, as the great Sanskrit scholar Pandurang Vaman Kane had opined, 'Dharma is one of those Sanskrit words that defy all attempts at an exact rendering in English or any other tongue.'[14] The meaning of Dharma is the subject of many scholarly works published over the centuries. In his masterwork *History of the Dharma Shastra*, Kane expounded thus:

> The writers on Dharma Shastra meant by 'Dharma' not a creed or religion but a mode of life or a code of conduct, which regulated a person's work and activities as a member of society and as an individual and was intended to bring about the gradual development of a person and to enable him to reach what was deemed to be the goal of human existence.[15]

Kane then goes on to cite Maharishi Devala, who had said 'Dharma is that one should not do to others what would be disliked by one's self.' In the context of national life and foreign policy, Dharma can thus be taken to mean 'good' conduct in the service of uncompromising national interest. Drawing a contrast between Dharma and religion, the scholar and philosopher Ram Swarup had observed:[16]

> The concept of Dharma is psychological and spiritual; that of religion credal and ideological. Therefore, the concept of multiple paths based on different psychological types and different starting points is very different in spirit from the current doctrine of equality and unity of all religions.

About the Book's Title, Cover and Outline

When the Constituent Committee finished the task of drafting the Republic of India's Constitution, India's leadership at the time—composed chiefly of figures from the Congress party—tasked the renowned Indian artist Nandalal Bose with illustrating the Constitution. Bose was a protégé of Abanindranath Tagore, a founder of the Bengal school of art and who was among the first to use *swadeshi* symbols in his iconography. Tagore's most famous work is *Bharat Mata*, completed in 1905 during the Swadeshi movement. The choice of Bose to lead the historic project says a lot about the leanings and philosophical orientation of newly independent India's political leadership. The front cover of the first edition of this book, featuring Ram, Sita and Lakshman from the Ramayana, is an illustration inspired from the fundamental rights section of the original Constitution of India whose artistic production was overseen by Bose. The front cover of this new, updated edition is inspired by the directive principles section of the same original illustrated Constitution, featuring a scene of Shri Krishna from the Mahabharata. The title of the first chapter, 'India, that is Bharat' is also taken from Article 1 (1) of the Constitution of India.

Renowned jurist Nani Palkhivala had written in 1974:[17]

> Freedom cannot be inherited in the blood stream. Each generation will have to defend it and fight for it—then alone will it be passed on to the next. Liberty can die surely, though not as swiftly, in a democracy as it does in a totalitarian state. Only the husk of democracy—the one man, one vote rite—may survive after freedom has perished.

This book makes the case that a 'civilizational republic'—a democratic polity based on the rule of law that in turn is rooted in India's millennia-old pluralistic ethos—is the surest guarantee of securing the freedom that Palkhivala held so dear. India is the only major civilizational republic in the world today. China is often described as a civilizational state,[18] and correctly so since it is not a democratic republic.

Chapter 1 lays the groundwork for the foundational philosophy of this book, that India is a civilization and not just a post-colonial entity. Chapter 2 describes how this civilization is transforming into a nation through the instrumentality of a democratic republic. In chapters 3 and 4, we look at individual rights within this framework, focusing on politics and economics, respectively. And finally, in Chapter 5, we further explore why this civilization needs a strong and honest, but limited, State. Such a State, can harness the size of India for numerous benefits, while minimizing the inefficiencies inherent in gigantism by focusing on federalism, markets and an explicit doctrine that recognizes the importance of both unity and diversity.

1

India, That Is Bharat

Who knows, and who can say
Whence it all came, and how creation happened?
The gods themselves are later than creation,
So who knows truly whence it has arisen?
Whence all creation had its origin,
He, whether he fashioned it or whether he did not,
He, who surveys it all from highest heaven,
He knows—or maybe even he does not know.

—'The Nasadiya Sukta' (Hymn of Creation)[1]
in the *Rig Veda* (10:129)

Eschewing certitude, embracing scepticism

The Vedas, the foundational texts of Dharma, created some three to five millennia ago, are filled with such scepticism[2] that would gladden the heart of philosophers and physicists even today. The great physicist Erwin Schrödinger, writing in 1944, observed that the Upanishadic concept that *atman* equals *brahman* or that 'the personal self equals the omnipresent, all-comprehending eternal self' was 'far from being blasphemous' and in fact represented 'the quintessence of deepest insight into the happenings of the world' in Indian philosophy.[3]

It is because of the sceptical tradition within the metaphysical aspects of what is now called Hinduism that even atheists and agnostics can be a part of the fold. Like other religions, hypocrisies and hierarchies exist in Indic religions as well, but they are primarily sociological—related to gender and caste—and less theological. This is not so because there are no 'holy texts' or doctrines, but because those texts and doctrines can be selectively followed. As Nassim Taleb expounded on the meaning of the word 'religion' in his book *Skin in The Game*:[4]

> For most Protestants, religion is belief with neither aesthetics, pomp nor law. Further East, for Buddhists, Shintoists and Hindus, religion is practical and spiritual philosophy, with a code of ethics (and for some, cosmogony). So when Hindus talk about the Hindu 'religion' they don't mean the same thing to a Pakistani as it would to a Hindu, and certainly something different for a Persian.

Scepticism is an indispensable foundation of what is called 'science'. The fundamental premise of scientific inquiry is that an unknown truth can be learnt through iterative experimentation and exploration. A school of thought that is dogmatic cannot profess to be scientific. As physicist Richard Feynman said, science is the belief in the ignorance of the experts.[5] Applied to the spiritual sphere, a 'scientific' religion would be one that can accept that its claims are wrong. Philosopher of science Karl Popper said much the same when he posited that for a theory to be scientific, it should be falsifiable. Popper also critiqued the historicist and teleological underpinnings of the Marxist and Hegelian world-views—that there were inexorable laws of historical destiny, all leading towards definite ends. In simple terms, the Indic world view is more cyclical than linear, and is not entirely deterministic.

Similarly, an economic system that imbibes such scepticism cannot, by definition, be centrally planned, for that would require an omniscient, omnipotent body to allocate resources. In this sense, socialism is analogous with obscurantist faith, while liberal capitalism is analogous to a 'scientific' religion.

Also, scepticism—and the intellectual humility that it engenders—is required to cultivate genuine tolerance in society, for it allows fellow human beings to accept mutual differences. This tolerance is also mediated through the mechanism of the social contract in the modern era of democratic nation-states, where the views of one person or group cannot be forced on fellow citizens.

Social diversity, too, is the product of scepticism. Only if individuals are allowed to build upon, that is, add and subtract from traditions and practices, without being required to dogmatically treat them as immutable rules, can diversity emerge within a group. This diversity is apparent and much celebrated in the land that is India, where the same festivals and rituals are celebrated in different ways by different communities and in different regions. Had the Hindu tradition been a dogmatic one, there would have been uniformity, not heterogeneity, in sociocultural life. Hinduism will never have a Pope, or a Vatican, or a final prophet, or a single unalterable holy text, or the one 'true God'. That is why the opposition from some groups to multiple interpretations of, say, the Ramayana, is very unfortunate.

India under Jawaharlal Nehru and his successors decided to pursue a development model partially inspired by Soviet Russia, with the State having a gargantuan participation in the economy. Under his leadership, Indian democracy came to be based upon the State brokering and negotiating settlements between groups of religions, castes and languages rather than guaranteeing equal rights and freedom to individual citizens.

Inevitably, the State favoured some groups over others, anointing itself as the referee. In both economic and social spheres, the Indian State exuded a certitude that chafed against the millennia-old pluralist and sceptical ethos of the society it sought to govern. But the governance philosophy was not limited only to certitude; it was selectively condescending as well. While Hindu personal laws were modernized, Muslim laws were not. Perhaps Nehru wanted to cultivate a committed voter base to support him as he pushed through his programme of leftist economics. As Stockholm University political scientist Ishtiaq Ahmed wrote:

The reason that Muslims were granted a separate set of personal rights was that the Jamiyat-Ulema-e-Hind, which supported the Congress against the Muslim League, had agreed to do so only if the Indian leadership pledged that the State would not interfere in Muslim personal law. Perhaps Nehru should have ridden roughshod over such a pledge to the ulema, but he kept his word . . .[6]

While he was deservedly criticized for appeasing Islamism, Nehru at least understood why India was united. In 1961, for example, addressing the All India Congress Committee session, Nehru had said:[7]

India has for ages past, been a country of pilgrimages. All over the country, you find these ancient places, from Badrinath, Kedarnath and Amarnath, high up in the snowy Himalayas down to Kanyakumari in the south, and throughout the ages people have gone on pilgrimage from north to south and south to north, and mixed with each other. For, from the very beginning of history, the people of India always thought of themselves as a people belonging to one great country. What has drawn our people from the south to the north and from north to the south in these great pilgrimages? What is the common thought that has made them travel from one region to another? It is the feeling of one country and one culture and this feeling has bound us together. This sense of a common urge and a common thought came to us hundreds, may be thousands of years ago. Our ancient books have said that the land of Bharat is the land stretching from the Himalayas in the north to the Southern seas. This conception of Bharat as one great land which the people considered a holy land has come down the ages and has joined us together, even though we have had different political kingdoms and even though we may speak different languages. This silken bond still keeps us together in many ways. Throughout these thousands of years, this land has been ours, ours in mind, ours in heart, and ours in spiritual heritage.

But Nehru's philosophy of centralization and certitude, carried forward with increasing intensity by the successor-members of

Nehru–Gandhi dynasty, had disastrous consequences for economic development and communal harmony. Today, the fact that the Nehruvians are hard pressed to even acknowledge the civilizational unity that seemed obvious to Nehru himself shows how far they have travelled from their roots. In the quest to brand themselves 'secular', and guided by narrow electoral interests, they have transformed into deniers of India's heritage. As the writer and former MP Swapan Dasgupta noted in his book *Awakening Bharat Mata*:[8]

> Till the lifetime of Indira Gandhi at least, the Congress—despite many secular adjustments—broadly represented the mainstream of Indian nationalism. However, as it progressively vacated the old ground and simultaneously lost its overwhelming political dominance, traditional Indian nationalism increasingly came to be identified with forces that had hitherto been on the fringes. The slow transition of *Vande Mataram* and Bharat Mata from being a mainstay of the Congress to being identified with the BJP epitomized the shift.

The shifting of the political landscape is evidenced by one of the early parliamentary debates on the issue of Article 370, held on 11 September 1964. Prakash Vir Shastri, an independent MP from Bijnor, introduced a private member's bill to abrogate Article 370.[9] In the ensuing four-hour debate, all seven Congress MPs who participated supported the abrogation. Even Sarjoo Pandey, a Communist Party of India MP from Rasra, supported the abrogation. Kengal Hanumanthaiah, the Congress MP from Bangalore City, said:[10]

> Not merely Members of Parliament from Kashmir, but irrespective of parties, from the extreme right to the extreme left of this House as it is constituted, we are all of one opinion that this Bill should be made into law. To go against it or to say anything against this unanimous opinion of this House is to disown constitutional responsibility in a convenient manner.

As the Congress party has been 'vacating the old ground', to use Dasgupta's words, the confusion between the State and society[11] has become more pronounced, ensconcing itself as the fundamental flaw of modern India's secularism as practised today. Nowhere is this confusion more evident than in the way secularism and communalism are routinely hailed as antonyms. The opposite of secularism is not communalism but theocracy, for secularism is a feature of the State; nation-states can be secular or theocratic. Communalism is a feature of societies. In a free, democratic and liberal country, when people who share the same ideas build coalitions and alliances, it is not only acceptable but sometimes even welcome. It is precisely through the creation of non-birth based, idea-driven networks and communities that ideational synthesis happens and social mobility accelerates.

High social capital catalyses networks of trust and cooperation that helps to bind together a society in myriad ways and thus encourages intercourse rather than creating distinctions, to use English–American political philosopher Thomas Paine's words. It is important to recognize that the 'type' of social capital is as important as its 'quantum', but the former is more a product of State policy than the latter. The degree of economic freedom determines the type of social capital; greater the economic freedom, the more likely it is that communities not tied exclusively to social, religious, linguistic or ethnic identity will emerge.

While it is true that State and society cannot be entirely divorced, the State has to be seen as a separate conceptual entity. For example, having an effective judiciary (or more generally, robust State capacity) means that social capital accumulation and business intercourse are more likely to happen across barriers of identity simply because contracts are likely to be respected, and hence people need not rely on social censure as a deterrence.

More broadly, this confusion between State and society rears its head when India is spoken of as a 'Hindu nation'. Whenever any politician, intellectual or public figure says so, there is much outrage and heartburn among a section of the intelligentsia, who wail that secularism is in danger. But these people fail to distinguish between nation and State. Because of India's civilizational ethos, demography and history, India is already largely a dharmic nation and society. However, it follows from the scepticism innate to India's philosophical tradition that the concept of a theocratic Hindu State is illogical. As former Deputy Prime Minister of India Lal Krishna Advani said, 'India is a Hindu rashtra, but can never become a theocratic state . . . a Hindu rashtra and a secular state are virtually synonymous.'[12]

Contradictions of an Indian renaissance

But the intelligentsia's fears are not entirely unfounded. One section of the Hindu nationalist spectrum is straying from the tradition that espouses scepticism and openness, under the garb of protecting Nehru's 'land of Bharat' from foreigners. In a delicious irony, while purportedly protecting the land from alien faiths, the self-anointed protectors have come under the influence of foreigners in their interpretation and practice of the Hindu tradition, aping the antediluvian diktats—which disregard scepticism and deny openness—of the same traditions from which they aim to defend Hinduism. As the philosopher Friedrich Nietzsche had observed,[13] those who fight with monsters should be careful lest they become monsters.

How else does one explain a so-called Hindu faction, however fringe, which beats up defenceless young couples, yet subscribes to the same broad Hindu tradition that worships Krishna, famed for his relationship with Radha, to whom he was never married? How does one reconcile a self-styled Hindu faction which attacks women for drinking alcohol, when Hindu festivals are celebrated by men and women alike with the consumption of a drink made from the cannabis plant, and when the potent *datura* is offered in prayer to Shiva? These groups seem to have internalized the anti-blasphemy attitudes of medieval Turks, and the prudery of Victorian England.

Marred by such confusions from all sides, the Indian State has not been in consonance with Indian society's highest metaphysical impulses. Given that the Nehruvian experiment has largely failed to create a prosperous and harmonious India, there is a slow but sure, if as yet unexpressed, realization that our idea of ourselves should evolve into seeing individual citizens as the unit of State policy. It is this philosophy—where salvation is ultimately individual and individualized—that is congruent with Indian society's heritage and best represents the possibility for India to emerge as a progressive, prosperous and strong nation for all its billion-plus citizens.

India's political 'Right', with the Bharatiya Janata Party (BJP) as its vehicle, has ensconced itself on the national centre stage only since the 1990s. Under Prime Minister Atal Bihari Vajpayee, the government embraced free-market reforms despite a powerful faction committed to anti-liberal economic policies, thanks largely to Vajpayee's visionary leadership. This push for market reforms created a new constituency committed to economic and personal freedom. Competitive capitalism, as opposed to crony socialism, is gradually dissolving the bonds of caste and community, as has been documented by intellectuals like Chandra Bhan Prasad.[14]

Cut to 2014—a 'low caste' leader of an ostensibly obscurantist party which won a simple majority in the Lok Sabha (and again in 2019), eloquently speaking about 'development for all', is something to be celebrated by even cynics. When it comes to the normative underpinnings of our public discourse, the orthodox have been defeated decisively, yet not completely. But this is a defeat of orthodoxy and not tradition per se, for it is the tradition of our civilization to be flexible. Through the ages, Indian tradition has been shaped by modernizing influences of the time. Hence, the adjective sanatana (or eternal) for Dharma.

The Indian Renaissance—the ground for which was cleared by the Marathas and Rajputs, amongst others—was initiated by its encounter with British imperialism. While India was humiliated, looted and impoverished like all colonies were, it got back a window to its ancient past—a culture that had influenced the Greeks with its scepticism, and to which the Europeans looked up for their own Enlightenment. The process of reform began in Bengal, where the Hindu elite finessed the acceptance of modernity and Western education while rejecting the Christianity of colonial missionaries. The deist and relatively egalitarian, views of Raja Ram Mohan Roy and fellow travellers in the

Brahmo Samaj were opposed by the orthodox Dharma Sabha led by Radhakanta Deb. Today, an increasing number of educated Indians are closer to Roy's ideas on rationalism and equality even as they confidently continue to worship their gods and have even resurrected the importance of *murtis* as symbols of piety, diversity and tradition.

A narrative for New India

There are four levels of political consciousness, in increasing order of depth—party politics, public policy, philosophical and psychological.

At the level of party politics, non-members including self-styled intellectuals—be they motivated more by economic or social concerns—should rise above partisan bickering and focus more on promoting ideas. Electoral politics should be left to the cadre, and that too is a critical role in any democracy.

At the public-policy level, there is room for substantial give and take. Everybody should agree to concede a little and drive change on connected issues such as how to deal with illegal economic migrants and religion-based personal laws: there is ample room for 'logrolling'. India has welfare schemes like Right to Food, which negate choice and competition and instead force distribution of food to the needy through a government-run body in a centralized, top-down model rife with waste and corruption.

In exchange for making these welfare programmes more efficient, more tax rupees can be spent for these normative objectives. On the administrative side, besides a Byzantine bureaucratic structure, India also has an enormous dearth of state capacity, with a woefully inadequate number of judges and police officers. This inadequacy seriously undermines rule of law and justice delivery. Contracts are often not worth the paper they are written on, which drives Indians to work only with people they already know and trust, restricting social mobility and concentrating certain types of social capital within specific communities.

At the philosophical level, the big question is what is it that India is aiming for? It is difficult to make the case that the India we have today lives up to the dreams and aspirations of the founders of the Indian Republic. Is there a Dharmic version of utopia or Ram Rajya besides rhetorical abstractions? If not, what is the point of communal cold wars in the face of changing religious demographics? India needs a different narrative. That is, the State must not discriminate based on identity. Also, 'swaraj' or democratic accountability at all levels is different from 'swatantra' which roughly translates to national sovereignty. Individual freedom and local self-rule are very different from independence.

Finally, at the psychological level, the real debate is between self-belief and a deep-seated inferiority complex. After more than seven decades of Independence, why are we as a nation still occasionally scarred? Is it due to the centuries of foreign rule experienced by our society? Despite all the bluster, do most Indians believe that India can take on the world? India will soon be the largest section of humanity but do we really belong at the high table, and what do we hope to contribute?

Do we say 'please' and 'thank you' to foreigners in the same way as we do to fellow Indians? Or is there something other than politeness involved? On average, is an Indian as important as a non-Indian? The answer varies and can often be uncomfortable. But this can be seen simply as human nature, when the underdog is excessively deferential. As a counterexample, former Australian cricket captain Michael Clarke went on record to say that Australia was 'too scared' to sledge Virat Kohli's India because of lucrative Indian Premier League deals and India's financial clout in the cricket world. Clarke asserted that 'Australian cricket, and probably every other team . . . actually sucked up to India.'[15]

Yet India's economy should boom not so that Indians can feel superior, but because it is reasonable to want the average Indian to be at least as well off as the average human. But for that India will have to make prosperity—and not merely the removal of poverty— its overarching aim. Indian society will be free and open when it focuses on self-improvement as our mantra. Indians should take responsibility for their destiny, channelize energies towards preparing to win, and as Krishna had advised Arjuna, do so without worrying about the outcome.

The pitfalls of Nehruvianism

To have a nation but not a State is the equivalent of having a body without a backbone—the society or culture looking to survive or thrive has simply no protection. The Jewish people realized this the hard and tragic way in twentieth-century Europe. Around six million Jews,[16] that is, more than a third of the global Jewish population, were massacred by Adolf Hitler's armies in just a few years. According to Bangladeshi estimates, three million Bengalis[17]—Hindus and Muslims—were killed by the Pakistani army in 1971. By some estimates, at least a few million Chinese civilians were killed by the imperialist Japanese forces during the Second World War.[18]

During the Partition, most deaths occurred in undivided Punjab—perhaps more than a million were killed. Around two and a half million Bengalis died during the famine of 1943—this tragedy could have been averted by the British[19] who had prospered by exploiting Bengal more than any province in India for two centuries, but the Indians were an enslaved people, neither white nor Christian (much less Anglo-Saxon Protestants from the colonial metropole). Through half a millennium of Central Asian Muslim rule in the Indo–Gangetic plains, millions of further deaths happened with famine, violence and discrimination being key interlinked reasons.[20]

After large parts of India were ruled by Turkic–Muslims and European–Christians for more than seven centuries, we won independence in 1947 symbolically breaking with not just Great Britain, the colonial power, but also with the claimant of the Mughal legacy, the Islamic nation of Pakistan. Even the liberation of Bangladesh in 1971 led to no demands in the Indian state of West Bengal or in what was East Bengal, now becoming a nation of its own, for any reunification with India or even for the creation of a Greater Bengal.

For the first half century after India's independence the dominant national narrative has been called 'Nehruvian'—not a surprise since Jawaharlal Nehru, his daughter and grandson (Indira and Rajiv Gandhi respectively) and then his granddaughter-in-law Sonia Gandhi have, directly or indirectly, ruled India for around five out of the seven decades since the British were ejected from India. Their idea of India—as defined by the court poets and philosophers of the Nehru-Gandhi dynasty—fundamentally viewed India as a post-colonial state with multiple groups that had to be reconciled in a collective pursuit of peace and progress. In this world view, Nehru was 'civilizing a savage world', to borrow from the title of a hagiographic volume on India's first prime minister by the writer (and Nehru's niece) Nayantara Sahgal.[21]

The political reconciliation of social diversity was attempted through democratic consociationalism—a long, difficult-to-pronounce word that essentially means power-sharing between identitarian groups. A subset of consociationalism is confessionalism, where the primary power-sharing is between religious groups, and this more than anything else defines the Nehruvian idea of India today. The other Nehruvian ideas of non-alignment in foreign policy and centralized socialism have become less relevant already, though we will visit those ideas in some detail in this book.

This Nehruvian world view, which again is not necessarily the view of the flesh-and-bone Nehru himself, saw India primarily as an accident of history and a collection of communities. It did not see Indians as individual citizens—no doubt this reflected the overwhelming ground reality of the early years of Nehru's premiership, but that later got calcified into a convenient political and ideological doctrine. But democracy in a universal adult franchise sense was also ostensibly foreign to India, just as it was globally. In a much broader sense, however, a 'democratic' culture has perhaps deeper but often invisible roots in Indian civilization. As French writer Guy Sorman observed in *The Genius of India*:

> The British may have given India parliamentarism of a certain kind but the democratic spirit was alive long before colonization. [Alexis de] Tocqueville had rightly sensed this. The distinction between the form and spirit of democracy makes it clear why other former British colonies—Burma, Iraq and those in Africa—have never taken to democracy. They never had a democratic culture and so parliamentary structures are mere facades to conceal dictatorships.

On the other hand the democratic ethos is firmly ingrained in the Indian culture . . . Let us assume that monotheism and the centralized church give rise to totalitarianism examples of which can be found in the history of Europe and present-day Islam; it would then appear that Indians are completely immune to the totalitarian temptation. Not only have the great religions like Jainism, Hinduism, Islam, Sikhism and Christianity coexisted for centuries, but each one in turn has been divided and subdivided into an infinite number of allegiances and communities. The dominant cult, Hinduism, which has several million gods and goddesses, is hardly likely to predispose the mind to political absolutism.[22]

Not everything about Nehruvian policies was incorrect, of course. Linguistic reorganization of states, for example, allowed for more coherent sub-sovereign entities without in any way sacrificing the unity of the nation or the idea of laws applying to all citizens equally though even this reorganization had its critics. Even caste and tribal quotas as an affirmative action programme were not problematic for this framework given the long history of marginalization and discrimination against Dalits and some tribal communities. Such quotas are based on birth and as long as one agrees conceptually that they should have a sunset clause, they are legitimate. The expansion of quotas for other backward classes (OBC) is more contentious, but again the above logic holds, though in a diluted form.

However, religion unlike caste can be changed and hence cannot be deemed to be a criterion for affirmative action in a secular State. It should be noted that many Muslims and Christians are already included in the OBC and ST reservation categories—they access reservation benefits based not on religion, but on other socio-economic criteria. Moreover, the ostensibly disadvantaged minority religions are often aggressively proselytizing whereas Hinduism—or other Dharmic systems such as Buddhism, Jainism and Sikhism—are not. Also, speech policing by the State when it comes to hurting religious feelings means that non-proselytizing religions have a further disadvantage. Hence any such policy legitmising blasphemy can in effect be an indirect incentive for conversion, especially with two minority Indian religious groups being the largest two religions globally.

Despite the carving out of Pakistan (and what is now Bangladesh) in the name of political Islam, and the secessionist insurgency seen in Kashmir due to similar motivations, so-called secular India did not adopt common personal laws. This happened even though Nehru changed, and rightly so, the Hindu personal laws by passing the Hindu code bills in 1955–1956. While the Hindu laws were made progressive, Muslim laws were left untouched.

The right thing would have been to have the same laws from the beginning as is the case in America or Australia, but even today something as classically liberal as this issue is painted as bigoted by many political parties as well as sections of the Indian intelligentsia. Just to take one example, an Indian Muslim man can have four wives, while a Hindu man cannot (and no woman can have multiple husbands). Whether this provision is used frequently or not is hardly the point; soft or symbolic secessionism within the Indian republic through a diluted sharia remains the norm.

The renowned jurist and Nehru's cabinet colleague, Mohammadali Carim Chagla, wrote in his autobiography *Roses in December*:[23]

> Consider the attitude of the Government to the question of uniform civil code . . . Government has refused to do anything about it on the plea that minorities will resent any attempt at imposition. Unless they are agreeable it would not be fair and proper to make the law applicable to them. I wholly and emphatically disagree with this view. The Constitution is binding on everyone, majority and minority . . . Jawaharlal showed great strength and courage in getting the Hindu Reform Bill passed, but he accepted the policy of laissez faire where the Muslims and other minorities were concerned. I am horrified to find that in my country, while monogamy has been made the law for the Hindus, Muslims can still indulge in the luxury of polygamy. It is an insult to womanhood; and Muslim women, I know, resent this discrimination between Muslim women and Hindu women.

Hence, Nehruvian secularism is like the erstwhile Ottoman system where different communities would have their own laws and ghettos, even though the Ottoman State was explicitly Islamic. But when it comes to economic redistribution and the welfare state, the ghettos disappear in the Nehruvian world view and we all become Indians once again, rather conveniently.

Similarly, there were and are no neutral regulations with respect to places of worship and educational institutions. Rich temples and privately-funded Hindu institutions—with some exceptions to the latter, run by linguistic minorities—have come to be regulated and often effectively controlled by the government, while many minority-run ones are exempt from various quotas and laws even while they receive subsidies from the government. Why? Because equality would be communalism—a lovely 'ism' with a neutral meaning in the rest of the world but with connotations of 'bigotry' in India.

Such allegations of bigotry hold little water today as political discourse coarsens and people develop thicker skins. In the age of the internet, crowd-sourced wisdom percolates through all the chaos, the abuse and the anger, however imperfectly. Political propaganda cannot camouflage the reality any longer. Those who complain selectively about fake news, social media and WhatsApp forwards are more often than not complaining about the loss of their monopoly in setting the narrative as they can no longer decide what should be discussed.

Indeed, India is changing ever more rapidly. As mentioned above, while the lived reality in the 1940s and 1950s was predominantly collectivist and rural, it is gradually becoming more individualistic and urban today. While the tendency back then was to focus on the immediate reality of a new post-colonial State, time has allowed Indians to take a longer and broader view of our history. India is not just a nation state manufactured in 1947, it is an ancient civilization with a remarkable—and unique—cultural continuity across space and time.

This is something that Nehru, Ambedkar and Gandhi understood, even if modern-day Nehruvians, Ambedkarites and Gandhians do not. India is an ancient, continuing civilization that is slowly being transformed into a nation through the agency of a modern State, as we explore in the first of the five chapters in this book. But what is this Indian civilizational State about? Is it just a load of humbug intentionally or otherwise being used to distract Indians from more pressing everyday issues of economic existence? Let us briefly explore that.

Indian exceptionalism?

As Indian society urbanizes, caste barriers gradually dissolve, joint families give way to smaller units, women begin to enter the formal economy in large numbers, the young attain universal literacy and start becoming digital natives, hitherto unheard of professions become more commonplace, a sexual revolution brews unheralded, and as civilizational awareness follows industrialization and in turn leads to self-assuredness, old certitudes as well as Orientalist cliches of a collectivist, traditional, rural, static India start to fall apart.

Living through these changes, the pace does feel glacial. But on a civilizational timeline—and Indian civilization has been around for many millennia—this transformation is blindingly fast. Even by global standards, what the West took a few centuries to achieve—'modernity' and 'progress'—Indian society (once described by the French political scientist Alexis de Tocqueville as 'petrified')[24] is aiming to do in a few generations, writing a unique playbook on the fly. Yet the sheer velocity is turning the proverbial generational gap into a generational chasm. Those born after Partition but before the Emergency have been sandwiched from both sides. They often followed their parents' directions, but are increasingly being questioned by their children. This formulation is true for urban India; rural India has been about a generation behind, but is fast catching up.

This quickly evolving India needs new ideas. The accepted pieties of the immediate past have become heavy cobwebs that need to be removed. But if these new ideas can still be anchored in an ancient, authentic yet somewhat conveniently abstract past, so much the better. The desire for robust anchors is only human.

That anchor in India's case is the idea of individual rights in a civilizational State, where Indian civilization is best encapsulated by the word 'Dharma'. Dharma is often understood as 'righteousness' but depending on the context many other meanings are possible— just like for the words, 'liberty', 'equality' or 'justice'. India's political philosophical grounding is open to external influences, but it is nonetheless not entirely derivative. In fact, Indians have been debating what is 'right' or 'wrong' from before the age of the Mahabharata, the world's longest epic by far (which also contains the Bhagavad Gita, Krishna's message to Arjuna about duty) and much before Chanakya penned the *Arthashastra,* a political economy manual.

Indeed, for an ever-increasing number of Indians, an ideal polity would be a State that is ideational and not just territorial, and one that also sees all citizens as equal individuals. It is not just a blood, language and ethnicity based State that aspires many if often misunderstood by critics of the civilizational state concept, but also about a broader world view only a part of which can be captured in the word 'religion'. This polity is not there yet, to be sure, but India must transcend the hitherto dominant 'idea of India' where the State sees people as members of (different and often warring) groups and not as individual citizens first.

Every important nation or civilization has its own credo: a North Star, or even a nebulous idea that makes the incoherent coherent, that magic which squares the circle in the minds and hearts of its people, the Schelling point that defines unstated but well-understood norms. This idea is often abstract, many times realized more in theory than in practice, occasionally downright ridiculous and indeed it can vary depending on the circumstances.

For the United States, it is the frontier spirit of the land of the free, home of the brave with the Founding Fathers being slave owners and 'Indian' killers. For France, it might be egalitarianism as seen through *laïcité* or hard secularism. For China, it might be *zhong guo* where China is the 'middle kingdom' of a harmoniously subservient universe. For Russia, it is probably order—yes, with a lot of rum and vodka. For Europe, it might be a rules-based order, both internally and externally, unless you are a German head of state (or an Italian head of the European Central Bank)—just do not be Turkish! For the United Kingdom, it might be a vague nostalgia for Victorian imperialism without Victorian values.

For Canada, it might be black faces in the Great White North. For Pakistan, it might be the era of the Great Mughal—when Sunni Islam was ascendant in the Punjab-Mohajir belt (it had already been eased out of Iran and Spain). For Bangladesh, it might be Joy Bangla—unless of course you are a Bengali Hindu, in which case there is paradise to your West. For Nepal, it might be that the Buddha was born in and only in Nepal. For Lanka, it might be that victory in the World Cup and the Civil War. For Bhutan, happy people and tasty jam.

Humans can be weird indeed, and India is hardly exempt from the beautiful infection of delusional daydreaming. Indians see no reason why they must be the first to improve in this regard. For nothing significant has come out of people aiming low. This brings us to the debate at hand, about 'the Idea of India'. The most troubling thing about that is not the 'idea' part, where we can partially agree and partially disagree, but the 'the' part.

As if a few people sitting together, often in the cafes of Washington DC's K Street or London's Piccadilly, or New Delhi's Khan Market, can decide, once and for all, this is Indian and this un-Indian. We do not think in this manner. We are only putting forward our opinion—one which a very large section of the country may share to varying degrees. Using 'A New' before 'Idea of India' in this book's title is deliberate. In the long run, ideas matter and not momentary majorities.

However, ideas do not just shape material reality—they are in turn shaped by it. India is on track to become the world's third-largest economy in dollar terms by 2025, after the United States and China, having overtaken Japan, Germany, France and the United Kingdom. India is already the world's third-largest economy in purchasing power-parity terms.

By 2023, India's population surpassed China's. So, by the second half of the 2020s, India would be not just the world's most populous democracy but also the world's most populous country, which is both an opportunity and a challenge. Already, India is home to the world's largest population of young people. According to some estimates,[25] India already has the third-largest defence budget. As per the 2020 Military Strength Ranking published by GlobalFirepower, India holds the fourth position today for conventional 'war-making capability across land, sea and air'.[26] With the current effort for defence technology development and production private sector-led indigenisation, India could surpass the firepower of the Russian armed forces by 2030 or so.

Given these economic and military dynamics, it does not matter beyond a point whether India becomes a veto-wielding permanent member of the United Nations Security Council or not—India's international influence will be palpable. By the 2030s decade, the key players on an increasingly multi-polar world stage are likely to be the United States, China and India as the great powers, and Russia as well as Japan as the middle powers. The European Union can be the fourth great power if Germany and France can forge a more coherent Europe, an uncertain but still plausible outcome.

All the countries in this list, except one, are used to being economically and politically powerful, having wielded power for decades if not centuries. The new kid on the block—rather, an ancient civilization returning to the global high table—is India. What India chooses to do with that renewed influence for itself and for humanity at large is of enormous import. India's successes and failures will have global repercussions. But like any magnificent metamorphosis, this too will begin internally at first. There is a great churning going on within India's soul—arguably, it never stopped. But it has accelerated in recent years and what the world will see tomorrow will be decided by what Indians discuss and decide today.

What is this great churn that we are witnessing? It is the mutually reinforcing and simultaneous rise of a modern, urbanized India and a deep Hindu political consciousness. As India industrializes and embraces technology, often pioneering ingenious innovations, old caste barriers and gender glass ceilings become weaker. The rise of nuclear families and steady migrations create an intermixing as well as numerous dislocations where the old certitudes give way to a broader

Hindu umbrella for the country's vast majority—an umbrella under which the spiritual and the political gradually fuse together.

As absolute poverty falls and Indians climb up Maslow's hierarchy of needs, questions of identity arise. The dangerous, contentious, but so-far-avoided facets of our historical narrative bare their fangs. Hitherto taboo topics are pulled out from under the carpet as lay people wonder, often unknowingly channelling the Bengal-born, St Paul's, London and-Cambridge-educated rishi of Tamil Nadu-surrounded Pondicherry, Sri Aurobindo:

> I say no longer that nationalism is a creed, a religion, a faith; I say that it is the Sanatan Dharma which for us is nationalism. This Hindu nation was born with the Sanatan Dharma, with it, it moves and with it, it grows. When the Sanatan Dharma declines, then the nation declines, and if the Sanatan Dharma were capable of perishing, with the Sanatan Dharma it would perish. The Sanatan Dharma, that is nationalism. This is the message that I have to speak to you.[27]

But these are not the Great Awakenings of a Christian America[28] that revive the Gospel every few generations. In the Californias of the world, the 1967 'Summer of Love' as well as the counter-counterculture[29] that was spawned were enemies. In India, a sexual revolution is underway precisely at the same time as the interestingly named Hindutva revolution, and except at the edges they might as well be talking past each other. But in some cases, the protagonists may overlap. For this is not as much a religious revival, as an ancient spirit embracing modernity—and finally doing so without much cant.

The gaze of the cocooned intellectual

In 2012,[30] writer Ashok Malik aptly described the problem with India's intellectual discourse, opining that 'the so-called opinion-shapers, in media and academia, have no stake in the real economy.'[31]

Malik was broadly referring to the permanent New Delhi, London and Washington DC-based intellectual set populating academic and media institutions for whom Indian affairs have become a spectator sport, and which is so ensconced in the inertia of Lutyens Delhi and global academia that it can scarcely fulfil its role as a contributor of new ideas and detached analysis.

Academics at government-funded universities and institutions see their pay and benefits go up with metronomic regularity.[32] A comparative study of faculty pay by the Centre for International Higher Education published in 2012 found that on a purchasing power parity basis, Indian academics receive the fourth-highest pay in the world, ahead of academics in the US, Germany, France and China.[33]

In his book *Intellectuals and Society*, economist Thomas Sowell wrote that intellectuals are judged by whether their ideas 'sound good to other intellectuals or resonate with the public'.[34] Sowell said that there was no objective test for the ideas that intellectuals offered, and 'the only test for most intellectuals is whether other intellectuals go along with them. And if they all have a wrong idea, then it becomes invincible' as the idea gets repeated and endorsed by the establishment *en masse*. Intellectuals have no accountability to anybody but their own community.

India's intellectual elite have often blamed political parties for not offering clear alternatives to the failed ideas of the past. But this fundamentally misunderstands the role of a political party in a democracy—it is the intellectual establishment's job to originate new ideas and educate the public about them, not that of a political party that faces electoral pressures every other month in a chaotic and large democracy such as India, with some local or state election always around the corner.

The reason India's intellectual establishment doesn't contribute new ideas to the public discourse is that it has been very comfortable with the status quo and is in broad agreement with the collectivist philosophy that has directed governance in India almost uninterrupted since Independence. While being a raucous democracy, it is routine in India for consequential policies with very large budgetary outlays shaping critical sectors such as education, defence and healthcare to be approved and implemented with scarcely any public debate about their costs and benefits.

This is not by accident. Intellectuals such as Amartya Sen were quick to conjure up morbid imagery of children dying every week when the legislation on providing food security was delayed. But the same intellectuals remained mute about the scope which the programme enjoys and the methods it employs. Specious arguments are spun circumventing fundamental issues concerning the design and scope of large government programmes like the those of food security and employment guarantee. The level of discussion is so abysmal that most commentators are unable to move beyond the anodyne suggestion that such policies make for clever politics.

Politicians are expected to commit electoral suicide and reject politically beneficial legislation, while the intellectuals cannot get themselves to unequivocally criticize the design of obviously flawed programmes, and just as importantly, offer actionable ideas for improvement should a political consensus exist in favour of such a policy. Eventually, we are proffered the defeatist view that the politicians and 'the system' are flawed and incorrigible. What the elite successfully hide is their own distaste for new ideas and for a new kind of governance, for such a change would undermine their influence and disturb the established privileges. They have so deeply internalized and accepted the shibboleths that India unquestionably needs to break out from, that they are unable to extricate themselves from their mental straitjackets.

The intellectuals have invented their own version of Godwin's law—no matter what the issue, it will be turned into a debate on secularism and liberalism, feeding upon old tensions centred on caste and religion. Economic growth is sometimes portrayed as favouring only certain communities despite evidence to the contrary and without regard for endogenous social factors that are partially responsible for holding certain communities back.

Threats to internal security are viewed through the lens of ideology or religion, with an infantilization of the perpetrators, as if the intellectuals are in collusion with brazenly opportunistic political parties who are evidently open to throwing India's security agencies under the bus of identity politics in their quest for the marginal vote. Even issues in foreign countries have been raked up and connected with

Indian identity politics. When Swiss citizens voted in 2009 to prevent the construction of Islamic minarets in their country, in a statement that would befit a rabble-rousing, bigoted politician, one television anchor here went so far as to call it 'a fundamental threat to millions of Muslims' in India.[35]

On almost every conceivable front, be it economic policy, foreign policy or internal security, India's deracinated and comfortably cocooned intellectual elite are unable to offer new ideas. They endorse or criticize an idea not based on whether it might work, but where it came from. Rather than their political positions being informed by a philosophical world view, their philosophical pronouncements derive from predetermined political positions. Some of the most eminent intellectuals write with pompous verbosity, as if showboating only to sound intelligent, and indulge in rhetorical games that would put the gobbledegook of a modern-day central banker or an erstwhile Soviet apparatchik to shame.

Often when they judge new ideas based on whether these ideas will be 'acceptable', the intellectuals forget that they are not politicians but analysts who should first and foremost enrich public debate on issues of the day. In truth, they are only clamouring for acceptability from others in the opinion-shaping industry, and are competing naively to influence the political party in government, which simply selects the ones which suit its political and electoral objectives. There are no winners in this virtue-signalling contest. It is a race to the bottom and degrades all discussion.

It is a telling fact that the intellectual whose work resonates with the public is almost extinct. Social media and the internet have made it easier to put out ideas for public consumption and break the monopoly enjoyed by the intellectual elite on setting the narrative for public discourse. The crumbling of the media monopoly has accelerated with the rise of Hindutva in the digital age.

The Hindutva movement is a civilizational movement, but it has not been the only such impulse in modern India. Savarkar, Gandhi, Nehru and Ambedkar, all saw India as a civilizational entity—unlike many of the ideological inheritors of all but the first. The idea that just 'constitutional morality' by itself is the only legitimate form of patriotism is deliberately vague and obtuse. The Hindutva movement is conservative only in the very broad sense of wanting to conserve and defend Indian civilization. But at the same time, it is radical—like the Indian Constitution—because it breaks from traditional Indian society on questions of caste and increasingly gender, to fashion an India-specific modernity within the confines of a globally connected, powerful, yet restrained State.

Of course, much of this may be less about being principled and more about *realpolitik*. The Hindutva movement may want a future without caste so that it can better mobilize Indic faiths. It desires an end to all religion-based personal laws, some of which are blatantly misogynist. It does not want to go back to a past where homosexuality was criminalized.

Contrary to popular fabrications, the Hindutva movement welcomes a women's right to choose when it comes to pregnancy and abortions. In contrast with maximalist bans and severe restrictions imposed on abortions by some American states in the aftermath of the US Supreme Court overturning the 1973 Roe v. Wade decision,[36] in 2021 the BJP-led government proactively liberalized the upper gestation limit for abortions from twenty weeks to twenty-four weeks. This recent amendment to the Medical Termination of Pregnancy Act further stated that the upper gestation limit would not apply in cases of foetal abnormalities, and permitted medical termination of pregnancy for unmarried women in situations where contraceptives had failed. The changes were hailed as a 'historic move' by the WHO, that would 'further empower women by providing comprehensive abortion care to all'.[37]

On the other hand, the present day Indian National Congress and various regional parties frequently align with the religious conservatives of minority communities, and want caste to thrive so that Hindus can be politically divided. In contrast, frontline organizations of the Hindutva movement have long espoused the annihilation of caste, as scholar–leaders like Dr B.R. Ambedkar had advocated. Speaking at an event in 2015 to mark the birth centenary of Swami Chinamayananda (philosopher–teacher and founder-president of the Vishva Hindu Parishad [VHP]), Prime Minister Narendra Modi had recounted the objectives laid out at the time of VHP's inception in 1964:[38]

> The two main tenets on which VHP was founded continue to hold lessons and have significance even today. The first message Swami ji gave was, *Hindavah sodaraa sarve* (all Hindus are equals). In our country, the taint of caste-based discrimination and untouchability were widespread. When a message of equality was given by a spiritual leader like Swami ji, people accepted and followed it. The second mantra given by Swami ji was *na Hindu patito bhavet* (the Hindu does not fall). If we take these two mantras forward in the same spirit, society will be freed from the evils plaguing it. From as early as 1953, Swami ji had included even the most backward and oppressed groups and persevered to link them with the great Dharmic mainstream. These steps may seem obvious today but were very courageous and unusual in the hidebound, orthodox context of that period, and Swami ji was exemplary in his thinking and action.

Along the same lines, Congress and its political–ideological fellow travellers do not support secular–liberal common personal laws that break the back of institutionalized misogyny. These groups are increasingly trying to exploit linguistic fault lines to break any consolidation of a national vote. They consciously or subconsciously want to keep India within an Ottoman-style millet system of religious ghettos. Beyond a point, it is futile to dwell on whether somebody philosophically supports classical secular–liberalism even though they do not support it in practice. What investor and leftist activist George Soros's theory of reflexivity says about markets also holds true for politics—that perception can become reality. As has been said, 'If you wear a mask for too long, there will come a time when you cannot remove it without removing your face'.[39]

Indeed, the Indian National Congress of the 2020s is very different from the Congress party of 1950, not in the least because the latter went through many splits and transmogrifications to become what it is today. Some Congress leaders such as Shashi Tharoor are writing books explaining the difference between Hinduism and Hindutva as they see it, owning the former while disowning the latter. Though without changes in key policy positions, this rhetoric is ultimately futile sophistry.

2

From Civilization to Nation

Indians are of course quarrelling, and no one can prophesy when they will stop quarrelling. But granting the fact, what does it establish? Only that Indians are a quarrelsome people. It does not destroy the fact that India is a single geographical unit. Her unity is as ancient as Nature. Within this geographic unit and covering the whole of it there has been a cultural unity from time immemorial. This cultural unity has defied political and racial divisions.

—B.R. Ambedkar[1]

Who are we?

Today, it is not uncommon for, say, a thirty-year-old educated Indian woman—let us call her Meena—to have her father's 'native village' in Punjab, her mother's in Uttar Pradesh, she herself having grown up in Mumbai, and having married someone whose family lives in Kolkata, with the couple having met at university in Ahmedabad and currently living in Bengaluru.

Nor are such relocation and intermarriage examples restricted to regional or caste boundaries. They also apply, though to a lesser degree, to class and religion. As Vinayak Savarkar, the freedom fighter and philosopher–theorist of Hindutva said, 'Sexual attraction has proved more powerful than all the commands of all the prophets put together.'[2]

So, what now is Meena's identity? It clearly is not just one. She is a human being, an Indian, a woman, a professional, a wife, a daughter, perhaps also a mother—and she can claim to be attached to six states. She can speak, though not very fluently, four languages and she may even understand the most important curse words in a few others. She has a soft corner for gurudwaras, Durga Puja, laughing Buddhas and feng shui.

She remembers the many Christian prayers from her convent school days (playing Santa and exchanging gifts on Christmas was a family tradition) and likes the Jain concept of *Micchami dukkadam*—having a day whereby you can sincerely apologize for any, deliberate or otherwise, pain caused by your words and actions. Like many urban millennials, Meena watches American shows on Netflix and the latest Bollywood movies with their Urdu–Hindi–Punjabi songs in the neighbourhood multiplex. She is from a Jat background, married to a Kannadiga. She zones out politics and hates taxes—all those curse words come streaming back on tax-filing day. Meena is, as you might have guessed, also a Hindu.

Depending on the situation, Meena, could easily have a dozen identities. India, home to a sixth of all humans, is obviously an almost unfathomably complex place. India's population in 2020 stood at approximately 1.35 billion. Soon, nearly a billion Indians will be forty years old or younger. China has more people overall for now, although India already has more young people. While China's homogeneity is often exaggerated by casual observers, it is undoubtedly less diverse than India.

Even in the United States, the world's third-largest country by population, there is incredible diversity in the metropolises. But on closer observation one finds that this diversity is relatively skin-deep, not soul-deep. The poor Mexican immigrants who cause so much heartburn in some parts of America do not want to change American laws, nor do they have a fundamentally different world view from most Americans. Mexicans, or broadly speaking, Hispanics, represent a bit of racial, linguistic and gastronomical diversity within the same Judeo–Christian and broadly Western construct.

In a 1998 speech at Union University in the United States, British Prime Minister Margaret Thatcher invoked this construct, saying that 'the moral foundation of this [Western] system is the Judeo-Christian outlook.'[3]

The United States is the current leader of 'the West', clearly a civilizational construct for there is no such political entity. Addressing the people of Poland in 2017, U.S. President Donald Trump echoed Thatcher when he said:[4]

> Americans, Poles, and the nations of Europe value individual freedom and sovereignty. We must work together to confront forces, whether they come from inside or out, from the South or the East, that threaten over time to undermine these values and to erase the bonds of culture, faith and tradition that make us who we are . . . The fundamental question of our time is whether the West has the will to survive . . . We can have the largest economies and the most lethal weapons anywhere on Earth, but if we do not have strong families and strong values, then we will be weak and we will not survive . . . Our own fight for the West does not begin on the battlefield—it begins with our minds, our wills, and our souls. Today, the ties that unite our civilization are no less vital, and demand no less defense, than that bare shred of land on which the hope of Poland once totally rested. Our freedom, our civilization, and our survival depend on these bonds of history, culture, and memory.

This construct of the West as a composite civilizational entity is broadly accepted even in Europe despite all their mixed attitudes about America as well their allergy to 'nationalism', which is an attitude coloured by the experience of the Second World War. In marked contrast, the notion that India is a civilization is surprisingly controversial in India itself. Even today, there are some who claim that India was created in 1947 or 1950, confusing the establishment of a constitutional democratic republic with the genesis of India.

A civilization of synthesis

The confusion on India's genesis is a relatively new one. Today, a section of intellectuals who call themselves Gandhians, Nehruvians and Ambedkarites, would like to pretend that India was created by these 'founding fathers'. But it is notable that Gandhi, Nehru and Ambedkar themselves never thought so. It is not a coincidence that Gandhi titled his 1909 book (originally published in Gujarati) on home rule and modern civilization, *Hind Swaraj*, echoing the terminology of *Hindavi Swarajya* coined by Chhatrapati Shivaji Maharaj in 1645. The leading lights of that era would be the first to recognize the voice of the colonial British in present-day arguments.

For example, Winston Churchill, who was responsible for exacerbating the 1943 Bengal famine that killed millions, could be a less-than-wholesome person in his rhetoric as well. He mocked Indians as a 'beastly people with a beastly religion'.[5] He is often lambasted for doubting the Indian nation's existence. On 26 March 1931, Churchill said at the Constitutional Club in London: 'India is no more a political personality than Europe. India is a geographical term. It is no more united than the equator.'[6]

While the 'equator' flourish can be ignored, it is true that at that time, India's political personality resembled Europe more than any European nation-state. British India of the 1930s eventually became five countries—India, Pakistan, Sri Lanka, Bangladesh and Myanmar (which was made a separate entity by the British in 1937).

Many modern-day Indian states do resemble European nations. Punjab and Andhra Pradesh have historically been as similar or dissimilar as France and Bulgaria. Both these pairs have different ethnolinguistic roots yet similar civilizational bases. Punjabi and Telugu are different languages just like French and Bulgarian. Yet the European Union is the modern secular inheritor of Christendom which in turn was shaped by its Greco–Roman heritage. In parallel, the Indian Union is the democratic manifestation of a dharmic polity.

Mahatma Gandhi believed that the 'soul of India' lived in her ancient villages, in her religiosity, in her determined non-violence and in her pursuit of truth. Gandhi may well be wrong on one or more of these accounts, but he clearly saw a pre-existing soul of India. He certainly did not see India as today's work-in-progress European Union—a Union that was necessary to prevent a third world war. As the French political economist, often hailed as the 'father of Europe', Jean Monnet had remarked, 'It is better to fight around a table than on a battlefield.'[7]

Europe's exclusivist linguist and sectarian nationalisms—for example, the French and the Germans murdering each other in three huge wars from the 1870s to the 1940s—would be akin to sub-nationalisms in the Indian civilizational framework if India's sub-nationalist thrust was much more militant and aggressive, which they have rarely been. India's divisions, as well as discriminations, have almost always been more vertical or caste-based, than horizontal or region-based. Yes, 'India' never had a singular state and political union for most of its long history (the Mauryas, Mughals and British being near-exceptions at their respective territorial peaks) but very large sections of Indian societies were always harmoniously interlinked.

From the third-century Gupta empire to Akbar to Ranjit Singh, providing protection to Sramanas and Brahmins as well as animals (such as cows) was a matter of prestige for kings and rich merchants. In our modern-day context, such an invocation has 'casteist' and 'majoritarian' connotations, yet reality then was more nuanced. Today, many Brahmins are in white-collar jobs and as motivated by financial success as any other Indian. The idea of reciprocal service in a non-monetary economy applies much less especially when the said service was defined in a hereditary context. Similarly, the cow was seen as key to both the economy—which was mostly agrarian earlier—and to post-Buddhist Hinduism.

The history of Indic spiritual paths taking up arms against one another on matters of theology has been relatively sparse unlike the history of medieval Europe, or medieval India itself. But then the latter fault line was due to violent proselytizing monotheisms entering the Indic mix, whose orthodox interpretations have never been a part of the 'soul of India'.

The State as a catalyst

The impossibly large number of languages, dialects, creeds and sub-ethnicities in India is peerless in the world. Since a nation has conventionally been the coming together of peoples who are generally bound by at least one of the three commonalities of religion, language or ethnicity in some form, India is indeed a very curious nation. As has often been said about India, '*Kos kos pe badle paani, char kos pe badle vaani*' (water tastes different after every mile and language changes after every four). How then does one try to understand this country which is soon to become the world's most-populated political unit?

One begins with a hypothesis that India has indeed not been a nation at least until recently. But it has been, and is, a civilization—a civilization that is slowly congealing into a functional, prosperous and peaceful nation aided by the instrumentality of a united State. And this process of conversion of a civilization into a nation will understandably have many growth pangs and homogenizing anxieties. It is important, therefore, to understand the differences between these terms—nation, State and civilization. While 'State' is self-explanatory and the word 'nation' has been much discussed, the word 'civilization' is a bit more elusive.

Firstly, the word 'civilization', while overlapping with 'culture', is, strictly speaking very different from it. North India and Pakistan may share a common culture when it comes to many cherished food items, movies and music, but all such congruities could not prevent the violent rupture of Partition. As political scientist Sunil Khilnani wrote in his book *The Idea of India*, Partition was 'the greatest violation of Gandhi's idea of India as a civilizational unity' by 'irrational forces'. Khilnani mentions the 'larger conceptual enigma of Partition' and wonders if it should be seen as the 'division of one territory between two 'nations' or peoples? Or the breaking of one civilization into two territories?'[8]

What Khilnani is unable to articulate, for that would cause too much cognitive dissonance, is that India and Pakistan undoubtedly represent two civilizations. Indeed, the India–Pakistan border may be the most severe civilizational fault line in existence around the world. Of all the modern states in existence today, India represents the pinnacle of syncretic polytheism and Pakistan probably the most unrestrained instincts of proselytizing monotheism. All the Urdu *shayari*, music and tasty kebabs, and even all the gods of our pantheon, cannot change that reality anytime soon.

This view was articulated by Samuel Huntington in his 1996 book *The Clash of Civilizations and the Remaking of World Order*[9] in which he responded to Francis Fukuyama's pollyannaish and premature *The End of History and the Last Man*.[10] Fukuyama, who has since nuanced his views, had argued that the fall of the Soviet Union had ended the great debate between democratic capitalism and totalitarian communism, and henceforth the world would simply see various versions of the former. Huntington responded, in essence saying, 'Not so fast.' He argued correctly that people would start asking deeper questions of identity: 'who are we?' as opposed to 'what do we believe in?' and henceforth global fault lines would be primarily civilizational ones.

Vidiadhar Surajprasad Naipaul, whose perspicacious travelogues on India and the Islamic world seemingly agreed with Huntington, took a step back and over the long horizon envisioned the development of 'our universal civilization'—a global, humane civilization whose genesis was nonetheless rooted in the liberal West. To that extent, he seemed to endorse Fukuyama more.

Thus, we see that while the word 'civilization' can have varying meanings, it is nonetheless a real and palpable concept.

What then is the Indian civilization all about? If there is one word that captures the essence of it, it is Dharma. A more mature Fukuyama, in his later book *The Origins of Political Order* notes about India:

> The Brahmin varna was regarded as the guardian of the sacred law that existed prior to and independently of political rule. Kings were thus regarded as subject to law written by others, not simply the makers of law as in China. Thus, in India, as in Europe, there was a germ of something that could be called the rule of law that would limit the power of secular political authority.[11]

However, there was much more to Dharma than the caste system being a proto-separation of powers. Unlike Europe which after the fall of Rome to Christianity was consumed by the Crusades—first against the Pagans in their continent, then against the Muslims in the Middle East and finally against itself after the rise of Protestantism—the Dharmic path did not see any theological civil wars.

In fact, Dharma in India represented the creative integration of various pre-existing local sects and cults into a broader pantheon through pilgrimages and the great epics Mahabharata and the Ramayana. Dharma is the original multiculturalism of our world—a civilization that is built on absorbing and being absorbed, so long as all sides approach one another with mutual respect. As Pandurang Kane wrote in *The History of The Dharma Shastra*:[12]

> The reason given for cultivating such virtues as *dayā* and *ahiṃsā* is based upon the philosophical doctrine of the one Self being immanent in every individual as said in the words *'tat tvam-asi'*. This is the highest point reached in Indian metaphysics . . . That doctrine requires us to regard the goodness or badness of one's actions from the standpoint of other individuals who will be affected by such actions. Dakṣa declares that 'one who desires happiness should look upon another just as he looks upon himself. Happiness and misery affect one's self and others in the same way'.

Daniel Patrick Moynihan, US ambassador to India from 1973–75, recognized the assimilative tendency and syncretic approach saying that 'the defining strength of Indian civilization is its ability to absorb synergistically the culture of outsiders . . . thereby conquering its conquerors.'[13]

Nehru, too, had paid homage to India's civilizational strength and unity in a speech made in 1961 at the end of his political life, where he said that 'from the very beginning of history, the people of India always thought of themselves as a people belonging to one great country.'

This conception is not very different from Atal Bihari Vajpayee's observation, made at a 1988 function[14] to pay tribute to Vinayak Damodar Savarkar in Pune:

At a fundamental level, India is a Hindu Nation . . . nobody can deny this, nobody can reject this. For me, Hindu Nation and Indian Nation are synonyms. When Savarkar spoke of a Hindu Nation, he also spoke of an Indian (Hindi) State. Savarkar envisioned a state that does not distinguish between citizens based on religion and worship . . . he spoke of a state that treats all equally, but Savarkar said the nation will be a Hindu nation. There is a difference between nation (rashtra) and State (rajya), and this difference must be made explicit.[15]

There is a lot to unpack here, for the import of the above quote depends on the word 'Hindu'. If it is meant in a broader dharmic and Indic sense, as Vajpayee and Savarkar used it, the assertion is unquestionable. If Hindu is used in a narrower sense, then the hypothesis is more debatable. The word itself obviously comes from the Indus (Sindhu) river and foreigners—as Oxford University comparative religion scholar Gavin Flood has argued[16]—often considered India to be the land of the Hindus or Hindu-sthan. It was quite literally a geographical term with no religious connotations. 'Religion' per se came to the Indian mainstream thanks to the Islamic invasions.

Initially (and earlier too, starting with the Arab conquest of Sindh in the eighth century), when the local converts to Islam were few, the distinctions between the Hindustanis and the Turks were obvious. As the converts grew in numbers, the word 'Hindu' became a default, catch-all phrase for Indians who were (primarily) not Christians or Muslims, as Flood has described. The broader Hindu terminology in that sense is a negative one, created in response to the advent of Abrahamic faiths in Bharat Varsha—the ancient term for the land that is India. According to Flood, the suffix '-ism' was added to 'Hindu' around 1830. The word 'religion' has different connotations for different systems. As Nassim Taleb has observed, 'Religions are not quite religions: some are philosophies, others are legal systems.'[17]

It was the Arya Samaj, from 1875, that tried to positively and exclusively define the new term 'Hinduism' as 'back to the Vedas'. With this conception, the paths of Sikhism, Buddhism and Jainism end up as separate 'religions'. The anxieties of Swami Dayanand Saraswati, the founder of Arya Samaj, were understandable. With Christian and Muslim evangelists gaining strength in undivided Punjab, the Hindu side had no answers to the accusations of polytheism, idolatry and the absence of any clear central scripture. While such an -ism (Hinduism) is a narrow conception with the possibilities of birth-based caste and dogma making a comeback, Dharma is a much wider canvas.

Even Ambedkar recognized this. When he denounced Hinduism, he made it a point to follow the Dharmic *panth* of Buddhism and not the exclusivist doctrine of Islam or Christianity. He said:

> I will choose only the least harmful way for the country. And that is the greatest benefit I am conferring on the country by embracing Buddhism; for Buddhism is a part and parcel of Bharatiya culture. I have taken care that my conversion will not harm the tradition of the culture and history of this land.[18]

In his classic work *Pakistan, or the Partition of India*, Ambedkar had written:[19]

> Islam is a close corporation and the distinction that it makes between Muslims and non-Muslims is a very real, very positive and very alienating distinction. The brotherhood of Islam is not the universal brotherhood of man. It is brotherhood of Muslims for Muslims only. There is a fraternity, but its benefit is confined to those within that corporation. For those who are outside the corporation, there is nothing but contempt and enmity. The second defect of Islam is that it is a system of social self-government and is incompatible with local self-government, because the allegiance of a Muslim does not

rest on his domicile in the country which is his but on the faith to which he belongs.

It is not well known that prior to becoming president of the Hindu Mahasabha in 1943, Bharatiya Jan Sangh founder Syama Prasad Mookerjee had been the president of the Maha Bodhi Society of India, the principal organization of the Buddhists, in 1942.[20] In 2022, Narendra Modi became the first Indian Prime Minister to visit Lumbini in Nepal, the birth place of the Buddha, on the occasion of the 2566th birth anniversary of the Buddha.[21]

Salad bowls and melting pots

Like all humans, Indians have been migrating and mixing for thousands of years with one another as well as foreigners. The size and geographical location of the subcontinent at the centre of the old worlds of Europe, Asia and Africa ensured that. Through the example of the Pandavas in the Mahabharata, Savarkar illustrates in his seminal text *Hindutva*, how Indians mixed freely before bottlenecks overwhelmed Indian groups and stratified identities.

> The sage Parashar was a Brahman. He fell in love with the fair maid of a fisherman who gave birth to the world-renowned Vyas, who in his turn raised two sons of the Kshatriya princesses Amba and Ambalika; one of these two sons, Pandu, allowed his wives to raise issues by resorting to the Niyoga system and they, having solicited the love of men of unknown castes, gave birth to the heroes of our great epic.[22]

But about seventy generations (or around 1500 years) ago, the populations seemed to have become more static despite significant mixing earlier as genetic research[23] by the National Institute of Biomedical Genomics in Kalyani, West Bengal has shown.[24] This could have been due to the many socioeconomic upheavals that the civilization went through owing to political or possibly even climatic factors.

As the caste system hardened and became much more hereditary by the later Gupta period, which is frequently described as India's Golden Age, society may have been a witness to the early ossification of caste during this era, turning to orthodox impulses. This complex and gradual phenomenon was, in ensuing centuries, exacerbated by the fact that the later invaders, unlike the earlier ones from the same regions in Central Asia, were more averse to assimilation. They had acquired a civilizational zeitgeist by then and had therefore agglomerated a transnational critical mass of their own.

Even two hundred years ago, when the British finally defeated the divided yet dominant Marathas in the Third Anglo–Maratha War of 1817, India was a very static place. Most Indians could not have just packed their bags and easily relocated from Maratha Pune to Mughal Delhi, or from British Calcutta to Sikh Lahore—much less from, say, from a small fort town in Rajputana to rural Mysore.

Besides logistics, language would have been a significant barrier and so would have social acceptance and work opportunities. The average Indian had almost nothing to fall back on without backing from the *biradari* or *gotra*. Society was overwhelmingly agricultural. The farm and the local market defined most people's lives, punctuated occasionally by a rare long-distance pilgrimage. Large-scale relocations would mostly happen during times of distress. Marrying contrary to parental wishes was unimaginable. Life was 'nasty, brutish and short', to borrow the famous Hobbesian description, and solace was found in the gods.

The so-called lower castes among Hindus as well as the non-Ashraf (those not of a foreign lineage) among the Muslims suffered more than the others, and so did women of all communities. Only a minuscule number of rich and powerful men lived lives of any real agency. Wider ideas of self-actualization and self-expression would have been considered ludicrous. Centuries of resisting colonization and invasion had seemingly sapped our energies, pushed us ever more inwards and made us even more rigid—a civilization to be sure, but a decaying and wounded one, to use Naipaul's evocative coinage.

Today, after 1500 years, that old instinct of moving, mixing and mating across various social boundaries is making a gradual comeback. This process, like almost everything else, has quickened over the last two decades, thanks to economic growth, urbanization and the empowerment of women. Of course, it is early days and a lot more needs to be done but the change is irreversible and the process will accelerate. 'The soul of India lives in its villages,' Mahatma Gandhi had declared. He wanted India's soul to remain there - the way India is urbanising today may not have pleased him. But it would be music to Ambedkar's ears. Introducing the draft Constitution of India on 4 November 1948, Ambedkar had said:[25] What is the village but a sink of localism, a den of ignorance, narrow-mindedness and communalism? I am glad that the Draft Constitution has discarded the village and adopted the individual as its unit.

Confusing State and society[26]

Since the meteoric rise of the BJP in the late 1980s and the emergence of Narendra Modi in particular, a great debate has been brewing in India. A section of intellectuals and writers warns Indians that the 'idea of India' is under grave threat. But what is the idea of India? Can there be only one idea of India?

Should certain religious groups have special rights over and above the individual rights that all citizens enjoy in a free, democratic India? This is the fundamental philosophical schism between the political Left and Right. While many intellectuals have long argued for the primacy of group rights over individual rights, and the protection of minority interests, there needs to be a detailed discussion on how this mindset might lead to withering of individual identity over a period of time.

An identity-based special 'minority group right' can broadly be of two types. It can either give the group members more liberty or enforce more restrictions. Canadian political philosopher Will Kymlicka, a leading proponent of multiculturalism, has developed a similar classification[27]. He supports the former, terming them 'external protections', and is less enthusiastic about the latter, which he calls 'internal restrictions'. But even external protections can be problematic. Examples of such protections in India include allowing members of certain groups to have multiple spouses, or increased autonomy in running educational institutions. The question is, why not extend this greater liberty to all citizens? If the rationale for not doing so is that polygamy is socially harmful, or that regulation of educational institutions is needed, then why have a policy that is condescending and detrimental to such groups?

Enforcing restrictions, like restricting alimony or adoptions, is worse, as they force individuals to choose between the State's definition of their faith or official apostasy. McGill University's Vrinda Narain argues in her book *Gender and Community: Muslim Women's Rights in India*: 'In a situation where religion is tied to organized national minorities, this (sexist) discrimination dictates a system of "differential citizenship" based on ascriptive belonging.'[28]

The prevailing intellectual consensus that affords special rights to minority groups manufactures resentment in the majority community. This consensus offers no comment on realities like State control over Hindu places of worship. It correctly brands as communal an assertion of majority group rights that manifests itself in episodes like the banning of voluntary conversions, while tacitly accepting similar rights for minorities in the name of protection. Is this secularism?

These double standards are principally illiberal. Labelling those asking for individual rights over group rights as 'radical' liberals or 'extremist' reactionaries, while claiming oneself to be a 'moderate' liberal, may be an effective rhetorical tactic, but it is a specious argument. Moreover, there is evidence to suggest that such a standard worsens communal relations. Political scientist Steven Ian Wilkinson of Yale University has shown that increasing consociationalism in India has led to rising ethnic violence.[29]

Consociationalism is a power-sharing arrangement in a democracy between different groups according them special collective rights, and confessionalism is a specific, religion-based subset of consociationalism. Lebanon is an example where seats in executive and legislature are divided between various religious groups. In India, Mohammad Ali

Jinnah and the Muslim League were essentially advocating a kind of confessionalism before demanding partition. As Wilkinson observed in a paper published in 2000:

> Only since the mid-1960s, as India has become more consociational, has there been an increase in Hindu–Muslim riots, caste conflict, and separatist violence . . . I argue that there are good reasons to think that consociational policies might even be responsible for the increase in ethnic violence in recent years.[30]

Wilkinson argues that no consociational arrangement can cover all ethnic groups in allocating political power and State resources. Some groups will always be left out. Caste-based agitations by socially dominant peasant castes such as Marathas, Jats, Patels and Gujjars over reservations in education and jobs is testament to that. Even if the impossible goal of satisfying each group is achieved, distribution within groups will tend to be unequal and lead to resentment.

To address these challenges, the Modi government constituted a panel, chaired by former Delhi High Court Chief Justice G. Rohini, to evaluate the allocation of the 27 per cent OBC quota to different categories for fairness, so that the stronger castes of the 2633 eligible notified castes do not corner the benefits.[31] The panel has found that less than 1 per cent of the communities notified as OBC corner 50 per cent of the reservation benefits in central educational institution admissions and recruitment to central services.[32] Wilkinson is thus right in pointing out the weaknesses of consociational agreements, 'most importantly the institutionalization and freezing of ethnic identities that by nature are multidimensional and oppositional—that seem to intensify rather than moderate ethnic violence'.

The tacit thrust of the propagators of this mindset of consociationalism is towards redistribution, from the majority to the minority, to ameliorate discrimination, while ignoring the fact that special minority rights pander to conservative elements that keep communities socially backward in the first place. Nobel laureate economist Gary Becker has shown that in a market system, discrimination hurts even those who indulge in it, not just those who are discriminated against.[33] It follows that in a non-market system, there are no substantive penalties upon indulging in such discrimination. In India, it is rare that those who bat for secularism come out in strong support of economic liberalization. Pseudo secularism[34] and socialistic economics are two heads of a polycephalic beast that increases its power by feeding on itself.

It dawned on Marxists by the 1950s that workers wanted to engage with, and reform, capitalism from within, not overthrow it altogether. In such a scenario, theorists of the New Left started scouting for virgin proletariats, based more on culture than class. Herbert Marcuse of the Frankfurt School was one of those who bridged Marx with his understanding of Friedrich Nietzsche and others, playing up the 'non-integrated forces of minorities, outsiders and radical intelligentsia'[35] in his 1964 book *One-Dimensional Man*. Integration would mean capitulation to the 'end of history', a euphemism for the victory of capitalism over communism. This furthered the legitimacy of liberalism and group rights being compatible in Left-leaning academia.

Left-liberals complain that 'radical' liberals—the former who support group rights, and the latter who support individual rights—ignore the reality of individuals existing in a world based on social intercourse. This misrepresentation ignores the fundamental difference between the State and society, between coercion and choice. It is no one's case that society should give primacy to individuals over groups. That is up to individuals in the society to decide and evolve, but this role of shaping the society, should not be in the hands of the State.

Thomas Paine, Alexis de Tocqueville, Mohandas Gandhi and Deendayal Upadhyay have argued along these lines as well. As Canadian philosopher Jan Narveson writes in his book *Respecting Persons in Theory and Practice*:[36]

Only individuals can make decisions, have values, engage in reasoning and deliberation: and the subject matter of morals is how entities capable of doing these things should do them. Facts about group decisions and actions are logically contingent on the occurring of acts of communication and responsive behaviour among individuals, who establish chains of commands and other patterns of behaviour responsive to the behaviour of others.

In India, where new ideas are in short supply, such a principled liberal stand in favour of individualism is rare. Indian intelligentsia's conflation of State and society has slowed down the natural evolution of India from a discrete salad bowl to a composite, dynamic melting pot. Their reasoning went that majority communalism is a bigger threat than minority communalism, partially because of the former's overlap with nationalism. But many of the mainstream Right's 'controversial' positions—in support of a uniform civil code and the abrogation of Article 370, for example—are not 'communal', but liberal and nationalist.

The directive principles in the Constitution of India call for a uniform civil code.[37] All laws should be applicable uniformly to all citizens of the country. Similarly, proscribing the autonomy of individuals to sell their lands to residents of other provinces, in the name of their province's autonomy—one of the perverse effects of the separate, special status granted to Jammu & Kashmir—also violates equality and liberty.

All well-meaning Indians, irrespective of political allegiances, should advocate for strengthening the law-and-order machinery so that no violence—irrespective of its antecedents—takes place and if it does, it does not go unpunished. Government welfare programmes should be targeted at those in economic need, and not just based upon a person's identity. To prevent politicians from fuelling competitive intolerance, the government should not have the discretion to decide what constitutes offensive speech.

When the State has no discretion to pick certain groups as winners, fraternity is more likely to prevail because socioeconomic intercourse, unlike political competition, is not a zero-sum game. India needs more genuine liberalism—rule of law, open markets and separation of religion and State—not a perverted, degenerate version of it.

It is pertinent to note here that advocating for a State that is agnostic to different sub-identities and a government that sees every citizen only as an equal and free individual Indian does not preclude the citizens from seeing themselves however they like, and from having as many hyphens as they want. Some might argue that 'If Indians can be Gujarati Indians or Hindu Indians, why can't there be Muslim Indians or Christian Indians?' This is a strawman. Nobody is saying Indians cannot see themselves and fellow citizens as belonging to any group. The argument is simply that the government should not see Indians as Hindus, Muslims, Christians and so on, and crucially, that it should not force an individual to self-identify as belonging to a particular group.

Other democracies, too, have had the debate India is having. This contrast is best brought out by the American and French approaches. France places curbs on certain clothing and accessories and the rule is applied equally, but it may still be considered illiberal. America, barring some exceptions, also has undifferentiated citizenship, while still retaining a normative attachment to liberty. Its jurisprudence is evolving in such a manner that even its taxpayer-funded, race-based affirmative action programmes have to increasingly show that they are not based exclusively on identity and instead have intrinsic pedagogical or diversity benefits.

A 2015 United States Supreme Court ruling[38] can be termed as a setback to building a classic melting pot society. In 2008, Samantha Elauf, a headscarf (hijab)-wearing Muslim, interviewed for a position at a clothing store owned by the retailer Abercrombie and Fitch, whose policy forbade black clothing and caps. When Elauf was graded lower for her appearance in the interview, she sued, claiming that the store had violated the US Civil Rights Act because the decision was based on the headscarf, a part of Elauf's religion. The district court ruled in her favour. A US Court of Appeals reversed the judgment but the Supreme Court overruled the Court of Appeals again. The problem here is that courts in the US would henceforth have to import some version of the Indian doctrine of 'essential religious practices' of mainstream religions as they now constitute a special category of protection undermining neutrality between religion and irreligion.

It is important to discuss in detail the terms 'salad bowl' and 'melting pot' and what they actually mean. Some politicians and intellectuals understand, or want to understand, 'salad bowl' versus 'melting pot' metaphor differently. Take India's former Vice-President Hamid Ansari. Speaking at a seminar on 'Nationalism and Culture' in Chandigarh in October 2017, Ansari said[39] that there were two ways of answering the question: What is Indian national identity? 'The first, premised on assumed infallibility of tradition, suggests uniformity, homogeneity, oneness; the second, based on ground reality, identifies diversity, heterogeneity, complexity.' Highlighting the vast diversity of India, Ansari said, 'It is not a melting pot because each ingredient retains its identity. It is perhaps a salad bowl.'

But we employ the salad bowl versus melting pot metaphor in a more nuanced way. To wit, a melting pot does not mean Indian society must necessarily be homogeneous, or that the State should social engineer any kind of conformity as Ansari seems to think of those advocating for the melting-pot model. If society, despite getting a classically liberal state, still wants to remain a salad bowl, so be it. It is just not likely to be so, and perhaps that is why certain vested interests do not want such a setup. Notably, in 2018 Ansari had supported the establishment of Muslim religious law-based sharia courts in all of India's districts, aligning with the All-India Muslim Personal Law Board. He asserted that 'each community has the right to practise its own personal law.'[40]

Ansari's position aligns closely with Indira Gandhi's views. In a 1981 speech at St Stephen's College in Delhi, Indira Gandhi had equated India to a salad bowl, where discrete identities should co-exist under the broader rubric of an Indian State.[41] In 1972, the All-India Muslim Personal Law Board, a non-statutory body, had been created when Mrs Gandhi was Prime Minister.[42]

Orwellian secularism and Hindu charters

In his 1939 address as president of the Hindu Mahasabha in Calcutta, Vinayak Savarkar had said:[43]

> The conception of this Hindu Nation is in no way inconsistent with the development of a common Indian Nation . . . in which

all sects and sections, races and religions, castes and creeds, Hindus, Muslims, Christians, Anglo-Indians could be harmoniously welded together into a political state in terms of perfect equality.

Nehruvians defend the rights of religious minorities to establish and administer educational institutions. Fair enough, but they do not answer a simple question—why not extend these rights, currently benefitting the global majority (adherents of Islam and Christianity) to the local 'majority' as well?[44] That was the critique of Will Kymlicka's 'external protections' in practice; if it is important for Muslims in Maharashtra to have more educational autonomy, why not extend this freedom to all citizens? If the reason is that it may lead to poor regulation and possibly harm students, then why deny minorities such prudence? Either way, the square cannot be circled.

Some intellectuals see only institutionalized discrimination against Muslims in the Rajinder Sachar Committee's findings submitted in 2006.[45] The worker-population ratio for Muslim women was just 25.2 per cent compared to 46.1 per cent for Hindu women and 47.2 per cent for other minorities. Is this the fault of others? A community reluctant to see women as financially independent will fall behind.

Socio-religious conservatism is probably as responsible as any institutionalized discrimination. Instead of creating a sense of victimhood, leaders and reformers need to address those interpretations of faith that are at the root of this disbalance. After the Supreme Court struck down the abhorrent practice of triple talaq as unconstitutional, the Modi government formulated the legislation to outlaw and criminalize instant divorce. Even so, a significant number of 'secular' politicians and intellectuals argue that this women-friendly reform should come from within the community. Former editor of *The Hindu* newspaper Malini Parthasarathy had said in 2013, that 'it's not for us, the majority, to dictate to minorities how to live their lives'.[46]

As far as quotas are concerned, a significant percentage of the Muslim population is already classified as OBC. That Muslims are disproportionately unsuccessful even in computer-evaluated, multiple-choice examinations undermines the argument that even more affirmative action is needed to correct for society's bias. Rather, it calls for, at the policy level, the supply-side liberalization of primary and secondary education, a cause that the Congress-led UPA (United Progressive Alliance) government had grievously harmed with the Right to Education Act's persecution of private schools and kowtowing to entrenched teacher unions.[47]

The same arguments can be made to oppose caste-based quotas too. But there are three points to consider.

First, in the case of Scheduled Castes and Scheduled Tribes (SC/ST) and to a lesser extent OBC quotas, there is a historical context of discrimination, which does not exist for Muslims. As the writer M.J. Akbar has observed, 'Only Dalits should be considered a minority' and Muslims should leave the 'politics of fear' and adopt the 'politics of development'.[48]

Second, while one cannot change one's caste, one can change religion. So, such quotas could incentivize conversions, and to expect Hindu taxpayers to quietly subsidize this would be absurd and unrealistic. When it comes to the State doling out welfare benefits based on identity, we need a proper test as to who ought to be the beneficiary.

The great tragedy of post-Sachar policymaking and discourse in India has been to put the minorities on the same (or even higher) pedestal than historically marginalized communities such as Scheduled Castes and Scheduled Tribes as far as affirmative action is concerned. Welfare benefits based on identity cannot be normalized and only *sui generis* cases need to be considered, if at all. A simple test could be based on two markers. If welfare is being granted to correct past wrongs, only the systematically and historically marginalized people should qualify for affirmative action.

If welfare is granted to set right the present economic and social inequalities, then affirmative action must not be based on malleable identities so as to avoid institutionalizing perverse incentives. A person cannot change their caste but can convert to a different religion. Likewise, a person cannot change their gender as easily as they can learn a different language and avail linguistic minority rights. Genetics is not malleable, religion is.

Third, saying that because caste quotas exist, religious quotas must also be introduced lacks logic. Why not fight identity entrenchment, rather than use one kind of quota to argue for even more quotas?

Of course, there are numerous interpretations of all these loaded '-isms', but the Indian Right, unlike the Right elsewhere, is potentially more at home with liberalism–secularism than the Left could ever be. When the Supreme Court was deciding on decriminalizing homosexuality, all three religious groups that were supporting Section 377 in the Court were Christian[49]—the Apostolic Alliance of Churches, the Utkal Christian Council and Trust God Ministries. A Christian pastor in Tamil Nadu barged into the Coimbatore district court premises and shouted slogans saying, 'Homosexuality is an evil against God' and assured, 'Jesus would come down to earth to punish the evil people who decriminalized consensual gay sex.'[50]

Milli Gazette, which describes itself as Indian Muslims' leading English newspaper, called the apex court's decision as 'a step towards self-destruction'.[51] The All-India Muslim Personal Law Board issued a release saying, 'Legalizing homosexuality is against Indian values and culture. No religion allows immorality. The government must pass a bill to protect the rights of women as they are the major victims of legalised homosexuality.'[52] Jamiat Ulema-e-Hind's general secretary Maulana Mahmood Madani said, 'Homosexuality is against nature, religion and cultural values of India. It should not have been allowed.'[53]

In contrast to these positions, the Rashtriya Swayamsevak Sangh's (RSS's) response to the issue was more mellow. In 2016, joint general secretary of the RSS Dattatreya Hosabale had said, 'Homosexuality is not a crime but socially immoral act in our society. No need to punish but [it should] be treated as a psychological case. Approach to homosexuality should be no criminalization, no glorification either.'[54]

On the LGBTQ community, RSS chief Mohan Bhagwat said in 2018:

Everyone is a part of society. How they are, they are, accept people for what they are. Society has changed. It is important that society prepares itself so people do not feel isolated.[55]

The BJP, in its affidavit before the Supreme Court said:

> In the event this honourable Court is pleased to declare Section 377
> viz. 'consensual acts of adults in private', to be unconstitutional, no
> other issue/issues and/or rights are referred for consideration and
> adjudication and therefore, may not be gone into.[56]

All these facts surrounding the repeal of Section 377 of the Indian
Penal Code, of course, did not prevent the popular show *Made
In Heaven* from painting right-wing forces as the villains who were
against homosexuality and LGBTQ rights.[57] In 2022, Muslim groups
in Kerala launched widespread campaigns denouncing 'homosexuality
and gender politics'[58]—notably, ideologically aligned political parties
like the Indian Union Muslim League who were part of the UPA
coalition and contested the 2021 Kerala assembly in an alliance with
the Congress party, had also railed against homosexuality.[59]

It should be remembered that the RSS or its allied organizations
do not wield any theology-based influence on what Hindus should
think about homosexuality or other issues, whereas the Christian
and Muslim organizations that supported keeping Section 377 and
opposed the Court's decision, have substantial sway over what their
adherents should see as right or wrong. This is a structural difference
between the decentralized, polytheistic Hindu way and the Abrahamic,
monotheistic faiths.

India's Hindu majority has no theological mandate against
blasphemy, apostasy, homosexuality or abortion,[60] and yet the country
was always spiritual enough to never fall for the materialist philosophy
of communism—'the god that failed'.[61] The fundamental question of
whether Indians should exist as groups in the eyes of the State and
whether these groups supersede individual rights is not new. This was
a pressing question during the decades preceding the founding of the
Indian Republic, through the tumultuous 1930s and 1940s. This
question, along with that of the position of Muslims as a minority
group in free India, gained importance with the political rise of the
Muslim League under Jinnah.

One of the reasons why the Congress party accepted the Partition and rejected the last-ditch compromise proposed by the Cabinet Mission Plan of May 1946 was its disagreement with the Muslim League, which demanded differentiated citizenship. Jinnah asked for separate electorates, grouping of provinces by religion and myriad other religious identity-based 'safeguards'.

In such a confederation based on power-sharing between religious groups, religious identity would have primacy by constitutional sanction. The League had earlier fought for and won these separate electorates with British connivance. Jinnah initially opposed separate electorates, but that was before he discovered the raw political power of demagogic dog whistles. The Congress had opposed separate electorates initially, before Motilal Nehru opportunistically constructed an about-turn with the Lucknow Pact of 1916 where the Congress party accepted religion-based separate electorates.[62]

The Muslim demand for separate electorates gave rise to other communities asking for the same. The idea of separate electorates for Dalits was supported by B.R. Ambedkar, and stoutly opposed by Mahatma Gandhi. The latter undertook a fast-unto-death, and 1932 Poona Pact, unlike the Lucknow Pact, was a compromise, not surrender—reservations, not separate electorates, carried the day.[63]

When the Indian Republic was established on 26 January 1950, reservations were announced with a clear sunset clause, but they have been extended and even expanded by successive governments. Ambedkar stood for the long-term annihilation of caste. In the absence of sustained economic growth, availability of affordable and quality education for all, reservations have, in fact, not completely ended caste inequities. Even within the affected communities, there are valid concerns that a small section, sometimes across generations, have disproportionately cornered benefits. There is a clear case for time-bound, caste-based affirmative action but reforms are now necessary.

Moreover, as we have stated before, it is important when designing policy to take cognizance of the fact that caste and gender identities are less easy to change than one's religious identity. Any government that creates minority religion-based schemes and reservations—it would be baffling to any rational, neutral observer how these are termed 'secular'—is incentivizing conversions from the majority community, especially if such reservations bestow socioeconomic and not just political benefits.

In the Constituent Assembly debates, some Indian Muslim leaders proposed separate electorates. Sardar Patel shot the idea down with great anger and pain saying, to thunderous applause:

> Those who want that kind of thing have a place in Pakistan, not here. Here we are building a nation and laying the foundations for one nation, and those who choose to divide again and sow the seed of disruption will have no place, no quarter here and I must say that plainly enough.[64]

The demand for separate electorates prior to Independence and the partition of India itself arose from the view that Muslims were a separate group. In a free, democratic India, if Muslims have to be treated as a group and not as individual Indian citizens, why then, did we accept the trauma of Partition?

Thanks to increased economic freedom since 1991, there are increasing numbers of Muslims who see themselves, first and foremost, as aspirational Indians. But ultraconservative Islamist leaders and 'secular' politicians, who are invested in denying the individuality of the Indian Muslim for maintaining their power, want to box these individuals into a group identity.

The mentality that seeks to view Muslims as a separate group in free India also thrusts upon them a separate civil code, once again in the name of an Orwellian kind of secularism.

Most intellectuals saw no wrong when Prime Minister Manmohan Singh launched separate, exclusive schemes for minorities. Instead, the 'secular' intellectuals derided the BJP as 'communal' for not fielding Muslim candidates in Muslim-dominated constituencies during elections, not realizing that their demand was akin to Jinnah's demand for separate electorates.

In the face of these grotesque distortions, one is reminded of George Orwell's 1946 classic, *Politics and the English Language* in which he wrote: 'The word "fascism" has now no meaning except in so far as it signifies "something not desirable". The words democracy, socialism, freedom, patriotic, realistic, justice, have each of them several different meanings which cannot be reconciled with one another.'[65]

Words of these kinds, Orwell says, are often used in a consciously dishonest way. 'That is, the person who uses them has his own private definition, but allows his hearer to think he means something quite different.' The same applies to the words 'secular' and 'communal' in Indian discourse.

Maulana Azad, as Congress president, in a seminal speech delivered in March 1940 at Ramgarh, spelled out how by emphasizing internal differences, British imperialism 'sought to use various groups for the consolidation of its own power'.[66] For a long time now, the Congress party and the 'secular' intellectual establishment has been championing a softer form of Islamic separatism.

Azad envisioned Muslims in free India to be confident and aspirational. But the Congress party has borrowed the Muslim League's demagoguery (which is itself derived from the British Empire's strategy) and adopted policies in state and Union governments that seek to enfeeble Muslims and keep them backward, adding to the efficacy of their enticements and thus maintaining its grip on political power. What would Azad and Patel, whom today's Congress party claims in its pantheon of icons, have said?

This mindset shackled India's Muslims and kept India behind, for no nation can become developed if 15 per cent of its population remains economically and socially isolated.

Similar attempts to sow seeds of alienation in the Christian community were made frequently, primarily by some senior community leaders.[67] An article written in 2015 by the highly decorated retired police officer Julio Ribeiro, initially headlined 'I feel I am on a hit list', ignited a debate concerning India's Christians and their security under the Narendra Modi government after a series of incidents of vandalism at churches in New Delhi came to light.[68]

The then eighty-six-year-old Ribeiro—who admitted later he had 'slightly exaggerated' the piece to attract attention—made a series of scathing allegations against the Modi government, writing, 'I feel threatened, not wanted, reduced to a stranger in my own country.'

Indulging in such hyperbole and scaremongering is the standard template adopted by Left-leaning public figures whenever a BJP government comes to power. Soon after the Atal Bihari Vajpayee government assumed office in 1999, stray incidents of church vandalism in a few states were presented as evidence of persecution of Christians and their institutions, with none other than Pope John Paul II raising the issue with the Indian Prime Minister.[69]

The discourse becomes so polluted and perverted that every incident of vandalism or crime where a minority community is involved is viewed through the lens of communalism and secularism. Investigations into these incidents sometimes find that they were petty crimes and localized incidents, not necessarily motivated by religious hatred. *Swarajya* magazine's Swati Goel Sharma has comprehensively documented the deep bias in media reporting on hate crimes and alleged lynchings of minority groups. Sharma identified three aspects of such bias—first, the reliance on English-language news reports to construct narratives and data bases; second, the disproportionate focus on minority victims of Hindu violence while often ignoring Hindu victims of minority violence; third, even the categorization of crime motives based on the already flawed selection is dishonest.[70] As Anand Vardhan wrote in Newslaundry, 'When two claimants on social justice find themselves in a victim-perpetrator equation, an influential section of the media either looks away or refuses to identify social or religious groups of the victims and perpetrators.' Even academic databases that rely on English-language media reports as their primary data source are not entirely representative of reality.[71]

Ribeiro's commentary citing media narratives was not the only controversial part of his article. He proclaimed that Mother Teresa was an 'acknowledged saint, acknowledged by all communities and peoples'. Mother Teresa is seen as a saint by some devout Christians. To assert that she was universally seen as a saint is not just false, but unacceptable. For example, RSS chief Mohan Bhagwat's comment in 2015 that Mother Teresa had an evangelical agenda[72] is simply a statement of fact—it is something which she herself proudly admitted.

A committed harvester of souls for her God, Teresa received criticism[73] for baptizing the impoverished on their deathbeds.[74] Speaking in 1992, Teresa said that 29,000 people who 'chose' to be baptized on their death beds received the 'ticket to St. Peter'.[75] It was owing to such unethical acts and her missionary zeal that British writer Christopher Hitchens called her the 'ghoul of Calcutta' and described her as 'a fanatic, a fundamentalist and a fraud'.[76]

Contrasting Teresa with Irish social activist and Swami Vivekananda's disciple Sister Nivedita, the writer Ram Swarup had observed:[77]

> Mother Teresa is a true daughter of the Church in having her mind and heart closed to the religions of the countries of her labour, even adoption . . . Let me clarify the point a little further by bringing in Sister Nivedita. She is a lady Hindus are proud of. She helped India by helping it to rediscover itself. No higher service could be rendered to a nation in the grip of self-forgetfulness. She stood for national justice for India and she helped us by giving us national pride. This explains why Sister Nivedita is Hindu India's hero. This also explains why Western nations shower praise and money on Mother Teresa while Sister Nivedita remained unsung in the West . . .

Julio Ribeiro then asserted that the Christian community had made significant contributions to India by building educational institutions and hospitals. It is true that many of India's leading schools and colleges are run by Christian organizations and have rendered yeoman service in the country for many decades. But this has not been entirely without an agenda. The missionary organizations running these institutions received substantial subsidies from the Indian public. In the British era and even after Independence, missionary-run institutions received prime land in city centres at subsidized rates.

More significantly, they were allowed autonomy and freedom in how they should run their institutions. Even today, top-ranked institutions like St Stephen's College in Delhi, Christian Medical College in Vellore, St Xavier's College in Kolkata and countless missionary schools across India clearly declare themselves to be minority institutions and admit Christian students through explicit quotas; all of this is done at a subsidy, implicit and explicit, from Indian taxpayers, who are largely Hindus. Apart from quotas, these minority institutions enjoy much greater autonomy in admission processes, faculty recruitment, curriculum, fee structure and other areas of administration which are denied to similar institutions, mostly on the basis of a single criterion—the religion of the individuals in charge of their administration.

Christian Medical College, for instance, clearly states in its 2019–20 admissions prospectus that its aim is to 'train individuals for service in needy areas, especially in Christian mission hospitals', and 'a large number of Christian churches and missions throughout India make use of these opportunities for training' that it offers in medical education. On the importance of 'service', the prospectus states:

> The central location of the chapels, both in the college and the hospital, reflect the centrality of worship in the life of the community. Sunday worship services in several Indian languages and in English are conducted in the town campus chapel and in English in the college campus. Staff and student retreats led by eminent Christian thinkers are an important feature of the spiritual nurture of the community.[78]

The medical college has a special sponsored category constituting up to 50 per cent seats, reserved for Christian applicants. For the nursing programme, 85 per cent seats are reserved for Christians.

St Stephen's College has a 50 per cent Christian quota and lower entry marks for Christian applicants. Valson Thampu, its principal from 2008 to 2016, came into national media limelight when a staff member alleged that he was being coerced by Thampu to convert to Christianity.[79]

While premier schools and educational institutions funded by public money have large religious quotas, the generous public subsidies as well as protection afforded by government regulation certainly helped them achieve their premier position. This then becomes incentive for Hindus to convert, since becoming a Christian, increases one's chances of getting admission to some of India's top schools and colleges. The obvious implication is also that India has a system of government-funded Christian evangelism. Is that secular?

However, if self-funded and independent institutions retain Christian quotas, that is their choice. The problem is such choices are not available to Hindus as the alternatives for them are restricted by regulations in the education sector that have created artificial shortages.

These are facts well known to even Left–leaning intellectuals. Writing in June 2007, when St Stephen's College talked of increasing its Christian quota, historian Ramachandra Guha had observed:

> According to the Union ministry of education, fully 95 per cent of the expenses of the college are met by the University Grants Commission. Why should a college that draws so heavily on the public exchequer be allowed to choose 40 per cent of its students from 2 per cent of the country's population?[80]

'If my DNA is tested, it will not differ markedly from Bhagwat's,' wrote an impassioned Ribeiro in his article. But the reality is the Indian State treats a Ribeiro or a John differently from a Bhagwat or a Gupta. In flesh and blood, Christians, atheists, Muslims, Parsis, Buddhists and Hindus may all be the same, but in the eyes of the Indian State they are not.

Take education. The government awards poor students from the six designated religious minorities (including groups such as Jains, Parsis, Sikhs and Christians that are socially and economically better off compared to the average Indian) with scholarships whereas students from Hindu communities who may be poorer or more educationally backward are denied the benefits because of their religion. The government allows these minority groups unparalleled autonomy to run educational institutions 'of their choice'. It exempts elite minority schools from the Right to Education Act while forcing even low-cost private schools run by the majority community to be burdened and even closed down by the pernicious legislation's financial liability. The government has also created an exclusive statutory body for minority educational institutions which can only have minorities as its members. These examples are just the tip of the iceberg.

Take religious institutions. A number of state governments have legislated their way into governing boards of major temples in which corrupt, inefficient and even non-Hindu government nominees sit as members, much to the chagrin of devotees, directing the day-to-day affairs of sacred Hindu sites. However, as regards governance of churches, mosques or gurdwaras, community members have the final say.

The application of laws is discriminatory and arbitrarily affords more freedom to one religious group than the other.

For now, concerned Hindu activists have begun to respond to the unequal treatment based on identities in their own ways, by crafting a 'core agenda', 'Hindu charter', or 'equality manifesto' as a counter to the prevailing discrimination. The rise of the internet has enabled both the spread of awareness about Nehruvian chauvinism, as well as enabled its opponents to organize and advocate its end, and bring equality. Some features of this core agenda include ending discrimination in education sector policy, ending government control of Hindu temples, and dissolving religion-based welfare and shifting to an economic-need based approach instead.

In September 2018, around 100 Hindus from all walks of life gathered in New Delhi and presented a charter of Hindu demands,[81] the most notable of which was to pass a private member's bill introduced in Parliament by Satyapal Singh, BJP MP from Baghpat in Uttar Pradesh. Singh's bill had proposed amendments to Articles 15 and 25–30 of the Indian Constitution which would give Hindus the right, at par with the minorities, to manage their religious and educational institutions.

Other demands in the charter included enacting a national Freedom of Religion Act to 'prevent interference in practise and propagation of native Hindu and Indic traditions'; establishing a government-funded national body for restoration of dilapidated temples and 'preservation and propagation of Hindu literature, arts, dance forms, culture and traditions'; banning all foreign contributions except by persons of Indian origin to non-governmental organisations (NGOs) in India; an equal-opportunity act to enable an environment where students schooled in Indian languages are not at any disadvantage vis-a-vis the English-medium educated set, among others.

While reasonable people can debate the specific proposals, practicalities and consequences of this charter, one thing is clear— the increasing feeling of revulsion towards the minoritarianism of the Indian State is resulting in pushback from members of the majority community.

But one should not be surprised if some political entrepreneurs make these proposals their own as and when these ideas start to gain sizeable electoral currency. History tells us that social movements and intellectual churnings long precede political and policy change, the most prominent example in the Indian context being the Ram Mandir movement co-opted successfully by the BJP in the late 1980s.

The BJP, for instance, promised to free temples from government control in its election manifesto for the 2018 Karnataka assembly elections. When BJP says 'appeasement for none, development for all', it is essentially promising an end to the idea of different rules for different religious groups. If BJP does not deliver, someone else will. The electoral forces of demand and supply cannot possibly remain in imbalance for too long.

It should be worrying for every genuinely secular Indian that Hindus and non-Hindus are treated differently by the Indian State. Under the Nehruvian template, differential treatment of minorities in several areas has become the norm in our country. It is also true that individual and equal freedoms have been denied in areas such as personal laws to minorities within minorities—the most egregious episode was the Shah Bano case of 1985, when the Prime Minister Rajiv Gandhi used his brute parliamentary supermajority to overturn a Supreme Court judgment providing alimony to a divorced Muslim woman.[82]

Correcting this institutionalized discrimination is part of Narendra Modi's mandate. It is telling that not one proponent of secularism ever asks that Hindus be granted this equality. During the 2014 general election campaign, Modi faced opprobrium from the intelligentsia for declining to wear the Muslim skull cap. Not wearing the cap amounted to an insult to Muslims and a violation of secularism, was the verdict. But Modi took the firm and principled position that as a practising Hindu, he could not and would not wear a religious symbol only to garner votes.

India should strive to remove all identity markers from the State's business—from the Hindu Undivided Family benefits to Haj pilgrimage subsidies, from St Stephen's College being 95 per cent taxpayer funded despite having a substantial Christian quota, to disallowing conversions and discouraging certain dietary habits simply because some dislike it and so on. Caste quotas should be gradually phased out with a sunset clause, in line with what Ambedkar envisioned.

In 2019, the Modi government enunciated need-based quotas[83] by passing the 103rd amendment to the Constitution providing quotas for economically weaker sections (EWS).

By doing so, India established the principle that economic backwardness in and of itself can be a sufficient criterion for government mandated affirmative action. The principle is not entirely new because OBC stands for Other Backward Classes, not castes. This is why a large part of the Muslim community is also included under the OBC quota, and also why there is already an income exclusion criterion within the quota. It is only for the Scheduled Castes and Scheduled Tribes that the criteria were based primarily on identity.

Yet it increasingly makes sense to have income cutoffs across all quotas for there is no convincing answer to a simple question: why should a rich Dalit or tribal be preferred over a poor Dalit or tribal Indian for the same seats or positions?

With the government preparing to impose quotas for the Scheduled Castes, Scheduled Tribes, OBC and EWS in all private universities, including minority institutions, all higher educational institutions could be on the same plane.

A shift from identity-based to need-based welfare strikes at the roots of the Nehruvian paradigm. The defining feature of Narendra Modi's move is that there has been an unambiguous assertion that a poor Brahmin, or a poor Ashraf Muslim, deserves affirmative action while a rich OBC does not. The political positioning of India's parties on this issue delineates the fundamental fault lines of Indian politics. The Nehruvian project relies on keeping Hindus divided through caste, class, region or language, while consolidating religious minority votes even at the cost of pandering to its ultraconservative elements.

It is notable and revelatory that just three MPs opposed the amendment in the Lok Sabha,[84] and all three were from Muslim-oriented parties: two from the Indian Union Muslim League and one from the All India Majlis-e-Ittehadul Muslimeen.[85]

These are incipient moves towards the State seeing citizens as unique individuals rather than as members of a group. In a diverse nation like ours, most individuals have overlapping identities—Shaivite, Buddhist, Bengali, Yadav, Sufi, agnostic, female, bisexual—and the State makes for a clumsy adjudicator. For example, if one religious group is not allowed to adopt children but others are, then the State is effectively giving them a rather unpleasant choice—accept our definition of your faith, or declare yourself an apostate. The writer and philosopher Ayn Rand was right when she said, 'The smallest minority on earth is the individual. Those who deny individual rights cannot claim to be defenders of minorities.'

In a land of over a billion minorities, the unifying strain that all of us share is that each of us is an Indian, and retaining this individuality amid the panoply of identities is the idea of India.

On Kashmir, Pakistan and Karl Popper

The philosopher Karl Popper wrote[86] in his classic work *The Open Society and Its Enemies* that if we want to see tolerance thrive, it is very important that we do not tolerate intolerance beyond a point.

I do not imply, for instance, that we should always suppress the utterance of intolerant philosophies; as long as we can counter them by rational argument and keep them in check by public opinion, suppression would certainly be unwise. But we should claim the right to suppress them if necessary even by force; for it may easily turn out that they are not prepared to meet us on the level of rational argument, but begin by denouncing all argument; they may forbid their followers to listen to rational argument, because it is deceptive, and teach them to answer arguments by the use of their fists or pistols. We should therefore claim, in the name of tolerance, the right not to tolerate the intolerant.

There is an inherent tension between, for example, support for absolute free speech and other liberties and the dystopia that may be caused by irrational and possibly violent intolerance of the chronically intolerant. Ideally, we would not like this tension to exist and prefer individual rights to be fully guaranteed by the State at all times. But there are cases where the exercise of such individual rights can lead to the demise of the very State that is supposed to protect these rights. How then does one square the circle once again?

Let us go from the abstract to the specific and consider the case of Kashmir. The issue there is much less complicated than has been made out by umpteen talking heads and commentators, who cannot see the obvious reality right in front of them due to their desire for political correctness.

The Kashmir Valley, an area of about 4000 sq. km, has an overwhelming demographic dominance of Sunni Muslims, a dominance that was secured by the violent and brutal expulsion of Kashmiri Hindus from there in 1990. The area being adjacent to Pakistan, a few want to secede from 'Hindu' India in the name of their religion. The media often conflates this relatively small area with all of Jammu, Kashmir and Ladakh, which has a total land area of over 22,2000 sq. km. There are obviously geographical, historical and legal factors that can be debated about this region until the cows come home, but the fundamental sore point for Pakistan is, how can

a Muslim-majority border region be a part of India and not of the
Islamic Republic of Pakistan?

Pakistan's supremacist posture towards Hindu India and
revanchist tendency to acquire Muslim-majority territories for itself
manifests itself in different ways. For example, where India names its
guided missiles Prithvi, Agni and Akash after the natural elements,
Pakistan names missiles after Mahmud Ghaznavi and Muhammad
Ghauri, two of the prominent early invaders and marauders of Hindu
India. Ghaznavi is particularly notorious for plundering the Somnath
temple seventeen times. In Pakistani military lore, the Gujarat theatre
of the 1965 India–Pakistan war has been portrayed as the eighteenth
attack on the Somnath Temple. Shah Mehmood Qureshi, who served
recently as Foreign Minister of Pakistan, had once compared himself
to Ghaznavi, proclaiming that he too would lead the destruction of
the Somnath shrine.[87]

Such is the lens through which Pakistan's senior-most military and
governmental leaders see India. Given this context, how should India
react to Pakistan's revanchism on Kashmir? One school of thought says
let us not hold any people, even if within a small valley, against their
will. But then, what would be the implications of a second religious
partition for India? It would imply that a minority that becomes a
majority in an Indian state can never be truly Indian, and this may
cause further fissures within the rest of India.

This is not just a hypothetical scenario. Demographic changes in
Kerala, West Bengal and Assam are moving in that direction, as census
data from 2001 and 2011 show. In West Bengal, the Muslim population
increased by 21.8 per cent between 2001 and 2011, compared to 10.8
per cent for the Hindu population. In Kerala, the Muslim population
increased by 12.8 per cent between 2001 and 2011, compared to 2.2
per cent for the Hindu population. In Assam, the Muslim population
increased by 29.5 per cent between 2001 and 2011, compared to 10.9
per cent for the Hindu population.

Should India just wait for that to happen? Obviously not. No State
would tolerate that, and the civilizational state of India, that is Bharat
certainly would not. For Bharat is nothing without Dharma, as Sri

Aurobindo said in his 1909 Uttarpara speech[88] before he retired to a life of spiritual exploration.

It is important to contrast the secessionist demands of the Sunni Muslim Kashmir Valley with such demands in, say, Catalonia (Spain), Scotland (United Kingdom) or Quebec (Canada). Any successful secession in the latter cases would result in a new nation-state within the broader West. In the first two cases, the new countries could be within not just the West but also within the European Union. Even a free Quebec would almost certainly be absorbed into the successor trade framework of the North American Free Trade Agreement (NAFTA) and the North Atlantic Treaty Organisation (NATO) security grouping. There is a civilizational logic to these inclusions and exclusions. Turkey, for example, could never enter the European Union and is plausibly going to leave NATO as well.

The renowned British philosopher Roger Scruton remarked while building on the work of constitutional jurist Jeremy Rabkin, 'The nation–state has been the greatest guarantor of freedom in the modern world, precisely because it establishes a territorial, rather than religious, jurisdiction. It is this that enables the nation–state to treat citizenship, rather than creed, as the criterion of membership.'[89] Still, his view must be seen in the European historical context of medieval religious wars.

It is important to belabour this point—if Northern Ireland unites with the Republic of Ireland and breaks with the United Kingdom of England, Scotland and Wales, as is plausible in the next few years,[90] it is partially because of demographic changes (possibly for the first time in centuries Catholics outnumber Protestants), but also because of ideological changes, namely, the Republic of Ireland as part of the larger civilizational entity of the European Union and in keeping with the zeitgeist of secular modernity, has given up draconian restrictions on abortion and has had a mixed-race Prime Minister from the LGBT community. No heretics are of course being killed, and there is no de facto concept of religious speech being declared as blasphemous by the State. With the sharp edges gone, the two Irelands can focus on the commonalities of their shared ethnolinguistic, Christian and now liberal heritage, egged on by the decision of Brexit.

Seen from this civilizational framework, any new Western country would simply mean a rearrangement of internal civilizational boundaries akin to the creation of a new state such as Telangana or Jharkhand within India. On the other hand, the so-called liberation of Kashmir—whether through 'azadi' or formal merger with Pakistan—would mean the loss of territory to a hostile civilizational unit. That is the reality.

Let us for a moment see Kashmir as Northern Ireland, Pakistan as the Republic of Ireland, and India as United Kingdom (in which case the rest of India is Great Britain). Some people can argue that for demographic and geographic reasons, Kashmir (more specifically the Valley districts) should go to Pakistan. But there are many objections to this. First, Partition was never about a one-to-one mapping to religious demographics even though that was the broad principle. Second, Pakistan is not like the Irish Republic in this thought experiment. Pakistan has not even remotely gone through any period of secular–liberal Enlightenment which would make the minorities, including many Shias and Muslim liberals, in the Valley comfortable about joining that setup (and even independence would be practically joining Pakistan, given the Valley's landlocked geography). The treatment meted out to Ahmadi Muslims in Pakistan is testament to the deeply intolerant ethos pervading its social culture.[91] Third, even if Pakistan miraculously went through a genuine secularization process, the principle of self-determination applies significantly less to a democratic, pluralistic setup such as India's as compared to a theocratic or authoritarian one. If the United States could sacrifice around 6,00,000 of its young men in the sparsely populated 1860s and temporarily suspend civil liberties to preserve the Union and break the back of slavery, India can and will fight to keep the Union and defeat theocracy. Finally, quite simply, Kashmir is integral to India's civilizational heritage,[92] given its millennia-old Hindu and Buddhist history.[93]

Post-partition India got a fraction of Bengal, Punjab and Kashmir, and should keep it that way. While the national anthem mentions an area called 'Sindh', today India doesn't have any such region. India should consider declaring some border districts of Gujarat and

Rajasthan as Sindh (perhaps as a union territory). India's division is final—any future litigation is best expressed by voting with one's feet, as it were. Those wanting religion-based political representation should move to a theocratic country,[94] to paraphrase Sardar Patel, for India will not compromise on its pluralistic ethos.

Speaking of Sindh and demographics, it is worth considering the case of some Hindu-majority areas in Pakistani Sindh, all next to the India border. Just like the Kashmir Valley has many sacred sites for Hindus, some areas in Sindh also have beautiful Hindu and Jain temples. Why did Tharparkar (in Sindh) not come to India with Partition? After all, Sindh province was separated from Bombay province in 1936.

Most of the Hindu-dominated areas are in present-day Tharparkar district, with Nagarparkar, even today, having a Hindu majority. This area is also where dozens of Hindu girls are being abducted, raped, forcibly married and converted regularly. By some estimates, 'at least 25 conversions of young Hindu girls and women take place every month in Umerkot's Kunri and Samaro talukas alone'.[95] Theocracies are not hospitable to non-adherents of the official State religion.

It was to rescue such hapless religious minorities in Pakistan and other Islamic countries that the Narendra Modi government implemented the Citizenship (Amendment) Act, or CAA in 2019. The CAA provided an accelerated path to Indian citizenship for persecuted minorities of neighbouring theocracies. As the writer Amish noted in the *Hindustan Times*:[96]

> In 1950, Prime Minister Jawaharlal Nehru signed the Nehru-Liaquat pact with Pakistani PM Liaquat Ali Khan, in which India promised to look after its Muslim minority and Pakistan, its non-Muslim minority. India has honoured its half of the pact. During this period, the population proportion of Muslims in India has increased from under 10% to over 14%. But in Pakistan and Bangladesh, perhaps one of the biggest ethnic cleansings of the past century has occurred with 60 million fewer minorities than there should have been. This amendment attempts to protect six besieged minorities from extinction.

Even as it offers a path to safety for such persecuted groups, the CAA does not impinge on the status of any Indian citizen. The CAA is similar to the Lautenberg Amendment in the US,[97] which prioritizes some Christians and Jews from the former Soviet Union, as well as religious minorities from Iran. The path for Muslims from any country to become citizens of India or to obtain asylum status in India remains open as before. Finally, the proposed National Register of Citizens as described by government leaders so far can and should have appropriate safeguards to ensure that no Indian citizen faces disenfranchisement.

It was a historical blunder that areas like Tharparkar and Nagarparkar in Sindh did not come to India. The logistical steps of executing the Partition were messy and arbitrary. The Boundary Commission tasked with dividing the populations was chaired by Cyril Radcliffe, a man who had never set foot in India before he was handed that job. Radcliffe also glibly said that no matter what he did, 'people would suffer' and he approached his task with casualness bordering on disdain, despite the enormous import of the decisions to be made.[98]

Some areas were left here, some there—demographic coherence was neither achieved nor aimed at by the Indian side, which is why the vast majority of Muslims in what are today's Uttar Pradesh, Madhya Pradesh, Bihar and West Bengal remained in India despite most of them (of those who could vote) having supported Muslim League in the 1946 elections, knowing very well that the clear demand of the League was Pakistan.[99, 100] Moreover, it was patently obvious even back then that Pakistan would become an Islamic state, Jinnah's confusing statements notwithstanding, and India a pluralist one, so India keeping a small Muslim-majority region is simply not comparable to Pakistan keeping a Hindu-majority region in the first place.

It is important here to step back and deal with the question of 'Akhand Bharat'. Some in Pakistan fear that India, especially if led by 'Hindutva forces', would try to forcibly annex Pakistan and Bangladesh to try to create a Greater India, Bharat Varsha or Jambudvipa of ancient times. In that context, many Pakistani critics argue, India's 'obdurate' stand on Kashmir is just the first step in a larger revanchist plan.

Nothing could be further from the truth. No Indian political group of any significance wants India to stop being a democracy—because there is a recognition that democracy is the only realistic way of keeping India united for the foreseeable future. And a democratic India simply cannot absorb 350 million more Muslim citizens when it has not been able to integrate the existing minority citizens legally (given that India still has religion-based civil laws), or more importantly, socially.

A small section of Indians may want to see Pakistan and Bangladesh back within the Indian fold but they realize that is only possible if those countries themselves choose such a path. Coercion, or even attempting persuasion, is out of the question. In the 2015 land-boundary settlement with Bangladesh, India actually conceded more land than it received,[101] transferring approximately 40 sq. km of territory to Bangladesh.

Partition, then, was not a generous concession but a recognition of the reality of a millennium-and-a-quarter's worth of Islamic presence in the subcontinent. Even Atal Bihari Vajpayee effectively confirmed this at the Minar-e-Pakistan in Lahore, when he visited Pakistan as Prime Minister in 1999.[102] Girilal Jain, the former editor of the *Times of India*, went on to say, only half in jest, that 'Muhammad Ali Jinnah was the greatest benefactor of Hindus in modern times, if he was not a Hindu in disguise.'[103] Ambedkar also wrote in favour of Partition to create a more coherent Indian nation-state, and in the Congress party, Rajaji was the first senior leader to see its wisdom before Patel and Nehru agreed with him.

Hence, India's insistence on Kashmir (and Jammu, Ladakh along with Pakistan-Occupied Kashmir, or PoK) being its integral territory in no way implies that what is currently Pakistan is also to be considered a part of India. The fear of such Indian revanchism (beyond PoK) among Pakistani strategists is actually a mirror to their own wild fantasies of Ghazwa-e-Hind.[104] One cannot do anything about such delusions, unfortunately, and Pakistan's strategic culture seems to be steeped in fantasies.[105]

In Jammu, Kashmir and Ladakh, until Article 370 and Article 35A providing special status were removed by the Modi government in August 2019, caste-based affirmative action and the laws promoting gender equity did not apply. Protections for homosexual Indians, thanks to the repeal of Section 377, were not extended to the region. Many Hindus and Sikhs who had come from what is now Pakistan or PoK could not vote in state elections (though they could vote in national elections), despite residing in the erstwhile state for decades. Since the revocation of the special status, Jammu, Kashmir and Ladakh have seen increased freedoms to women and historically oppressed communities.[106] Citizens of the region who were deprived of voting rights in state elections and even public-welfare benefits are now receiving equal access.[107]

The end of separate, special status through a de facto abrogation of Article 370 has rightfully and irrevocably integrated Jammu, Kashmir and Ladakh with India, and brought Indian constitutional values and legal guarantees to millions of people residing in the region.

3

Saving Secularism from the Secularists

I believe that the word 'secular' is the biggest lie since Independence. Those that have given birth to this lie and those that use it should apologize to the people and this country. No system can be secular. The political system can be sect neutral. If someone were to say that the government has to be run by one way of prayer, that is not possible. In UP, I have to look at 22 crore people and I am answerable for their security and their feelings. But I am not sitting here to ruin one community either. You can be sect-neutral but not secular.

—Uttar Pradesh Chief Minister Yogi Adityanath[1]

Nehru's soft bigotry of low expectations

Speaking in 1955 during the parliamentary debate on the Hindu Code Bill[2] that sought to reform personal laws for the Hindu community, Acharya J.B. Kripalani said:

I charge you with communalism because you are bringing forward a law about monogamy only for Hindu community. Take it from me that the Muslim community is prepared to have it but you are not brave enough to do it.[3]

69

Kripalani, who was decidedly not from the Hindu Right, was castigating Prime Minister Jawaharlal Nehru for being an appeaser, a charge we agree with. Yet, it is Nehru who is upheld as a paragon of liberal and secular values, and generation after generation of intellectuals has internalized his dubious standards.

Some intellectuals and commentators peddle Nehru's line of argument that reform in the Muslim community should happen through 'persuasion' rather than 'imposition'. India must take group rights seriously 'if we want the world to believe that we are a genuine democracy,'[4] former editor of *The Hindu* newspaper Malini Parthasarathy asserted once. But that does not answer why citizens affiliated to one religion should have had to face difficulties in formally adopting children,[5] for example—and if their religion is indeed opposed to adoption or other practices, why not let those individuals decide? Why should the Indian State make itself an arbiter of what a given scripture says, and why should it align itself with conservative religious dogma that undermines an individual's rights? Business magnate and founder of Infosys N.R. Narayana Murthy, too, has argued in the past that reform in the Muslim community should come from within.[6] Delivering the first Darbari Seth Memorial Lecture on 21 August 2002 on the issue of having a uniform civil code, Murthy said that the onus to introduce it should be on leaders of a given community 'if they want their community to prosper':

> There are many people who believe that the country must have a uniform civil code. My own view is that this is not necessary as long as the country's economic progress is not hampered. The leaders of a given community whose personal code is not progressive or modern should be the ones to take up this issue . . . Let the onus be on them.

Should Indians not care about the welfare and prosperity of their fellow Indians? Is it sustainable for a nation to have socially liberal ideals for one section of society, while condemning another section to religious orthodoxy? There are severe social and economic implications of encouraging 'separateness' between religious communities. Successive

Indian governments did little to change regressive gender practices in the Muslim community under the garb of protecting them. The result is that Muslim women today are far less likely to be a part of the economic mainstream of the country. It is not that they do not have aspirations—the sad reality is those aspirations were sacrificed at the altar of electoral politics and political convenience by successive pseudo-secular governments, almost all of them led by the Congress party.

Advocates of religion-based group rights deny that social backwardness has an endogenous basis. Instead, they insist any differences between groups, even if adjusted for education and income levels, are mostly due to discrimination. In the case of the Muslim community, it is clear that some backwardness is present because of the community's attitudes towards women, especially when it comes to education and employment, as documented in the much-touted 2006 Rajinder Sachar Committee report itself. This affects not just the Muslim community, but India's economy as well as broader societal harmony.

Many intellectuals and politicians dismiss as 'communal' those advocating for dissolution of identity distinctions enforced by the State. Acharya Kripalani would have been called communal today.

India rejected Nehru's economic ideology of State control and government-led industrialization, embracing economic liberalization in 1991 with impressive results for all sections of society, as Columbia University economists Jagdish Bhagwati and Arvind Panagariya have comprehensively documented in their book *Why Growth Matters: How Economic Growth in India Reduced Poverty and the Lessons for Other Developing Countries.*[7]

In the interest of social harmony and national integration, it is high time the Indian State breaks from Nehru's construct of seeing religious minorities as 'separate from us' and stops indulging in the 'soft bigotry of low expectations'—to borrow the phrase used by former US President George W. Bush—from certain communities. This kind of mindset only produces distrust in society and encourages Indians to be suspicious of one another because the State emphasizes our differences, rather than our common heritage, while making us compete for goods and services for which an artificial shortage was created by faulty economic policies. The correct stand a government should take is not to label its citizens, but to simply step aside and let the individual decide how she or he wants to identify themselves.

Hamid Dalwai, a Marathi Muslim who faced ostracism from his community for being a radical reformist, understood this. He advocated women's emancipation through education and employment at the social level, and for a liberal–secular government at the political level. In his 1969 book *Muslim Politics in Secular India*, he critiqued minority politics for continuing to further the separatist mindset of the pre-Partition Muslim League.[8]

The real problem, Dalwai wrote, was Muslim obscurantism. Dalwai also argued that the right answer to Muslim communalism is not its Hindu variant, but genuine secularism. Hindu communalism is largely reactive whereas the Muslim opposition to separation of State and religion is theologically central, a reality that is globally observable today. Despite this reality, the Left-leaning intelligentsia attempts to falsely draw an equivalence between both.

Dalwai wrote that Indian Muslim intellectuals are more likely to blame Hindus rather than introspect. As early as 1967, Hamid Dalwai led a protest march demanding that the government should end the practice of triple talaq.[9] On 20 March 1970,[10] Hamid Dalwai founded the Muslim Satyashodhak Mandal to bring social reforms in the Muslim community. Speaking at a function of the Samajwadi Mahila Sabha in March 1973,[11] Dalwai had said that purdah should be legally banned, and family planning be made compulsory. Rejecting claims that sharia laws were made by God and thus must not be changed, he said that 'leaders of other religions had said the same thing and yet changes were made to their laws'.

After Hamid Dalwai passed away at the age of just forty-four in 1977, his many colleagues carried on the struggle for social reforms to no avail. His wife Mehrunnisa Dalwai, who went on to lead the Muslim Satyashodhak Mandal, argued that 'laws applying 1400 years ago cannot be applied in today's situation'. Mrs Dalwai regretted in 1986 that 'Muslim fundamentalists are using this issue to retain their hold over the community.'[12] After a lifetime of activism, Mehrunnisa

Dalwai passed away in 2017 at the age of eighty-seven, just two months before the Supreme Court struck down triple talaq as unconstitutional.[13]

Things have not changed much over the decades despite spirited advocacy for such reforms by members of all communities, including prominent Muslims.

Reform is the need of the hour, and entails confronting what Hamid Dalwai characterized as 'obscurantist medievalism'[14] rather than evading it under the deceptive labels of 'minority protection' and 'secularism'. The new standard should be that anyone who claims that such reform is only a 'Muslim problem' is 'communal', for it is a problem for all Indians if a large section of India's society is consumed by religion-sanctioned and State-enforced orthodoxy.

Scholars like the anthropologist Partha Chatterjee have pointed out that the Indian Right is simply not threatened by genuine secularism, and that if a strict separation of religion and State is accepted, this would—in his Left–Liberal view—be incompatible with religion-based positive discrimination.[15]

This exposes the game of Left–Liberals: 'formal' equality is not enough, the ever-subjective 'substantive' or 'contextual' equality is what will be demanded. Unfortunately, sections of the so-called Right fall in this trap by failing to advocate the former, which would force the Left to explicitly defend the latter.

There is also the question of India's changing demographics, that has been analysed in detail by Dr J.K. Bajaj of the Chennai-based Centre for Policy Studies. Commenting on the decadal population trend, Bajaj wrote that 'very significant changes in the relative numbers of different communities that have taken place in the course of 2001–2011'.[16] Bajaj groups Indic-origin religions (Sikhism, Jainism and Hinduism) together as 'Indian Religionists' (IRs) and then compares the growth rate of the group with that of the Muslim community over the decades, noting:

The gap between the growth rates of Muslims and IRs, normalized to the absolute growth of IRs, widened to as much as 49 percent during 1981–91; it became marginally narrower in 1991–2001

and has widened again in the last decade. The commentators, who
have been pointing out the decline of the Muslim growth rate from
29.69 to 24.65 percent as an indication of the halting of the religious
imbalance, are wrong; because, the normalized gap between the
growth rates of Muslims and IRs has only widened. The Muslims in
the country have grown by nearly 50 percent more than the Indian
Religionists for the third decade in a row.[17]

Widening Normalized Gap in the Growth of Muslims and Indian Religionists			
Census Decade	Growth of Indian R (percent)	Growth of Muslims (percent)	Normalized Growth Gap (percent)
1951-61	21.16	24.43	15.45
1961-71	23.84	30.84	29.36
1971-81	24.09	30.74	27.60
1981-91	22.79	33.89	48.70
1991-01	20.34	29.50	45.03
2001-11	16.67	24.65	47.82

*Difference as a proportion of Growth of Indian Religionists,
including Hindus, Sikhs, Jains and ORPs.*

Table 3.1: Comparing growth for Indic-origin religion adherents and
Islam adherents[18]

Given that these are national figures, there are states where the
dynamics of religious demographic change are more pronounced.
Political leaders also acknowledge the demographic change underway:
speaking about the activities of Christian evangelical groups, YSR
Congress MP Raghu Ramakrishna Raju said in May 2020[19] that
'conversions are happening at many places in the country. It is the
money power of the Christian missionaries that they are pumping

in money from abroad to carry out their proselytizing activities and strengthening their religion. This is happening throughout the country.' Changing religious demographics is not a problem in and of itself, but the picture is complicated by the primacy accorded to group rights and religion-based welfare schemes in India, as well as the history of secessionism along this axis.

In their everyday lives though, Indians continue to resist the divisive messages issued by the political class and are forging a deeper, common identity. In India's melting pot—and urbanizing landscape—customs are cross-pollinating more than ever before, making for a unique and constantly evolving culture. Nowhere is this more visible than in the tradition of the great Indian wedding, in the form of mehndi and Bollywood-style *sangeet* functions in Christian weddings, and Sufi music performers invited to Hindu weddings. It is the government's insistence on telling Indians what their identity is that creates fissures in society.

The pseudo-secularist fraud

In his book *The Hindu Phenomenon*, eminent journalist and author Girilal Jain had written:[20]

> As a group, the secularists, especially the Leftists, have not summoned the courage to insist that in order to ensure the survival of the secular India state, Muslims should accept one common civil code, and that Article 370 of the Constitution, which concedes special rights to Jammu and Kashmir mainly because it is a Muslim-majority state, should be scrapped . . . I find it extraordinary that those who call themselves modernizers and secularists—the two terms are interchangeable—should shirk the logic of their philosophy of life.

Identity politics, the principal driver behind the partition of India in 1947, has only worsened since Independence. Rather than placing primacy on the universal rights of individuals, successive governments divided the population into groups and arbitrarily allocated rights to these groups, forcing individuals to self-identify as members of this group or that.

As described earlier, even as Hindus enjoyed increased social freedoms, they were denied control over their temples and their ability to run Hindu-oriented educational institutions was eroded to the point of complete debilitation. Where Muslims and Christians enjoyed freedom from State interference over their places of worship and retained control over educational institutions, they were deprived of social freedoms that Hindus now take for granted. More perniciously, political parties belonging to the 'secular' fold have openly doled out government welfare on religious grounds. One can only bluntly describe this practice as bribery, and it has enjoyed the highest judicial endorsement and constitutional protection. This bribery, euphemistically called 'minority appeasement' in popular parlance, saw a dramatic escalation during the Sonia Gandhi–Manmohan Singh era, and that escalation has escaped scrutiny and critical commentary.[21]

In November 2004, the UPA government formed the National Commission for Minority Educational Institutions (NCMEI) ostensibly to protect educational institutions established by India's religious minorities. In 2018, the Supreme Court held that NCMEI had the power 'to decide all questions relating to the status of an institution as a minority educational institution and to declare its status as such'.[22] By law, a Hindu cannot be a member of this Commission. While non-Hindu Supreme Court judges or a local district collector can be trusted to judge knotty theological issues pertaining to Hinduism and the government has powers to appoint non-Hindus as the trustees of Hindu temple trusts, the government thinks it fit to explicitly exclude Hindus from a statutory public body such as NCMEI. Even though a Christian or a Parsi can define policy and adjudicate issues concerning Muslims and vice-versa, somehow a Hindu is particularly disqualified from doing the same.

In March 2005, Prime Minister Manmohan Singh appointed the Sachar Committee to study the social and economic condition of India's Muslim community.[23] In January 2006, the government carved out a separate ministry for minorities. In the same month, the 93rd constitutional amendment came into force, with the BJP's efforts to dilute the communalist elements in the amendment being rejected by the 'secular' coalition. This amendment cleared the way for the government to implement caste quotas in private educational institutions while explicitly keeping institutions run by the minorities exempt.

In June 2006, Prime Minister Manmohan Singh announced the 15-Point Programme for the welfare of minorities.[24] Under it, he declared that a certain percentage of the Integrated Child Development Service (ICDS) projects or Anganwadi Centres, government schools and new Industrial Training Institutes (ITIs) would be located in areas with a substantial population of minority communities. He promised Central assistance for recruitment and posting of Urdu-language teachers in primary and upper primary schools in areas where 25 per cent of the population spoke Urdu. The government created special scholarship schemes for minority students, discriminating between Indian citizens on the basis of religion.[25]

The government also committed under the Programme that ministries would 'earmark 15 per cent of the physical targets and financial outlays for minorities'. The 'secular' alliance of UPA didn't blink while asserting that 'in the recruitment of police personnel, state governments will be advised to give special consideration to minorities'.[26]

The Programme also stated that 'in the areas, which have been identified as communally sensitive and riot prone, district and police officials of the highest known efficiency, impartiality and secular record must be posted'. By now, we are all too aware of the connotation of the word 'secular' so there is no need for clarification on what the Programme was referring to. But this raises an obvious point, why should officers with a secular record be posted in communally sensitive areas only? Would it be alright if those with a 'non-secular' record are posted in 'normal' areas? Such are the absurd and artificial fissures that the 'secularized' idea of India has manufactured.

On 30 November 2006, the Sachar Committee Report recommending various sectarian schemes on the lines of the Programme was tabled in the Parliament. On 9 December 2006, Prime Minister

Manmohan Singh asserted that Muslims would have first claim on India's resources while addressing the 52nd meeting of the Planning Commission's National Development Council (NDC).[27] The Union government then went on to classify a host of minority-only schemes in education and skill development as 'core of core' schemes which were given top priority in the allocation of public resources. In the same year, the government tried to conduct a survey on the religious affiliations of India's soldiers, inviting the ire of Army Chief J.J. Singh.[28] 'Our system for entry into the armed forces and for enrollment is based on merit and on the ability to perform the task that might be assigned,' said General Singh. Starting in 2007, the government began doling out sectarian, minority-only pre-matric and post-matric scholarships. The National Advisory Council chaired by Sonia Gandhi had even recommended that the National Rural Employment Guarantee Scheme should have a special minority focus.[29]

In 2009, after bringing the 93rd Amendment to India's Constitution, the Union government enunciated the Right to Education (RTE), from the provisions of which minority schools were exempted completely but with which most Hindu schools should comply. In 2013, the Congress–UPA government brought the Communal Violence Bill, which did not recognize communal violence committed by minority communities against the majority community. This bill was withdrawn after strong opposition to it from many parties, including the BJP.[30]

In January 2013, Union Home Minister Sushilkumar Shinde asserted that 'reports have come during investigation that BJP and RSS conduct terror training camps to spread terrorism . . . This is saffron terrorism.'[31] In March 2013, Shinde wrote to Minority Affairs Minister K. Rahman Khan that special Muslim-only fast-track courts would be set up for trial of terror cases.[32] Why not reform the whole judicial system to speed up justice delivery for all Indians?

In January 2014, in an astounding display of New Delhi's executive interference in the functioning of states' police and legal process, Shinde wrote to all chief ministers asking them to set up special screening committees to look at cases where minority youths had been jailed, following up on a communication in September 2013 by the home minister that asked all chief ministers to ensure 'wrong arrests' of minorities were not made.[33]

In January 2014, Jains were declared a national 'minority' community by the Union government,[34] the same month when the Union minority affairs minister said the government was seriously looking into religion-based reservations for minorities. Like in the case of the RTE, the government created incentives for the balkanization of India's society, since becoming a 'minority', results in benefits flowing from the minority affairs ministry, and various exemptions become available with minority status under existing laws.

In 1980, similar perverse incentives drove Swami Vivekananda's Ramakrishna Mission to try and declare itself non-Hindu in a bid to escape the Indian State's intrusive hand.[35] In 2018, we saw a promise made during the Assembly election campaign by the Congress party in Karnataka to provide the coveted tag of minority to Lingayats,[36] a prominent Hindu community that traditionally votes for the BJP.

Other parties subscribing to this malignant mutation of secularism follow the Congress party's lead closely.

Uttar Pradesh, which was run by a 'secular' Samajwadi Party government during 2012–2017, created a number of Muslim-only government welfare schemes. The state government introduced an education scheme only for Muslim girls—spare a thought for the Hindu girl denied aid because of her faith. The government created special tribunals to expedite the hearing of cases relating to Muslim-owned property.[37] The state government went so far as to attempt unilaterally dropping charges against those accused of terrorism[38]—something it had promised it would do before the 2012 Assembly elections—but was restrained from doing so by the Lucknow bench of the Allahabad High Court. 'Today you are withdrawing cases against them, tomorrow will you give them the Padma Bhushan?', the court had said to the state government when it tried to let two terror accused in the 2006 Varanasi bomb blasts—a heinous attack that claimed 25 lives—off the hook.[39] In August 2013, Chief Minister Akhilesh Yadav announced that a 20 per cent share in spending in all eighty-five state-administered development schemes would be reserved for minorities. In September

2013, India saw heinous violence in UP under the Samajwadi Party state government and a Congress-led Union government, both of them said to be secular. Over four dozen people were killed, and 50,000 were displaced, yet, scarcely any question was asked of Chief Minister Akhilesh Yadav or the Union government.[40]

In 2017, UP supposedly turned 'communal' on Yogi Adityanath's election as chief minister. The result was for all to witness—communal clashes dropped drastically on Holi in 2018.[41] According to the UP Director General of Police (DGP), only fourteen communal clashes took place compared to fifty-nine in 2017, ninety-seven in 2016, fifty-five in 2015, sixty-four in 2014 and fifty-one in 2013 during 'secular' rule. Among the first actions taken by Chief Minister Yogi Adityanath was to introduce English language education at the nursery level. 'The traditional and the modern should blend. We should have an education system which promotes nationalism but is modern,' Adityanath said.[42]

The propensity to ban English language education in government schools should be seen in terms of whom it helps. When public schools don't offer English as a language of instruction, it is schools run by Christian missionaries and evangelical forces—which are exempted from government control and whose agenda it is to pursue religious conversions—that stand to benefit.

Some of the Hindu temples in India would rank among the wealthiest religious institutions in the world. For example, the Tirupati temple in Andhra Pradesh and Padmanabhaswamy temple in Kerala, both controlled by the respective state governments, together have an asset base running into several tens of billions of dollars. Tirupati Tirumala Devasthanams (TTD) trust alone has over Rs 12,000 crore or $1.5 billion in cash deposits, nearly 9.2 tons of gold,[43] and vast land holdings among other assets. The Padmanabhaswamy temple's asset base is valued at over Rs 1 trillion or over $12 billion.

There is a long-standing practice of state governments dipping into the coffers of temple trusts to supplement government revenue and fund the state's expenditure. In 1983, the Andhra Pradesh state government nudged the TTD trust to transfer its surplus funds to the government coffers. BJP's M. Venkaiah Naidu, a legislator at the time who went on to serve as India's Vice-President, had said, 'It is an encroachment on the affairs of a Hindu religious endowment.' S. Jaipal Reddy of the Janata Party, who subsequently went on to have a long career in public life with the Congress party, at the time had said that 'Government should not tamper with the funds of religious organizations. It is more difficult and sensitive to touch funds of organizations of religions other than Hinduism.'[44]

This channelling of funds donated by pious Hindus into government welfare and public schemes never makes the progressives wince. Under the Andhra Pradesh Charitable and Hindu Religious Institutions Act, 1966, all temples receiving above Rs 5 lakh per year are required to pay 21.5 per cent of their income to the state's Endowments Department.[45] Not only do Indian governments not shy away from taking temple money for public schemes, they pool such funds with taxpayer's money and create subsidies for Christians to travel to Bethlehem, as the Congress party Chief Minister Y.S. Rajasekhara Reddy (YSR) had done in Andhra Pradesh.[46]

Andhra Pradesh, under YSR and the unquestionably 'secular' Congress party, set a new benchmark for persistence in the pursuit of minority appeasement. As the politician–scholar Arun Shourie documented in his masterful work *Falling Over Backwards*,[47] the YSR government tried relentlessly to create job reservations for Muslims, starting June 2004, but kept being rebuffed by the judiciary which held that such reservations were unconstitutional. The state government eventually secured religion-based reservations within the OBC quota for a subset of 'caste' Muslims only.

Besides giving a special allowance to Christians for visiting Bethlehem, on the lines of the Haj subsidy provided for Muslims, YSR doled out taxpayer funds to Christian organizations for the refurbishment and construction of churches.[48] YSR's son-in-law, Christian evangelist Anil Kumar, held large-scale evangelism programmes with assistance from the state government.[49]

In the most tragicomic manifestation of Nehruvian economics combined with 'secularism', government-controlled temples in Andhra Pradesh—such as the renowned 300-year-old Varaha Lakshmi

Narasimha temple at Simhachalam—were so inefficiently managed that they were unable to deal with the large number of cows being donated by devout Hindus and stopped accepting such donations. YSR government's response was both reprehensible and insensitive—the cows were auctioned to slaughterhouses apparently because the temple authorities were unable to care for them, despite receiving crores of rupees every year in donations from devotees.[50]

In 2012, three TTD employees, who are duty-bound to administer the temple, were taken into custody by vigilance officers for carrying out proselytization activities on behalf of other (non-Hindu) religions atop the temple.[51] In another incident, an official enquiry found that forty-four non-Hindu officials had been recruited in Tirumala temple by the government. Most of them were appointed even after the guidelines made it clear than only Hindus could serve in the administration of the temple.[52]

In 2018, Andhra Pradesh Chief Minister Chandrababu Naidu boasted that his Telugu Desam Party (TDP) was the only party 'that constructed Haj houses in Hyderabad, Vijayawada and Kadapa. We promoted Urdu and built thousands of mosques across the state.'[53] In 2019, YSR's son Y.S. Jagan Reddy replaced Naidu as the chief minister of Andhra Pradesh. In May 2020, as the coronavirus pandemic raged in the state, the government faced allegations that it was selling off 23 land holdings of the TTD trust to its own cronies. TTD Chairman Y.V. Subba Reddy said that 129 properties owned by the trust had been divested since 1974.[54] Jagan Reddy also enhanced benefits and welfare for the Christian community—travel doles were increased for 'Christian pilgrims visiting Jerusalem in Israel and other Biblical places from Rs 40,000 to Rs 60,000 (for those with annual income up to Rs 3 lakh), and from Rs 20,000 to Rs 30,000 (for those with annual income over Rs 3 lakh)'.[55] He also added destinations in Jordan and Israel to the list of places qualifying for Christian pilgrimage subsidy, with the permitted tour period being increased from eight to ten days. ThePrint reported in November 2019 that 'the government is preparing to fulfil other YSR Congress Party manifesto promises for the Christian community—like plots and house construction for pastors, and financial assistance of Rs 1 lakh for wedding of Christian girls.'

In Telangana, Chief Minister Kalvakuntla Chandrashekar Rao (KCR)-led government passed a bill in the state assembly to triple reservation for Muslims in education and employment, from the 4 per cent to 12 per cent.[56] He also promised to bring a bill to give the state Wakf Board judicial powers with the justification being that 'Wakf land is being illegally grabbed'. As Arihant Pawariya wrote in *Swarajya* magazine, 'How can the state give power of adjudication to one participating party in a legal battle? This is akin to giving judicial power to an alleged victim over the alleged accused.'[57]

In 2015, KCR started a new tradition of hosting Christmas dinners every year and distributing expensive gift hampers to lakhs of poor Christians.[58] Since then, KCR has allocated crores for repairing old churches and building new ones in addition to giving subsidy to Christians for pilgrimage to Jerusalem.[59] In 2016, he promised to build seventy residential schools exclusively for minorities at a budget of over Rs 2,000 crore.[60] Later, he cleared the formation of a separate board for recruitment of teachers in these schools.[61] In 2017, he declared Urdu as the second official language of the state on the grounds that 12.69 per cent of the state population was Urdu speaking.[62] The KCR government also announced that it would construct an exclusive industrial estate and information technology corridor for Muslims in the state apart from an International Islamic Cultural Convention Centre, built to global standards at Kokapet.[63]

In 2017, the Telangana Social Welfare Residential Educational Institutions Society, which operates under the state welfare department, created a special category consisting of Scheduled Caste people who converted to Christianity and gave them 2 per cent reservation in admissions, even though conversion to Christianity or Islam is supposed to nullify[64] caste status.[65]

West Bengal, also governed by the 'secular' Trinamool Congress since 2011, provisioned a monthly allowance for Muslim clerics and imams in April 2012, costing a near-bankrupt state government Rs 126 crore per year, until the Calcutta High Court held it unconstitutional in September 2013.[66] The chief minister also gave thousands of bicycles and special scholarships to Muslim students in 2012.[67] In 2016, 10,000 Muslim clerics decided to hit the streets protesting that the amount wasn't enough. 'We believe that the amount, which was already too small, had no appreciation in over five years now,' Mohammed Kamruzzaman, general secretary of the All Bengal Minority Youth Federation (ABMYF) said, as if he was a government worker talking about the Pay Commission.[68] A news report quotes aggrieved protesters thus:

> 'Mamata had promised that imams would receive homes under the 'Nijo Jomi Nijo Griho' housing scheme but no imam has received anything so far. The process of giving money to 52,000 imams should also be streamlined,' said A.T.M. Rafiqul Hassan, president of All Bengal Imam and Moizzin Samity. 'The amount of Rs 2,500 is too small. It should be raised to at least Rs 20,000 for imams and Rs 10,000 for moizzins,' said Shafique Qasmi, imam, Nakhoda Masjid.

It is an enduring enigma of '*the* idea of India' as to how and when public funding for salaries and benefits doled out by a state government to religious chiefs became normalized as 'secular'.

In September 2012, the West Bengal state government provided for an exclusive Muslim-only medical college and hospital in the South 24 Parganas district.[69] The government also sanctioned Rs 298 crore to Aliah University, a minority-oriented university under the state Minority Affairs and Madrassa Education (MAME) department, created by the 'secular' Communist-led Left Front government in 2007. The All India Survey on Higher Education prepared by the Union human resource development ministry in July 2017 reported that the student body of Alia University was 98 per cent Muslim, in a state with 27 per cent Muslim population. The same survey reported that the Muslim population at Presidency College and Jadavpur University was 3 per cent, signalling a total separation of the minority and majority populations in West Bengal higher education.

There was much consternation in the Muslim community when control of Aliah University was shifted from the MAME department to the state Higher Education Department in September 2017. News reports quoted Syed Ruhul Amin, the national president of All India Minority Association (AIMA), West Bengal, as asserting that 'if the order comes true, it will be a great loss for the whole Muslim community.' The district president of AIMA in East Medinipur, Sanaullah Khan, claimed that if the government moved ahead with the decision, 'a massive protest march would be arranged'. Dr Amzed Hossein, the head of Aliah's Department of English, doubted whether the Higher Education Department officials would have 'the same intensity of community sentiments for Aliah as shown by the Minority officials'.[70]

In addition to providing funds for Aliah University, the Mamata Banerjee government created six industrial training institutes and six polytechnic colleges exclusively for Muslims.

In January 2013, Banerjee complained that she could only allow job reservations for Muslims under the OBC quota and not directly because 'the Constitution does not allow it', citing the experience of the 'secular' YSR government in Andhra Pradesh.[71] On 12 September 2013, the state public prosecutor Pradip Chatterjee told the courts that cases against rioters who ran amok in Kolkata in 2007 and attacked writer Taslima Nasrin should be dropped.[72, 73]

This was a riot in which the army had to be called in to control the violence and arson, and in which the president of the All India Minority Forum, Idris Ali, who demanded that Nasrin be deported, had been charge sheeted. Ali was in the news again in December 2013, when he managed to get a TV serial written by Taslima Nasrin banned with Banerjee's help.[74] In the 2014 general election, Idris Ali was elected as a Trinamool Congress Member of Parliament from Basirhat.

Where was the army of self-described secular–liberal intellectuals and activists when the state government dropped charges against arsonists and rioters to appease religious bigots? None of the guardians of secularism dared protest against Idris Ali despite his record. Ali completed his term in the 16th Lok Sabha, but did not receive a ticket to contest the 2019 Lok Sabha elections, with Trinamool Congress picking film personality Nusrat Jahan in his place.

Before the 2014 general elections, the West Bengal chief minister declined to meet the US ambassador to India, Nancy Powell, out of fear of antagonizing the minorities[75]—she immediately received plaudits from the powerful shahi imam of Kolkata's Tipu Sultan Mosque, Noor-ur Rehman Barkati, who said, 'She will get the results' in the polls and 'secure maximum votes' from Muslims. Mohammad Quamruzzaman, general secretary of the All Bengal Minority Youth Federation, hailed Banerjee's decision as a 'historic move'. 'She has in fact never disappointed us,' Quamruzzaman added. 'When controversial author Salman Rushdie wanted to visit the Calcutta Book Fair, we requested her not to allow him into the city. We also appealed to her not to allow a television show based on a story by Taslima Nasreen to be aired on a Bengali channel recently, and it was taken off air,' he stated approvingly.[76]

Barkati endorsed Banerjee as 'prime minister material'.[77] In 2017, when the Modi government banned the use of *lal battis* (red beacon lights in VIP cars) to end the VIP culture in the country, Barkati refused to give up his red beacon-fitted car, saying it was his right to have it as a religious leader. 'Who are they to order me?' Barkati asked, referring to the Union Government.[78]

Until 2019, India had the dubious distinction of allowing the abominable practice of triple talaq, whereby a Muslim man could divorce his wife by simply uttering the word 'talaq' three times. When the BJP-led Union government introduced the pro-women rights bill to end the practice of triple talaq, Mamata Banerjee said it 'will not help women and that it was only intended to incite the Muslim community'.[79] Banerjee's party wasn't the only 'secular' outfit who wanted India's Muslim women to bear the brunt of a practice outlawed in even Muslim majority countries such as Saudi Arabia, Pakistan and Afghanistan—the Congress party declared that it would bring back 'triple talaq' if it won the 2019 general election.[80]

Karnataka, which used to be governed by the 'communal' BJP till May 2013, also turned suitably 'secular' when the Congress government led by Siddaramaiah took office. Within two months of taking office, the chief minister announced a housing scheme for homeless minorities,[81] financial assistance of Rs 50,000 each for marriage of minority-community girls[82] and minority-only education scholarships too. The state Congress chief G. Parameshwara said in October 2013 that it didn't matter if minorities did not repay loans to the government and 'it was part of the development process'.[83] Before the assembly elections in 2018, the Karnataka Director General of Police fired off a letter, marked 'extremely urgent', to police chiefs of major districts asking their opinion on dropping cases of communal violence registered against members of minority community in the previous five years.[84]

Before the state polls, in February 2018, the state government's Muzrai department issued a public notice inviting suggestions from stakeholders on whether Hindu *mathas*, temples and religious institutions should come under the control of Karnataka Hindu Religious Institutions and Charitable Act, 1997.[85] The Congress party claimed that this was done to comply with a Karnataka High Court order requiring the Muzrai department, which administers 34,559 temples across the state, to bring all Hindu, Jain, Sikh and Buddhist religious institutions under its ambit[86]—of course, institutions belonging to the minority communities were not to be touched. Interestingly, the 'minority' tag in this case was not extended to Indic faiths like Sikhism, Buddhism and Jainism.

To appease Muslims in the state, the Siddaramaiah government also started celebrating the birth anniversary of Tipu Sultan—a ruler known as the 'Tyrant of Mysore' who destroyed many Hindu temples and murdered thousands of innocents. With his illustrious 'secular' record, Chief Minister Siddaramaiah asserted, without a hint of hesitation or irony, in the run-up to the 2018 state assembly elections, that the contest was between secularism and communalism, with the Congress party supposedly championing the former.[87]

The Congress conclusively lost the assembly elections in 2018 but to protect 'secularism', it formed a post-poll alliance with the Janata Dal (Secular) which had come third, installing H.D. Kumaraswamy as chief minister. This 'secular' government announced in September

2018 that it would give monetary rewards to those students from minority communities who passed examinations with first class marks.[88] Meritorious students from other communities, no matter how poor or needy, were ignored only because of their faith.

In 2017, the Kerala state government announced a new housing scheme for divorcees and widows from the minority communities with an outlay of Rs 30 crore, with each beneficiary getting Rs 2.5 lakh of financial support.[89] The Communist Party of India (Marxist) government's minister responsible for the administration and management of Hindu temples under the state government's control, Kadakampally Surendran, participated in a beef fest and was photographed relishing beef.[90] In 2018, the decision of the executive committee of the Travancore Devaswom Board to dismantle a Veda school and convert it into a non-vegetarian, beef-serving restaurant generated much outrage.[91]

In 2013, the United Democratic Front (UDF) government, an alliance between the Congress party and the Indian Union Muslim League, made a push to legalize child marriage. Supporting the UDF government, a community leader commented that 'the Shariah law allows Muslim girls to marry when they attain puberty.'[92] As of June 2020, child marriage in the Muslim community is not banned in India.[93] The Indian government is now pushing to increase the minimum age of marriage for women from eighteen years to twenty-one years, the same age as men.[94]

In 2017, former Vice-President of India Hamid Ansari attended an event organized by radical Islamist outfit Popular Front of India (PFI).[95] Thirteen members of PFI had been convicted by the Kerala High Court in 2015 for chopping off the hand of T.J. Joseph, a professor at Newman College, Thodupuzha.[96] Joseph had committed blasphemy, according to the attackers. PFI members had also been accused in several criminal cases such as the murder of RSS leader Rudresh[97] in Bengaluru, organizing terror training camps in Kannur from where the police had seized bombs and swords and the Islamic State Omar Al-Hindi module matter, among others.

In June 2018, Hyderabad MP and chief of All India Majlis-e-Ittehadul Muslimeen (AIMIM) Asaduddin Owaisi exhorted all

Muslims to vote for Muslim candidates 'if you want to keep secularism alive'. 'If Muslims become a political power, secularism and democracy will be strengthened,' he asserted.[98]

This was not very different from Sonia Gandhi's appeal during the 2014 general election campaign, jointly issued with the Shahi Imam of New Delhi, to India's Muslim community that they must vote to reject Narendra Modi and protect 'secularism'.[99] Only in India can open calls for sectarianism be passed off as an appeal to strengthen secularism. As the writer Sita Ram Goel wryly observed in his book *Freedom of Expression: Secular Theocracy Versus Liberal Democracy*:[100]

> The concept of Secularism as known to the modern West is dreaded, derided and denounced in the strongest terms by the foundational doctrines of Christianity and Islam . . . It is, therefore, intriguing that the most fanatical and fundamentalist adherents of Christianity and Islam in India—Christian missionaries and Muslim mullahs—cry themselves hoarse in defence of Indian Secularism.

On 21 June 2018, when the world was celebrating International Yoga Day, Mizoram decided to give it a miss because 'there is no practice of celebrating the International Yoga Day in Mizoram as it is a Christian-majority state.'[101] In Tripura, a mosque didn't allow a few Muslims to pray inside the premises because they had joined the BJP.[102] Before the 2018 state polls, Nagaland's biggest church organization, the Nagaland Baptist Church Council, issued a fatwa of sorts asking all the believers to choose between Trishul and Cross.[103] The entire country mourned the passing of Bharat Ratna Atal Bihari Vajpayee on 16 August 2018, and his ashes were immersed in rivers across the nation to honour his memory. But only in Nagaland did this move encounter pushback. The BJP was accused of imposing 'alien rituals' on a 'Christian-majority state'.[104]

Before the Gujarat assembly elections in 2017, the Congress questioned the arrest of the alleged mastermind of the terrorist attack on Gandhinagar's Akshardham temple in 2002.[105] The Archdiocese of Gandhinagar alerted the faithful in a letter saying that 'nationalist forces are on the verge of taking over the country' and emphasized the need to elect the correct people in Gujarat polls.[106] The Delhi Archbishop called for nationwide prayers to influence 2019 general elections.[107] 'We are witnessing a turbulent political atmosphere which poses a threat to the democratic principles enshrined in our Constitution and the secular fabric of our nation,' Archbishop Anil Couto asserted—no prizes for guessing who in his view was threatening the secular fabric of India. In December 2018, three states turned 'secular' from 'communal', as BJP lost state elections in Chhattisgarh, Rajasthan and Madhya Pradesh.

In November 2019, Rajasthan Chief Minister Ashok Gehlot doled out Rs 1.88 crore[108] as a grant to madrasas in the state, after the Union government stopped central funding. State Minority Affairs Minister Saleh Mohammad accused Prime Minister Narendra Modi of not fulfilling promises of taking everybody along. Such is the sense of entitlement, and so spectacular the intellectual gymnastics of 'secularism' that declining to fund religious instruction in madrasa institutions can be passed off as a 'communal' act of betrayal. The Union government had not ended religion-based welfare—shortly after winning the general election, the Modi government announced changes to the programmes funded by the Union minority affairs ministry, deciding that madrasa education should be modernized. Scholarships for minority students continue to be given out for pre-matric and post-matric education, with the objective of fifty million beneficiaries by 2024.

The difference is that while the BJP-led Union government is attempting to bring minorities into the mainstream through modernizing instruction and formalizing institutions,[109] certain 'secular' governments seem more interested in continuing with the orthodox mode of religious instruction. It is clear which path is in the interest of both the minority community as well as India. Additionally, it is worth investigating how many minority leaders and politicians push for orthodox instruction for 'their' community practice what they preach and have their own family members shunning modern education.

Delhi Chief Minister Arvind Kejriwal, whose rise in politics was proffered as the emergence of a new kind of educated leader, also could not resist cashing in on the political payoffs of providing salaries from the public exchequer to imams. In January 2019, with an eye on the general election, he increased the salary of the imams of 185 mosques who come under the Delhi Waqf Board from Rs 10,000 per month to Rs 18,000 per month while helpers received a bump up from Rs 9000 to Rs 16,000 per month. Expanding the scope of this 'secular' dole, Kejriwal even added imams who were not affiliated with the Delhi Waqf Board, and they would receive Rs 14,000 per month with their helpers getting Rs 12,000 per month.[110]

In February 2020, Madhya Pradesh Chief Minister Kamal Nath announced an increase in the salaries of imams from Rs 2200 to Rs 5000 and muezzins from Rs 1900 to Rs 4500 per month. Striking a statesmanesque tone, the chief minister proclaimed that 'our country India and our culture is great because we have the speciality to live together with a sense of respect for each other.'[111] It is not clear how doling out public money to religious preachers contributed to India's culture or increased mutual respect between communities. In March 2020, communal forces took power again in Madhya Pradesh, with BJP led by Shivraj Singh Chouhan forming the state government.

When in 2017, India voted at the United Nations against the decision of the United States to recognize Jerusalem as Israel's capital, Badruddin Ajmal, the Lok Sabha MP from Dhubri in Assam, thanked Sushma Swaraj. When she tweeted in jest asking for his support, he said, 'The day BJP does not differentiate between Majority and Minority community, our vote will be for you.'[112]

The reality is completely opposite. History tells us that the day BJP starts treating the majority and minority community members as equal citizens before the law, all we will witness is organized scaremongering that minorities are under threat. It's not without reason that the faithful are exhorted by their religious clergy to vote against the BJP.

By maintaining a studied silence in the face of all these episodes, India's self-proclaimed secularists have helped discredit the ideal of secularism. This stems from their flawed conception—or worse, calculated distortion—of what secularism actually is.

Secularism should mean the State treating all individual citizens as equals, irrespective of their religious identity. But under a template pioneered by Nehru that all the Indian 'secular' leaders follow dutifully even today, secularism has been perverted to mean discriminating between citizens on religious grounds. For example, hardly any intellectual seems to think that government control over Hindu places of worship is a violation of the principle of secularism.

Some intellectuals might assert that the government is only intervening for better administration of the temples. Member of Parliament Subramanian Swamy wrote an essay in 2014 on how the government control of temples is proving to be disastrous for the Hindu community. Swamy wrote:

> Tamil Nadu temples, under the Hindu Religious and Charitable Endowments Department, has control over more than 4.7 lakh acres of agricultural land, 2.6 crore square feet of buildings and 29 crore square feet of urban sites of temples. By any reasonable measure, the income from these properties should be in thousands of crores of rupees. The government, however, collects a mere Rs 36 crore in rent against a 'demand' of mere Rs 304 crore—around a 12 per cent realization.[113]

As scientist and writer Anand Ranganathan has pointed out, just five states in southern India control 90,700 temples, with Tamil Nadu controlling 36,425 temples and 56 *mathas*, from which the state government leeches huge sums of money at will.[114] While temples suffer from maladministration of the government and fritter away what should be their due income, Christian religious institutions raise funds from abroad and build schools and hospitals, with such educational and health institutions often enjoying liberalized regulations, giving them a competitive advantage in the marketplace. In many cases, these institutions are even subsidized with public money to protect and promote 'secularism'. As described earlier, established institutions such as the haloed St Stephens College received 95 per cent of their funding from the government even as they ramp up their Christian quota.[115]

As early as 1951, T.S.S. Rajan, a minister in the Madras state government, had said that it was the wish of Jawaharlal Nehru that there should not be any private temples.[116] This thinking cemented

State control on Hindu temples but allowed minority places of worship to remain outside the State's influence.

Secularism has come to mean government showing favour to specific religious groups and those groups in turn voting to keep the political party showering such favours when in office. This is nothing but bribery, and those who raise their voice against such bribery are immediately deemed communal by the keepers of the 'secular' flame. Whenever elections come closer, journalists, historians and activists of the Nehruvian creed go to town warning Indians about secularism being in danger should communal forces win.

Indian voters always need be on guard so as not to allow themselves to be misled by hypocritical intellectuals and journalists who are in cahoots with the 'secular' politicians. These politicians should have been held accountable for their perversion of secularism by intellectuals and journalists in the first place.

India needs a government that works for the development and security of all citizens and enunciates laws that are the same for all individuals—only such a government would be worthy of being called secular.

For decades, India made the mistake of conflating its internal minority appeasement with its foreign policy. It was not until 1992, under P.V. Narasimha Rao, that India gave official recognition to the Jewish state of Israel and established full diplomatic ties. The contortions of the 'secular' mindset are spectacular. While India shied away from recognizing Israel and building a formal relationship with the Jewish State, under the same rubric, a chief minister of an Indian state, Y.S. Jagan Reddy, has poured taxpayer money into funding Christian pilgrimages to Israel. India's policy towards even the Islamic Republic of Pakistan was often ambivalent, as opportunistic politicians infantilized India's Muslims by tying their allegiance to Pakistan.

Prime Minister Narendra Modi showed unprecedented courage by allowing the Indian army to cross the Line of Control and launch a surgical strike to hunt down terrorists in Pakistan Occupied Kashmir in the aftermath of the 2016 Uri terror attack, and by sending in fighter jets to attack terror camps in Balakot after the 2019 Pulwama attack.

Modi introduced a new dimension to India's response options on Pakistan's policy of supporting terrorism and transformed our strategic calculus. On both these occasions, a section of politicians sought to scare Indian Muslims through linking their identity with Pakistan.

Narendra Modi was elected on the promise of '*sabka saath, sabka vikas*' (together with all, the progress of all). One of the defining moments of the 2014 general election campaign was when Congress President Sonia Gandhi issued an appeal to Muslims alongside New Delhi's Shahi Imam to protect secularism, even as Modi refused to wear the Muslim skull cap.[117] It was a stark contrast—Modi took the position that as a practising Hindu, he could not wear an Islamic religious symbol only to be deemed electable.

He boldly refused to pander to Muslim sentiments, while those who promised new politics, the likes of whom included IIT-educated engineer Arvind Kejriwal,[118] donned the Muslim skull cap to court the Muslim vote bank.

On the 2014 campaign trail, Modi distinguished himself as one who stood for individual rights when he spoke of his personal right to practise a faith of his choosing, even as he simultaneously reaffirmed the constitutional rights afforded to all citizens of India, including minorities. This was the record on the back of which Narendra Modi was elected as Prime Minister.

But securing equal individual rights for all citizens requires navigating the minefield of pernicious and illiberal legal–constitutional provisions planted by Congress party governments over the decades that, in an Orwellian turn, have institutionalized religious discrimination in the name of secularism.

For example, the 93rd constitutional amendment, as discussed earlier, expanded reservations to all educational institutions, except those run by minorities, discriminating against Hindus. Following Indira Gandhi, who amended and changed the structure of India's constitution repeatedly through the 1960s and 1970s because her draconian orders were struck down by the courts, the Congress–UPA government amended India's Constitution in 2005 to discriminate against Indians who were Hindus after its ideologically driven policies were rejected by the courts. The 93rd amendment was designed to overturn two key judicial pronouncements given in favour of individual and equal rights. The first was the verdict of the eleven-judge bench in T.M.A. Pai vs State of Karnataka (2002), which held that all citizens should have equal rights in the domain of education and the second verdict was of the seven-judge bench in P.N. Inamdar vs State of Maharashtra (2005), which ruled that unaided institutions (whether minority or non-minority) could not be subjected to the government's reservation policy.

For the rights of citizens, the BJP has stood for bringing a uniform civil code since its inception, drawing on the legacy of Bharatiya Jan Sangh founder Syama Prasad Mookerjee.

In government policy, BJP's stand favours stronger individual rights with respect to personal laws and equality before the law for all Indian citizens—BJP governments both in states and at the Centre, have generally favoured need-based welfare. Of course, the self-described 'secular–liberal' establishment is stoutly against such equality. The path to achieving this equality, through appropriate legal–constitutional reforms that will be necessary to overturn Orwellian secularism entrenched over decades, will not be easy as a powerful political–intellectual alliance of collectivists and religious conservatives is redoubling its efforts to hold India back.

Cutting through the carefully laid thicket of legal defences built by the Congress party and combating the propaganda of the deep intellectual–academic ecosystem it has nurtured over decades on this issue will require majorities in both houses of Parliament as well as winning public opinion by highlighting the issue of equal rights for Hindus.

Just as Muslims and other minorities must be afforded the increased personal liberties that Hindus enjoy, Hindus too should be allowed to run educational institutions freely and be given administrative control of their places of worship, both liberties that their minority compatriots enjoy. It is unconscionable that after centuries of colonial rule and seven decades of independence, the modern Indian State should make arbitrary distinctions between individual citizens based on the religion of the citizen.

A critical piece of the post-liberalization Indian social reform project is to dismantle this legal minefield and to enshrine equal individual rights for all Indians, irrespective of their religion. Such a reform would make the society equal and just, and help bridge religion-based fissures. The Narendra Modi government has a historic opportunity to deliver on this paradigm shift.

The tautology of rationalism

Rationalism needs to be rescued from India's 'rationalists' just as secularism needs to be extracted from the grip of 'secularists'.[119] In fact, with very few honourable exceptions, the rationalism movement in India is only an extension of the pseudo-secularism movement. Rationalists are acutely secular in that they seem interested only in weeding out superstition and malpractices from Hinduism, a polytheistic system where any Hindu or non-Hindu can challenge as well as even reject or denounce a given prescription from the panoply of scriptures and books that are a part of the Hindu way.

One cannot say whether rationalists have condescension towards minority faiths, a fear of physical retaliation from religious extremists or if they simply have a devotion to reforming only the majority religion. There is no doubt that fixating exclusively on the flaws of Hinduism is hypocritical, and this makes the rationalists pliant bedfellows of the 'secular liberals'.

India in general and Hinduism in particular has a long history of making saints out of reformers. From Buddha to Swami Dayanand Saraswati, the nation's history is replete with examples of common folk embracing and worshipping spiritual reformers even if they used harsh language and methods for their admonition. But rationalism movements of the recent past, led by the likes of anti-superstition activist Narendra Dabholkar and writer M.M. Kalburgi have resulted in more antipathy than sympathy.

The killings of Dabholkar in Maharashtra and Kalburgi in Karnataka are worthy of unreserved condemnation. Both campaigned for decades against practices and ideas that they deemed to be superstitious and were apparently killed because of their activism.

These heinous acts were rightly censured by an array of prominent individuals. But some lionized them and lamented how 'we didn't deserve these 'rationalists'.'[120] This adulation is something we disagree with and find to be completely wrong.

In both Maharashtra and Karnataka, activists have sought to criminalize, through anti-superstition laws, what they deemed to be irrational and superstitious practices. Maharashtra accepted and implemented such a law in 2013,[121] and Karnataka followed in 2017,[122] with the anti-superstition laws proffered as a tribute to rationalism and rationalists. Narendra Dabholkar's daughter wanted a bill against superstitions brought at the national level as a tribute to her deceased father.[123]

In the din surrounding these events, common sense seems to have been the casualty. Should the heinous murder of an activist be a pretext for the deployment of State power to control an individual's choices on matters of belief and faith? Isn't it troubling that a bunch of activists are being allowed to enforce their ideas of what is rational and what isn't in an ostensibly liberal, democratic republic and a free country without adequate debate?

Let us examine some of the positions taken by the activists. The draft law proposed by Dabholkar's Maharashtra Andhashraddha Nirmoolan Samiti (MANS) had mentioned a list of practices it wanted outlawed including those acts that 'defame, disgrace the names of erstwhile Saints/Gods, by claiming to be there (sic) reincarnation'.[124]

One would be forgiven for thinking this to be a satirical dig or intentional jocularity from a self-described rationalist organization, but this statement is made in all seriousness. Its absurdity doesn't really merit elaboration, but nevertheless one must persist, for it reveals the intellectual bankruptcy of the activists, who lobbied successfully and were able to force governments to enact legislation for their absurd ideas. Does this group of activists believe that there was once an era of gods and saints, and there cannot be one today? What is the basis for an approach that legitimizes ancient dogma and effectively creates entry barriers for modern-day faith entrepreneurs?

The activists claim that their effort to stop what they deemed superstitious practices through legislation doesn't try to distinguish between faith and blind faith—what is categorized as blind faith is included in a 'separate schedule', and this schedule can be 'updated periodically'. This is a strange distinction, for faith, by definition, is blind. This arbitrary differentiation seems to have been introduced because the activists don't have the intellectual capacity or more likely the moral courage to make a consistent case against faith per se, and instead want to anoint themselves arbiters of 'rationality' through the instrument of government power.

Matthew Inman, creator of the web comic *The Oatmeal*, brought out this kind of hypocrisy memorably, showing how fundamentalist Christians mock scientologists for having strange beliefs.[125] As the saying goes, 'A cult is a church down the street from your church.'

At a rigorous and non-colloquial level, rationality has to be but tautological. This is so because to deem a practice as irrational implicitly accepts a standard of rationality, and attributes anything else to a certain form of 'false consciousness'. But, to paraphrase what Chicago School economists had famously asked: is it really irrational to be a chain-smoker? Who decides the costs and benefits, except the concerned individuals? Are non-religious superstitions more rational?

As Nassim Taleb writes in *Skin in the Game*:[126]

> When we look at religion and, to some extent ancestral superstitions, we should consider what purpose they serve, rather than focusing on the notion of 'belief', epistemic belief in its strict scientific definition. In science, belief is literal belief; it is right or wrong, never metaphorical. In real life, belief is an instrument to do things, not the end product.

This group of activists has been feted as a group for advocating scientific thinking. But to quote Taleb again: 'Judging people on their beliefs is not scientific. There is no such thing as 'rationality' of a belief, there is rationality of action.'

This assertion of 'scientific thinking' is on weak footing—the activists seem to be clueless about the science of why animals, including human beings, are ostensibly superstitious. Writing in *Nautilus* magazine, Carleton University cognitive scientist Jim Davies said that 'any of us can become superstitious given the right circumstances' and brought out how 'the tendency to resort to ritual in an effort to manage a challenging situation isn't exclusive to humans.'[127] As early as 1948, Harvard psychologist B.F. Skinner showed how pigeons could be induced to partake in ritual and superstition.[128]

Davies elaborated on how pattern detection was critical to helping us interpret the world around us, and the neurotransmitter dopamine helped the brain in detecting patterns. An uncertain environment generates an excess of dopamine, and this tends to make humans paranoid and incredulous, leading us to imagine patterns and connections where none exist.

The phenomenon of an uncertain environment triggering ritualism is also visible in sport—countless highly successful sportspersons have practised all kinds of superstitions. Steve Waugh always carried a red handkerchief when batting. Sachin Tendulkar used to put on the left pad first.[129]

Given the grave, life-threatening uncertainties many Indians—especially the poor—have to contend with, from the lack of medical facilities to the absence of educational opportunities, gainful employment and even personal security, they are predisposed towards believing in all kinds of supernatural phenomena, especially those that might allay these uncertainties. The legislative solution to ban superstitions hardly addresses this problem—it only criminalizes what is a natural human tendency. Thus, those lionized as advocates for the cultivation of scientific temper, as encouraged by India's Constitution, are blissfully ignorant of the scientific reasons behind what makes us superstitious.

All superstitions are not meaningless ritualism emanating from ignorance and illiteracy. Some are highly constructive. Geographer and anthropologist Jared Diamond in his classic work *Guns, Germs and Steel* narrates an interesting tale of the paranoia of residents of Papua New Guinea who warned their guests not to pitch a tent under a dead tree as it could fall and kill them. It might seem irrational to most people given the low probability of a dead tree falling but the risk increases every time you sleep under such a tree. It's only a matter of time, before the dead tree actually falls. This 'irrational' heuristic developed by New Guineans is rooted in the need for safety and survival.

To quote Taleb again, 'Superstitions can be vectors for risk management rules.' According to him, 'The only definition of rationality that is practically, empirically, and mathematically rigorous is that of survival . . . Anything that hinders one's survival at an individual, collective, tribal, or general level is deemed *irrational*.'[130]

Taleb presents rationality 'in terms of actual decisions, not what is called "beliefs" as these may be adapted to prevent us in the most convincing way to avoid things that threaten systemic survival'.

While Taleb builds an intellectually sound case on how to think rationally about rationality, clinical psychologist Jordan B. Peterson is scathing in his assessment of those who turn rationalism into a cult. He says[131] that 'the worship of the rational mind makes you prone to totalitarian ideology' because 'the rational mind always falls in love with its own creations'. Taken further, religion serves the purpose of preventing a person from thinking he is a God. Superstition kills solipsism.

In a television debate, Peterson said:[132]

Rational thinking can go in a variety of directions. It depends on your initial presuppositions. If you believe that life is worth living . . . you're going to come up with a pretty optimistic conclusion. But if you've looked at life and you think that the suffering of most people is unbearable and life is evil, which is what Stalin thought, you have no problems whatsoever mobilizing everything you can to kill as many people as you can.

And here we have a tiny cabal of activists harnessing State power to outlaw what they think is irrational. It is astonishing how so few in

India's intellectual establishment find this legislation-based approach odious. It seems to be the case that almost all writers and commentators have conflated the enactment of a law with recompense for the murders of activists.

Narendra Dabholkar's criticisms weren't restricted to attacking the activities of those he considered to be charlatans. In an astounding display of self-righteousness, he frequently argued that rice was being wasted during weddings and that rituals were a waste of resources. He campaigned against such conspicuous consumption.[133]

The truth is that it is impossible for anyone to draw a line defining what is waste and what is legitimate consumption in a society. If a bunch of activists argue that there is a wastage of resources caused by bad television shows, should such content be outlawed? The solution lies in allowing markets to set a price on the transaction—those who are willing to pay the price should be allowed to 'waste' and consume. At best, there may have to be some adjustments for negative externalities but any kind of outright bans or coercive policies make no sense. It is each individual's choice what they should or should not spend in weddings, and it does not behove the government to intervene and try to regulate the choices.

Moreover, those who like to publicly shame rich families celebrating weddings on a grand scale should ask the beneficiaries of the spending—the numerous decorators, cooks, kitchen helpers, cleaners, photographers, videographers, electricians, sound technicians, waiters, bartenders, clothes designers, makeup artists, stylists, tailors, security guards, hoteliers, florists, musicians, disc jockeys, singers, entertainers, wedding planners and others who make their livelihoods from such events—about their earnings from the 'ostentatious' celebrations. The classic big, fat Indian wedding sustains many services jobs.

In another leap of sanctimony, MANS has gone so far as to want to completely outlaw certain sects and practices of the Hindu tradition. The opposition of the Warkari sect to Maharashtra's Anti-Superstition law (officially, the Maharashtra Prevention and Eradication of Human Sacrifice and Other Inhuman, Evil and Aghori Practices and Black Magic Act) has been well-documented[134]—the plight of the

Aghoris, whose way of life has become criminalized under the law, is not even mentioned. Aghoris are Shiva devotees who often live in Hindu cremation grounds, smear ashes from cremated dead bodies onto themselves, use human bones as ornaments and even consume organic or human waste. The criminalization of the Aghori identity is lamentable, for the existence of sects like the Aghoris captures the deepest strains of liberalism in the Hindu faith—their way of life pushes the boundaries of what is considered morally acceptable by mainstream society.

To be sure, anything that curbs the freedom of a citizen or harms another person should not be allowed, but for that a specific law against superstition or black magic is not required. What does it say about India's liberal democracy that we have laws turning a microscopic minority like the Aghoris into criminals because of who they are, not because they did something harmful to anyone else?

Curbing superstition would involve bringing a semblance of predictability to the lives of ordinary Indians, who contend every single day with incredible uncertainty to gain access to facilities and services that should be commonplace. This requires, amongst other things, that governments should govern better and provide the public goods that assuage uncertainty in the life of an individual.

Spectacles where activists blackmail governments into turning their pet ideas into law should not be encouraged. All of India does not need to embrace statist paternalism, and Indian society does not have to accept the arbitrary diktats of moralistic activists on what is rational and what is not. Anti-superstition laws are unnecessary and harmful, and yet another instance of the deep confusion that persists in India about what the State should be doing and what should be left to the society.

The importance of free speech

The Indian State has, since the passage of the First Amendment to the Constitution, appointed itself a referee in deciding what is acceptable speech and what is not.[135] The State censoring speech and content out of its own volition is bad enough—what makes matters worse is censorship in response to threats by some group claiming to be offended. But when there is a referee with the power to decide one way or the other, there is no use blaming offended groups for lobbying and pressurizing governments to get what they want.

By taking a stand either way, the State exposes itself to several charges, especially when it has a history of seeing its citizens as members of groups rather than as individuals. More often than not, a group's right to get offended and enforce censorship trumps an individual's right to freedom of speech and expression.

In 2012, Salman Rushdie was prevented from participating at a literature festival for having written *The Satanic Verses* two decades earlier. In 2015, Hindu Mahasabha leader Kamlesh Tiwari was arrested and detained under the draconian National Security Act by a 'secular and liberal' Samajwadi Party government for making 'derogatory remarks' about the prophet of Islam. In 2019, Kamlesh Tiwari was murdered, and those who conspired to kill him confessed that their motive had been to avenge what Tiwari had said. Celebrity TV anchors and the liberal intelligentsia seen pontificating about press freedom also looked the other way when Shirin Dalvi, former editor of the Urdu newspaper *Avadhnama*, was arrested for reprinting the Charlie Hebdo cartoons. Dalvi subsequently lost her job and the newspaper had to be shut down.[136]

Despite a religion-based Partition of Bharat, nothing much has changed since 1929 when it comes to blasphemy. Mahashay Rajpal, the publisher of an allegedly incendiary book, was stabbed to death by a twenty-year-old Muslim fanatic carpenter who was then hailed as a hero by none other than Muhammad Iqbal, whose song *Saare jahaan se achha, Hindustan hamara,* is still sung by Indians. Iqbal had said about Rajpal's killer, that 'This uneducated young man has surpassed us, the educated ones.'[137] Rajpal's killer continues to be lionized as a religious hero to this day in Pakistan. Cut to 2022—a spokesperson of the BJP received death threats for 'blasphemous' statements, and some of the people who spoke up for the rights of individuals to express their views, were murdered in a gruesome fashion similar to Rajpal's killing.[138]

These episodes, predictable to a fault, are illustrative in the way politics has been conducted and the free speech debate in India has played out over the years. Employing wily statecraft and plausible deniability, the Congress–UPA government achieved its political objective of stopping Rushdie from attending the event. Speaking at the same literature festival in 2012, *Outlook* magazine editor Vinod Mehta, a self-described Left–Liberal, berated the Congress party for its 'shameless communalism' in using the episode to court Muslim votes in poll-bound Uttar Pradesh.

While there was highfalutin outraging from the chattering classes and the customary online petition imploring the government to remove the bar on Rushdie's book, almost nobody came to the defence of Kamlesh Tiwari and other victims of Islamist violence—the principle of free speech be damned.

Every time an episode of this nature occurs, television channels conduct debates on the state of free speech in India. It doesn't matter that one of the television journalists frequently seen pontificating on free speech had bullied into silence critics of this journalist's own work, by employing legal tactics similar to those used by opponents of the artist M.F. Husain. Another leading television journalist opined that the right to free speech did not include the right to offend, and the real question was who should decide what is offensive.

It is worth thinking about why the same cycles of outrage repeat again and again, yet nothing really changes. Since Independence, movies and books have been banned under pressure from different interest groups in various states all over India. The list is simply too long to reproduce in full, but includes movies such as the *Da Vinci Code*, *Jodhaa Akbar*, *Aaja Nachle* and several books deemed offensive to Muslims, Hindus, other identity groups and even members of the Nehru–Gandhi family. In a new low created in 2011, columnist Anish Trivedi, who had supposedly written an 'anti-caste' article was convicted and jailed for six months by a court of law.[139] The world's largest democracy can also take credit for jailing writers, like a totalitarian State.

The bans and censorship don't apply only in the case of causing offence to an identity group. India's Censor Board, that indispensable institution, often finds itself in controversies when it decides what is fit for public consumption and what isn't. Bizarre as it may sound, it is accepted practice for the board to ask theatres to display warnings on cigarette smoking—comically enough, in the 2012 film *Agneepath*, with a plot centred around drug peddling, underworld gang wars and human trafficking, there were many anti-smoking messages inserted in the film. Much to the shock of India's Tibetan community, the Censor Board decided that Tibetan flags shown in the song 'Sadda Haq' (celebrating rebels) from the 2011 film *Rockstar* must be blurred out so as not to offend the Chinese.[140] The song is an anthem against authoritarianism and for individual freedom performed by the singer Mohit Chauhan and written by the poet Irshad Kamil. The mandarins thus ended up hilariously and emphatically making the musical masterpiece's point.

All these instances are assaults on free speech. No celebrity writer or journalist protested these attacks on free expression. This is because free speech and its importance to a democracy isn't widely understood or championed in our country. Salman Rushdie said it best after he had been prevented from visiting his home country in 2012:[141]

> I have been fighting this battle, not just on behalf of myself . . . but on behalf of the great principles that have evolved here; the principles of freedom of expression, which is the principle on which all other democratic freedoms rest. If you don't have freedom of expression, you don't have any other freedom. That's the corner stone and the bedrock of any free society and that's why I fight this battle.

Free speech is about preventing the State from forcing individuals to remain silent as well as not forcing individuals to say something they do not want to. The right to offend is fundamental to free speech. Free speech is also about the State protecting individuals from being at the receiving end of physical attack from others. Such protection is needed especially for speech considered offensive by some people. Let us go back to a debate from our own Parliament, and look at a historical case study from a foreign land many Indians love.

Clarence Brandenburg, a leader of the racist Ku Klux Klan, was allowed to take out inflammatory rallies by the US Supreme Court in the landmark Brandenburg vs Ohio case—just one year after the tragic assassination of civil rights icon Martin Luther King Jr. The Court ruled that so long as any speech is both unintended and unlikely to incite imminent lawless action, it must not be curtailed. The Court held that the intent of violence, the probability of violence, as well as the imminence of violence, all three must be present. Mere abstract advocacy of violence, much less hate, cannot be proscribed.

Therefore, what is hate speech in some countries qualifies as protected speech in American jurisprudence. The difference in the ways the Indian Constitution and the American Constitution guarantee free speech is telling. Article 19 clause (1) (a) of India's Constitution states that all citizens shall have the right to freedom of expression, and then goes on to list the 'reasonable restrictions' on this freedom. These 'reasonable restrictions' were inserted into the Constitution by India's first Prime Minister Jawaharlal Nehru. This First Amendment was supported by B.R. Ambedkar, and staunchly opposed by Syama Prasad Mookerjee.

Mookerjee called out Nehru's intolerance as 'scandalous', to which Nehru retorted that those who thought the amendment curbed liberty were liars.[142] Mookerjee argued that India should have unrestricted, absolute freedom of expression, on the lines of what Sweden had.[143]

Nehru told the Parliament that the free press was 'poisoning the minds of the younger generation, degrading their mental integrity and moral standards'. He accused some of the media properties of propagating 'vulgarity, indecency and falsehood'.[144] Jawaharlal Nehru, feted by historian Ramachandra Guha as a man who 'respected the press',[145] succeeded in pushing through the amendment, including vague generalities like public order, decency or morality, friendly relations with foreign countries and other arbitrary causes in the interest of which restrictions on speech could be imposed. *Time* magazine, reporting on the issue, said at the time that Prime Minister Nehru was more interested in muzzling criticism of his foreign and domestic policy from news weeklies such as *Blitz* and *Current* published at the time in Bombay (now Mumbai).[146] The petulant Nehru who had jailed the poet Majrooh Sultanpuri in 1951 for writing '*Commonwealth ka das hai Nehru*' (Nehru is slavish to the Commonwealth) wasn't above defiling the Constitution for settling petty battles.[147]

With the passing of the First Amendment, free speech became constitutionally restricted in India. In stark contrast to India's caveat-filled constitutional right to free speech, the First Amendment to the American Constitution simply states 'Congress shall make no law . . . abridging the freedom of speech, or of the press'. India's Constitution doles out 'rights' to individuals. The American Constitution assumes pre-existing rights and freedoms, and places limitations on government power instead. For India, the State is supreme with practically no constitutional limits because of all the broad caveats. For America, the State is but a constitutionally restricted agent of the individual. In India, the onus is on the individual to show that he or she is within their rights to do something. In US, the government has to prove that it is constitutionally valid to regulate an undeniable freedom.

This is the difference between lip service to freedom and true freedom. The State should exist merely as a guarantor–protector of rights that individuals inalienably have. The true battle that free speech votaries should fight is to eradicate the outdated, colonial laws governing free speech in India and to argue for the dissolution of patronizing, anachronistic institutions such as the Censor Board.

The defence of free speech as the cornerstone of individual rights should not be merely on normative or utilitarian grounds. The defence must also take into cognizance practical realities of politics. America's First Amendment causes heartburn to many Americans when their identity is under relentless attack. Nonetheless, they have the comfort that their government is not permitted to choose winners and losers in the public square and everybody can respond with equally fervent speech. This is not the case in Europe. For example, in the name of a dubious multiculturalism, Dutch politician Geert Wilders's speech was banned in some countries but Islamist preacher Anjem Choudary was allowed free reign—while being on government welfare.

Such double standards have been witnessed in India too. The objection that many Hindus had wasn't just with M.F. Husain's painting of Hindu deities in the nude, but it was also indignation at the fact that art deemed offensive to other religions had been enthusiastically banned by the government to garner votes. India kept company with Syria and Lebanon, when a number of states banned Tom Hanks-starrer *The Da Vinci Code* under pressure from Christian and Muslim groups.

Competitive intolerance results when opportunistic governments choose what to censor based on their political preferences. Even if we had a Solomon to sieve art into sacred and sacrilegious, it would inevitably be perceived as unfair by one party or the other. That is why it is better to allow all speech in the public sphere. Any restrictions on the grounds of public order or security should therefore follow something like the Brandenburg standard.[148]

If certain types of speech are curtailed based on the threat or actuality of violence, it creates a perverse incentive for those taking offence to indulge in more violence, knowing that the State is likely to give in to their demands for censorship. Some sceptics obviously raise doubts over the Indian State's capability to manage the fallout when the limits of free expression are tested. They are not wrong. But the answer to this challenge is not to continue with restrictions out of fear but to shore up State capacity to enforce the law and take violators to task. That's where the problem lies as prison and police personnel statistics illustrate.

The incarceration rate in India hovers around 30 to 40 people per 1,00,000 while it is about twenty times higher in the United States. Nations such as Russia (411), Brazil (328), Israel (236) and Australia (167) are also way ahead of India.[149] On top of that, our prisons are overcrowded compared to other countries. Similarly, India has 150 police officers per 1,00,000 compared with Spain (533), Turkey (524), Russia (515), Israel (345), France (340) and US (284). An analysis of state-level spending shows that India cumulatively spends just 4.1 per cent of state budgets on policing, almost entirely going to payment of salaries with nominal sums left over for modernization and capital investment.[150] There is systemic under-investment in law enforcement—no wonder then that governments choose the easy alternative of silencing the Tiwaris and the Rushdies of the world rather than try to control the mobs baying for their blood. The Indian State needs to build the capacity to deploy force and order the mobs to stand back or face the wrath of the law.

Kamlesh Tiwari's murder has echoes of the assassination of Swami Shraddhanand by Abdul Rashid in 1926. Shraddhanand's crime was to propagate *shuddhi* (or reconversion to Hinduism), a movement started by Swami Dayanand Saraswati. More recently, Pakistani politician Salman Taseer was assassinated in 2011 by his own bodyguard for suggesting that Pakistan should do away with the blasphemy law. Taseer's assassin was hailed as a hero by not just dozens of Islamic clerics, but also by common citizens in Pakistan.[151] When an individual says something that another person or group finds offensive, that individual needs to be protected and his or her rights unequivocally defended by the government. It is for India to decide whether it wants to be like Islamist Pakistan or a free republic, as envisioned by our Constitution makers.

Curtailing speech that violates somebody's privacy is very different, as that is less about free speech and more a violation of implicit trust. Libel is more complicated, but libel prosecution must rely on the defence of truth without regard to complaints about sullied reputation, with the burden of proof on the person suing.

Additionally, the threshold for suing on grounds of privacy violations or libel should be higher for politicians, celebrities and other public figures. It would be a travesty to treat defamation of a politician by a citizen and defamation of a citizen by a politician equally. We are witnessing the instances of the latter a lot these days where powerful politicians have gone so far as to openly name and target prominent social media figures on the floor of the Parliament.[152] Barring parliamentary privilege, the threshold for suing by private citizens should be very low in such cases. In this digital age, where some internet celebrities have more influence than many traditional public figures, what we should be discussing is the nuance around who qualifies as a public figure.

But how can we do that when we haven't yet settled the debate over foundational principles?

It would be pertinent to emphasize here that support for free speech does not entail support for leaking of State secrets, trade secrets or military intelligence as has been done by organizations like Wikileaks. No liberal doctrine says that speech cannot be curtailed by contracts entered of one's own volition, and such information is privileged.

Above all, we all must grow thicker skins. The legendary Atal Bihari Vajpayee's advice is in order here. In 2003, the Maharashtra state government had banned a book on Chhatrapati Shivaji Maharaj by American academic James Laine after protests by Maratha groups. Prime Minister Vajpayee, who had been invited to unveil Shivaji's statue at Mumbai airport, told the audience that he 'could understand criticism of books but not ban or boycott . . . If you want to make a line appear short, do not erase it but draw a longer one beside it,' he had said, with none other than Balasaheb Thackeray sitting on the dais. In other words, reply to a bad book with a better one. If you do not like what someone says or writes, consider saying or writing something more persuasive.[153]

Vajpayee's position on free speech was closer to his political mentor Syama Prasad Mookerjee's who, as mentioned earlier, had advocated 'unrestricted, absolute' freedom of speech when opposing Nehru in Parliament.

Lala Lajpat Rai, writing in 1924 from the vantage point of undivided Muslim-majority Punjab, would probably have disagreed with Mookerjee and Vajpayee.[154] Lala Lajpat Rai believed that 'unity has a price which they will have to pay before it can be achieved'. Rai was speaking in the context of Hindu–Muslim unity and the price was the compromise that adherents of both the religions needed to make so as to live together peacefully. He wasn't a votary of absolute rights, be it religious freedom or speech. 'I contend that there is no such thing as an absolute right vested in any individual or in any community forming part of a nation; that all rights are relative, that no society can remain intact even for twenty-four hours on the basis of absolute rights,' he wrote.

He believed that 'All the rights of an individual are subject to the equal rights of others, which in fact creates duties and obligations on the part of the different members of a society towards each other.' While it is perfectly fine to create legal boundaries for action, it's not advisable to have such limitations on speech. Rai's view was essentially that 'My right to swing my fist ends where your nose begins.' This is a specious position, as no entity, much less a legal one consisting of mandarins, can define where the boundary of 'acceptable' speech ends and where the offence begins. This is especially so in a diverse society such as India. Two individuals might even come to a compromise and define limitations—as partners usually do in relationships—but attempting to do so for entire societies and nations would be a hopeless endeavour.

Giving the example of the liberty of speech and the liberty of the press, Rai submitted that even the United States during the First World War didn't shy away from taking away the fundamental rights of the people and forcing them to fight against their will. But this is also a questionable argument. It is no one's case that in extraordinary circumstances such as a global war, rights should not be curtailed.

For Lala Lajpat Rai, the unity of India was paramount. In the pursuit of unity, he went as far as suggesting that citizens 'make a clear distinction between essentials and non-essentials in religion' and shun those 'observances and practices which affect the just rights of other communities or otherwise injure their feelings'. One cannot emphasize enough on the impracticality of arriving at such an arrangement which would require consensus among tens of millions of people. Lofty idealism is often the graveyard of common sense. That is why, for any idealism to fructify, it must remain rooted in reality.

From the perspective of enforceability, Rai was essentially advocating the present-day French model which actively discourages all public displays of religiosity. He wrote, 'Ceremonial aspect of religion should only be the concern of individuals or of communities, and should not be permitted to create barriers or political distinctions between the followers of different religions, or between different religious communities as such.' This works as long as a society is homogenous but becomes increasingly difficult to implement as diversity increases.

This is exactly what the French—including the Quebecois people in Canada—are struggling with. In a country like India, where already so many groups with their own non-negotiables exist, it's impossible to limit religion or speech to the area of private sphere. The only way out is to let people do or speak what they want as long as they there is no imminent threat to public order.

Rai believed that 'In the interest of peace and neighbourly goodwill, to avoid social collision, [we] have to sacrifice a certain amount of our freedom.' But truly liberal principles should stop us from seeing fellow citizens as Pavlovian dogs who get violently provoked by any religious or socio-political speech.

Moreover, citizens will rely on the authority of the government to use force on their behalf as necessary to protect them from violence. Individual freedom implies individual responsibility and those who initiate violence must be held responsible for their actions—not those who offended them. We must never forget American statesman Benjamin Franklin's warning, 'Those who can give up essential liberty to obtain a little temporary safety, deserve neither liberty nor safety'.

Nellie and Delhi: communal riots, contorted discourse

In an interview[155] to the *Financial Times* when asked why she had not acted earlier to stop the violence during Assam's Nellie massacre of 18 February 1983, when the state was under President's rule, Prime Minister Indira Gandhi had said: 'One has to let such events take their own course before stepping in.'[156]

Mrs Gandhi was never probed about what she meant when she said this, and neither has the Congress party ever had to answer for what was one of the worst riots in independent India's history, with the official number of dead said to be 2191, most of them Muslims.

When Manmohan Singh was re-elected to the Rajya Sabha in 2013 as a representative of Assam, he said, 'It's a great opportunity for me to rededicate myself to the service of the people of Assam.'[157] Singh entered the Rajya Sabha claiming to be a resident of Assam and a tenant of the Congress party's Hiteshwar Saikia, the man who took over as Assam chief minister on 27 February 1983 after the Nellie riots.

It was under Saikia's chief ministership that the Assam Accord was executed in 1985 by Prime Minister Rajiv Gandhi. As part of the Accord, 310 charge-sheeted criminal cases related to the Nellie violence were dropped by the Union government[158]—a curious case of the Union government exonerating itself, given that the violence took place when Assam was under President's rule and hence under the control of Indira Gandhi.

Indira Gandhi's remark is lesser known than Rajiv Gandhi's disgraceful comment that justified the Congress-sponsored pogrom against Sikhs in 1984—the worst riots in the history of the republic. 'When a big tree falls, the earth shakes,' Rajiv Gandhi had said referring to his mother's killing and the subsequent pogrom of Sikhs in Delhi.[159]

The government-controlled Doordarshan television, immediately after Rajiv Gandhi's first speech as Prime Minister, showed shots of H.K.L. Bhagat and his supporters beating their breasts and shouting 'Khoon ka badla khoon se lenge' (Blood will be avenged with blood).[160] It should be remembered that Doordarshan was the only TV channel in India then, and played an outside role in public communications at the time. Bhagat had also showed up at Rajiv Gandhi's residence after his assassination, asking if it was Sikhs who had killed the Prime Minister. Bhagat died in 2005 and in fine Congress tradition, his son Deepak Bhagat was made the general secretary of the Delhi Pradesh Congress Committee.

Immediately after Rajiv Gandhi was assassinated, he was posthumously awarded the Bharat Ratna. Manmohan Singh as finance minister announced a donation of Rs 100 crore in the 1991 budget (equivalent to about Rs 1,000 crore today) to the Rajiv Gandhi Foundation,[161] a private trust created in the former Prime Minister's name controlled by Sonia Gandhi. With India reeling under an economic crisis, Singh deemed it fit and responsible to dole out a huge public grant to a private foundation. After protests by opposition parties, the government was forced to cancel this donation.

Singh claimed while campaigning during the 1999 general elections that the 1984 pogrom had been orchestrated by the RSS and that the

Congress organization had nothing to do with it.[162] He made this wild assertion because no investigation till then had been able to pin down the Congress party or any of its leaders for perpetrating the 1984 pogrom, even though there were eyewitness accounts of prominent Congress party functionaries leading mobs to kill innocent Sikhs. The Misra Commission constituted in May 1985 kept the names of the accused secret from the public. More committees and commissions were created to act on the findings of the Misra Commission. The entire exercise made a mockery of justice as the Congress-controlled governments did not act on their recommendations, and there was political connivance to delay and protract the process.

In August 2018, Congress President Rahul Gandhi flatly denied that the party had a role in the 1984 riots.[163] In October 2017, Manmohan Singh shared the stage with 1984 riots–accused Sajjan Kumar.[164] In December 2018, Sajjan Kumar was convicted for his role in the riots.

The 1984 pogrom wasn't even investigated properly till the A.B. Vajpayee government constituted the G.T. Nanavati Commission in 2000. When the Commission submitted its 185-page report in 2005, it was Singh, who as Prime Minister issued an apology in the Rajya Sabha and not Sonia Gandhi who lays claim to the legacy of Rajiv Gandhi. Her stance on 1984 has been notable. Speaking at Chandigarh in January 1998 on the storming of the Golden Temple and the Sikh killings, she said rather conveniently, 'There is no use recalling what we have collectively lost. No words can balm that pain.'[165]

Contrast the farce that the investigations of 1983 Nellie riots and the 1984 anti-Sikh pogrom were reduced to, with the thorough investigation that Narendra Modi faced in the cases pertaining to the 2002 Gujarat riots. Not only did the Special Investigation Team (SIT) constituted by the Supreme Court fully exonerate Modi, with the 541-page SIT closure report recording that 'Modi was busy with steps to control the situation, establishment of relief camps for riot victims and also with efforts to restore peace and normalcy', completely contradicting the false narrative manufactured by denizens of the intellectual–media complex.

Eminent philosopher–economist Amartya Sen once commented, 'There is no philosophy of killing Sikhs in the Congress.'[166] This line is often regurgitated by many Left-intellectuals aligned with the Congress party. Left parties too have employed incredible violence to achieve their ends. According to an article in the *Mainstream Weekly* published in 2010, the Communist Party of India (Marxist)-led Left Front coalition that governed West Bengal from 1977 to 2011 committed over 55,000 political murders.[167]

The riots in Nellie and Delhi are just two examples of the many tragic incidents that have taken place in independent India, the vast majority under Congress governments. What is especially notable about Nellie and Delhi is that they happened under members of the Nehru–Gandhi dynasty, (who are not just relatives but self-described role models for the party's most powerful leaders, Sonia Gandhi and Rahul Gandhi) and for which none of the people at the top have been held accountable.

Paraphrasing billionaire investor Warren Buffett's response to his academic critics—responding to academia that asserted it was not possible to outperform efficient markets, Buffett had essentially said that he couldn't beat the market in theory, but was beating it in practice—we wholeheartedly agree with Amartya Sen when he says that there is no philosophy of attacking minorities in the Congress party—because they can actually kill in practice, there is no need to kill in theory.

The Patelian heirs of Ambedkar, Savarkar and Rajaji

Speaking at the convocation ceremony of Aligarh Muslim University in 1948, Jawaharlal Nehru had said:[168]

I am proud of India, not only because of her ancient magnificent heritage, but also because of her remarkable capacity to add to it by keeping the doors and windows of her mind and spirit open to fresh and invigorating winds from distant lands. India's strength has been twofold: her innate culture which flowered through ages, and her

capacity to draw from other sources and thus add to her own . . .
I have said that I am proud of our inheritance and our ancestors
who gave an intellectual and cultural pre-eminence to India. How
do you feel about this past? Do you feel you are also sharers in it
and inheritors of it and, therefore, proud of something that belongs
to you as much as to me? Or do you feel alien to it and pass it by
without understanding it or feeling that strange thrill which comes
from the realization that we are the trustees and inheritors of this
vast treasure . . . You are Muslims and I am a Hindu. We may
adhere to different religious faiths or even to none; but that does
not take away from that cultural inheritance that is yours as well
as mine. The past holds us together; why should the present or the
future divide us in spirit?

Nehru went a step further when, in a May 1964 interview, he said
that[169] 'Hindus . . . are not a proselytizing race . . . Muslims were keen
on proselytizing and getting converts. Nearly all Muslims of India are
descendants of Hindus. Only a handful came from outside.' A 2009
genetic study on the origin of Indian Muslims confirmed[170] Nehru's
instincts, concluding that 'the spread of Islamic faith in the Indian
subcontinent was predominantly cultural transformation associated
with minor gene flow from West Asia.'[171]

Nehru defined the philosophical debate in Indian politics from
Independence till his death in 1964.[172] The world view he espoused
has come to be known as Nehruvian, even if its present-day version
does not entirely overlap with his own views. The Nehruvian view
entailed pervasive state control over the economy, an idealistic stance
in foreign affairs and special consideration to minority communities
in domestic policy.

But the Congress was far from a one-person or one-ideology
party in the 1950s—it was a big tent with a vibrant right wing, too.
Its decline as a political institution began under Nehru, who was the
first Prime Minister to abuse Article 356 and dismiss Kerala's elected
state government in 1959. Even if Nehru was not inclined to take this
position, he allowed himself to be overruled by the Congress president,
his daughter Indira Gandhi, whom he had helped install as party

president in 1959.[173] This Stalinist template, where no distinction is made between the party and State, and the executive is debased at the expense of the party, was pioneered by Nehru and has been followed by almost all successive Congress prime ministers—Sonia Gandhi carried it to a new high during the UPA government years.[174] The emasculation of inner-party democracy accelerated under Indira Gandhi, was continued by her son Rajiv Gandhi and has been dutifully carried forward by his wife Sonia Gandhi and son Rahul Gandhi.

Acharya J.B. Kripalani opposed Nehru vigorously on the issue of allowing separate personal laws for Muslims in 1955, charging him with 'communalism' on the floor of the Parliament. Rajaji quit the Congress at age eighty in 1959 to establish the Swatantra Party, espousing economic liberalism.

Speaking at the launch of the Swatantra Party in August 1959, Rajaji had said:[175]

I have come to the conclusion that a movement for freedom, as important and as serious as the movement for independence against British rule, has now to be inaugurated against this misconceived progress of the Congress towards what will finally end in the suppression of individual liberty and the development of the State into a true Leviathan. The State is becoming a giant entity by itself, menacingly poised against the citizen, interfering with his life at all points, mistrusting the people, imposing restrictions, introducing a series of controls and regulations, stepping into the fields of agriculture, industry and trade, creating an army of officials, tremendously increasing the cost of administration and therefore the taxes paid by the nation, hypnotising the people with slogans that are mistaken for thought and wisdom, a scheme of government in which it is taken for granted that the citizen is ignorant of what is his own interest.

'The Congress Party has swung to the Left, what is wanted is not an ultra or outer-Left . . . but a strong and articulate Right,' he wrote in his essay 'Our Democracy'.[176] In the dusk of his illustrious life, Rajaji founded the *Swarajya* journal[177] to push back against Nehru's statist-collectivist policies:

There is before the country the great problem of how to secure welfare without surrendering the individual to be swallowed up by the state, how to get the best return for the taxes the people pay and how to preserve spiritual values while working for better material standards of life. This journal will serve all these purposes.

After Rajaji's demise in 1972, Swatantra was ably led by Minoo Masani and N. G. Ranga, among others. Threatened that Swatantra was gaining traction and had secured forty-four seats in the 1967 general election to become the principal opposition party, Indira Gandhi went out of her way to crush Swatantra Party's backers—the former royal families and the business community—which included many of the industrialists who had funded the Congress during the independence movement. It was a classic case of undermining economic freedom to subvert political freedom as well. It is not surprising that this approach led to the Emergency in some years. But Nehru's most formidable ideological opponent was Sardar Vallabhbhai Patel and it was Patel's death on 15 December 1950 that accelerated India's tilt towards the Left.

Patel's world view was substantively different from Nehru's in many important spheres. Despite opposition from Nehru, Patel got a mosque shifted[178] to rebuild the temple at Somnath that had been repeatedly destroyed over the centuries by Muslim invaders. Mahatma Gandhi gave his blessings to Patel but wanted no public funds to be used for the construction of the temple. Gandhi viewed the pillaging and usurpation of Hindu temples by Islamic invaders in a strongly negative light. He wrote in 1937:[179]

It is a very heinous sin to damage any place of worship. During the Mughal period, due to religious fanaticism, the Mughal rulers occupied many religious places of Hindus. Many of these were looted and destroyed and many were converted into mosques. Although both temples and mosques are holy places of worship of God and there is no difference between the two, the worship tradition of both Hindus and Muslims is different. From a religious point of view, a Muslim can never tolerate that a Hindu loots the mosque where he has been praying. Similarly, a Hindu will never tolerate that his temple, where he has been worshipping Ram, Krishna, Vishnu and other gods, be demolished. Where such incidents have happened, these are signs of slavery.

On China, their views differed, with Patel advocating help to Tibet when it was invaded—and Patel turned out to be right.[180] On Kashmir's accession to India, Patel's realism was again overruled, and Nehru needlessly internationalized the issue by inviting intervention from the United Nations.

On economic issues, too, they had significant differences, with Patel repeatedly opposing Nehru's demand for establishing the Planning Commission. It was on Patel's insistence that the Commission was given an advisory role only, with its policies subject to the Union Cabinet's review and approval. Nehru wanted to define the purpose of planning as the elimination of 'the motive of private gain in economic activity or organization of society and the antisocial concentration of wealth and means of production'. Patel prevailed over him and got this language deleted.[181]

That Nehru sought to endow such a body with sweeping powers only betrays his affinity for a centralized, anti-market, if not communist, approach to economic development.

As the writer and historian Hindol Sengupta has recorded in his biography of Sardar Patel, in a January 1948 speech, Patel said that before any ideas of nationalization could be considered, a vibrant environment for private industry needed to be created.[182] Their positions on zamindari abolition and the use of eminent domain for land acquisition further illuminate their philosophical leanings. Patel wanted compensation at market price plus 15 per cent while Nehru favoured no compensation. Patel also successfully supported Rajendra Prasad for President of India and Purushottam Das Tandon for Congress party president in 1950, not just for ideological reasons but also to show Nehru that he couldn't always dictate terms.

Only Patel commanded the political heft to counter Nehru, and with his demise the 'conservative' wing within the Congress lost its strongest ballast. By 1955, Nehru had consolidated his hold on both the party and the government, and the Avadi session of the Congress marked a definitive tilt towards a 'socialist pattern'.[183] Nehru proclaimed that the 'national aim is a welfare state and a socialist economy'.[184]

The freedom fighter S. Ambujammal noted that 'a new Congress was born at the 1955 Avadi session, shunning its old image.'[185] Nehru's new stance on both economic and social policy thus hastened the exit of many stalwarts. K.M. Munshi, who was an ally of Sardar Patel and had been instrumental in the re-establishment of the Somnath temple, also joined the Swatantra Party in 1959.[186] Munshi was a founding member of the Vishva Hindu Parishad in 1964. V.P. Menon, Patel's close associate who was a key figure in the integration of the princely states after Partition, was also a leading light of the Swatantra Party.[187]

Just as with towering figures like Swami Vivekananda, Nehruvian intellectuals are confused whether to re-appropriate the legacy of Patel, or to escalate their attacks to try and toxify Patel's place in history. They are tempted to try re-appropriation because of his titanic stature, but at the same time they are unable to reconcile the views of titans like Patel or Vivekananda with their own dogma.

In such a political–historical context entered Narendra Modi. His economic record as chief minister of Gujarat was debated threadbare during the 2014 general election campaign. When it was proved beyond reasonable doubt that Modi's leadership of Gujarat accelerated the state's economic progress, his opponents trained guns on another front.

Prime Minister Modi's critics have long argued that he isn't inclusive and is autocratic. Above all, they say, Narendra Modi is not secular—he has been painted as someone too divisive and obdurate for a diverse nation like India despite having secured two consecutive, comprehensive electoral mandates in the world's largest democracy.

The charge of not being inclusive is also inaccurate. The word 'inclusive' has become a euphemism to justify irresponsible and wasteful government spending, usually based upon identity, and it is parroted by all who promote the type of socialism that kept India impoverished for decades. In India, one is branded communal if one doesn't support State welfare of citizens based on religious criteria.

This is a hideous perversion of secularism. The ugliness of secular politics has plumbed unimaginable depths, with even murders by terrorists being used for vote bank politics. During a rally at Azamgarh at the time of the 2012 Uttar Pradesh Assembly elections, Congress MP Salman Khurshid said that the Congress president 'wept bitterly' on seeing images of the encounter that took place at Batla House in Delhi.[188] Congress leaders like him insisted the encounter was fake before a judicial verdict was delivered. Tears were shed for the terrorists killed in the encounter, but there were no tears shed for the policeman Mohan Chand Sharma, who was killed by the terrorists at Batla House.

The pseudo-secularists try to keep Hindu society divided for electoral reasons. But Ambedkar stood for the long-term 'annihilation of caste',[189] and as Shri Ram College of Commerce Professor Abhinav Prakash Singh has observed:[190]

> Savarkar understood that an agrarian society, fractured by the caste system, could not become a nation. Consequently, along with advocating the embrace of industrialization and the modern world, Hindutva was also an anti-caste movement. In fact, Hindutva was among the most powerful reform movements that emerged in colonial India and aimed at eradicating caste and regional differentiations to create social unity by fostering a Hindu identity.

Patel had severe disagreements with Nehru and Abul Kalam Azad over the allocation of housing in Delhi that used to be occupied by Muslims who, after Partition, migrated to Pakistan.[191] Nehru and Azad insisted that only Muslims should stay in those homes, whereas Patel held that no secular government could take such a stand. The gatekeepers of secularism would have charged Patel as communal today, just as they attack Modi as communal for upholding similar principles. Patel unreservedly condemned the methods adopted by Communists as being against the rule of law. He said, 'Their philosophy is to exploit every situation, to create chaos and anarchy, in the belief that, in such conditions, it would be possible for them to seize power.'[192]

The same charges—fascist, communalist, capitalist—were made against Patel during his lifetime and since Patel's demise have been levelled against Modi. This only shows that the Nehruvian consensus has never been so threatened in India as it is today—and those wedded to such ideas will do everything they can to prevent the implosion of this consensus.

4

Profit Is Not a Dirty Word

Never talk to me about the word profit; it is a dirty word.

—Prime Minister Nehru to J.R.D. Tata when the
latter talked about the need for the public sector
to make a profit[1]

The morality of markets

No strain of the modern socialist movement—in India or elsewhere—subscribes to individual freedom as an end in itself.[2] For socialists, equal material outcomes within the country are paramount. Freedom for the socialists has meant freedom from the State when it comes to personal choices and civil matters but on economic issues, the State is suddenly transformed into a benign institution. Freedom, then, becomes the fulfilment of needs such as food, healthcare and a minimum income through the agency of the government.

To paraphrase the philosopher Isaiah Berlin, socialists do not believe in 'negative liberty' or freedom from the State beyond protection of life, liberty, and property but instead in 'positive liberty' or material freedom through the State.[3]

Yet, ensuring one person's (say, Ram's) negative liberty does not significantly affect another person's (say, Shyam's) negative liberty unless one insists that murder or theft is liberty. But ensuring

Ram's positive liberty of a cradle-to-grave State support does mean downgrading Shyam's negative liberty with respect to his personal property. There is also a very practical problem with positive liberty—how would the ever-expanding welfare state, built and geared to deliver material equality for all, be funded?

The point here is not to oppose any attempt at redistribution, but to press for intellectual honesty. Now, socialists often call welfare policies 'insurance', but if the spreading of risks is what primarily motivated them, they would not be opposed to private or foreign companies providing the same services more efficiently—in life insurance, property insurance, health insurance and even limited forms of income or unemployment insurance. The insistence on government involvement for welfare delivery gives the game away.

To press for State-enforced egalitarianism is a legitimate position to have and one which we support in a still-poor nation such as India. But there is much greater scope for efficiency in welfare. Welfare programmes designed by the State, delivered through public–private partnerships in the social sector, are welcome and India would be better off with lesser socioeconomic engineering by top-down bureaucracies sitting in New Delhi.

But to pretend that mandated redistribution is somehow consistent with negative liberty and individual freedom—indeed is the very essence of liberty or freedom itself—is to indulge in Orwellian sophistry. Yet, this is precisely what the socialists do. Nobel laureate Amartya Sen is not above this either. One of his books is titled *Development as Freedom*, where he proclaims that development is 'a process of expanding the real freedoms that people enjoy'.[4] According to Sen, land redistribution, government-run schools, government-operated hospitals and public make-work schemes constitute development.

But inefficiently run programmes are certainly not consistent with individual freedom, especially of the taxpayer, and it must be remembered that the poor also pay indirect taxes and perhaps even more perniciously, the 'inflation tax'. Of course, the taxpayers could be dismissed as greedy but what is undeniable is that their private property has been expropriated by the State for redistribution.

Socialists and economic collectivists understand the natural attraction to freedom in the hearts of all humans, and so they paradoxically undermine and discredit the idea of individual freedom, while still co-opting its message. In *Development as Freedom*, Sen writes, 'The uncompromising priority of libertarian rights can be particularly problematic since the actual consequences of the operation of these entitlements can, quite possibly, include rather terrible results.' That may often be the case. For example, a government that refuses to intervene during a natural calamity or redistribute during a famine would be a good example, as we are sure Sen would agree, but two points remain unanswered.

First, what is preventing noble individuals like Sen (pun not intended) from getting together and helping others during crises like natural calamities? It is presumptuous to assume that only people who agree with Sen's statist philosophy care for the poor, while others do not. It would be hypocritical, too, because one does not know of many socialists who voluntarily pay more in taxes than they are required to, although many of them goad others to do so. On the other hand, classical liberals have said freedom requires responsibility that must be voluntarily discharged—towards oneself, one's family and the larger society. But here, too, Sen has a masterful answer. He writes, 'Responsibility requires freedom.' What he means is that if his kind of welfare state is not realized, people will not be free to be responsible enough!

Second, if one were to discredit a philosophy based on extreme conditions, Sen, who has hailed communist prophet Karl Marx as a 'great intellectual',[5] should remember what turned out to be actually problematic in communist countries such as China, the former Soviet Union and other nations where tens of millions of people died because of policies such as the forced collectivization of agriculture.[6]

During a tour of Soviet Russia in 1955, Prime Minister Jawaharlal Nehru was completely taken up by the Soviet economic model, including its practice of collective farming. Nehru was like a 'kid in a candy store', according to one editor.[7] After Sardar Patel's passing, the Congress party's economically liberal groups had been weakened.[8]

Nobody in the Cabinet had the standing to counter Nehru at the time, and his scheme for cooperative farming mimicked the Soviet drive for collectivized agriculture under a palatable label.[9] The Second Five-Year Plan noted that India would 'provide sound foundations for the development of cooperative farming, so that over a period of 10 years or so, a substantial portion of agricultural lands are cultivated on cooperative lines'.[10] Fortunately for India, collectivization of agriculture was prevented due to resistance from farmer groups and firm pushback provided by leaders like Sucheta Kripalani and Chaudhary Charan Singh—who went on to become Prime Minister in 1979. Singh opposed collectivization in 1957, saying that 'it has not proved a success anywhere in the world.'[11]

To return to Sen's positions, let us take the example of the British policies responsible for the deaths of about 3 million people during the Bengal famine of 1943. As Sen himself has documented, government policies—such as a ban on interprovincial trade in rice—that were anything but laissez-faire greatly exacerbated the situation. As the historian Madhusree Mukerjee has shown, India exported over 70,000 tons of rice between January–July 1943, just as the famine was setting in.[12]

Winston Churchill deliberately denied food supplies and showed a cruel 'will to punish' Indians, according to Mukherjee. IIT Gandhinagar's Vimal Mishra showed in a paper published by *Geophysical Research Letters* how policy failures and deliberate decisions plunged Bengal into one of the worst famines India ever saw, killing millions from starvation and disease.[13] In any case, it is nobody's case that extraordinary exigencies created by natural disasters or war should not be responded to by the government. Most votaries of liberal economic ideas do support some redistribution and are not opposed to transfers in the form of food stamps or conditional cash transfers, and so on.

The contortions that socialists go through to depict State coercion as freedom are impressive. Jagdish Bhagwati wrote in his book *In Defense of Globalization* about this garbled state of affairs:

Deconstructionism . . . amounts to an endless horizon of meanings . . . Derrida's technique will deconstruct any political ideology, including

Marxism. Typically, however, it is focused on deconstructing and devaluing capitalism rather than Marxism . . . Foucault's emphasis on discourses as instruments of power and dominance has also led to what is often described as an 'anti-rational' approach that challenges the legitimacy of academic disciplines, including economics, and their ability to get at the 'truth'.[14]

The confusions and distortions that manifest in the intellectual realm flow downstream into politics. Rahul Gandhi and the Congress party have never missed an opportunity[15] to label the Modi government as '*suit-boot ki sarkar*'.[16] His aversion to market-friendly or pro-business policies is not new. Like his mother, he believes in doling out 'rights' to citizens.[17]

In the 2019 general election campaign, Gandhi had promised distributing Rs 72,000 per year to the poorest 20 per cent of the population under the Nyay minimum income guarantee scheme.[18] 'We are empowering India by giving the common man all kinds of rights,'[19] Gandhi had said at an election rally in 2013. 'We run a government at the Centre which gives rights to the people . . . We believe in inclusive growth,' he had said in a speech at Aligarh the same year. While campaigning in Madhya Pradesh in 2013, he had launched a scathing attack on the BJP's 'capitalist politics'.[20]

Obviously, Gandhi intended the label as a slur, just as he did with the 'suit-boot' jibe. It shows how socialistic his economic vision is. One could dismiss the Congress leader's pronouncements as naive or ignorant—but even technocratic voices within the Congress firmament have made celebratory utterances of 'rights-based development' that Rahul Gandhi has claimed is a guarantee of progress.

The rights-based development paradigm fundamentally misunderstands the reasons behind India's poverty, and it points away from the direction that governance in India needs to take so that many more Indians can become wealthy and prosperous.

The negative effects of government interventions are often borne by the poorest—for example, when onion prices rise, the State snatches away the bonanza from onion farmers by introducing export and price controls. On other occasions it bans imports, raises procurement prices and adds numerous regulations. Only recently has there been a welcome policy shift by the government. As part of the Atmanirbhar Bharat economic reforms package of 2020, certain agriculture commodities were removed from the Essential Commodities Act, 1955, reducing market distortions.[21] Agriculture Minister Narendra Singh Tomar described farming as a 'business', saying that:[22]

> Farmers . . . are perhaps the only producers who neither decide the price of their produce nor sell it to the buyer of their choice. Moreover, they are tied to all sorts of rules and regulations. If you take any other business, the producer is free to produce his goods, sell to whoever he wants, and at any place of his choice. Therefore, these big reforms were badly needed for boosting farmer income.

As eminent agriculture economist Dr Ashok Gulati observed, 'the reforms . . . could be a harbinger of major change in agri-marketing, a 1991 moment of economic reforms for agriculture.'[23] But it was not to be—these important structural reforms brought protests from the same groups[24] who would be losing out had the reforms been implemented.[25] The agitation resulted in the blockade of entry points into New Delhi, obstruction of railroads and coordinated marches to New Delhi by thousands of protesters. The protests reached a crescendo on Republic Day in 2021 when in an unseemly display of street power, thousands of tractors entered New Delhi and hordes of protesters caused disruptions throughout the city. Over 300 police officials were injured by violent mobs. The occupation of roads and highways, disrupting traffic and goods movement around New Delhi, continued all through 2021. On 19 November 2021, Prime Minister Narendra Modi withdrew the bold agriculture reforms, stating that while he had brought the reforms for the benefit of India's vast agriculture-dependent workers, he was taking them back in the interest of national security.[26] The relentless protests—possibly funded by foreign countries, according to some press reports[27]—had exacted their price.

The protests against the farm laws were concentrated in a few northern states near Delhi, because the benefits of public procurement disproportionately favoured those few states.[28] Resetting agriculture policy is a critical structural reform that in the future could be preceded by making public procurement more evenly spread out across India. Rather than micromanaging the supply side, the State should construct an efficient safety net that helps the poor, irrespective of whether they reside in cities or villages and whether they work on farms or factories. In this context, the recent reform measure by the Modi government to introduce portability of ration cards is an excellent first step.[29]

But there have been criticisms of the failure of market liberals to situate economic arguments in ethical terms. Doing so would make the efficiency argument more politically saleable. Private school access, for example, could be a great issue based on which a talented politician could explain free market competition in rural India. The question of why the economic liberals have failed to do so is, indeed, an important one.

Economic arguments against socialism in mainstream Indian public discourse are a relatively recent phenomenon. For a variety of reasons, India never had a sizable liberal constituency committed to free enterprise. In the early decades after Independence, pioneering thinkers like the banker–industrialist (and Tata group director) A.D. Shroff, who had founded the Forum Of Free Enterprise, the economist B.R. Shenoy[30], were largely ignored. Shroff had presciently said at the founding of the Forum in 1956, after the landmark 1955 Avadi session of the Congress:[31]

> With the announcement of the Socialist pattern of society as our goal, the raising of the tempo of planning and the inevitable concentration of economic power in the hands of the State, the question of the relation between Free Enterprise and Democracy has assumed great significance . . . democracy is a political concomitant of Free Enterprise, and with every step towards a diminution of Free Enterprise, democracy is hastening towards its end. It is not a

mere accident or coincidence of history that democracy has grown and flourished along with the system of free enterprise. Issues are unfortunately confused by the dogma of Marxism, identifying ends with means.

Intellectual discourse on such issues from Independence till the 1990s was stoutly against liberal ideas—the reform proposals of trailblazing intellectuals such as Jagdish Bhagwati were largely ignored through the 1960s, 1970s and 1980s, despite mounting evidence of the failures of central planning and the Nehruvian socialist approach.

All opposition parties simply adopted different hues of the same socialist thinking that the Congress, as the pre-eminent political party in independent India, championed under Jawaharlal Nehru and Indira Gandhi. Apart from the Swatantra Party, only the Bharatiya Jan Sangh differed more sharply from the Congress. It differed more on issues of secularism, national identity and foreign policy than on economics, though in economics, too, the Bharatiya Jan Sangh's 1952 election manifesto stated that State ownership of industries 'had generally not worked efficiently and economically in this country'. Marking a break from the dogma of the day, the manifesto continued that the Bharatiya Jan Sangh would 'encourage private enterprise . . . under the general control and regulation of the State in the interests of consumers and producers alike'.[32]

The cardinal error pro-market ideologues made was to accept the charge of the socialists that capitalism was about materialism. For example, political ideologues such as Deendayal Upadhyaya of the BJP's predecessor, the Bharatiya Jan Sangh, articulated integral humanism, taking a broader metaphysical view of the economy.

Upadhyaya believed that both communism and capitalism were unsuited to India and sought to amalgamate features of both philosophies into a new theory grounded in humanism. Though he rightly understood communism to be anti-individual, he narrowly viewed capitalism not as a force that favoured—and emerged from—individual freedom, but as one that promoted materialism at the expense of spiritual self-actualization.

But it is communism and socialism that promote materialism by placing primacy on achieving material equality for individuals through State coercion. The very notion that the material equality of individuals should be the yardstick by which to measure the morality of the society betrays the obsession of the Left with materialism. The emphasis placed on such equality shows how Leftists seek to project their own obsession onto ideological opponents.

A socialist system force-fits individuals into narrow professions and vocations. Democratic capitalism, in contrast, creates space for individual self-discovery without an obsessive regard for material outcomes being equal. It can be more egalitarian because it leaves each individual free to define their own standard for economic success as a subset—but not the entirety—of their unique path to satisfaction and happiness.

Moreover, the economic system most compatible with India's spiritual heritage is capitalism that works towards equal opportunity and social mobility, for such a system both accepts and allows for a collection of pathways towards the end goal of self-realization. This is not to say that a primarily materialistic world view is incompatible with the Indic world view—but it can only be one part of it. As Prime Minister Narendra Modi had acknowledged during a May 2019 interview, in the Dharmic system even the hedonism of the Charvaka world view has been given due recognition,[33] despite a large number of people disagreeing with it.

Capitalism is the economic analogue of the philosophy that pervades and defines the highest traditions of India's spiritual life, if one agrees that Indic traditions are rooted in pluralism. It also follows that communism and socialism are antagonistic towards these traditions. As writer Charles Wheelan had observed, 'market economy is to economics what democracy is to government: a decent, if flawed, choice among many bad alternatives.'[34]

While some may have intuitively understood this, unfortunately many who espouse the cause of India's cultural renaissance don't see capitalism as a philosophy in consonance with Indic values, because these values themselves were distorted by British rule, when a Victorian morality seeped into social life in India. Simultaneously, votaries of economic liberalism have failed to see India's spiritual heritage as complementary to economic liberalism and they reflexively revolt at any discussion of spirituality or religion.

The practical case for markets

An infographic capturing the leading causes of death in the twentieth century,[35] published by a London-based journalist in 2012, is now a popular and powerful internet meme.[36] The artwork says that 142 million had been killed because of ideology, of which 94 million deaths were caused by communism, with massive killings taking place in its name in China, the Soviet Union, Eastern Europe and North Korea. The death count because of communism exceeds deaths caused by fascism, terrorism and even both the World Wars. India usually doesn't figure in the public mind as a nation that has been communist, though it was frequently described as the seemingly more benign-sounding 'socialist'. Conventionally, India is not counted among countries affected by communism.

One of the great mistakes is to judge policies and programmes by their intentions rather than their results.[37] Cato Institute research fellow Swaminathan Aiyar published a paper in October 2009 titled 'Socialism Kills: The Human Cost of Delayed Economic Reform in India'.[38] Aiyar wrote that '14.5 million more children would have survived, 261 million would have become literate and 109 million more people would have risen above the poverty line' had India initiated economic reforms in 1971.

It wasn't always this way, but the Indian Constitution has a commitment to socialism and doesn't recognize property rights as a fundamental right. When India became independent, the right to private property was a fundamental right. The First Amendment to the Constitution championed by Prime Minister Jawaharlal Nehru started the process of diluting this right. He inserted new articles 31A and 31B reasoning that land reforms were being held up due to property being a fundamental right.

Eminent jurist Nani Palkhivala had written presciently in 1974, that 'property' has become a dirty word today, '"liberty" will become a dirty word tomorrow. If we permit the right to property to be abrogated, the denizens of the mansions of power will not jib at taking away the right to personal liberty.'[39] Less than a year after this prognostication, Indira Gandhi declared the dictatorial Emergency in 1975. In 1978, the Janata Party government delivered the final nail in the coffin, further degrading the right to property by removing it from the list of fundamental rights altogether by passing the 44th constitutional amendment. Right to property became just another legal right. Palkhivala had written that the right to property was 'the essence of a sound body politic and of a democracy which aims at marching forward economically.'

The word 'socialism' was inserted into the Preamble of the Constitution by Prime Minister Indira Gandhi via the 42nd constitutional amendment in 1976, during the dictatorial Emergency. This historical context is not merely of academic interest, but is very relevant to the debate on economic development and liberalization in India, which is far from settled despite what many intellectuals seem to believe. There is a popular view that after the reforms of 1991, India has already become a free-market capitalist economy. This is not entirely correct, because economic reforms are an ongoing journey.

Under the Representation of People Act, all Indian political parties are required to swear allegiance to 'socialism' to become registered and contest elections.[40] The government considers it perfectly acceptable to own and operate hotels, steel manufacturing companies, power generation firms, chemicals manufacturers, telecommunications providers, electronics manufacturers, mining companies and myriad other businesses.

Since the liberalization era began in 1991, many industries have seen a sea change, but perhaps few sectors have been as comprehensively transformed as the telecommunications industry. Unfortunately, there has been a concerted attempt[41] to ascribe India's telecommunications boom to the vision and work of former Prime Minister Rajiv Gandhi and his adviser Sam Pitroda. A segment of media commentary has asserted that it was Gandhi and Pitroda's efforts, starting in the 1980s, that set the stage for the telecom revolution that has put mobile phones in the hands of India's masses.

'You got mobile phones because Rajiv Gandhi heard you,' Congress's Rahul Gandhi is often heard boasting in public.[42] At one such rally during the 2013 Uttar Pradesh elections, Gandhi said '*Badaai hai woh*',[43] pointing out Sam Pitroda's carpenter caste. The technocrat Pitroda had accompanied Rahul Gandhi at some of these election rallies despite such crass politics to gain votes by using his caste identity. Pitroda has been more than willing to take credit for India's mobile revolution. The inside cover of the *March of Mobile Money*, a book coauthored by him, declares him to be 'the man behind India's telecom revolution'.[44]

The rapid growth of mobile telephony in India ranks inarguably as one of India's greatest success stories. It is important to trace the history of telephony and draw lessons from this success story, for such successes have been rare in Indian business and policy history. This is a case study for how changing the role of government from business owner to regulator can enable an industry to pole vault ahead.

Under Prime Minister Atal Bihari Vajpayee, the New Telecom Policy (NTP) announced by the Government of India on 3 March 1999 recounted some facts about the status of the telecom sector in India at the time. It noted that India had 'over 1 million' mobile phone subscribers. Ten years after Rajiv Gandhi's government left office in 1989 and eight years after Pitroda returned to the US following Rajiv Gandhi's assassination, tele-density in India had moved from 0.6 per cent in 1989 to 2.8 per cent in 1999.[45]

Does that constitute a revolution and does that make Rajiv Gandhi and Sam Pitroda the progenitors of the mobile revolution?

The 1999 NTP far exceeded its own target of achieving 15 per cent tele-density by 2010, which would have probably sounded overly optimistic when announced in 1999. How did this massive growth happen? Does any specific individual or policy deserve more credit than others?

Speaking at a corporate awards function in December 2009 where his company was felicitated, Idea Cellular's then managing director

Sanjeev Aga was asked to identify what in his view marked the turning point for India's telecom sector. Aga pointed to the 1999 NTP, saying, 'When I read it today, it is still contemporary and comprehensive.' Aga characterized the NTP as a 'watershed event'.[46]

In his magisterial work, *India: The Emerging Giant*, Columbia University's Arvind Panagariya also addresses the question of what catalysed the growth in telecom. Panagariya writes that key policy reforms were implemented by the government in 1999, with one of the most important measures being separation between policy formulation and service provision, culminating with the birth of Bharat Sanchar Nigam Ltd (BSNL) on 1 October 2000.[47] Getting rid of this very obvious conflict of interest freed the telecom sector from political control.

Vajpayee, who also held the telecom portfolio at the time, took the politically difficult step of corporatizing BSNL, and Panagariya writes that the Prime Minister personally intervened to push through this deep structural reform. The creation of BSNL wasn't easy—Panagariya writes that 400,000 department of telecommunications (DoT) employees went on a long strike to oppose it. Though the Vajpayee government conceded almost all their demands, there was no going back on the fundamental principle of separating policy formulation from service provision and the accompanying corporatization. Besides this step, the 1999 NTP separated the DoT's regulatory and dispute settlement roles too, with the creation of the Telecom Dispute Settlement Appellate Tribunal.

Before these reforms, the DoT was deciding policy for the sector, adjudicating disputes and providing telecom services. That such glaring conflict of interest persisted for so many decades, reflects on the calibre and intent of the governments that preceded the Vajpayee administration. Unbundling these conflicting and overlapping roles required strong political will and concerted administrative action.

Under the 1999 NTP, the fixed licence fee payable upfront was lowered with the government introducing a revenue-sharing regime. The media was very hostile to the new policy. *Frontline* magazine ran a stinging criticism of the policy, holding Prime Minister Vajpayee guilty of 'a new standard of impropriety'.[48] *Outlook* magazine said that Vajpayee's moves had 'all the trappings of a financial scam'.[49]

On 15 August 2000, 'unlimited competition' was introduced in domestic long-distance telephony services. On 1 April 2002, VSNL's monopoly on international telephony ended. Panagariya documents all these changes painstakingly in his book, and it is these changes that deserve credit for the rapid increase in tele-density since then.

Pitroda, in fact, had torpedoed attempts to bring mobile telephony to India in 1987, as Panagariya records. DoT had received World Bank funds to deploy a cellular network in Mumbai (or Bombay, as the city was called then) with Sweden winning the project. Panagariya writes that Pitroda, who was heading the Centre for Development of Telematics (CDoT), created at his behest by Indira Gandhi in August 1984, went to the media arguing that 'luxury car phones' were 'obscene' in a nation where 'people were starving'.

Pitroda's intervention escalated the issue to Rajiv Gandhi, who pulled the plug on what would have been India's first cellular network deployment. Panagariya cites this case as an example of how turf wars within government arise in response to policy changes— because Pitroda felt that mobile telephony threatened his work at CDoT, he did not hesitate to use his influence to stop what may have been a better way to achieve the desirable outcome of increasing tele-density.

The results speak for themselves—Rajiv Gandhi and Pitroda's model of promoting growth through the DoT trying to meet the demand for telephones failed conclusively, whereas the Vajpayee government's policies curtailed the State's role and created space for private entrepreneurs to deliver cheap and reliable telecom service speedily on a massive scale. The former tried to grow by State-led indigenization, the latter threw open the sector to competition and entrepreneurship.

Pitroda did not return to India till 2004, when the Congress party formed the Union government once again. Yet, Rajiv Gandhi's son claimed that the telecom revolution was his father's achievement and Pitroda felt no compunction in claiming to be the driving force behind India's telecom revolution.

India's telecom story is a shining testament to how policy clarity, political conviction for reforms and private entrepreneurship can deliver outcomes quickly that government intervention and well-intentioned bureaucratic thinking cannot even conceive of. Reform is ultimately driven by a commitment to national interest, as there is always some interest group or the other looking to prevent change from happening. For example, Vajpayee did not give in to a strike by the 400,000 DoT employees in 1999,[50] who were protesting against the creation of a corporate entity for provision of telephone services. Vajpayee stuck to his guns, defied the unions and pushed through the creation of Bharat Sanchar Nigam Ltd (BSNL).

The lesson from India's telecom boom is that curtailing government control and public-sector clout in sectors such as agriculture, mining, defence, power, ports and banking can deliver similar outcomes—and no amount of spin doctoring by any individual or political party should be allowed to detract from this lesson.

The telecom experience of unbundling the regulation, dispute resolution and service-provision functions offers a sound playbook for driving reforms in other sectors too. Let us take the example of the financial sector, which holds the key to capital allocation in the economy.

Borrowing large sums from banks and not repaying loans—effectively robbing the banks—had become a reliable, profitable business model for unscrupulous owners. Working in connivance with a corrupt political class in New Delhi who pulled the strings at public sector banks under the infamous 'phone banking'[51] approach, the business owners successfully normalized the recapitalization of public sector banks as a fit-and-proper use of taxpayer money.

This was the legacy of Indira Gandhi's 1969 bank nationalization, a step hailed as a visionary masterstroke that saved India from the 2008 global financial crisis, by then Finance Minister Pranab Mukherjee,[52] and frequently by the Nehru–Gandhi dynasty.[53] The nationalization brought banking under political control, with even unviable projects and questionable businesses obtaining bank loans by getting the right people to call the bank managers or by greasing palms. Every few years, the government would bail out public sector banks.

The restructuring and recapitalization helped to transfer wealth from taxpayers to the pockets of a clique of business houses who were close to the Congress party and the Nehru–Gandhi family. Even the media was co-opted successfully, as it celebrated these paper tigers as respectable industrialists. The happy nexus of mutual accommodation between crony business groups, media and politics carried on for decades. The high noon of this corrupt circle was seen during the credit bubble inflated by the Sonia Gandhi–Manmohan Singh UPA government.

The denouement of the binge commenced around when Narendra Modi became Prime Minister. Responding to the rise of non-performing assets on the books of the banks, most of whom were in the public sector, the government and the RBI took several measures.

Among these measures has been the merger of public sector banks, reducing their number from twenty-seven to twelve, implemented from 2017 to 2020. This consolidation has created the opportunity for the ultimate privatization of some of these banks.

Bank bailouts have cumulatively consumed several trillion rupees since 1990 alone[54]—transferring ownership into private hands would reduce costs and make many of these institutions viable. This will depoliticize credit extension and help align incentives between owners and managers.

A signature reform of the Modi government in this context has been the insolvency and bankruptcy code (IBC). The IBC has brought accountability to business groups for the first time in India's history. With the creation of the IBC, there is a powerful instrument for banks to take company owners to task, and some of India's most powerful businessmen have lost control of their crown jewels.[55] The policy of bank consolidation and privatization along with the IBC will both do a world of good to fairness in credit extension and the long-term health of India's banking system.

But public opinion on privatization as a correct policy is mixed. The confusion about the appropriate role of the government is part of the reason why India has had so many scams as well as sub-par governance, both of which happen largely because the State chooses to enter domains where it should have no direct role to play, even as the State stays weak in areas where administrative capacity is needs to increase substantially.

India's digital transformation

As we have argued, India is transforming from a civilization to a nation through the agency of a State. The State is penetrating deeper into all sections of society, which have long been accustomed to disparate existence. Simultaneously, the State is also transforming from a blunt hammer to a more precise scalpel.

Until recently, the Indian State lacked what Yale University political scientist and anthropologist James C. Scott has called 'legibility'.[56] In his classic work *Seeing Like a State: How Certain Schemes to Improve the Human Condition Have Failed*, Scott writes: 'The premodern state was, in many crucial respects, partially blind; it knew precious little about its subjects, their wealth, their landholdings and yields, their location, their very identity.' This blindness or lack of legibility made State interventions 'crude and self-defeating'. Scott describes how the practice of taking universal last names was a recent historical phenomenon:[57]

> Tracking property ownership and inheritance, collecting taxes, maintaining court records, performing police work, conscripting soldiers, and controlling epidemics were all made immeasurably easier by the clarity of full names and, increasingly, fixed addresses. While the utilitarian state was committed to a complete inventory of its population, liberal ideas of citizenship, which implied voting rights and conscription, also contributed greatly to the standardization of naming practices.

The Indian government, too, has for decades faced the challenge of accurately identifying, recording, and categorizing who its citizens are. This is necessary for multiple facets of governance, especially for designing poverty alleviation programmes and delivering welfare efficiently. The problem is now comprehensively being addressed with the advent of digital technologies in the public sphere and the creation and provision of new kinds of digital public goods.[58]

As Infosys chairman and former chairman of Unique Identification Authority of India (UIDAI), Nandan Nilekani said at the start of the Aadhaar project rollout that Aadhaar 'isn't just a number, it is an identity'. Obtaining an Aadhaar number made individuals legible in the eyes of the State, and vice versa[59]—for the social contract to hold, legibility needs to be a two-way street. If the State doesn't know who its citizens are, it cannot serve and protect— or when necessary, litigate and prosecute—them. Simultaneously, if citizens don't see the State, they are in national communion with fellow citizens only in name.

Another manifestation of citizens not seeing the State is when qualified persons don't receive government welfare from a programme ostensibly created for them. In the throes of the COVID-19 pandemic, as the government prepared a relief programme for the poor, a significant challenge was that there was no comprehensive, up-to-date national database. The 2018–19 Economic Survey had identified this gap in the government's toolkit. 'While private sector does a good job of harnessing data where it is profitable, government intervention is needed in social sectors of the country where private investment in data remains inadequate,' it said.[60]

Governing a land as vast and diverse as India has always been a logistical challenge. As the statesman and founding Prime Minister of Singapore, Lee Kuan Yew, had observed about India: 'If you stand up in Delhi and speak in English . . . maybe 200 million will understand you. If you speak in Hindi maybe 250 million will understand you. If you speak in Tamil maybe 80 million will understand you.'[61]

India's language diversity is one of the reasons why Indian leaders, from Mahatma Gandhi to Narendra Modi, have used symbolism and grand gestures to mobilize masses.

It is no accident that the expansion of British rule in the mid-nineteenth century occurred in the aftermath of the Industrial Revolution—the British brought with them technologies such as railways transportation and telegraph communication that were necessary to establish the writ of a ruler and maintain control over the enormous geographical footprint of India.

The importance of telecommunications and digitalization, seen from the lens of legibility, is in how these technologies are recasting the citizen-State relationship with the creation of a unique digital commons composed of made-for-India public goods and utilities.

Nilekani was not exaggerating when he said that Aadhaar gave Indians 'an identity'. Over 1.25 billion Aadhaar IDs have been issued in the last decade, covering more than 90 per cent of India's population. Another piece of the Jan Dhan-Aadhaar-Mobile or 'JAM' trinity is the Pradhan Mantri Jan Dhan Yojana (PMJDY), Prime Minister Modi's financial inclusion programme that has equipped hundreds of millions with a bank account, connecting them to the formal financial system. In his first Independence Day speech after taking office as Prime Minister—a speech where he also laid out the criticality of driving digitalization not just for economic growth but also for efficient governance—Narendra Modi had said:[62]

> I have come here with a pledge to launch a scheme on this festival of Freedom. It will be called Pradhan Mantri Jan Dhan Yojana. I wish to connect the poorest citizens of the country with the facility of bank accounts through this yojana. There are millions of families who have mobile phones but no bank accounts. We have to change this scenario.

In an April 2018 report[63] assessing global financial inclusion, the World Bank noted that in India, 'a strong government push to increase account ownership through biometric identification cards helped narrow both the gender gap and the gap between richer and poorer adults' and 'the leakage of funds for pension payments dropped by 47 percent (2.8 percentage points) when the payments were made through biometric smart cards rather than being handed out in cash'.

Commending the impact of PMJDY, the report stated:

In India the share of adults with an account has more than doubled since 2011, to 80 percent. An important factor driving this increase was a government policy launched in 2014 to boost account ownership among unbanked adults through biometric identification cards. This policy benefited traditionally excluded groups and helped ensure inclusive growth in account ownership. Between 2014 and 2017 account ownership in India rose by more than 30 percentage points among women as well as among adults in the poorest 40 percent of households.

By April 2022, PMJDY had brought in an additional 450 million people into the formal banking system, according to the World Bank.[64] The final piece of the JAM trinity is mobile connectivity, which was achieved thanks to private sector competition stoked by the entry of Reliance Industries in the telecommunications sector. The Jio phenomenon grew India's active internet user base past 560 million by September 2018, within two years of entering the industry, and India is projected to have over 800 million users (about 60 per cent of the population) by 2021. Simultaneously, the price per gigabyte of data collapsed by over 95 per cent, making India the lowest priced as well as highest per capita data consumption market in the world. Data consumption rocketed between 2014–2017 at a scorching pace of 152 per cent annually.[65]

With the JAM infrastructure as the foundation, as of September 2022 the government has converted over 300 welfare schemes from across fifty-three executing Union ministries into direct benefits transfer (DBT) or direct cash transfer programmes, with qualified individuals receiving their dues totalling over Rs 25 trillion with minimal leakage and friction,[66] with Rs 2.2 trillion saved from wastage or leakage according to government estimates. In the long history of Indian civilization, never has the legibility between citizen and State been so high fidelity. The direct cash transfer capability built up by India proved to be an extraordinary strength during the global pandemic, with 56 per cent of this cumulative value being distributed during March 2020–September 2022. The DBT platform enabled hundreds of millions of people receiving payments directly in their bank accounts at a time of recurring lockdowns and disruptions.

The payments segment of the digital value chain has also seen a transformation. With a commitment to a 'less cash' economy, India developed RuPay, a payments network, and Unified Payments Interface (UPI), a real-time payment system. As made-for-India products created by the National Payments Corporation of India, RuPay and UPI have made online and digital payments a snap. Prime Minister Modi's move to demonetize high-denomination currency notes in November 2016 provided a measurable boost to digital payments and UPI, with digital payment volumes leapfrogging by 2.5 years.[67]

From a standing start in April 2016, UPI has grown at an explosive pace that has surprised industry analysts.[68] Analysts at the investment bank Morgan Stanley termed it a 'juggernaut', writing in September 2019 that 'almost every Indian business or activity which involves payments now either has a UPI strategy or is working aggressively on it. This ranges, among others, from P2P payments to bill payments to investing (even in IPOs) to loan servicing.'[69] UPI transaction volumes stood at 900 million (annualized value at Rs 19 trillion) September 2019 and climbed nearly 50 per cent to 1.32 billion (annualized Rs 26.4 trillion in value) by February 2020.[70] In May 2022, UPI processed nearly 6 billion transactions (annualized Rs 120 trillion in value). After clocking a compounded transaction volume growth rate of 104 per cent per year between March 2019–2022, RBI projects that till 2025, UPI volumes will keep growing at around 50 per cent annually.[71]

RuPay, India's home-grown payment network, has also shown exponential growth, with value transacted growing over 100x in four years since its inception, up till April 2019.[72] For the financial year 2021–22, RuPay aggregate transaction value had crossed Rs 2.5 trillion, up 40 per cent from 2019–20.[73] By creating an indigenous payment network, India has also avoided paying a fee of about 2 per cent on value transacted to global card issuers on a recurring basis, saving many billions of rupees every year. The success of RuPay has caused much heartburn among foreign payment networks. In June 2018, Mastercard complained to the US government that 'Prime Minister

Narendra Modi was using nationalism to promote the use of domestic payments network RuPay.'[74] RuPay and UPI are now entering foreign markets, starting with Bhutan, Singapore[75] and UAE, with countries like Oman,[76] France,[77] Brazil, Nepal and Japan also in the process of partnering with India.

With RuPay and UPI, India's payments infrastructure is significantly better than that found in many of the advanced economies.[78] Since the implementation of the GST, there is a now a digital trail of cash flows that lenders can access. This eases credit access and enables more precise credit analytics, reducing the cost of capital for deserving businesses that consistently generate cash while being asset light. India has created a set of application programming interfaces (APIs) that across four layers—presence-less, paperless, cashless and consent. Taken together, this collection of APIs known as India Stack, is a horizontal toolkit that unshackles information sharing. UPI works by harnessing India Stack for payments.

Another instantiation of India Stack is the Aadhaar-based electronic-Know Your Customer (eKYC) for identity verification. The eKYC approach has dramatically reduced time and friction associated with activities such as opening bank accounts and brokerage accounts, strengthening the formalization and financialization process. As writer Hindol Sengupta noted,[79] eKYC 'brought down the cost of authenticating say a mutual fund beneficiary identity by 99% (from ₹1,500 to ₹10)'. When Western powers took the unprecedented action of requiring Visa and Mastercard to suspend their Russian operations, effectively cutting off Russia from global payments networks in the aftermath of the February 2022 invasion of Ukraine, the wisdom of India's strategy of building national capabilities in payments and retaining control of critical financial infrastructure was further borne out.

As impressive as these achievements are, these are the basic building blocks, and on this foundation of India Stack, JAM and digital payments, a new class of financial firms and lending institutions is poised to come up. In July 2019, India launched the Sahamati account aggregator framework,[80] an infrastructure layer for enabling consent-driven sharing of private data. The account aggregator system went live in September 2020, and is onboarding all major Indian financial institutions and banks. Similarly, the Open Credit Enablement Network (OCEN) through its reference app Sahay is an online lending marketplace, bringing together private data via consent-driven account aggregation, GST data and UPI to enable faster cash-flow based credit deployment for small enterprises[81]. In April 2022, India launched the Open Network for Digital Commerce (ONDC) to promote 'open networks for all aspects of exchange of goods and services over digital or electronic networks'[82]. ONDC is modelled on the hypertext transfer protocol, the foundational protocol for data exchange undergirding the internet, and is designed to curb the rise of marketplace monopolies that derive from network effects in online commerce.

India's suite of digital public goods and utilities is world-class,[83] unique, and opportune, given that 5G networks and the fourth industrial revolution are knocking at the door. The United Nations Development Programme (UNDP) acknowledged India's work in the development of digital public goods, observing:[84]

> India has emerged as a global leader in building population-scale digital public goods. India Stack for example is an ambitious project to build a unique digital infrastructure to help solve population-scale problems through creating a set of open APIs. The project has made presence-less (Aadhaar), paperless (eKYC, eSign, Digilocker), and cashless (UPI) services available for healthcare and urban governance.
>
> India's leadership in digital public goods offers unique lessons and digital public solutions that can be adapted by countries worldwide. This is especially relevant for lower middle-income countries, which face similar challenges as India, including barriers to access, connectivity, and digital literacy. UNDP is working with the Government (of India) to help drive the South-South cooperation agenda and leverage these programmes.

In 2022, India joined several leading economies and launched ultra-high-speed and low-latency 5G services. When 3G and 4G networks finally came to India, entrepreneurs were handicapped because data access was expensive and, consequently, the domestic market for digital services was too small. But subsequent consolidation in the market and private- sector competition made India the lowest-cost data provider in the world. The dramatic increase of the 4G user base has expanded the market and opened new opportunities for entrepreneurship. This is where deploying 5G networks at scale and without delay matters enormously.[85]

One of the most interesting aspects of the fourth industrial revolution will be its impact on global trade. Globalization enabled Asian countries to export their way to a higher standard of living. Manufacturing to export was the mantra adopted across Southeast and East Asia—India was an oddity that focused on services instead and built a $135 billion[86] export industry in IT services. Notably, both the goods and services export models hinge on labour cost arbitrage.

With 3D printing and industrial automation, production is shifting closer to the final place of consumption. Technological advances are, once again, turning manufacturing from a labour game into a capital game. As these advances gather momentum, what are today deemed tradable goods will not necessarily be traded in the future. Conversely, what we characterize as non-tradable services will be traded despite physical distances. A yoga instructor in Bihar may be able to offer classes globally, or a receptionist in Mumbai will be able work in a Manhattan office, as the confluence of robotics, holography, augmented reality and digital payments forges a new global-services arbitrage model.

Immigration control that imposes barriers on movement of human capital will be rendered largely irrelevant by the fourth industrial revolution's virtualization wave. Given India's traditional strength in services and its young population at a time when the rest of the world is ageing, this can be a huge growth opportunity. In its impact on global economic transformation, this shift will match the influence that the shipping container had on the physical trade of goods. With this sea change on the horizon, India did well to implement new rules for the business process outsourcing and IT-enabled services industries, the so-called 'other service providers' who provide telemarketing and telebanking services, in November 2020.[87] The import of the new rules was what liberated small enterprises in these sectors from several compliance burdens and permitted remote work.

As we stand on the cusp of the fourth industrial revolution, the government needs to take a bespoke view of laws and policy in areas such as antitrust, data localization and privacy. The explosion and application of data in both the private and public spheres requires safeguards for data security and privacy,[88] as debates across the world on these topics are already showing—but these technologies should not be shunned in the name of civil liberties. Leadership in the fourth industrial revolution will have foreign policy implications too. India's rise will bring balance and stability to the world as authoritarian China casts a long shadow on the international order.

Misfits, rebels, troublemakers

Film-making is both creative and entrepreneurial.[89] The role of a producer is analogous to that of a venture capital (VC) investor. Successful movie producers, like smart VC investors, know that large amounts of capital, star billing or marketing alone cannot guarantee success. Just like entrepreneurs execute on a business plan, actors and directors work to bring the script to life. More than anything else, making a good film and building a business from scratch both requires creativity and street smarts.

India, home to the world's largest film industry by output, has a storied and rich heritage in the cinematic arts. Given the country's linguistic diversity, every region has its own significant-sized entertainment and media industry. What has been common across regions over the decades has been the portrayal of Indian society and business, with tropes about the typically corrosive effect of commerce and money on society. The usurious moneylender, the corrupt businessmen (and they are all men), the powerful smuggler, the righteous union leader, the inept police, the likeable thief or dacoit, the stereotyped minority, the pathos-inducing mother, the helpless damsel-in-distress—these have all been recurring characters in popular Indian cinema.

This reflected the dismal state of India's economy and society. India's GDP per capita (2010 US dollars) crawled at the Nehruvian rate of growth, from $330 (1960) to $581 (1990)—a compounded growth rate of just 1.9 per cent per year for three decades.[90] Commenting on the economic state of the country, the eminent industrialist Shantanurao Kirloskar wrote in 1982:[91]

> All the Governments—the pre-split Congress, the first Indira Government, the Emergency Government, the Janata Government and today's second Indira Government—have shut their eyes to the damage which the controls are doing. All they see is the advantage of these controls to the politicians. Hence, in spite of any desire they may feel to eliminate restrictions on the economy and to make progress on the economic front, they neither wish nor dare to reduce any of those controls or restrictions which effectively inhibit business.

This despondency was shared by other business leaders of the time. In a 1986 interview, Tata group chairman J.R.D. Tata was asked whether he had achieved what he had set out to achieve in industry. The 82-year-old Tata, who was awarded the Bharat Ratna in 1992, replied that 'I must confess that I've been very frustrated. When I was young, I was an angry young man: we were under foreign rule, people were oppressed. Now I'm an angry old man because of all the opportunities that have been missed.'[92]

G.D. Birla, an icon of the freedom movement and titan of modern Indian industry, had anticipated the disastrous direction being taken by India early on after Independence. He wrote in an article for *Hindustan Times* on 26 January 1950:[93]

> Under the regime of a thousand 'don'ts,' the man who is interested in producing more, feels a bit bewildered at all this talk of hard work when he finds himself bound hand and foot and yet asked to run. The truth is that there is no task before the public into which it

can throw itself with zeal and fervour. The achievement of Indian industry thus is not small. It built itself up against heavy odds when there was no encouragement. It could achieve much more in a free atmosphere. It is a paradox that it should have stagnated only after we got Independence. The explanation is simple. The doors of creation, organisation, efficiency and incentive have been bolted and barred under the directives of 'don'ts'. The government only tells us what not to do. As long as this regimentation continues, we have a straitjacket imposed on us which allows no freedom of movement. That precludes teamwork; creates inefficiency, black markets, scarcity and corruption; and brings down the standard of the people, morally as well as economically. The so-called controls take away the creative genius of the people; make them servile and dependent on government; create unemployment, misery and poverty and consequently deep dissatisfaction and discontent.

Economic stagnation led to hopelessness about India's viability as a nation-state. Those depicted as successful in popular movie narratives were often government bureaucrats, professionals such as lawyers or doctors, or non-resident Indians. The other pronounced marker of success shown on the silver screen was dynastic power—in India's stratified society only those who had already been wealthy for generations were expected to be wealthy, and there was hardly any scope for new wealth creation. What's notable is that only a minuscule segment of the population could fit into these roles and professions, with the vast majority shut out of any possibility of prosperity. This never really bothered India's elites and the perfumed classes. As writer, poet and lyricist Javed Akhtar observed:

I believe that at any point in history, we can see that art, literature, and music and the contemporary socio-political movements are not in watertight compartments. They reflect one another. There was a sort of moral decline in the 1980s. Our sense of values had nose-dived. There is no doubt that in those years, the worst kind of film was being made in India, and by and large, the worst kind of film music was appreciated. Compare this to the era of 1950s, a time when the best film songs were written. A time when culture, decency and idealism prevailed, those were the days of Jawaharlal Nehru.[94]

As a prolific screenwriter, Akhtar popularized the persona of the 'angry young man', reflecting a dynamic among India's youth of the 1960s and 1970s that later contributed to separatist movements in different regions as well as a full-blown Maoist insurgency, characterized in 2006 as 'the single biggest internal-security challenge ever faced by our country' by Prime Minister Manmohan Singh.[95]

What Akhtar does not seem to have grasped was the reason for the anger. The basis of the rage was systematic economic suppression, with its roots in the supposedly golden era of Nehru's premiership. Whatever integrity and idealism that may have prevailed under Nehru and his political–intellectual successors, were not enough to fill the stomachs of the impoverished.

It was economic liberalization that changed the landscape—from the dynastic family business inheritor, today's films frequently portray new economy entrepreneurs as the standard bearers of industry. Between 1990–2015, India's GDP per capita (2010 US dollars) grew from $581 to $1751, more than doubling the Nehruvian-era growth rate to 4.5 per cent. Several films came up that challenged the conventional wisdom propagated in India till then that it was best to strive to become bureaucrats, doctors, lawyers or worse, smugglers. The question of why the older generation would want their children to join what are essentially professional guilds has not been explained or understood widely enough.

In Nehruvian India, which had strangulating government control over economic activity, these vocations were the only ones which came with credible guarantees of a reasonable standard of living. Since economic liberalization and the boost to economic freedom, career opportunities have expanded dramatically. As the satellite television industry opened up and private radio channels were established, Indians could be productively employed as TV actors and radio jockeys, for example. Rising incomes led to an explosion of consumer products, and the consumer economy created scope for successful sportspersons to promote those brands and earn incomes that were unheard of just a generation earlier. Today, the top sportspersons and athletes enjoy a cult status with commensurate financial rewards, much like top-tier movie stars and business leaders.

There are other markers of how economic growth has changed social attitudes, creating new kinds of jobs in the process. The emergence of a technology sector and accompanying internet economy is creating vocations and jobs that baffle the older generation. The story of Israil Ansari, a 20-year-old from an Uttar Pradesh village with over two million followers on a social media platform, illustrates this phenomenon.[96] Ansari became a celebrity not just in his village and region, but even in major Indian cities. With a steady flow of endorsement offers and brand sponsorships, Ansari has earned more money than anybody in his family ever did. The consumer economy that is enabling individuals like Ansari to make an honest living will continue to expand faster than India's overall growth.

A controlled, constricted economy forces individuals to enter a very specific, limited pool of professions. It also forces individuals to cultivate political connections, besides straitjacketing society into sacrosanct hierarchies—this is the experience India had until the dawn of economic liberalization in 1991, before which even the wealthy lived in mortal fear of leading politicians.

In contrast, a freer economy accepts individuals as they are and allows them to grow into what they want to become—whether it is an entrepreneur, musician, actor, radio jockey, chef, business executive, danseuse, doctor, fitness instructor, fashion designer, singer or stand-up comedian. It is no coincidence that there has been an explosion of different types of professions in India only since liberalization took off. If somebody in the 1980s was told that India's youth could one day aspire to become dieticians, makeup artists, or interior decorators, they would simply not believe it because these professions did not exist as legitimate, remunerative career options.

The great American artist Andy Warhol had once thus observed the beauty of American-style capitalism:

What's great about this country is that America started the tradition where the richest consumers buy essentially the same things as the poorest. You can be watching TV and see Coca-Cola, and you know that the President drinks Coke, Liz Taylor drinks Coke, and just think, you can drink Coke, too. A Coke is a Coke and no amount of money can get you a better Coke than the one the bum on the corner is drinking.[97]

But popular attitudes have taken time to catch up with the growth of opportunities and a large number of Indians continue to believe that the field of one's education should dictate the career path.

Creating an environment that allows people to pursue excellence in a field of their choosing is what makes for a prosperous and happy society. Moreover, without liberalization it is not possible for different and new industries to evolve and create space for novel ideas and fresh talent.

Just as new kinds of jobs and vocations were dismissed, the technology entrepreneurship revolution India has seen in the last two decades went through a similar cycle of rejection and denial. Two events mark the broader acceptance of entrepreneurship as a 'respectable' path in the eyes of the older generation.

The first was the emergence of Ratan Tata as a VC investor after he retired as chairman of Tata Group in 2013. Tata, the most recognized and respected Indian businessman in the last three decades, started making investments in technology ventures from his personal funds. Almost overnight, what was seen as a speculative, even reckless, activity acquired a halo of respectability. After all, if India's most prominent business leader was choosing to participate in the field, it must be something really good. Parents and grandparents across India softened up to the idea of supporting their children if they wanted to start a business, as they too gained confidence from seeing Ratan Tata endorsing entrepreneurship and staking his personal reputation and capital on new ventures.

The second was the sale of Flipkart to Walmart in 2018 for over a trillion rupees, which remains the biggest acquisition in India's new technology industry and turned many early employees and backers into multi-millionaires. The two events changed the perception of technology entrepreneurship by enhancing the social acceptability of starting a new venture. Successful initial public offerings of multiple technology enterprises in 2021, and the emergence of over a 100 private ventures valued north of one billion dollars have now completely mainstreamed entrepreneurship in India.

There was a time when India celebrated *jugaad*, the curiously Indian way of getting things done. In 2001, Fevicol ran an advertising campaign showing a truck overloaded with people making its way across a rough and barren landscape.[98] Even though the terrain is rocky and the truck overflowing with people, none of the passengers fall off, bonded together, viewers are to think, with the same strength and reliability as India's leading adhesive brand. This award-winning advertisement captures the ethos of jugaad very well.

Some VCs and management gurus praised this approach of doing more with less, but jugaad was more an outcome of limited access to capital, resources and infrastructure, than innovation. It is the textbook example of how innovating for the bottom of the pyramid can degenerate into a paternalistic condescension of creating low-quality products that have poor usability. Many innovations which claim to be for the bottom of the pyramid assume that their users will remain stuck at the bottom, for if they managed to increase their income levels, they'd choose better solutions.

As Warhol had observed, the great thing about American capitalism was that 'the richest consumers buy essentially the same things as the poorest.' This is precisely what we are witnessing in India's new technology and consumer boom. The telecom revolution ignited by Atal Bihari Vajpayee's government turned the telephone and long-distance calling—once considered status symbols—into commonplace consumer utilities, accessible to all Indians. Industrialists and their bankers, or house cleaners and their employers, could all become customers of the same telecom service provider.

When domestic workers of an urban upper-class family shop on Flipkart and Amazon or watch movies at a multiplex just like their wealthy bosses, it erodes the class divide. This is the new India, built by private entrepreneurs in a liberalizing environment, that is enabling next- generation Indians to pursue careers of their choice, while helping erase social divisions.

Market feminism and Dalit entrepreneurship

As Karl Marx and Friedrich Engels wrote in the foundational text of communism, *The Communist Manifesto*:[99]

> The bourgeoisie, wherever it has got the upper hand, has put an end to all feudal, patriarchal, idyllic relations. It has pitilessly torn asunder the motley feudal ties that bound man to his 'natural superiors', and has left no other bond between man and man than naked self-interest, than callous 'cash payment'.

Nobel laureate economist and renowned University of Chicago academic Gary Becker's insight on how competitive markets undercut social discrimination offers an effective policy solution to eradicate discrimination in India.[100] Unfortunately, casteism still rears its ugly head in India even today. In many schools, it has been reported that young children face discrimination due to their caste. In some cities, members of the Muslim community in particular face difficulties in renting or buying apartments. A prominent Chennai-based English-language newspaper was known for banning the consumption of non-vegetarian food in its canteen. Colleges in Kanpur,[101] Bhiwani and Bhopal banned women from wearing jeans.

All these are examples of discrimination, a subject typically studied by sociologists, anthropologists and psychologists. Becker was the first to apply economic reasoning to study discrimination. Becker's pathbreaking research on racial discrimination in the US was published in 1957 in a book titled *The Economics of Discrimination*.[102] His work was largely ignored at the time. Few economic journals reviewed his findings. Racial discrimination was a subject of fierce public debate in post-war America. Over time, Becker's original work stood vindicated, and he won the Nobel Prize for economics in 1992.

The parallels with India are striking. Nearly seventy-five years after Independence, discrimination based on group identity continues to be an ugly reality of our society. What lessons can India draw from Becker's work to eradicate such discrimination? The key insight one derives is that in competitive markets, discrimination hurts those who practise it as much as those who are discriminated against. As Becker and his fellow University of Chicago economist Richard Posner wrote in a 2008:

> An employer discriminates against untouchables, women, or other minority members when he refuses to hire them even though they are cheaper relative to their productivity than the persons he does hire. Discrimination in this way raises his costs and lowers his profits. This puts him at a competitive disadvantage relative to employers who maximize their profits, and hire only on the basis of productivity per dollar of cost. Strongly discriminating employers, therefore, tend to lose out to other employers in competitive industries that have easy entry of new firms.[103]

There is empirical evidence to support this position. In a 2008 paper titled 'Labour Market Discrimination in Delhi: Evidence from a Field Experiment' published by Nobel laureate economist Abhijit Banerjee and others, it was reported that there was 'no evidence of discrimination against non-upper caste (Scheduled Castes, Scheduled Tribes and Other Backward Classes) applicants for jobs in the software industry, one of the most competitive sectors in India. There was also no evidence of discrimination against Muslims.[104] That is because the software industry is intensely competitive, and discrimination hurts profits.

The same logic that applies to labour markets also applies to land and capital markets. A buyer or seller who discriminates against another individual or entity based on their identity stands to lose in industries that are competitive. It follows that to reduce discrimination, it is imperative that India should promote market competition. Two contrasting examples illustrate how competitive markets promote individual freedom and choice.

Kasturi and Sons Ltd., owner of *The Hindu* newspaper, was in the news in 2014 for the wrong reasons, after it implemented a corporate policy to bar the consumption of non-vegetarian food in its canteen.[105] As a private organization, the company was entitled to set policies that do not otherwise violate any laws in India. There was, however, much outrage on social media, both at the discriminatory attitude of the company and its hypocrisy in promoting 'liberal' values for others while itself staying true to ostensibly socially conservative choices.

In contrast, the chairman of Aditya Birla Group, Kumar Mangalam Birla, wrote an essay titled 'Butter Chicken at Birla'[106] for the book *Reimagining India: Unlocking the Potential of Asia's Next Superpower*, describing how his conglomerate had to change as it globalized. Birla wrote about how after completing the acquisition of a copper mine in Australia, the employees there expressed concern on whether 'they have to give up their Foster's and barbecues at company events'. They were assured that no such thing would happen, but then that led to pushback by employees in India, who asked why 'they should have to go meatless at parties, if employees abroad did not'.

Expectedly, the Aditya Birla Group had to liberalize rules and amend company policy that had been against non-vegetarian food. The difference between Kasturi and Sons and the Aditya Birla Group was that while the former was in a protected, quasi-monopolistic industry where the entry of regional competitors was difficult, the latter was more subject to the forces of competitive capitalism. The promoters of Kasturi and Sons knew that their employees did not have a realistic alternative. It was the only option for journalists who wanted to work at a major English-language newspaper headquartered in Chennai, while the Aditya Birla Group was competing with other large global corporations in the metals industry.

Becker posited that in competitive markets, discrimination hurts both those who discriminate and those at the receiving end of discrimination, but the former are affected more. In the case of

Kasturi and Sons, discrimination hurt primarily the employees. In the case of Aditya Birla Group, it can hurt both the company and its employees; market competition will transfer the cost of discrimination from the individual to the global corporation, which has to adapt to stay competitive, or pay the price for being a discriminator by losing competitiveness.

Frequently, when there is discrimination in India, there is the predictable clamour for a new law to protect the specific group being discriminated. Unfortunately, a barrage of such laws has often failed to check discrimination. For too long, socialist economics and anti-discrimination legislation have made happy bedfellows. The former creates the basis for discrimination which the latter is supposed to check. If more industries in India become as competitive as the software industry, this social problem can be ameliorated. The debate in India needs to turn towards how competitive market forces can be deployed in more sectors of the economy.

Take another example from the food and restaurant industry. Writer Chandra Bhan Prasad had observed that 'home delivery of pizza and other foodstuff is caste-neutral'.[107] It is difficult for those not from a so-called low caste to appreciate the experience of Dalits (who have been told that nobody will accept food from their hands) when they serve food at restaurants or deliver food to homes, without anybody even asking their caste. This is enabled by competition in the restaurant industry. Prasad argued, 'Capitalism, like caste, is a social order and therefore uniquely qualified to subvert and destroy the caste system from the inside, as opposed to the State, which is a political order and intervenes in the caste society from the outside.'[108]

Members of religious groups that find it hard to rent apartments in Mumbai and Ahmedabad would not feel like outcastes if the real estate markets become as competitive as the software industry's labour market. A number of bottlenecks need to be removed by the state governments, since land is a state subject, to achieve this. But in the case of housing, it should be remembered that Indian jurisprudence allows for discrimination. In the 2005 Zoroastrian Cooperative Housing case,[109] courts had ruled that the private cooperative housing society was allowed, under the Constitution's freedom of association provision, to discriminate based on religion. Even then, should India contemplate having an anti-discrimination legislation for housing, it should be ensured that such a law applies uniformly to all citizens, and no exemptions are carved out for any community.

A student empowered with education vouchers can leave the institution where he or she is discriminated against because of their caste. Girls attending colleges with strict dress codes can choose to go to those that offer a more liberal environment if the market grows and the higher education sector is opened to supply-side competition (by allowing foreign and for-profit players) and demand-side competition (by letting subsidies follow the student, not the institution). Becker's economic insight has transformational implications for India's diverse society. All politicians who speak for social harmony would do well to adopt policies that promote choice and competition, because such liberal economic policies are beneficial for both growth as well as social equality.

Atmanirbhar capitalism

In his seminal treatise *Capitalism and Freedom*, first published in 1962, Nobel laureate economist Milton Friedman wrote that economic freedom was a necessary condition but not a sufficient one for political freedom. Friedman defined political freedom as 'the absence of coercion of a man by his fellow men'.[110]

By this benchmark, Indians are not politically free. Those wielding power and influence, from top politicians to corrupt local bureaucrats, can coerce entrepreneurs and fellow citizens with impunity. It is commonplace for politicians to dole out freebies at election time that include everything from loan waivers to colour televisions and laptops. That many citizens barter their vote for short-term material benefits often reflects their unfortunate economic weakness. [111]

The use of money and muscle power during election time is well documented—the media, which is also heavily dependent on government advertisements, has been known to be paid off by political parties to manipulate the public discourse. Cutting across party lines, local *bahubalis* or strongmen are routinely given tickets to contest elections because of the clout they have at the constituency level. This results in law-making bodies in states and in New Delhi that are packed with several individuals who have criminal backgrounds. The vicious cycle is complete—once law-making institutions are controlled by such elements, they push back against proposed laws that could potentially dislodge them.

Indians will be more politically free when they are able to say no to such freebies and are able to stand up to such muscle power. This would require a two-pronged approach: economically empowering individuals so that they don't depend on government dole and making law enforcement and justice delivery substantially more effective.

The question then is: which political interest groups stand to gain from an India that is politically free and which interests will be certain to lose? The Congress and the BJP are India's two major political parties with a national footprint—but the political interest group that stands to lose the most short-to-medium term is the Congress party in its current form, and the group that will gain the most is the BJP. There are several reasons for this.

The Congress party's economic world view is rooted in Nehruvian socialism, and ever since Indira Gandhi cemented her control on the party in 1966 after the demise of Lal Bahadur Shastri, its instincts have been decisively towards control of economic activity. After the Congress party split in 1969, with Indira Gandhi separating from more centrist leaders like the then Finance Minister Morarji Desai (who resisted bank nationalization), the Indira Gandhi faction allied with the communist parties.[112] It was around this period that the communists entrenched their ideological cronies into academia[113]— the committed leftist Saiyid Nurul Hasan became the education minister in 1972, running the ministry till the end of the Emergency. His tenure saw the creation of several new 'social science' research institutions backed by public funding,[114] staffed by similarly minded communists and leftists who were motivated to whitewash India's history and culture, and even had a disregard for scientific method and research process. When Hasan was appointed vice-president of CSIR in 1980, there was fear and resentment in the scientific community that the intellectual corruption injected into social sciences would also find its way into the physical sciences and engineering institutions run by the CSIR system.[115]

Partially driven by the motive to contain the rise of C. Rajagopalachari's Swatantra Party, which was largely funded by India's erstwhile royals and wealthy industrialists, Gandhi abolished privy purses to the royals and proceeded to nationalize industries on an unprecedented scale. On the abrogation of the privy purses, eminent jurist Nani Palkhivala had said:[116]

> It is the highest guarantee, the highest assurance, the greatest security known to our law. What has come of that security and assurance? . . . I'm not talking of those individuals [the royals] . . . those individuals are not worth saving, but the honour of India is worth saving . . . If the greatest guarantee known to law, enshrined in the Constitution is of no avail, what do you make of verbal assurances given by individuals? . . . To me, as to Rajaji, it is only a matter of principle. Is it worthwhile dragging in the mire the name of your country?

Palkhivala, despite his distaste and indifference towards the former royals, was against the abrogation of the privy purse on the principle that India should not go back on its word. By going back on a commitment as fundamental as the privy-purse guarantee, Indira Gandhi signalled that any commitment can be broken on political grounds and that everything was up for grabs. Nothing was sacred anymore.

By legitimizing the Nehru–Gandhi dynasty's grip on the Congress, Indira Gandhi's ascent also transformed the Congress from a political institution to a party that was irredeemably beholden to one family. Regrettably, Indira Gandhi's Congress defined a Stalinist template for organizing political parties that has been copied by several regional parties since then.

This has imposed a great cost to India's democracy and economy, for dynastic politics requires centralizing decision-making and controlling citizens, rather than empowering them. The Congress, once a pioneering national institution that counted among its ranks some of India's finest leaders and thinkers, has today been reduced to a rump—it is 'a crowd around a family', to use the late statesman–politician Arun Jaitley's sharp and blunt description, that the exists only to preserve the Nehru–Gandhi dynasty at all costs.

Liberalization and economic development are not the natural instincts of any dynastic party because their effects undercut the legitimacy of the dynasty. This is true for all such parties, whether it is the Samajwadi Party, Shiv Sena, Shiromani Akali Dal, Telangana Rashtra Samithi (now Bharatiya Rashtra Samithi) or the Trinamool Congress. Such parties may never want that the populace to become truly independent and prosperous—that would be inimical to their political interest and long-term sustenance.

BJP's predecessor, the Bharatiya Jan Sangh, was opposed to the Congress since its founding in 1951. Jan Sangh's founder Syama Prasad Mookerjee vigorously opposed the First Amendment to India's Constitution implemented by Jawaharlal Nehru that curtailed free speech and eliminated the right to property as a fundamental right.

The governments led by the BJP from 1998 to 2004 under Atal Bihari Vajpayee and 2014 onwards under Narendra Modi, have arguably been the most reformist in India's history if one only looks at reforms implemented without a crisis facing the country, as was the case with the bold reforms that P.V. Narasimha Rao unleashed.

During Vajpayee's government, Congress chief Sonia Gandhi had mocked the then Union Finance Minister Jaswant Singh's projection of 8 per cent GDP growth as daydreaming or 'Mungerilal ke haseen sapnay'.[117] Under the BJP-led NDA government, public sector companies were privatized, taxation rationalized, foreign exchange rules relaxed and capital markets and insurance reforms executed. Plans to privatize Air India and the oil marketing companies fell through—had they succeeded, the national exchequer would have saved several trillion rupees in the subsequent years. Twenty-two hotels were privatized by the Vajpayee government, though fifteen are still run by the Government of India.

But too often free markets and a competent State are seen as opposites, whereas the fact is that the two cannot survive without each other. Speaking at a conference on 2 March 2019, Prime Minister Narendra Modi said, 'In the last five years, we have persevered to strengthen the foundations of India, and it is on these foundations that the New India will be built.' Cynics may dismiss the comment but Narendra Modi has made concerted efforts to augment the Indian State's capabilities in principal areas such as welfare delivery, digital governance, national defence and internal security.

This has been accompanied by a range of internal liberalization measures to enable the economy's formalization along with permitting or increasing foreign direct investment (FDI) across industries. Better than anybody else perhaps, Modi has understood that India needs to have Thomas Hobbes before John Locke and John Stuart Mill—in others words, order precedes liberty and freedom. Without order, there can only be anarchy.

But when the economy was weighed down by the licence-permit-quota raj and society was ravaged by an extractive State during the pre-liberalization era, indulging in corruption and hiding income became a normal practice. The all-powerful State acquired a deservedly terrible reputation and a belief took root in the people's psyche that the Indian State, even if it was democratic, was incorrigibly predatory. There was little public discussion on restructuring the State and changing its focus to the provision of necessary public goods. This extracted a very high cost by undermining Indian society's trust in the government. Only now, however gradually, is this changing. Historically, the State grew to make war and facilitate trade. It is worth diving into the second aspect for post-Independence India.

India has been an agriculture-centric economy since Independence, even as the contribution of agriculture to GDP has slipped from 41.7 per cent in 1960, to 27.7 per cent in 1991 and even lower to 16.8 per cent in 2021.[118] This is because about two-fifths of India's population continues to directly or indirectly depend on agriculture.

India's experience has been unique in the world as an economy that shifted from agriculture to services, without growing in manufacturing.

In 1960, manufacturing contributed 15 per cent to GDP, and in 2021, the number has stagnated at 14 per cent.[119] The contribution of manufacturing to GDP has never crossed 18 per cent or about one-fifth in India's recent history.[120] The services sector, in sharp contrast, has grown from strength to strength.

Economic figures in India also obscure what are essentially subsistence jobs or 'forced entrepreneurship' for many, rolling them up into agricultural or services data. There are millions of individuals in India who take up farming, for example, for want of formal employment opportunities. The challenge before India is how to create jobs, especially in the long underperforming manufacturing sector.

The solution lies in a policy response combining both internal liberalization and time-bound and moderate external protection, an idea that would be considered deeply heterodox by present-day conventional economic thinking.

The case for internal liberalization—a bucket encompassing factor market reforms in land, labour and capital, besides improving the ease of doing business, contract enforcement, opening up more sectors to foreign direct investment and generally bringing rules-based capitalism to India—is well established and accepted by all reform-oriented economists and analysts. In a nutshell, labour laws need to be made more flexible while ensuring protections for occupational health and safety. Land acquisition needs to be streamlined and made faster, and capital markets require reforms so that access to equity funding as well as credit is eased. While the rise of private equity investment has made it easier for first-generation entrepreneurs to grow businesses, India needs far wider and deeper debt capital markets to meet the needs of the manufacturing sector, which is a lot more capital intensive than the services sector.

The second piece of our policy suggestion—the one on having external protections in the form of limited tariffs, is admittedly controversial. This is so because it triggers a confirmation bias among the generation of pro-liberalization economists who fought hard for India to open up and integrate with the world economy. The Columbia economist Arvind Panagariya—an authority on free trade and widely

regarded as the foremost expert in the world on India's economy—
critiqued the Modi government for 'erecting the wall of protection all
over again'.[121] As Panagariya has correctly pointed out, the danger with
such protections is that instead of being limited and temporary, they
become more extensive and permanent.

We would still draw a leaf from the history of America's
economic development to make the case for internal liberalization
along with limited external protections. In 1790, President George
Washington, the first President of the newly created republic of the
United States of America, said that the interest of the American
nation required that 'They should promote such manufactures as
tend to render them independent of others for essential, particularly
military, supplies.'[122] Washington's colleague Alexander Hamilton,
one of the founding fathers of the United States and its first treasury
secretary, presented the Report on Manufactures to the US Congress
in 1791,[123] which laid out 'a broad-ranging and powerful case for
the government promotion of manufacturing' (through moderate
protectionism).[124]

Rebutting Adam Smith's position that the invisible hand would
enable industry to 'naturally find its way to the most useful and
profitable employment', Hamilton said that 'the incitement and
patronage of government' was required to kickstart industrial activity
in new areas to get over 'the strong influence of habit and the spirit of
imitation' that gets ingrained in entrepreneurs, where success attracts
new players to an industry but fear of failure prevents industrialists
from trying something new. In other words, Hamilton laid down the
classical 'infant industry' argument. More crucially, especially in the
present global context, Hamilton pointed to 'the bounties, premiums
and other artificial encouragements', with which foreign nations second
the exertions of their own citizens' as a reason to pursue what can today
be called a defensive, mercantilist trade policy.

The rise of China in the last three decades has transformed global
trade and the world economy, as genuine and 'artificial' encouragements
drew manufacturing away from advanced economies to China, turning
it into the factory of the world. There was no historical precedent when

a country with the size and weight of China entered the trade scene and started integrating with the world economy.

To draw an analogy from physics, Albert Einstein's theory of general relativity posited that space and time are bent by matter, and the greater the mass of that matter, the more severe the distortion of space–time. Similarly, large economies in the world can wield disproportionate power in trade, both as buyers as well as producers. The former endows partial monopsony power, while the latter provides oligopolistic influence. Furthering the analogy, Newtonian mechanics works within a certain scale range, but breaks down at the extremes.

In other words, what works for a Singapore or a Romania may not necessarily be the correct policy for a China or an India, given the difference in sizes. In several studies advocating unilateral free trade, the econometric methodology nonetheless treats all these countries as equal data points.

Viewed through the lens of the prisoner's dilemma framework, global trade is a multi-step game of negotiations where small countries with very limited negotiating power are better off embracing free trade by default, but larger economies with the capacity to shape the fabric of global trade can bargain for more, especially when other large countries go down the route of political authoritarianism and economic mercantilism.

It is critical to appreciate that the range of policies in favour of internal liberalization and further opening of sectors to foreign direct investment as pursued by the Modi government is not at cross purposes with the external-sector policy of moderate tariffs. In this way, India is positioning itself better to build its manufacturing base and generate jobs. A glimpse of this break from liberal economic orthodoxy can be seen in the early successes made by India's fast-growing mobile phone manufacturing industry.

In 2014, India had two mobile phone manufacturing facilities, and by 2018 the number had increased to 268.[125] In value terms, mobile phone output increase from Rs 189 billion in 2014–15 to Rs 1700 billion in 2018–19, as per government data.[126] While the sector started with mobile phone assembly, a component production ecosystem is also emerging swiftly. India is now the second-largest manufacturer of mobile phones by volume,[127] behind only China. According to media reports, electronics exports increased by 38 per cent between 2018 and 2019.[128]

For 2022, mobile phone exports from India hit $5.5 billion, up 75 per cent from $3.2 billion in the prior year.[129] Data for 2021 showed that India's share in the world's aggregate goods exports had reached an all-time high 1.9 per cent, with substantial growth contribution coming from manufacturing.[130]

Some analysts opine that India has only been assembling phones, and there is hardly any value addition.[131] But as the Indian Trade Service officer Tirumala Venkatesh has written, 'usually such screwdriver technologies are the stepping-stones to upper levels of value chain. And while at it, the millions who turn the screwdrivers have a job.'[132] India's initial success in promoting mobile device manufacturing is now sought to be replicated for electronics items such as air conditioners and other consumer goods.[133]

The key to understanding this revival of moderate protectionism is not to confuse import substitution with licence raj. The Nehruvian controlled economy certainly attempted industrialization with import substitution (through tariffs and other barriers) as one of its planks, but it also included the need to get licences for capacity expansion (hence the name 'licence raj') and consequent corruption, restrictions on imports, a fixed—and often overvalued—currency and a general political and policy environment which was not conducive to growing businesses honestly. Today, except for the very moderate tariffs, none of the other conditions apply.

Just as moderate protectionism on the trade policy front can turbocharge manufacturing, similarly targeted incentives on the industrial policy front can also boost output and exports. Both assume competent and honest state capacity, or at least a trajectory towards that. These trade and industrial policies should be implemented with sunset clauses. In 2020, building upon the early push to onshore electronics manufacturing, India announced production-linked incentive (PLI) schemes for the same. The PLI schemes, envisaging a cumulative outlay by the government of about Rs 2 trillion to private firms who achieve output targets,[134] have been subsequently extended to a number of sectors, such as semiconductor manufacturing, advanced chemistry cell energy storage, specialty steel, automotive components, textiles and food processing.

Synchronization between trade and industrial policy is necessary to fulfil India's manufacturing potential and create large-scale jobs. To better understand the trade–industrial dynamic, it is worth contrasting India's experience with the automobile and electronics sectors over the last few decades. In the former, India is relatively well placed including in the auto components segment. In the latter, until recently, as described earlier, India has been far behind China, Taiwan and Southeast Asian countries.

In the auto sector, FDI has long been liberalized and the leading players are foreign companies. Suzuki or Hyundai may not be Indian companies (though Suzuki's subsidiary is listed in India) but so long as they are manufacturing cars in India, they are treated the same as domestic companies. They bring their technology, keep the profits and expand the industry by themselves or with local partners. Unlike Australia, for example,[135] India does not import its automobiles but mostly consumes its own manufactures while also exporting automobiles and auto components.

On the other hand, for electronics, on joining the World Trade Organization (WTO) and signing the Information Technology Agreement (ITA) in 1996, India immediately went for zero tariffs in the entire sector.[136] While in the short term, it certainly helped customers since they were able to buy cheaper mobile phones and computers, it completely hollowed out domestic manufacturing of the same.[137]

India's indigenization attempt with respect to the electronics sector was severely affected. It was similar to what happened to the textile sector in Bihar, Bengal and Gujarat under the British,[138] except this time the decimation was much faster. If we had followed the same strategy in automobiles, chances are that Indian entrepreneurs in the sector would have remained importers and wholesalers as opposed to industrialists and innovators.

It may make sense for Australia to not build most of its own cars given that it is a country of 25 million people focusing on other industries. Moreover, the geopolitical setting is conducive. Not only is Australia a member of the political West that still dominates the world, it is its core constituent as a member of the 'Five Eyes' intelligence alliance along with US, UK, Canada and New Zealand. Protected by oceans and guaranteed security by the United States, Australia reaps multiple benefits. However, the much larger European Union bloc is now considering the use of 'trade defence instruments (TDIs)', a euphemism for protectionism, against the sharp rise in imports of Chinese-made electric vehicles and auto ancillaries. The European automotive industry contributed 10 per cent of manufacturing jobs and one-third of the bloc's trade surplus in 2019.[139] The EU, being a very large market with superior bargaining power, can push for policies that an Australia or a stand-alone European country may not be able to.

Additionally, while India may be content being a half-member of the geopolitical West, it has a difficult neighbourhood and has to balance economic ties with China and military ones with Russia, along with increasingly closer ties with the United States. Not only that, as a country with low per capita income India must industrialize or stagnate. A smaller nation such as Paraguay or Kenya by itself may not be able to put up auto or electronics tariffs and industrialize, as foreign manufacturers would just skip the country. In the post-COVID-19 world, as the US and China enter a new cold war, global just-in-time supply chains may anyway be disrupted by trade wars and geopolitical rivalry. This does not mean that India should avoid international supply chains, but it is worth remembering that the domestic market as a springboard for exports may be an effective strategy.

India is liberalizing FDI across industries unlike in the licence-raj era. This opening up has increased competition and therefore domestic players are not mollycoddled even when there are moderate tariffs. Of course, there is no scope to overdo it, raising the barriers so high that it invites significant geo-economic retribution. Like Alexander Hamilton, the present-day Indian trade policy makers want at best moderate protectionism. Indian manufacturing, and the jobs that manufacturing growth will bring, needs infrastructure, better contract enforcement, factor market reforms, low corporate taxes, ease of doing business, as well as a gentle push through time-bound protectionism. Several steps have been implemented across these vectors, and more needs to be done. Alongside these internal reform measures, a comprehensive administrative restructuring of the commerce ministry is also underway to achieve the stated goal of $2 trillion in exports by 2027, with measures such as the creation of a trade promotion body and capacity-building for sourcing local market intelligence in Indian missions on the anvil.[140]

In the post-pandemic world, many countries are realizing that when it comes to supply chains, 'just-in-case' is as critical as 'just-in-time'. This is further exacerbated by Chinese bellicosity (including towards India) and the Russian invasion of Ukraine which is leading to the disruption and even disintegration of formerly reliable commercial networks. Events have borne out that trade policy needs to be aligned with broader strategic and geopolitical considerations and does not exist in a vacuum.

5

Decolonizing the Indian State

The political institutions of a society are a key determinant of the outcome of this game [of the distribution of political power in a society]. They are the rules that govern incentives in politics. They determine how the government is chosen and which part of the government has the right to do what. Political institutions determine who has power in society and to what ends that power can be used. If the distribution of power is narrow and unconstrained, then the political institutions are absolutist, as exemplified by the absolutist monarchies reigning throughout the world during much of history.

—Daron Acemoglu and James A. Robinson[1]

From *matsya nyaya* to rule of law

Given that in large parts of the country, Indians did not have a State for centuries, we understandably forgot the art and science of statecraft. The last seven decades have been a time of re-learning. Hence, focusing too much on the foibles of individuals, families and parties, while important for introspection, should be seen in the broader historical context. Some mistakes in economics, law and foreign policy may now seem obvious but often that is because we, looking back decades after the Republic was forged, have the benefit of hindsight. Some mistakes were avoidable, but many were inevitable. Importantly, a few gargantuan tragedies were avoided.

China, for example, is economically far ahead of India now even though until a generation ago we were at the same level. Even if we adjust for population, consumption, inequality and cost of living, the common Chinese still earns about twice as much as his or her Indian counterpart. However, what matters for the purpose of this analysis is that just a few decades earlier the Chinese went through the tragic famines that killed tens of millions during Mao's Great Leap Forward and the Cultural Revolution of the 1960s, but democratic India avoided such mass starvation.

Nonetheless, the Chinese have a near-unbroken experience of statecraft for two millennia. Even the Jurchens, Mongols and the Manchus got 'sinicized' in a way that the Turks or Mughals never fully Indianized. Yet, the Chinese messed up the first few decades of their Communist State and India, despite—or more likely because of—being a democracy did not achieve extreme results, good or bad. Hence just having a State is not enough—it has to be simultaneously accountable and effective, strong yet limited.

What is a State? The simplest definition of a functional State is: it is the authority that has a legitimate monopoly on conducting violence. As Thomas Hobbes wrote in the *Leviathan*, 'during the time men live without a common Power to keep them all in awe, they are in that condition called Warre (War).'[2] To prevent such an ongoing civil war, allegiance was historically owed to the monarchy or an oligarchy. Today such loyalty may be expressed for a democratic republic. In any case, without having a strong State, it is difficult for peace to prevail. Without peace and order, economic growth is unlikely to take place.

Occasionally, wars may have been important to establish a more just peace, in which case economic growth suffered for some time. For example, in the eighteenth century average per capita income in India (in 2011 US dollars) declined from $1200 to $1067 while that in the UK increased from $1591 to $2210.[3] There are other estimates as well, but the broad directionality is not contested. Starting with the twenty-seven-year war initiated by Chhatrapati Shivaji in 1680, and then the further rise of the Maratha empire after Mughal Emperor Aurangzeb's death in 1707, output suffered. Cities from Surat to Calcutta were threatened and merchants were harassed—it was a missed opportunity for the Marathas to collaborate with the Rajputs, Jats and Sikhs—but this still bought enough time for Indian civilization to catch its breath. The temples built by Ahilyabai Holkar, the Queen of Malwa who reigned during 1767–1795, across the length and breadth of India[4] are but a small proof of that respite. The British effectively captured Delhi not from the Mughals but from the Marathas.[5]

Yet in the long run without an effective State, growth is impossible. A strong State is a necessary but not sufficient condition. For growth to be sustained, the State must be restrained while still being effective in specific areas. Mao and Stalin certainly had very strong States, but the lack of any sane restrictions meant that they consigned tens of millions of Chinese, Russians, Kazakhs and others to death through their policies.

Less dramatically, the Indian State, while avoiding mass famine, caused a lot of misery nonetheless and millions of early deaths indirectly because of its wrong socialist and overly interventionist policies for many decades, not to mention a lack of focus in the areas where a State must be strong—namely national defence, internal security and provision of public goods such as basic education, public health and good roads.

That the Indian State is inefficient is true. Any discussion about first principles in public policy can't possibly paper over as deep-seated a problem as poor State capacity.[6]

Things are improving, though gradually. As India urbanizes, expectations from politicians will shift from doling out arbitrary group-based largess to the creation of public goods. Some advocates of economic freedom argue for a smaller State, and in some specific domains correctly so, but without realizing that India's size of government is anyway smaller compared to many Western countries where such libertarian rhetoric may find a wider audience.

India's problem is having 'State flab' in the wrong places in the government and no muscle in areas that matter. There are bloated ministries at the Centre as well as in the states but many vacancies in departments entrusted with actually executing critical programmes and policies. Indian bureaucracy is too generalist and an average IAS officer usually does not spend enough time in a particular ministry to develop any real expertise. For example, the finance and defence ministries, two of the most important ministries of the Union government, each see about half a dozen people take the post of secretary across multiple departments over the five-year term of an elected government. What makes matters worse is that there is hardly any room to bring in external talent to the higher echelons of the government—it took the Modi government six years to select and appoint nine lateral entrants as joint secretaries. But to the government's credit, at least the process has now been initiated.[7]

India has a comparatively smaller State in terms of employees per one thousand Indians compared to developed economies, but the government pays much higher in salaries as a ratio of per capita income. Yet, senior officers need to be paid much more—with less non-cash benefits and more variable cash compensation—and middle- as well as lower-ranked officers need to be paid less. The high non-cash component of compensation to senior government officers is a relic of the usurious high tax legacy of the Indira Gandhi years, when the tax at the top bracket was 97.75 per cent.[8]

Like market salaries, government salaries need to have greater divergence if the goal is to attract talent while staying within fiscal constraints. Unfortunately, the union leaders of government employees are against this and without the public at large understanding this issue better, inertia rules the day.

According to the Seventh Pay Commission report released in 2015, the sanctioned strength of India's Central government departments was around 4 million, with about 3.3 million of these positions were filled. The report stated:[9]

Available literature indicates that the size of the non-postal civilian workforce for the US Federal Government in the year 2012 was 21.30 lakh. This includes civilians working in US defence establishments.

The corresponding persons in position in India for the Central Government in 2014 was 17.96 lakh. The total number of federal/Central Government personnel per lakh of population in India and the US works out to 139 and 668 respectively.

In the top echelons of India's elite civil services, the situation is just as worrying. The size of India's diplomatic corps is tiny compared to its global ambitions—there are only 2700 staff members and 912 foreign service officers. Countries like China (4500), Japan (5700), France (6000) and the US (20,000) are way ahead of India.[10] Moreover that 'the annual intake into IFS [Indian Foreign Service] tops off at 35 officers tells its own sad story', the hawkish analyst Bharat Karnad correctly mentions.[11]

Not only should India ramp up its diplomatic strength, the selection process too needs to be revamped with a separate exam to select foreign officers, assessing them on 'parameters such as international aptitude, curiosity about the world, knowledge or demonstrated interest in foreign affairs, communication skills' as recommended in the report by the Parliamentary Standing Committee on External Affairs chaired by Congress MP Shashi Tharoor.[12] The report also asked for mid-career entry where even ambassador-level appointments could be made from outside the IFS, selecting people from fields like 'community affairs, diaspora issues, foreign policy, area studies, literature, journalism'.

India could also use more experts from the private sector as consultants across important external affairs ministry divisions. In February 2020, External Affairs Minister S. Jaishankar implemented a comprehensive restructuring of the ministry, initiating long-overdue administrative reforms necessary to align the ministry with the changed trade and security objectives of India. For example, the administrative and consular work of the ministry was consolidated and separated from the diplomatic work.[13]

The IFS is not the only civil service facing capacity constraints. As many as 1449 posts of the IAS (22.11 per cent of sanctioned strength) and 970 posts in the IPS (19.64 per cent of sanctioned strength) were lying vacant in the country,[14] according to government data released in July 2018. On top of this, the government is reducing civil services intake each year. It has fallen from a high of 1291 candidates in 2014 to 782 in 2018—quantitatively similar to the intake in 1996.[15]

Talking about police forces across the country, in all the states, over five lakh posts are vacant with the highest—around 1.80 lakh—being in Uttar Pradesh.[16] Why is it surprising then that there is no rule of law, and any group can extract special benefits from the State based on its violence potential?

The UPSC examination which selects civil service officers for the IAS, IPS, IFS and around twenty other central government departments, needs a complete overhaul. The recruitment process needs to be more aptitude-based and less content-based. After selection, there needs to be specialized training in public administration and public policy (for the IAS), law and policing (for the IPS), diplomacy and international affairs (for the IFS) and so on. There is reason to change even the examination and intake methodology. Sanjeev Chopra, former director of the Lal Bahadur Shastri National Academy of Administration, the national training institution of the civil services cadres, has written:[17]

> The Civil Service Exam template of three-phase selection— Prelims, Mains and Personality Test—has continued from 1979, even though the structure, syllabi, and relative weightage of each of the three components has changed from time to time ... Should India not give civil service aspirants the option to sit for an exam of the specific service they want to join . . . is it fair to any Service to induct officers who never wanted to join it in the first place? Would it not make sense if the Prelims and the compulsory papers for the Mains were common to all services, but service-specific papers introduced for the IAS, IPS, IFS and Revenue Services with focus on public policy and governance, criminal law and internal security issues, international affairs, and tax policy respectively?

Once in the service, there must not be any automatic, practically guaranteed promotions—promotions must be performance based. Praising the Agnipath scheme, that will recruit about 50,000 soldiers per year for a fixed tenure of four years after which most soldiers would leave the armed forces, retired Indian Police Service officer Prakash Singh noted that the All India Services (AIS) comprising IAS, IPS and other officer cadres 'have become very, very top-heavy' and they too should have an Agnipath-type programme:[18]

> It has been noticed that once an officer is selected for the AIS, he/she develops a smug attitude that his/her career for the next 30/35 years is now secure and that, under normal circumstances, he/she would be able to reach the top level. There is no pressure to perform, no incentive to innovate, and no desire to excel. No wonder, many of these officers become laid-back and are, most of the time, feathering their nests. There is no *agni* in them.

The brief of the civil service is to execute the policy of the government of the day. The argument that bureaucracy acts as a check on the whims and fancies (even corrupt proclivities) of the politicians isn't sound. That's not their job, but that of other institutions entrusted specifically with the task of maintaining transparency.

There needs to be ample time for bureaucrats to develop expertise based on their interest and governmental needs. An analysis of the executive record sheets of over 2000 officers with at least a decade in service shows that only 7.9 per cent of the IAS officers remain in one post for more than two years.[19] In every bureaucratic shuffle, it is quite common to read, for example, that the urban development secretary has taken charge as the home secretary, the information and broadcasting secretary is now in the department of personnel and training, the steel secretary moves to the finance ministry, a senior agriculture ministry official is shifted to the power ministry, and so on. Such a system based on primarily generalists doesn't allow officers to build domain expertise and is highly detrimental to improving administrative efficiency.

On the other hand, a very narrow functional role for an entire career—as was the case in Indian Railways for more than a century until the creation of a generalist railway cadre was approved by the

Union cabinet—is also suboptimal. Writing about the rationale for the railway administrative reforms announced on 25 December 2019 that turned the Indian Railways into a more functionally-oriented unit, Aashish Chandorkar observed:

> To understand why these reforms were necessary, one needs to understand the existing work process of the Indian Railways. The organization still carries the British legacy of departmentalization. The eight key departments—accounts, civil, electrical, mechanical, personnel, signal and telecom, stores and traffic—are integrated vertically, and have their own hierarchies. Each department works in silos, with reporting staying within the department.[20]

There also needs to be a mechanism for absorbing outside talent which has domain expertise and experience. This will require an overhaul of compensation practices. Pay at the highest levels of bureaucracy should be much higher than what it is today. The reason why India has a relatively small, central State (in terms of number of employees) is precisely because we pay peanuts in salaries to the most experienced officers at the top, whose number is low, while doling out relatively attractive pay to those at the bottom. As the Pay Commission report stated:[21]

> Of the total 33.02 lakh civilian workforce 89 percent are in Group 'C', 8 percent are in Group 'B' and 3 percent are in Group 'A' . . . While 89 percent of civilian Central Government personnel are in Group 'C', the Railways, Department of Posts and MHA have a significantly higher proportion in Group 'C' at 99 percent, 96 percent and 92 percent respectively . . . Scientific and technical focused ministries/departments have a high percentage of Group 'A' Officers.

This disproportionately high pay granted to lower levels compared to the market rate for similar jobs distorts the labour market. It wastes the youth of tens of millions of people who keep trying their luck to somehow land a government job with its lifelong job security and multiple non-cash perks. Even the cash component at the lower levels is higher than for comparable private sector jobs. This results in advanced degree holders applying in tens of thousands for entry-level posts in the government.[22]

Of course, asking for higher salaries for the senior officials and lower pay for junior staff can be politically difficult. But it is required. An October 2015 study conducted by IIM Ahmedabad which was commissioned by the Government of India found that 'Government is paying higher salaries compared to the private sector . . . for jobs at the lower levels of skill requirement and hierarchy (but) salary in government is relatively lower compared to the private sector, particularly in later years, for some highly skilled jobs.'[23]

Take the post of a driver. In 2015, the government paid around Rs 25,000 to those without any experience, while in the private sector, their salary was around Rs 12,000, depending on the city they were in.[24] A nurse made about Rs 7000 to 17,000 in the private sector but entry-level pay for a nurse in the government was about three times more. The government paid around Rs 50,000 for entry-level engineers while they received barely half of that in the private sector.

But salaries rise in the private sector at a much higher pace than in the government, with experience and acquisition of skills. There is no such incentive to improve for someone working in the government thanks to lock-step promotions and fixed increments irrespective or performance.

Moreover, Article 311 of the Constitution[25] gives such near-ironclad job security that 'an employee has to be a sexual offender or a lunatic before the government will act against him or her,' as T.C.A. Srinivasa Raghavan writes.[26] Clause 1 of the article states, 'No person who is a member of a civil service . . . shall be dismissed or removed by an authority subordinate to that by which he was appointed.' Since the President of India appoints the civil servants, he alone can sack them. This needs to change.

Improving the efficacy of the Indian State is not just about getting the incentives for public servants right, but increasing accountability and transparency. It is almost impossible for even the most law-abiding citizens to be aware of what rules they need to follow.[27] Economist Sanjeev Sanyal has opined that India needs a 'Transparency of Rules Act' so that all rules and procedures are notified in a real-time manner on the website of the relevant government agency or department, in one coherent document, rather than as a series of circulars.[28]

Sanyal is spot on. Transparency of rules would not just make life easier for all citizens as they go about their mundane business, whether it is obtaining a driving licence or registering a new company. Transparency of rules will be a meta-reform that can catalyse new debates on what rules are needed, and how existing rules may be expanded or curtailed. Greater transparency of rules would significantly improve the existing Right to Information (RTI) Act.

The RTI Act has helped the cause of accountability. It has shaken the system, especially the bureaucracy that had coalesced into an unimaginable labyrinth of sinecures. Thanks to the indefatigable idealism and persistence of activists such as H.D. Shourie and building on the NDA government's Freedom of Information Act (2002), the UPA government passed the RTI Act in 2005. This has allowed many citizens to demand, and usually obtain, more transparency from the government. But marginal returns from RTI are diminishing—it is in the interest of transparency and even economic efficiency that RTI be reformed and its objectives be broadened.

The embedded time lags in the RTI process—it can take months to obtain information, if re-appeals are included—and the associated paperwork deter queries on the relatively minor issues that citizens face in their daily lives. The transaction costs are simply too high for most people to use RTI for routine matters, not to mention how some of the smartest and most resourceful talent available to the government is employed in churning out clerical work of replying to RTI questions, many of which are inane. The high-stakes queries go unanswered. The uncomfortable ones can invite physical threats too.

The issue right now is that the State has locked up all the information by default and will dole out some information only to those who are persistent and curious. It's a typically bureaucratic way of ushering in transparency—in theory, but not in practice. Humphrey Appleby of the British TV show on government, *Yes Minister*, would be proud of the architects of this great wall of stymied accountability.

In a democracy, public information should not be rationed by bureaucrats. If one commits to the principle of openness, the envelope can be pushed even further. Jaideep Prabhu has noted how declassification of government documents and opening up of the National Archives could cure the Indian establishment's allodoxaphobia, or fear of opinions.[29] Prabhu rightly suggests that such openness could dramatically boost scholarship and analysis of India's governance, both past and present.

If one wants to know comprehensively about local laws and regulations, and the local department website offers incomplete, incoherently presented information, then the resultant high transaction costs mean that it makes rational sense to take the risk of being on the wrong side of the law, and often to simply bribe a middleman or a tout to 'do the needful'. If the rules were presented coherently on the websites of government departments with timestamps to record amendments on an ongoing basis, it would save substantial time and effort for both citizens and government, as well as reduce the need for citizens to indulge in petty corruption.

Freely available and properly formatted government data could be the second plank towards a transparent State. There is a larger movement among governments and institutions to make available standardized, machine-readable data by default. India's stock exchanges have already taken the lead in putting out financial information on their websites in this way. While the Union government's annual budget is analysed threadbare, state government and local body budgets—which are more consequential for the lived reality of citizens—are hardly discussed.

If analysts could compare education or healthcare spending across cities and states thanks to standardized data, public engagement with policy making would be much more constructive. Many democracies have already moved to release significantly more information in the public domain. US President Barack Obama's administration had decided to make most data collected by the government available to the public for free, and that too in a machine-readable format by default.

Public data can also allow for better pricing of private goods and services. *The Economist* correctly assessed the benefits this would bring to citizens, saying, 'Pollution numbers will affect property prices. Restaurant reviews will mention official sanitation ratings. Data from toll-booths could be used to determine prices for nearby billboards.'[30]

In India, the possibilities are endless as we have already constructed a world-leading basket of digital public goods and utilities with India Stack.[31] For example, in 2016 the Bangalore Metropolitan Transport Corporation (BMTC) introduced an Intelligent Transport System (ITS) with functions like electronic ticketing and vehicle tracking. As a result, BMTC is collecting huge amounts of data. Thanks to e-ticketing, it is now possible to track exactly how many people are boarding and deboarding at specific stops on a route. Live tracking has made it possible to arrive at an exact travel time for a route at different times in a day. If the data is utilized properly, the government can increase the number of buses on routes in peak hours depending on demand and reduce when not needed, instead of continuing with monotonous fixed schedules. If the government doesn't have the capacity, it can give open access to the data and let entrepreneurs take the lead in coming up with innovative solutions.

Team India's economic federalism

India will soon have the world's largest population, growing per capita income and increasing its economies of scale.[32] It is possible to buy or build expensive aircraft carriers that smaller or poorer nations cannot. A large consumer base provides what experts call partial monopsony power to attract investments given the size and growth of the national market. India's voice will increasingly be heard in global matters even as the average citizen is still poor because the country's size ensures influence.

But there are problems, too. With excessive centralization of power, the right solutions do not get designed or customized as per varying local requirements. Devolving most policy making to the states—and even to the local bodies—may make much more sense. In this manner the state governments can act as the 'laboratories of democracy'.

A Tamil Nadu can come up with the idea of school lunches, a Bihar with bicycles for girls, a Chhattisgarh with better public distribution system—and then the good ideas can be copied or tweaked. It makes a lot of sense that policing, agriculture and public health are in the state list. Obviously, something like defence needs to be in the Union list. During the Emergency imposed by Prime Minister Indira Gandhi, some subjects such as education were brought into the concurrent list, which is open to both the Union and states for formulating policy but where the former generally prevails.

When states compete, either with lower taxes or with better infrastructure as well as more honest and competent governance to attract business investments, there is competitive federalism. In some cases, such competition can be destructive but generally it is healthy and is an important mechanism, or a meta-reform, to keep sub-national governments efficient. Citizens and capital should be able to vote with their feet.

When states cooperate with each other or collectively with the Union, a good example of which is the GST Council, we can consider it to be cooperative federalism. This can be critical in some other areas such as education or health policy, but in general is difficult to pull it off in an institutionalized setting given the diffusion of accountability and the eventual increase in partisan rancour, which is to be expected in any closely-fought-over democracy.

Of course, federalism is not just about economics or even principally about it. The Muslim League in the mid-1940s wanted a very loose federation with residual powers in the provinces after the British left, insisting that the provinces would fund the Central government, rather than the latter raising any taxes directly. Nehru and Patel foresaw that such an arrangement would destabilize the Union, and rightly rejected the idea even though it meant accepting Partition. Speaking on 10 July 1946, Nehru said: 'If anyone suggests that some kind of contributions or doles are going to be given by the Provinces or States, it is bunkum. No Central Government carries on on doles.'[33]

Rejecting the dubious structure of the Cabinet Mission Plan was better, even though deeply tragic, as it cut the losses at one go instead of not being able to control future centrifugal forces.

Does that mean that over-centralization in a free but partitioned India due to Nehruvian economics made sense? Not necessarily. For example, freight equalization was one of the reasons that led to the dense fertile plains of the north and the east of the country being underdeveloped[34] even though they were closer to many natural resources, whereas the coastal areas of the south and the west raced ahead. The north was still saved due to the Green Revolution, and Delhi being the national capital. Besides regional inequalities, India as a whole suffered, insisting the areas that did relatively well. It is in this context of the three issues of growth, equity and federalism that the GST is an important topic worth discussing, along with related policies being set by the various finance commissions.

In July 2017, India got a new indirect tax system—the goods and services tax (GST)—that subsumed a dozen different taxes and levies, unifying the vast but fragmented Indian market. The transition has been difficult, though expecting anything else for a political economy as massive and complex as India's would have been overly optimistic, even silly. The Narendra Modi government certainly deserves credit for pushing through this reform by ensuring revenue certainty for some time to the state governments. Finance Minister Arun Jaitley deserves significant credit for his role in building the political consensus to deliver the tax overhaul, in a country that has around Africa's population and per capita income.[35] In April 2018, the total gross GST monthly revenue crossed Rs 1 trillion for the first time. By February 2020, it crossed that figure for three successive months in spite of many tax cuts—not necessarily impressive but nonetheless reassuring. More broadly, how does one evaluate the GST?

First, on growth. The GST is positive for long-term sustainable economic growth compared to the earlier tax regime. The GST is expanding one of the most important benefits of the value added tax (VAT) system (offsetting credit from final tax outgo based on the taxes paid on purchased supplies) in two directions—goods purchased across states, and services purchased within and across states. This represents India signing a revolutionary 'free trade deal with itself'.[36] A second-order effect is of course higher tax revenue first, with existing firms paying more due to growth, and second, through the impact of formalization as unorganized firms find it much more difficult to remain a part of larger supply chains without coming into the GST system. Millions of new businesses have registered and entered the indirect tax system as a consequence.[37] There is also a tertiary impact of indirect tax returns being matched against direct returns through analytics, and the consequent higher compliance with direct taxes as well, over time. Finally, the digital trail of GST returns will improve credit access as discussed earlier.

Second, is the impact of GST on equity or fairness. It is true that having fewer tax rates would be good for growth in the neoclassical economics view. Moreover, having less tweaking of rates by having fewer rates certainly reduces the chances of cronyism or political favouritism. But this should be weighed against concerns about fairness (or 'progressivity')—indirect taxes are generally considered 'regressive' because a poor person pays the same percentage of tax on his or her consumption as a rich person when they buy the same product. This of course accepts the normative view that the rich must not only pay more in absolute taxes but that they should also pay a higher share of their income or spending as well. Within that framework, it would be absurd to tax an expensive car and apparel at the same percentage levels. Further, even if there were no fairness concerns, a case can be made that incentivizing savings and discouraging luxury or 'sinful' consumption through tax-rate tweaks may help economic growth and social stability. Just because equity concerns are valid does not mean we tax some goods to oblivion. The government eventually reduced tax on many products from 28 per cent to 18 per cent,[38] and this should help increase compliance.

Third and last, on federalism. The GST as it stands today has been a brilliant example of cooperative federalism, but it is still a potentially worrying development when it comes to competitive federalism. Once the states start thinking beyond the guaranteed revenues, they will realize that they do not control the tax setting policies, except collectively with other states and the Union government. This is likely to lead to higher expenditure at the state level as chief ministers who can no longer significantly cut taxes may resort to increasing spending. The Union government is likely to face the consequences of these misaligned incentives over time. The good news is that whatever needs to be changed has been provided by the system itself, namely, the critical GST information technology-enabled network. Hence, what matters is not the same GST rates across states but rather the verification of inter-state purchases once the computerized system stabilizes with e-way bills.[39]

This flexibility will become even more important as India may gradually include alcohol, diesel, petrol and real estate under the GST, which is why some proposals are already talking about letting states levy additional duties if these items are included in the GST ambit. Hence, instead of having such a halfway house, India should consider a central GST and a state GST, with the states free to have different rates for the state GST so that we can preserve the autonomy of states and enhance healthy interstate fiscal competition.

There should be a fixed number of rate categories in all states to prevent favouritism and crony socialism. By having the same tax bases, state politicians would not be able to offer arbitrary tax breaks. Federalism means allowing maximum flexibility (in terms of rates but not tax bases) as far as the rule of law is not violated. To prevent excessive or destructive competition, India can adopt an EU-type structure with minimum tax rates.

Now, some sceptics of interstate tax competition might still say a 'race to the bottom' could take place, with states potentially cutting spending in drastic ways to cut taxes. But taxpayers, like consumers, operate on two variables, namely, cost and quality. Tax competition makes state spending more efficient and does not necessarily decrease it—a state could choose to have great infrastructure and social insurance, and firms might be ready to pay higher taxes to locate there.

We need to learn from the European, American and Canadian models to figure out how to have an integrated market while still having separate tax rates within. A few countries such as Australia have gone for uniform rates—but a huge economy and heterogeneous polity such as India's needs to be aware of the dangers of fiscal centralization.

The GST roll-out is an ongoing process and, in one form or the other, should keep our mandarins busy for years. It is more than worth all the troubles that occurred in the short-term. We are finally able to leverage our size, our population and our internal market. While growth will be boosted over time and equity concerns have been addressed, the federalism aspect is more mixed. However, there is no need to throw the baby out with the bathwater, and whatever needs to be improved in the system has been provided in the system itself.

Another approach for states to gain a fiscal lever is through direct taxes, where levying an income tax on agriculture can be a starting point. Under India's direct tax code, agricultural income is not taxed at all by the Union government. As D.P. Sengupta and R. Kavita Rao of the National Institute for Public Finance and Policy, New Delhi, have observed: 'the Constitution empowers Parliament to make laws with respect to taxes on income "other than agricultural income".' Similarly, Article 246(3) read with Entry 46 in List II of the Seventh Schedule empowers the state legislature to make laws relating to tax on agricultural income.[40]

With the implementation of state-level reforms and uptake of digital technology in the agriculture sector that are likely to bring more corporate and commercial activity, there is a case to tax agriculture income just like any other income. Taxing agriculture income is odious in India because of the history of colonial rulers brutally extracting the farmer's earnings, to the point at the millions dying in famines was not unheard of. The Indian economy stands transformed today and it is much less agriculture-centric. A transition to an agriculture income tax should be gradual, and initially only the ultra-rich farmers or corporate participants should be taxed. In any case, given that the personal income tax slab starts in India effectively at a level of about Rs 0.5 million, most farmers would not be taxed anyway.

Liberating the education system

In 2013,[41] Karthik Muralidharan of the University of California, San Diego, and World Bank's Venkatesh Sundararaman released a paper, titled 'The aggregate effect of school choice: evidence from a two-stage experiment in India,'[42] dropping a gigantic bombshell on the cobwebs engulfing education policy in India. Their paper analysed the Andhra Pradesh School Choice Project that was based on the concept of randomized controlled trials (RCTs), for which Massachusetts Institute of Technology (MIT) economists Abhijit Banerjee and Esther Duflo were awarded the 2019 Nobel Prize in economics.

Before discussing those results, let us understand what RCTs are, and what school choice is. An RCT tries to have reasonably large control and sample groups, with their constituents randomly chosen and differing in only one way—the intervention. In this process, the law of large numbers says that any significant difference between an output parameter post-intervention for both the groups should be attributable to the intervention.

In this manner, the theory goes, one can avoid complicated statistical analyses using randomized controls and avoid caveats like 'correlations are not causations' which haunt other kinds of economic studies. Of course, there are limitations of RCT, the most significant one being the high cost of such trials, because of which experiments are often localized and the results cannot always be extrapolated globally or even nationally. Yet RCTs are a valuable and exciting research tool in economics.

Vouchers allow poor students options beyond the free government school by compensating them if they want to attend a private school instead.

School choice is a broader concept. It includes autonomous schools (known as 'charters' in the United States) with less teacher union interference. It could also subsume the concept of government-aided private schools, where the aid may or may not be calculated on a per-student basis. The broad idea is that having more market-like structures in fees, salaries and subsidies leads to greater choice, better teaching and more bang for the buck. Why? Because teachers who cannot be fired or given bonuses are not very motivated teachers.

Unfortunately, the Right to Education (RTE) Act brought by the Congress–UPA government in 2009 achieved exactly the opposite. RTE militates against the right to equality, right to property and right to free association. Economist Bibek Debroy succinctly summarized his opposition to RTE in the *Indian Express*. The RTE, he writes 'imposes high compliance costs on many of these low-cost private schools while simultaneously tacitly admitting that the government school system cannot deliver'.[43]

Another Nobel laureate economist, Milton Friedman, had come up with the idea of school vouchers. James Tooley's book *The Beautiful Tree* popularized the existence of low-cost private schools, often operating in the regulatory shadows, in many emerging economies of Asia and Africa.[44] As a reviewer wrote about Tooley's book:[45]

> We are used to thinking of private education in terms of green playing fields and elites. But in the slums of Hyderabad, where the book begins, and in Nigeria, Ghana, Kenya and China, where it goes next, private education confounds our stereotypes.

Coming back to Muralidharan's paper, the first thing he found was that those students who attended private schools by using the voucher they won in a lottery, performed slightly better than those who did not. There was 'no difference between the test scores of lottery winners and losers on Math and Telugu. However, private schools spend significantly less instructional time on these subjects, and use the extra time to teach more English, Science.' On an average, across all subjects, lottery winners did better.

The significant result was that the average cost per student in private schools was just a third of the cost in public schools, suggesting, 'Private schools in this setting deliver (slightly) better test score gains than their public counterparts, and do so at substantially lower costs per student.' To illustrate, suppose a rural government school spends around Rs 6000 per student per month in Andhra Pradesh. Then, an average private school in that area charging students Rs 2000 per student per month is actually delivering slightly better results on average across subjects. How do the private schools manage this seemingly incongruous result?

In one word, incentives. Among other factors, private schools pay their teachers lower salaries while making the teachers work harder. This is because jobs in private schools, unlike government schools, are not secure. If teachers do not perform, they will be fired. Now consider, if the government were to give students a Rs 4000 monthly voucher which they could redeem at a government or a private school. The output of academic teaching at private schools, which is already slightly higher to begin with, will only go up because they will now have more resources. Of course, educational outcomes and quality will not go up linearly with increasing spend. The amount of the proposed voucher could vary but such a policy reform will improve the outcomes over the present arrangement, while saving substantial taxpayer money. Rupee for rupee, private schools outperform government schools by a large margin. And even if we were to raise government funding and the size of the voucher, school choice would still make sense.

The 'how much' of the educational and other subsidies to give out is a political and normative question, whereas the 'how to' is simply a matter of being smart and efficient. Indian politicians, especially of the socialist persuasion, routinely try to fool voters and analysts by bragging about how big the budget allocations and expenditures are, instead of focusing on what results a particular welfare scheme has delivered. It is outcomes that matter, not outlays.

The usual caveats of RCTs apply. What is true in Andhra Pradesh may not necessarily apply to the rest of India, although the sheer size of the cost-adjusted outcomes is extremely noteworthy. So, to be sure, let us evaluate some more evidence.

In a paper for the Friedman Foundation for Educational Choice, Greg Forster found that of the twelve American RCTs about school choice, improvements were seen in eleven—in six all students benefited, in five some students benefited, in one there was no impact and there were none with a negative impact.[46]

Twenty-three empirical studies employing all methods (not just RCTs) examined school-choice impact on academic outcomes in government schools—twenty-two found it improves public schools and one found zero impact. Six studies examined school choice's impact on taxpayers—all found that it saved money, and none found a negative impact. Then one can peruse the monograph titled *Educational Vouchers: Global Experience and India's Promise*, coauthored by Dr Parth J. Shah of the New Delhi–based think tank Centre for Civil Society (CCS), which compiled evidence from countries as diverse as the US, Chile, New Zealand, Hungary and Denmark.[47]

The evidence for school choice (i.e., adjusted for money spent, educational outcomes are better at private schools than government schools) is overwhelming and robust. Obviously, the government-teachers union leaders represent a powerful interest group that blocks reform. But they are not alone.

They are supported by the outdated mindset that education should not be a profit-making industry. There is only one real reason why profit continues to be illegal in parts of the education industry—because profit in modern India continues to be a dirty word for some ideologues. Never mind that these ideologues turn a blind eye to politically connected education-sector incumbents who want the sector to remain off limits to profit-making, such that their de facto businesses enjoy protection. It is a classic case of bootleggers and Baptists coming together to ban alcohol.

Private schools have longer school days, fewer holidays, lower teacher absence, lower pupil-to-teacher ratios and less cross-grade teaching. They provide better school facilities (more toilets, for example) and yet spend far less. Yes, the teachers at private schools are less educated and less experienced, but as the CCS study has documented, experience from all over the world shows that incentives to perform are much more important than mere qualifications.

As Geeta Gandhi Kingdon observed in her 2017 paper 'Private Schooling Phenomenon in India: A Review':

Official data show a steep growth of private schooling and a corresponding rapid shrinkage in the size of the government school sector in India, suggesting parental abandonment of government schools. Data show that a very large majority of private schools in most states are 'low-fee' . . . This suggests that affordability is an important factor behind the migration towards and growth of private schools. The main reason for the very low fee levels in private schools is their lower teacher salaries, which the data show to be a small fraction of the salaries paid in government schools; this is possible because private schools pay the market-clearing wage . . .[48]

That school vouchers are yet to gain endorsement from India's intellectual establishment is extremely unfortunate and detrimental to the future of tens of millions of children. Moreover, centralized systems are hardly innovative. As mobile phones and the internet transform lives, the education system should be opened up to create more incentives for technology-based competition too. Many government schools have no students and they continue to receive subsidies. Between 2010 and 2015, over Rs 1000 crore was spent on government schools that had no students at all.[49] Why ignore the lessons of price-decreasing and quality-increasing impact of competition in sectors such as telecom and aviation?

India needs to break the stranglehold of special interest groups involved in schools, hold teachers accountable and dissolve the 'dictatorship of the salariat'.[50] The regulatory stranglehold applies not just to primary and secondary schooling, but also extends to higher education.

Higher education is one sector where the United States enjoys a globally dominant position[51] even more than in technology, pharmaceuticals, defence or aerospace.

Every year, around half of the top twenty universities globally are US universities.[52] No country comes close when it comes to attracting the best students, retaining the best researchers and producing output that pushes the boundaries of knowledge in practically every field of human inquiry. America's commanding strength in higher education powers its economy and endows the country with a formidable strategic edge.

It is worth studying what has made US institutions so markedly better than others in the world. Key factors are 'national wealth, large population, government support especially of science' along with the migration of talent from Europe to the US because of the Second World War, and the 'American habit of private philanthropy'.[53]

Henry Rosovsky, former dean of Harvard University's faculty of arts and sciences, also points to certain specific features in the governance structure, such as the fact that all senior and middle management of an institution 'are appointed, not elected, and they can be dismissed', and the 'unitary governance' approach,[54] with the university president being answerable only to the board of trustees and holding full executive responsibility.

Freedom and autonomy matter deeply to knowledge creation. Academic research and scientific inquiry cannot coexist with dogmatism, top-down control and doctrinaire thinking. Finally, inter-institution competition for talent and resources spurs universities to do better.

Most Indian universities do not have autonomy and freedom in important areas such as deciding their curriculum, fees and salaries. Shailendra Mehta, in his analysis of why the US has been so successful in higher education, identifies the key innovation that the US brought, which propelled its universities to the top ranks globally, as 'alumni control of the board of trustees',[55] not surprisingly pioneered by Harvard University, whose board was de facto controlled by alumni starting in 1710, with de jure control cemented in 1865. Harvard had been founded by the state of Massachusetts, and the Massachusetts legislature retained the right to appoint the board of trustees until 1865 (though it usually appointed only Harvard alumni). Thus, as Mehta writes, Harvard remained a public university or a 'State School' for over two hundred years after its founding.

Securing de jure alumni control over the board of trustees was anything but easy. In a nail-biting win, as Mehta records, the 'Act in Relation to the Board of Overseers of Harvard College' was passed on

29 April 1865 by a margin of just one vote in the Massachusetts State Senate, and by a margin of two in the House. The legislation expressly barred government officials from becoming trustees of the institution and insulated the trustees from faculty influence by preventing faculty from voting in trustee elections. Harvard was already America's pre-eminent university in 1865 and its rise was accelerated after this critical—and hard-fought—change in its governance structure. Seeing its effectiveness, other American universities promptly emulated the Harvard model, and the rest, as they say, is history.

Why is this story relevant for India today? Because there is a surge in technology entrepreneurship across the country. There are huge expectations that India's youth have and they wish their country to emerge as a leader in education, research and innovation.

The Narendra Modi government has implemented policies to enhance India's global competitiveness in higher education. The Indian Institute of Management Act, 2017 that came into effect in 2018 has devolved complete autonomy to the IIMs in areas such as selection and removal of the chairperson and director, fee regulation, student intake, institute expansion and other key aspects. The government has a policy to award 'Institutions of Eminence' status to selected public and private universities which are best suited to rise in global rankings.

These institutions will be freed from regulatory control that has been the scourge of the education sector. The government is also taking steps to scrap the biggest impediments to the liberalization of higher education sector—the University Grants Commission and the All-India Council for Technical Education—and replace them with a single regulator called the Higher Education Commission of India.[56]

Similarly, in a stellar reform move, the Medical Council of India, notorious as a den of corruption and cronyism, was replaced with a new body called National Medical Commission in August 2019.[57]

India's capacity for scientific research is linked inextricably to the quality of our higher education institutions. If America dominates the world in higher education, India would today win top honours for being a powerhouse exporter of high-quality human capital.

Much of our elite human capital ends up in US institutions, sometimes never to return. Between 2007 and 2017, the number of Indian students in the US doubled, and currently India is the 'second leading place of origin for students coming to the U.S., comprising 17.3 per cent of all international students'. A study by the Institute of International Education reveals that over 1,86,000 Indian students were studying in the US in 2017. By 2019 the number of Indian students in the US was more than 2,00,000.[58]

But this is largely a self-inflicted problem. India has high economic aspirations with an outdated and decrepit higher education system. The Times Higher Education World University 2020 ranking had just six Indian universities in the top 500, with no Indian institution making it to even the top 300.[59] Without world-class universities that are free to grow and compete with one another, tomorrow's innovators and entrepreneurs who would strengthen India's knowledge economy are often left with no choice but to move abroad.

The other error made by Indian policymakers was to cleave research from teaching. Creative ideas and breakthrough advances often come from the combination of young minds and experienced scholars studying and researching together. Unfortunately, the Council of Scientific and Industrial Research (CSIR) and the IITs, for example, constitute two disparate systems. In 2008, the Government of India had introduced the Protection and Utilisation of Public Funded Intellectual Property (PFIP) Bill. The PFIP Bill, modelled on the American Bayh-Dole Act of 1980 that has been described as 'innovation's golden goose',[60] aimed to catalyse commercialization of publicly funded research and creation of incentives for technology entrepreneurship in academia. The Bill was withdrawn in 2014, but there is a strong case for reviving this Bill and for changing it as needed.[61]

These reforms are critical to transform research and education. The institutional governance change, in particular, would empower alumni of Indian institutions who have proven themselves and run public institutions and global corporations to contribute to running their alma mater.

One symptom of stagnation in Indian academia is that instead of prioritizing nation-building and knowledge creation, what is often seen is that universities tend to become political battlefields. That is not necessarily wrong, but balance is needed.

For example, the Indian Left enjoyed State academic patronage and has a long history of being viciously intolerant towards not just contrary viewpoints, but even to those who resist political control over educational institutions.[62] The treatment meted out to Santosh Bhattacharya, vice-chancellor of Calcutta University from 1983 to 1987, speaks volumes about the viciousness of the communist leaders, who stooped to unspeakable lows in their attempts to abuse, harass and intimidate the scholarly Bhattacharya through his vice-chancellorship, only because he upheld academic standards and resisted undue political interference, much to the angst of the Left Front-controlled state government. Bhattacharya lamented:[63]

> . . . the CPI(M) in West Bengal . . . has always chosen the populist path of unmerited expansion and compromise with standards in higher education even for attaining and retaining control over university-level education, rather than pitching for the best, thus encouraging mediocrity in the process. Calcutta University has gone downhill because of such politically motivated interference by the present political masters, who dictate appointments, lay down academic policies even and fine-tune the university's executive actions too in step with political exigencies.

Economist Bibek Debroy recounted how Columbia University economist Jagdish Bhagwati was 'essentially made to leave' the Delhi School of Economics in the 1950s.[64] As economist Sanjeev Sanyal has written:

> The Left dominance over the intellectual establishment has its roots in the systematic 'ethnic cleansing' of all non-Left thinkers since the 1950s . . . the result of the systemic cleansing was that there were no non-Left academics remaining in the social sciences field in India

by the early 1990s . . . there needs to be a wider national debate about bringing greater plurality of thought in India's intellectual establishment.[65]

As Sanyal was careful to point out, it is not that 'the overwhelming dominance of the Left should be replaced by a similar dominance of the Right'. What India needs is a marketplace of ideas, and like any market, one certainly cannot expect the incumbent force (that is, the Indian Left-wing) to willingly cede space to new entrants. The most effective way to ensure the long-term impairment of India's entrenched Left-wing is to throw open the education market to competition. It is also the cheapest, for it would not require spending government money, thus freeing up resources for other areas.

Nothing matters more to most Indian parents than providing a good education to their children. On the back of the demographic changes, demand for quality education far outstrips supply. Corruption is rampant, and even reputable private institutions frequently extort under-the-table money from hapless parents. As always, it is not the rich that are hurt the most, but the poor and middle class.

With reforms underway to merge higher education regulatory bodies,[66] the creation of the Institutions of Eminence designation, granting of complete autonomy to qualified universities, granting unprecedented autonomy to the IIMs, and an overhaul of medical education regulation, the Modi government has made strides in the correct direction to both enhance academic efficacy as well as broaden intellectual diversity on campuses. The National Education Policy announced in 2020 is ambitious, and has a 20-year timeline for implementation given the scale and depth of reforms it envisions across schooling and higher education[67]—among other critical changes, it seeks to reduce the focus on board examination results, implement a unified university admissions process, ensure that all higher education institutions become multidisciplinary by 2040, and shift schooling from a 10+2 structure to a 5+3+3+4 modular structure encompassing pre-schooling, preparatory schooling, middle schooling and secondary schooling.[68]

Pandemics, State and incentives

The coronavirus pandemic, which has not gone away at the time of this writing but has faded in its impact, has brought to the fore the critical importance of public health. As UNDP noted,[69] India's efforts to modernize and digitize its public health delivery and vaccination ensured it was better prepared than most countries going into the pandemic:

> In India, thoughtfully developed digital infrastructure formed the backbone for an inclusive, resilient, and adaptive pandemic response. Back in 2014, India's Ministry of Health and Family Welfare began digitizing the vaccine supply chain network, training some 50,000 public health workers with support from UNDP and GAVI, the Vaccine Alliance. Thanks to this early investment, the Government of India already had significant experience digitally implementing population-scale vaccine infrastructure when the COVID-19 pandemic hit.
>
> Similarly, prior investments in building the capabilities of the country's health system through the electronic vaccine intelligence network (eVin) became the backbone for the COVID-19 vaccine management and delivery system. As part of India's routine immunization programme, eVin digitized the vaccine supply chain in over 29,000 vaccine storage centres, across all districts in India's 28 States and 8 Union Territories. eVin also saw the installation of over 27,000 digital temperature loggers for remote temperature monitoring and helped train 50,000 personnel for vaccine and cold chain management. These efforts resulted in over 80 per cent reduction in vaccine stock-outs, assured a 99 per cent vaccine availability rate, increased immunization coverage in children, and significantly reduced wastage and mismanagement.

India adopted a technology-led approach for vaccination with registration, appointment booking and certificate delivery being primarily digital, with the Covid Vaccine Intelligence Network (CoWIN) as its backbone.

The same technology infrastructure in turn allowed India's fiscal response to be targeted towards the vulnerable (in-kind benefits, cash transfers or loan guarantees) which enabled India to conserve resources compared to many richer nations (which spent money with less means-testing.) As an IMF paper by Surjit Bhalla, Arvind Virmani and Karan Bhasin summarized:

> Extreme poverty was as low as 0.8 percent in the pre-pandemic year 2019, and food transfers were instrumental in ensuring that it remained at that low level in pandemic year 2020. Post-food subsidy inequality at 0.294 is now very close to its lowest level 0.284 observed in 1993/94.[70]

Grouping the pandemic response measures under three heads of fiscal impulse, deferrals and liquidity provisions, the Brussels-based think tank Bruegel analysed each country's stimulus programme.[71] Where countries like Brazil (89 per cent), China (67 per cent), US (63 per cent) and Indonesia (60 per cent) focused their response on fiscal impulse, India's package was weighted just 12 per cent towards this segment, with heavier emphasis on deferrals and liquidity provisions—both of which served as shock absorbers through the unprecedented economic dislocation. This decision proved to be far-sighted, as India was better positioned to stimulate the economy when lockdowns were lifted, and the vaccination effort gathered momentum.

By adopting this data-driven, calibrated and agile policy approach—characterized by then Principal Economic Advisor Sanjeev Sanyal as 'wait, watch and then respond'[72]—India did not exhaust its fiscal and monetary bullets in the first one or two waves of the pandemic. Efficient targeting along with lower inflation[73] compared to richer economies was certainly noteworthy. Another paper found that inequality fell during the pandemic, despite the initial temporary rise in poverty:[74] 'We observe a sharp spike in poverty, peaking during India's sharp but short lockdown. However, there was a striking decrease in income inequality outside the lockdown. There was a smaller decrease in consumption inequality, likely due to consumption smoothing.'

Indeed, the foreign exchange reserves that India built up were useful during the Russia–Ukraine war (still underway at the time of writing) even as the pandemic had not fully ended. Hence the relative outperformance of the Indian rupee against the US dollar compared to many other currencies in 2022 thus far.[75]

But perhaps even more critically important than the economic response was India's COVID-19 vaccination programme. By October 2022, India had delivered over 2 billion vaccine shots, with over 90 per cent of the eligible population having completed vaccination. As Ram Sewak Sharma, CEO of India's National Health Authority (NHA), wrote:[76]

> The journey of CoWIN has been critical in helping us gain confidence that digital health systems can be run at the scale of billion-plus successfully, while being inclusive . . . The story of CoWIN has truly been one of national impact and importance. And while the story started during the pandemic, it won't end with the pandemic: it will segue into a repurposed digital platform for more health use-cases.

The NHA is tasked with implementing the Ayushman Bharat Digital Health Mission, which integrates governments, insurers, healthcare providers, medical professionals and patients onto a unified platform to facilitate consent-driven sharing of health records and trusted information with data portability. Invoking the success of UPI-driven digital payments, infotech pioneer and architect of Aadhaar Nandan Nilekani prophesized:[77]

> Today, you simply use any UPI app to pay anyone without worrying about what app or bank they use. Similarly, the vision is to use any Unified Health Interface (UHI) app to connect with any doctor, book an appointment, make a payment, share health records and get the prescription added to health records. Doctors will also have the choice to use the best UHI app that helps them manage their patients' interactions digitally. Interoperability will accelerate digital adoption. This will be a boon to Bharat as a lot of our healthcare talent

is still in the cities. Low-cost mobile connectivity, high smartphone penetration combined with these new digital public goods provide the right environment for a transformation.

In a broader sense, immunization, sanitation as well as aspects of health insurance are public goods with significant positive externalities—for example if X does not get infected, chances of Y getting infected are also lower and vice versa. That means smart government interventions are called for. While many governments tried to address the difficult challenges inherent to provisioning high positive externality public goods, such as expanding sanitation coverage and drinking water availability, the Modi Government has been especially successful in delivering mass-scale impact. Public welfare programmes like Swachh Bharat Mission (SBM), which aims to make India open-defecation free and has constructed over 110 million latrines across the country,[78] and Jal Jeevan Mission (JJM), which has increased the number of rural homes with tap water supply from 32 million (17 per cent) in 2019 to over 100 million (52 per cent) as of August 2022, are successful examples. Alongside programmes like Pradhan Mantri Ujjwala Yojana (PMUY) which provides clean cooking fuel to rural households to prevent them from having to burn wood, thus reducing exposure to toxic fumes when cooking meals, large-scale public welfare with significant positive externalities has a multiplier effect on health as well as economic growth. SBM, JJM and PMUY have reduced the number of hours per day that are expended on fulfilling some of the most basic human needs, thus creating mind space and bandwidth[79] among the rural poor so that they think beyond day-to-day sustenance.

Healthcare policy in all countries is one of the most complex fields of public policy. There are difficult trade-offs, and the solutions very much depend on the national or even regional context. For example, end-of-life healthcare anywhere tends to be very expensive[80] whereas saving children can be relatively inexpensive and, in terms of expected life years saved, much more rewarding.

Prioritization of tax resources designated for healthcare can be morally complicated everywhere—remember former vice-presidential candidate of the United States, Sarah Palin's barb about 'death panels' when it came to 'Obamacare' in the United States healthcare expansion. In an emerging economy, however, it is even more critical to get it right.

According to India's latest National Health Policy document released in 2017 there is a need to look at

> solutions holistically with [the] private sector as strategic partners. It seeks to promote quality of care; focus is on emerging diseases . . . It addresses health security and 'Make in India' for drugs and devices. The main objective . . . is to achieve the highest possible level of good health and well-being, through a preventive and promotive health care orientation in all developmental policies, and to achieve universal access to good quality health care services without anyone having to face financial hardship as a consequence.

As of now, this is very much work-in-progress. In India's smaller towns, one can see general physicians, dentists, vets and others operating from makeshift clinics near the main markets. Often, there is no clinic; there are just a few chairs for the doctor and his clients from the town and nearby villages. Often, there is no doctor either at least officially—many such service providers have no formal medical training.[81] Yet, without them many a tooth cavity and stomach ache would go untreated.

Central and state government spending on health programmes stands at about 1.2 per cent of our GDP and is just a small fraction of the total healthcare spending.[82] Since India's average per capita monthly income for 2019–20 was around Rs 12,500 (the median income is significantly lower), it is not possible to run high-quality hospitals with well-qualified doctors who provide free or highly subsidized services in all of India's villages and towns. The State should stop trying to force qualified doctors to perform compulsory rural service and instead encourage medical colleges to start shorter training programmes to equip practitioners in providing basic care. This concept has been largely accepted by the Modi government when the medical regulation regime was overhauled, with the new National Medical Commission being set up.[83]

A lot more needs to be done. India's global Human Development Index rank is 129th.[84] But there are some positives too—diseases like tuberculosis, smallpox, leprosy and polio have either been eliminated or significantly controlled. The sex ratio has stopped falling. The infant mortality rate has been almost halved to 33 in 2017 from 57 per 1000 live births in 2006.[85] Similarly, the median under-five mortality rate per 1000 live births in India was 37 in 2018 (compared to 71 in 2006[86]) while the figure is around 120 for Nigeria, 69 for Pakistan and just 9 in China. Also, life expectancy in India has gone up to sixty-nine years in 2019.[87]

The broader question is: does India need an entitlements-based centralized welfare state whose roll-out the UPA government started accelerating in 2004? The question is a complex one, with both normative and positive aspects, because there is a lot of confusion between 'how much help' and 'how to help'. The latter is more of a policy question, whereas the former is a political one.

What gives some hope is that many policy debates often presuppose a wider normative disagreement than what truly exists. Many on the so-called Right are not Uncle Scrooges when it comes to tax rupees and often have more efficient ideas on how to spend public money. For example, laws passed to guarantee employment, education and food access are often debated especially with respect to aspects that promote corruption and inefficiency. Market proponents tend to focus on cash transfers, school vouchers and food stamps instead. India does not have enough well-designed public private partnership (PPP) models in our developing welfare State though that is evolving rapidly, partially thanks to the JAM (Jan Dhan–Aadhaar–Mobile) foundation.

Consider the Ayushman Bharat Yojana. It builds on the success of the Rashtriya Swasthya Bima Yojana (RSBY) which reached millions of Indians who were below the poverty line (BPL) through family smart cards. RSBY provided coverage up to a certain amount—the premiums were mostly funded by the Centre. Insurers were chosen based on competitive bidding, and they collected premiums from the government and refunded the hospitals as needed. Both public and private organizations were involved, and information technology was used extensively.

RSBY has evolved into NHPS (National Health Protection Scheme) which, together with prevention-focused wellness centres, constitutes the Pradhan Mantri Jan Arogya Yojana (PMJAY), also known as Ayushman Bharat. Coverage has expanded and most treatments are covered except those included in the negative list. According to government data, as of June 2020, over 22,000 hospitals across India were part of PMJAY, with 6.3 million claims amounting to more than Rs 73 billion paid out.[88] Ayushman Bharat relies more on cooperative federalism, and notably three states (Odisha, West Bengal and Telangana) are yet to be onboarded.

To further augment healthcare based on government subsidies but still through viable market incentives, it would be useful to learn from the Singaporean example of medical or health savings accounts (HSAs). California, since 1993, and some other regions of the United States since 2003 have also had a similar concept, even though the ongoing debates may eventually supersede them. Even China has been thinking along similar lines.[89]

HSAs often give steep tax benefits as well as direct government subsidies to individuals and families which in turn helps them buy catastrophic insurance so that regular care has relatively high deductibles and co-payments with genuine emergencies almost fully covered. This aligns incentives and reduces waste.

Given India's State-dominated health insurance system, there is not much incentive for the average citizen to compare different insurers as of now and Ayushman Bharat's design needs to go through further iterations. India should incorporate HSA-type ideas to save taxpayer rupees without sacrificing healthcare quality. In addition, all hospital pricing should be negotiated strictly between the hospitals and the insurers. Recent moves to fix prices for certain procedures and instruments by the government could be considered a retrograde move which can increase inefficiency.

There will always be a component of direct government spending on primary healthcare, immunization and sanitation—as they have significant positive externalities. But when it comes to personal healthcare services, India should unabashedly combine private competition with targeted public subsidies. India must not repeat other countries' mistakes of creating too many open-ended commitments. A demographic boom does not last forever, whereas entitlements will have a long life.

The experience of the COVID-19 pandemic has also shown that novel health challenges will require flexible approaches and mindsets. Countries that were successful in containing the spread of the virus did so by harnessing information technology for identifying and tracking individuals.[90] Governments will need to develop rules and safeguards on appropriate use of such contact tracing during times of epidemics and other health emergencies. State capacity or legibility, to invoke James C. Scott's concept again, is critical for public health too.

Refocusing government

Most Indians, irrespective of political or economic ideology, would support some combination of spending more on social welfare and cutting taxes, instead of funding government-owned white elephants in the business world, especially in industries where several businesses already provide better products and services compared to public sector unit (PSU) providers. The only long-term, fiscally sustainable solution is for the government to reduce its shareholding in these companies and transfer management control to the private sector.

The State will perform best when it restricts itself to roles and responsibilities that cannot or should not be carried out by the private sector. These areas include the domains of internal security, national defence, justice delivery, market regulation and facilitation as well as welfare in those specific domains where markets do not work very well. Keeping this sharp focus entails that the government should extricate itself from business by privatizing PSUs, and India's decision to segregate sectors into two categories of strategic and non-strategic, with non-strategic sector PSUs committed for privatization, should be seen in that light.[91]

But privatizing always must be done in a certain political economy and global macro context, and there is an element of luck regarding market timing. In 2001, Prime Minister Vajpayee went to the extent of shifting coalition partner Janata Dal (United) chief Sharad Yadav out of the civil aviation ministry because he was against privatization.[92] The Vajpayee government came close to divesting Air India to a Tata–Singapore Airlines joint venture but the transaction was shelved due to a global economic slowdown. As Prime Minister Modi said in an interview to *Swarajya* magazine,[93] 'We don't want to make a sale where we will be accused of selling something for X amount when we could have got more.' Moreover, if the government has to promise PSU staff generous voluntary retirement schemes (VRS), the chances of extensive privatization look uncertain until the economy starts growing much faster.

The Modi government also took up the task of privatizing Air India, finally succeeding in 2021 when the Tata Group acquired the airline. When announcing the transaction, the government noted that Air India had incinerated Rs 1.1 trillion of public money since 2009.[94] Where Union government-owned PSUs receive some scrutiny—and there is a consensus emerging on the need to privatize companies in non-strategic sectors—there is barely any discussion on the colossal wastage by state government–owned PSUs. In a 2019 article, the columnist and author Shankkar Aiyar laid out the unconscionable state of affairs in the states, citing data for 2016–17:[95]

India's states own 1,309 public sector enterprises of which 989 are deemed working. The data reveals a horrifying story. Analysis of data on 19 states shows there isn't a single state where the profits earned by PSUs are more than the losses registered. The quantum of losses incurred by states' public enterprises was Rs 97,078.61 crore—which is nearly three times that of central PSUs—and the profits earned were Rs 17,537.38 crore. Translated, the state enterprises were losing five rupees against every rupee they earned as profit. Net of profits, the state PSUs lost Rs 79,541 crore or roughly Rs 218 crore per day—that is more than what the central government will spend this year on providing income support to farmers or what it has allocated for rural employment under the National Rural Employment Guarantee Scheme.

Aiyar noted that 'outstanding loans of the entities is nearly Rs 7.5 lakh crore and state governments were sitting on losses of Rs 3.81 lakh crore accumulated by the public enterprises'. State after state, across the length and breadth of India, continues to indulge in this bacchanalia of capital destruction, and yet there is no outcry for course correction. The deficit in policing capacity seen across states described earlier should be seen in the light of these figures, where states are frittering away precious resources on running companies while failing to deliver necessary public goods.

Inefficiency has been an inalienable feature of governance for decades, and not just in PSUs. Many sectors have multiple ministries— until the creation of the jal shakti ministry in May 2019, water-related ministries included the ministry of drinking water and sanitation and ministry of water resources, river development and Ganga rejuvenation. A steel business, for example, is connected to at least three ministries—steel, coal and mining. Similarly, transportation has four ministries—civil aviation, railways, road transport and highways and shipping. Also, the agriculture, food processing and consumer affairs ministries oversee India's food sector. Why should it then be surprising that forging a consensus on policy matters proves to be difficult and contentious?

The truth is that almost half of India's ministries could vanish tomorrow and nobody would really miss them.[96] Honest entrepreneurs would be delighted with the State having fewer discretionary powers, and India would have an economy with faster growth. The only people adversely affected in the long run would be crony socialists and their intermediaries.

It is worth understanding why India has scores of Union ministers. In any polity, especially in a large and diverse one like ours, there will be many power centres. In democracies, powerful politicians need to be accommodated in various institutions.

For example, an American senator who is a member or chair of an important Senate committee almost has as much influence in global capitals as the secretary of state, because elected representatives in the United States can take on the executive. But in a democracy, such as India, where power can be concentrated in the Union government's cabinet, such arrangements are difficult. Ministries have to be literally invented to accommodate leaders and, when required, coalition partners. This situation also arises as India's polity is restricted when it comes to internal democracy.

Embracing leaner government is necessary to make governance more efficient. For ministries to be downsized, political incentives need to be realigned through structural reforms such as abolishing the anti-defection law,[97] which would make elected representatives more answerable to their constituencies and important leaders could be 'accommodated' in parliamentary committees.

The concurrent list must be abolished with many of the responsibilities devolved to states. Expanded through the 42nd amendment to the Constitution during Indira Gandhi's dictatorship, the concurrent list has created a thicket of jurisdictional issues. Indeed in 2018, Telangana Chief Minister K. Chandrashekar Rao had called for the concurrent list to be abolished.[98] Where important areas such as law and order are on the state list, policing requires more funding and attention. This is where state governments need to shift focus: rather than running up gargantuan losses in their PSUs, they should invest capital for public goods like policing and primary schooling. Downsizing ministries, creating transparent regulatory institutions and privatizing public sector enterprises—both at the Union government level and in the states—would also go a long way towards facilitating a level playing field for first-generation entrepreneurs. These reforms concern the efficiency of the executive branch.

Equally critical is capacity creation in the judicial branch.[99] In 2019, over 30 million cases were pending in district and subordinate courts, 4.3 million in high courts, and nearly 60,000 in the Supreme

Court.[100] The pandemic exacerbated the backlog and by May 2022, over 47 million cases were pending in courts at different levels across the country, of which 87.4 per cent were in lower courts and 12.4 per cent were in higher courts. The waste and sloth impose a severe human cost—as of September 2022, 76 per cent of India's prisoners (the global average is 34 per cent), totalling 3,71,848 persons, were in pre-trial detention, spending time incarcerated while awaiting trial. A fourth of these undertrials had stayed in jail for at least one year.[101] According to a January 2019 report by the Centre for Budget and Governance Accountability, the total spending on judiciary and justice delivery amounts to less than 0.40 per cent of the aggregate gross budgetary expenditure of the Union and state governments.[102]

An overhaul of the supporting staff and human resources, digital infrastructure as well as physical infrastructure of the court system would help raise the productivity[103] of courts.[104] The 13th Finance Commission (2010–2015) provided a special grant of Rs 5000 crore for investment in judicial infrastructure, but 80 per cent of the sum went unspent.[105] Given the capacity bottleneck, it is hardly a surprise that a gargantuan number of cases are pending. Justice delivery is delayed, and the rule of law is not enforced. This protraction in law enforcement from judiciary has resulted in what entrepreneur and writer Manish Sabharwal has described[106] as a 'sense of humour about the rule of law'.

Apart from filling up the vacancies, there is a clear need to ramp up the sanctioned strength as well. As of February 2020, against a sanctioned strength of 1079 judgeships for twenty-five high courts across the country, 396 posts were vacant.[107] The Supreme Court of India has increased the number of judges from twenty-five in 1986 to thirty-four in September 2019.[108] Thousands of judgeships lie vacant in subordinate courts, and hundreds of positions are unfilled in the high courts.[109] Former Chief Justice of India T.S. Thakur had said during his tenure that India needs 70,000 more judges,[110] but by other estimates, India doesn't need that many judges at one go. To clear all the pending cases, perhaps a total of 25,000 judges would suffice, that is, an increase of around 8000 from present strength.[111]

The 2018–19 Economic Survey dealt extensively with the issue, even recommending the use of technology to raise productivity. A start was made during the COVID-19 pandemic and these institutional and process changes need to be sustained and deepened.[112] It is the need of the hour that all arms of the State—that is, the central executive, the legislature (including the Opposition) and the higher judiciary—sit together and move forward on building capacity. Moreover, it is not just about the number of judges but also how the valuable bandwidth of existing judges is used, especially in the lower judiciary. Judges in subordinate courts spend most of their time in administrative matters which shouldn't be their remit. According to a study, 'A subordinate court judge spends 45–55 percent of court time each day in calling out matters and adjourning them rather than on hearing evidence' because 'the institutional mechanism that supports the judge is not geared up to assist him in managing his time in court better.'[113]

Such a comprehensive restructuring of the judicial arm of the Indian State is a colossal task. A beginning must be made now itself, given the grim prognosis on justice delivery and contract enforcement. Despite rapidly improving its overall ranking in the World Bank's 2020 Ease of Doing Business study to 63rd out of 190 countries, on contract enforcement India is at an abysmal 163rd position.[114] This pathetic performance extracts a very heavy cost and hobbles Indian manufacturing enterprises. In their 2020 paper 'Misallocation in the Market for Inputs: Enforcement and the Organization of Production',[115] Johannes Boehm and Ezra Oberfield showed that

> firms tilt their input basket toward the use of more standardized inputs, for which spot markets exist, and for which enforcement by courts is not necessary . . . distortions associated with poor courts are sizable and that improving courts would increase welfare: reducing the average age of pending cases by a year would, on average, increase a state's aggregate productivity by about 2 per cent.

These frictions, along with the byzantine compliance requirements imposed on enterprises—especially those in manufacturing—

contribute to a litigious culture and pummel India's economic potential. In a landmark study on the criminalization of business lapses, Gautam Chikermane and Rishi Agarwal noted:[116]

> . . . the criminalization of business laws violates Indian business traditions: from the *Mahabharata* to the *Arthashastra*, criminality was never a part of punitive action against businesses in ancient India— only financial penalties were. Reforming these clauses is necessary to restore dignity to entrepreneurship in India.

The litigiousness of the State itself is a major issue—according to an official government estimate, government departments, autonomous bodies, regulatory authorities and PSUs are party to nearly half of all court cases, and thus the State and its entities are themselves the biggest litigants in the country.[117] One of the critical investments that the Indian State needs to make is in lower and middle judiciary, not necessarily the higher judiciary, which usually gets media attention. Reforms in the recruitment of public prosecutors are required, and such prosecutors need to be afforded leeway to operate freely from external influences.[118] Another principal issue is the low compensation offered to judges.[119] Moreover, there is a two-speed judicial system in the country—one in the higher echelons and one at the entry level. A small section of the judicial elite controls higher court appointments, and the perks and benefits of becoming a judge come only with those appointments.

The balance of power that must be maintained between the executive, legislature and judiciary has been disturbed with the scales tilted in favour of courts. The activist encroachment of judiciary into policymaking needs to be dialled back.

Who judges the judges?

Justice Jasti Chelameswar, the sole dissenting voice in a decision by the Supreme Court of India which struck down the National Judicial Appointments Commission (NJAC) in 2015 with a 4–1 majority, said in his dissenting opinion:[120]

We the members of the judiciary exult and frolic in our emancipation from the other two organs of the State. But have we developed an alternate constitutional morality to emancipate us from the theory of checks and balances, robust enough to keep us in control from abusing such independence? Have we acquired independence greater than our intelligence, maturity and nature could digest? Have we really outgrown the malady of dependence or merely transferred it from the political to judicial hierarchy?

Passed by both houses of the Parliament, ratified by sixteen state legislatures and finally assented to by the President of India,[121] this historic bipartisan, herculean effort was undone by the five-judge bench which termed the 99th Constitutional Amendment establishing NJAC as unconstitutional.[122]

Why? Because, in their exalted opinion, it would have eroded the independence of the judiciary, which is a part of the 'basic structure'—a unique innovation introduced by India's highest court that seeks to cast arbitrarily selected features of India's Constitution in stone, such that they cannot be amended by Parliament.

There was no attempt to recommend or to suggest to Parliament on how to come up with a better framework for the creation of the NJAC. Instead it was rejected in toto, clearly sending a message that 'independence' of judiciary could only be maintained as long as the power to appoint judges vested with the judiciary. It is notable that India is unique among democracies in this respect, where judges effectively appoint themselves. For example, in the United States, Supreme Court justices are appointed by the President and confirmed by the Senate.

Justice Chelameswar was right in stating:

The assumption that primacy of the Judicial Branch in the appointments process is an essential element and thus a basic feature is empirically flawed without any basis either in the constitutional history of the nation or any other and normatively fallacious apart from being contrary to political theory.

Among the principal beneficiaries of the basic structure doctrine are those who sit at the very top of the hierarchy in India's judicial system. The Supreme Court has gifted to itself the so-called collegium system in which the topmost judges themselves appoint their colleagues to serve in constitutional courts. In November 2019, a nine-judge bench of the Supreme Court declined to undo two rulings that created the collegium system, whereby the five senior-most judges determine appointments and elected representatives in the executive or legislative branch of the government can do little about who is appointed as a judge.[123]

The founders of the Indian republic treaded a unique path while devising a mechanism for the appointment of judges. Article 124 of the Constitution stated:

> Every Judge of the Supreme Court shall be appointed by the President by warrant under his hand and seal after consultation with such of the Judges of the Supreme Court and of the High Courts in the States as the President may deem necessary for the purpose and shall hold office until he attains the age of sixty five years: Provided that in the case of appointment of a Judge other than the Chief Justice, the Chief Justice of India shall always be consulted.

Two things are clear from reading Article 124—it is the President who shall appoint judges. He or she shall do so after consulting with such judges as deemed necessary. For appointment of judges other than the Chief Justice of India (CJI), the CJI shall always be consulted.

The eminent judges wielding the basic-structure doctrine have turned this arrangement on its head. In a series of back-to-back cases (collectively called the Three Judges Cases, namely, *S.P. Gupta v. Union of India* of 1981, *Supreme Court Advocates-on-Record Association v. Union of India* of 1993 and *In Re: Under Article 143(1) of the . . . v. Unknown* of 1998—the last was not a case per se but an opinion delivered responding to a question raised by the then President of India), the apex court came up with a completely new creature, the collegium system, after it ruled that neither the executive nor the legislature can have a say in the appointment of judges. This specific understanding of the independence of judiciary, which in the opinion of the honourable judges was a part of the basic structure of the Constitution—a deliberately ambiguous and anti-democratic construct—was to be kept intact.

Under this new system, the CJI and four senior judges, who together form the collegium, recommend names for appointments and transfer of judges, to the government on whose advice the President gives approval. The government can send the recommendation back for reconsideration of the collegium only once. If rejected by the collegium, it will be binding on the President to give his assent.

So, what was initially the primary prerogative of the executive has been taken over by the judiciary. The President was supposed to only consult the senior-most judges in making the appointments. Now, the President and the executive, and by extension the people's representatives, have been relegated to just a rubber stamp, doing the bidding of the five senior-most judges. It is important to add that judicial appointments made by the legislature can be required to be done in a bipartisan manner, so the fear of packing the courts with 'committed' judges[124] is unfounded.

Ambedkar would have been shocked to see how Article 124 has been mangled. Explaining the scheme of judicial appointments in 1949, he had said:

> With regard to the question of the concurrence of the Chief Justice, it seems to me that those who advocate that proposition seem to rely implicitly both on the impartiality of the Chief Justice and the soundness of his judgment. I personally feel no doubt that the Chief Justice is a very eminent person. But after all the Chief Justice is a man with all the failings, all the sentiments and all the prejudices which we as common people have; and I think, to allow the Chief Justice practically a veto upon the appointment of Judges is really to transfer the authority to the Chief Justice which we are not prepared to vest in the President or the Government of the day. I therefore, think that that is also a dangerous proposition.[125]

In another interpretive leap, the role of appointment itself was usurped in a most bizarre manner. In its pursuit to protect one basic feature of the Constitution (viz. the independence of the judiciary), the Court defenestrated the other basic feature (separation of powers).

The collegium system in judicial appointments has given rise to nepotistic tendencies in the judiciary which the Constitution makers would never have fathomed—the rot is so deep that it competes with the scourge of dynastic politics, but while the latter has been widely critiqued and nonetheless has to pass frequent electoral tests, the lack of public knowledge about the extent of dynastic sway in the legal world has saved the judicial establishment from scrutiny.

Out of thirty-three names sent for appointment in 2018 by the Allahabad High Court Collegium, one-third were found to be related to sitting or retired judges.[126] In 2016, the country's largest high court faced a similar embarrassment when the then CJI T.S. Thakur had to reject eleven out of thirty names.[127] Consider the case of other chief justices. Ranjan Gogoi is the son of former Assam Chief Minister and Congress leader K.C. Gogoi. Dipak Misra is the nephew of former CJI Ranganath Misra. T.S. Thakur himself is the son of former J&K High Court judge and former Assam Governor D.D. Thakur. R.M. Lodha's father Justice Srikrishna Mal Lodha was a Rajasthan High Court judge, as was his uncle Chand Mal Lodha who was the chief justice of Rajasthan High Court and also served in the Guwahati High Court. Another uncle, Guman Mal Lodha, was the chief justice of Guwahati High Court.

Former CJI Altamas Kabir's father Jehangir Kabir was a leading Congress politician and minister in the West Bengal state government. His sister Shukla Kabir Sinha was elevated to the Calcutta High Court when Justice Kabir was in the Supreme Court.[128] Justice S.A. Bobde, who succeeded Ranjan Gogoi as CJI, is the son of former Attorney General of Maharashtra Arvind Bobde. Justice U.U. Lalit is the son of former Delhi Court judge U.R. Lalit. Justice D.Y. Chandrachud, who is serving as India's CJI from 2022 to 2024, is the son of former CJI Y.V. Chandrachud. And it goes on. In September 2016, *Outlook* magazine reported that out of twenty-eight sitting Supreme Court judges, eleven 'had either judges or legal luminaries as relatives'.[129]

This type of culture extends further, with family relations of sitting judges practising law as advocates and counsels in the same courts. A 2014 news report stated that over a third of the judges of Punjab and Haryana High Court had their kith and kin practising law in the same institution.[130] This entrenchment of apparent nepotism in the constitutional courts can sound the death knell of competence and integrity. We needn't look further than the kind of Public Interest Litigations (PILs) that the courts have entertained in the past few years—banning certain jokes[131] for ostensibly hurting religious sentiments, bringing back the Kohinoor diamond from the United Kingdom,[132] checking if condom packaging was in contravention of obscenity laws[133] and so on.

Next, consider the blatant and brazen violation of the principle of separation of powers—a basic feature of the Constitution according to the Supreme Court's own admission, except this principle is repeatedly pulverized at the whims and fancies of the judiciary.

Arbitrary judgments on PILs as well as other cases before the higher courts have caused severe economic damage. The Supreme Court has been pronouncing on, and deciding how, a private sports body like the Board of Control for Cricket in India should be run. In 2016, the Bombay High Court ordered all Indian Premier League matches to be shifted out of Maharashtra because of drought in Latur.[134] In the same year, the Supreme Court ordered a ban on sale of liquor within 500 metres of national highways,[135] disrupting the lodging and restaurant industries overnight. In 2018, the Uttarakhand High Court banned river rafting, paragliding, and other sports activities[136] which hit the livelihoods of thousands of people working in the tourism industry in that state. Such arbitrary decisions increase economic uncertainty and amplify the perception of policy instability in India, putting off global investors and entrepreneurs. In 2013, the Supreme Court halted all pharmaceutical clinical trials in India, and overnight 162 such drug trials that were going on in the country were jeopardized.[137]

Commenting in 2019 on the impact of arbitrariness of judicial pronouncements, one of India's most respected jurists, Harish Salve, said that it is the Supreme Court that should be squarely blamed for the economic slowdown, given the havoc created by the Court's decisions in a number of cases where entire sectors were singed and where foreign investors were scarred by how random doing business in India could be.[138] Notably, of the 1293 judgments delivered by the Supreme Court in 2019, just 3.3 per cent dealt with the Constitution.[139]

The violation of separation of powers and constant encroachment into the domain of the executive and legislature is often justified by proponents of judicial activism on the grounds that the judiciary is forced to pass orders in areas outside its purview because the government or the legislature is not doing its job. This is a specious argument. As the late statesman, jurist and politician Arun Jaitley said in a speech at the 2017 National Law Day function:

> If any organ of the state is not doing its duty, it can be directed to do its duty. Usurpation of power . . . by any other organ would never be the correct constitutional approach. What if the same argument was used the other way round against the judiciary? Arrears were pending, judges are not doing their job. So must somebody step in and now exercise that power? The answer is no . . . And therefore, it's extremely important that the dividing line on separation of powers is maintained. And therefore, by creating arguments, the thin dividing line itself cannot be lost.[140]

When in 2016 the Supreme Court ordered the government to create a National Disaster Mitigation Fund, even the usually unflappable Jaitley lost his temper. In Parliament, he took the Court to task and said that, 'Step by step, brick by brick, the edifice of India's legislature is being destroyed,' lamenting that 'India's budget-making is being subject to judicial review.'[141] Harish Salve, too, had taken issue with judicial activism in May 2020[142] saying that 'unelected people think they can impose their will on government through courts.'

Then there is the grave matter of the Indian judiciary not evolving any first principles to base judgements on. No one knows which way it will swing on a given day. When there are no judicial principles, or any regard for precedents, and cases are decided on the fly, it is no wonder then that there is an influential cabal of senior advocates, many of whom are former or current politicians.

Of course, judicial review is one of their most important prerogatives of the higher judiciary, but when courts start making about-turns more frequently than politicians, it's time for some serious introspection. For instance, the Supreme Court modified its own 2016 order on banning liquor sale near highways within few months of pronouncing the orders. While the reversal is welcome, what remains unconvincing is the rationale for both the earlier and later decisions.

Similarly, the apex court passed an order in 2016 making singing of national anthem mandatory before the screening of movies in cinema halls. Irrationally, the media painted this as a directive of the Narendra Modi government. The Court made a volte-face in 2018,[143] wondering, 'Should we wear patriotism on our sleeves?'[144] Why didn't this revelation dawn on the Court earlier, prior to passing the order?

In 2009, the Delhi High Court ruled Section 377 of the Indian Penal Code which criminalized homosexual acts between consenting adults as unconstitutional. In 2013, the Supreme Court upheld Section 377. Five years later, the same court made an about-turn and waxed eloquent about the importance of sexual autonomy, with constitutional morality taking precedence over societal morality.[145] The interesting question is what exactly is 'constitutional morality' and how often does it change?

Moreover, the apex court has been adjudicating on religious matters in an arbitrary manner. Interfering in centuries-old traditions that are not otherwise harming any citizen has become a habit. While hearing and deciding on cases related to Dahi Handi, Jallikattu and Sabarimala temple, the judiciary has apparently given little thought to the diversity of traditions within Hindu Dharma.

Take the Sabarimala case.[146] Since the Supreme Court's judgment on 28 September 2018, overturning the bar on the entry of women aged 10–50 years into the 800-year-old Sabarimala temple in Kerala,[147] there has been a spirited debate on the issue of State interference in religious affairs.

Interestingly, those projecting the Sabarimala issue as one of gender justice and women's equality are quick to draw comparisons with ending the practice of triple talaq. There is an argument that permitting the entry of women into Sabarimala is not only about ensuring women's rights, but should also be seen in the context of the so-called innately discriminatory attributes within Hinduism—if the entry of women is to be barred, will banning individuals from lower-caste groups from worshipping at Hindu temples also be accepted?

Both these arguments are specious. The Sabarimala issue is not about caste or gender justice. The Sabarimala temple has a well-defined raison d'être—the Ayyappa deity here is worshipped as one who has renounced the world and is celibate. The richness of the Hindu tradition is that there are other Ayyappa temples across southern India where the deity is worshipped in different forms and through varying methods. At the Kulathupuzha temple, Ayyappa appears as a child. At the Achankovil temple, Ayyappa is worshipped as one who participates in family life.

This is not different from how Ravana is worshipped in some parts of India,[148] even as his likeness is set on fire on Vijayadashami all across the country. The key fact is that no centralized and institutionalized gender or caste discrimination is being corrected by the Court's diktat on allowing a certain age group of women to pray at the temple.

Just as Sabarimala temple bans the entry of women of a certain age group, there are prominent Hindu temples that do not permit the entry of certain men or women based on age and marital status. For example, the Kamrup Kamakhya temple in Assam disallows men from worshipping on specified days, and celebrates the power of the female form for creation and conception of life.[149] The 600-year-old Brahma temple in Pushkar, Rajasthan does not permit married men to worship the deity.[150]

The Supreme Court, in its wisdom, overturned the 1991 judgment of the Kerala High Court that upheld the customs of the Sabarimala temple. The Supreme Court judgment itself is discriminatory in that it does not seek to provide equality to all women irrespective of religion—non-Hindu women can still be barred from entering their places of worship and Hindu women who may be barred from entering other Hindu temples are also not affected by the apex court's judgment.

The Court has picked on a particular temple and provided for a specific judgment that only applies to that temple, rather than pronounce that equality in worship applies to all religions and regions, and that women (or men) cannot be discriminated against by anybody in the matter of access to a place of worship. If they did that as an interpretation of the Constitution's right to equality, that would be a different argument altogether but a more consistent one. But is it justice to say, as the Court has done, let another PIL be filed and only then the honourable Court would decide on other issues?[151]

An even more problematic issue is with India's judges anointing onto themselves spiritual–theological exegesis powers in their drive to determine what is 'essential religious practice'. The genesis of this unfortunate situation emerges from shying away from stating that there is a basic minimum standard of human rights and constitutional guarantees available to each and every Indian, irrespective of any ascriptive identity.

Unable to raise itself to the level where it can proclaim that a given set of liberties is inviolable, no matter what any religion or group asserts, Indian jurisprudence has taken refuge in selectively picking on the Hindu faith under the Nehruvian rubric of protection to minorities. Ironically, this has often, but not always, been to the advantage of Hindus, where State power has pushed them towards more reform.

The absurdities created by these selective actions can manifest in ugly ways—when the Lok Sabha moved a bill removing leprosy as a ground for divorce in January 2019,[152] All India Majlis-e-Ittehadul Muslimeen (AIMIM) MP Asaduddin Owaisi opposed it, saying, 'Don't interfere in Muslim personal law,' holding up the example of the Islamic republics of Pakistan and Bangladesh, which still allow divorce on this discriminatory ground.[153] Owaisi echoed Nehru's position, who also wanted to protect Muslims and declined to reform Muslim personal laws in 1955 when Hindu laws were reformed, for that would have been 'interference'.

But leaving minorities out in the cold in the name of protecting them only widens the fissures in Indian society, where one section of the population experiences liberal State policy—such as freedom to divorce with mutual consent—but a large minority is subjected to ultraconservative religious laws that are provided State backing in the name of protection.

There is a fundamental difference between monotheistic, centralized Abrahamic faiths and the polytheistic, pantheistic, 'pagan' Hindu ways. When individuals decided to build temples for living figures such as Amitabh Bachchan, Rajinikanth and Sachin Tendulkar, no 'Hindu authority' could stop them. Hinduism has no barriers to entry. There is no codified directive to the Hindu on how to worship, where to worship, when to worship or even whether to worship. An attempt to homogenize Hindus using State power erodes the diversity of Hinduism and only semitizes it. Such attempts stem from the impulse of the judiciary to rule on what is 'essential religious practice'.

Article 25 of the Indian Constitution guarantees all citizens the right to practise any religion of their choice. Just like the other fundamental rights, there are limitations on the freedom to practise one's religion. The right is subject to public order, morality and health, and the power of the State to take measures for social welfare and reform. This coupled with the 'essential religious practice' idea is a recipe for sociopolitical tension. Proving that a religious practice is essential is much easier for adherents of the Abrahamic faiths who follow particular books.

The Supreme Court, which ruled 4–1 in the Sabarimala case, refused to designate Lord Ayyappa's devotees as a 'religious denomination'—another onerous task the judiciary has taken upon itself to adjudicate on without the competency or knowledge to do so. It reasoned that since people of other faiths also visit the temple, it cannot be called a separate denomination. Imagine the incentives at play—if temples admit people from other faiths, they risk losing their independence. Does this really further pluralism and national integration?

Moreover, the higher judiciary is quite proactive in intervening in Hindu traditions whether it is setting the maximum height of pyramids for Dahi Handi or a ban on Jallikattu on the premise of safety or animal cruelty. But when it comes to reforming other religions, the judiciary has a history of backing out. When a PIL was filed to ban the practice of butchering animals as a form of religious practice or at the very least employ trained butchers so as to cause the animals the least pain and trauma, the Supreme Court said: 'This Court has to balance between the law and religious practices. This is a sensitive matter better dealt by the representatives of the people in the appropriate forums. We cannot shut our eyes to centuries-old traditions.'[154]

Such arbitrary interpretation of the law not only breeds resentment but also calls into question the basis on which judgments are being delivered. What made the Supreme Court interfere in the centuries-old tradition of Jallikattu when in the case of another faith, similar interventions were none of its business?

On the double standards and singling out of Hinduism for judicial intervention and the danger this poses to freedom of religion, the writer Arihant Pawariya observed:

> Unlike a certain book with well laid out rules in Abrahamic religions, rituals form the core of Hinduism. It will wither away without them. But the Supreme Court has no time or inclination to understand the nuances attached to these traditions. What is outright dangerous is its interpretation of these customs from the Abrahamic point of view. What the judiciary is trying to do is define (or shrink?) the boundaries of Hinduism by striking down one ritual after another citing that this or that practice is not essential.[155]

While hearing the Jallikattu ban review petition, the court asked, 'What is the necessity of such a festival like Jallikattu? There was no festival for four years.'[156] Is this even an argument? India didn't have freedom until 1947. Should we give that up too? Moreover, can not a religion evolve and devise new practices and customs with time? Not only do the Court's verdicts spell doom for any internal innovation, they would force the religious institutions to be static and orthodox.

All these issues can be addressed readily. The beginning has to be made by revisiting the basic-structure doctrine which says that even parliamentary and legislative supermajorities cannot change an ever expanding and ambiguous list of tenets. The basic structure doctrine wasn't provided in the original Constitution nor spoken of in the Constituent Assembly debates. Where was this basic structure when fundamental liberties were destroyed in the period leading up the Indira Gandhi's dictatorial Emergency? This doctrine couldn't stop the Emergency when all the fundamental rights were being trampled upon.

As the Supreme Court advocate and legal scholar Aankhi Ghosh wrote:[157]

> The Basic Structure doctrine has, in effect, not upheld the supremacy of the Constitution. What it has upheld in effect, is the supremacy of the judiciary and that has evidenced itself in various judgments in the following years. The Court has repeatedly ballooned the contours of the Basic Structure using the certificate of authority given to it by *Kesavananda Bharati,* and in the process, imposed upon the people of India its own morality and ideology from time to time.

In fact, the words 'secular' and 'socialist' inserted in the Preamble of the Constitution during the dictatorial Emergency have also been accepted by the judiciary as new features of the basic structure! This when Dr B. R. Ambedkar had specifically shot down attempts to add these words:

> What should be the policy of the State, how the Society should be organized in its social and economic side are matters which must be decided by the people themselves according to time and circumstances.' He had said, 'If you state in the Constitution that the social organization of the State shall take a particular form, you are . . . taking away the liberty of the people to decide what should be the social organisation in which they wish to live.[158]

Eminent jurist Nani Palkhivala critiqued the insertions of these words into the Preamble as 'singularly ill-conceived'. 'The Preamble sets out . . . what the people of India resolved in 1949 to do for their unfolding future. No parliament can amend or alter the historical past,' he lamented.[159]

None other than H.M. Seervai, regarded as the foremost jurist on Indian constitutional law, described the method by which the Preamble was amended by Indira Gandhi as 'historically false'. He wrote thus in his magisterial *Constitutional Law of India*:

> . . . an amendment to the Preamble moved by Maulana Hasrat Mohani, namely 'We, the people of India having solemnly resolved to constitute India into a Union of Indian Socialist Republic to be called UISR on the lines of USSR' was rejected as inconsistent with our Constitution. Secondly, the word 'secular' is not precise and would itself require to be defined . . . Good drafting would require that ambiguous words should not be put into a Preamble without a reason and as far as one can see, there is no reason for putting in the word 'socialist' and 'secular', for the content of those concepts themselves would have to be found in the enacting parts of the Constitution and by themselves the two words have certain associations which are inconsistent with the enacting provisions of our Constitution.[160]

Given the importance of the judicial branch for society as well as business, expansive and comprehensive reforms are necessary on multiple fronts—first, to change the way appointments and promotions are carried out; second, to focus higher courts on issues of constitutional importance; third, to build capacity in the lower court system.

Saraswati, Lakshmi and Durga

Dr Raghunath Mashelkar, one of India's most renowned technologists, has frequently spoken about the importance of Saraswati (the goddess of knowledge) and Lakshmi (the goddess of wealth) coming together[161] for India's prosperity. As the director-general of CSIR, Mashelkar spearheaded a movement to 'patent, publish and prosper', so that India would be able to convert its knowledge into wealth, and emerge as a leader in science and technology.

The rise—and social acceptance—of technology entrepreneurship is a recent phenomenon, as described earlier in this book. Where there is knowledge and wealth, power is sure to follow—Saraswati and Lakshmi are joined by Durga, the goddess of war.

The great poet Ramdhari Singh Dinkar concludes his poem '*Shakti aur Kshama*' (Power and Forgiveness) with the following lines:

सहनशीलता, क्षमा, दया को
तभी पूजता जग है,
बल का दर्प चमकता उसके
पीछे जब जगमग है।

Tolerance, forgiveness, mercy are seen as virtues
Only in those, behind whom shines the light of strength

Dinkar says that the world respects the virtues of tolerance and mercy only when they are found in strong persons.[162] In the context of nations, power has multiple components—military power, economic power and sociocultural power. The latter is seen as a soft power, which is increasingly important but irrelevant without the first two. In recent decades, economic strength is becoming more important even within hard power.

Vijay Kelkar, chairman of the 13th Finance Commission and former finance secretary, had said in 2012 that a 10 per cent GDP growth rate was the best foreign policy for India. This erudite observation by the distinguished economist merits greater public debate.

In the early decades after Independence and during the Cold War, India styled itself as a 'non-aligned' nation. Non-alignment had its critics even at inception. As early as 1962, in response to Prime Minister Nehru's highfalutin rhetoric about the principles behind non-alignment, a 36-year-old Atal Bihari Vajpayee called non-alignment 'not a principle but a policy' in Parliament.[163] He said, 'Policies are made for the country, not the country for the policy . . . non-alignment is not a holy raiment; the day it no longer serves the national interest, it should be discarded as one would an old, torn garment . . . the nation comes first, policies later.'

Conventional military strength, despite its great importance, offers diminishing marginal returns. Possibilities of asymmetric power projections preclude any simplistic linear comparison of military resources. Offence is always more difficult than defence, but within offence the element of surprise can be crucial. In addition, morale and organizational structures can be very important.

This is especially true for those who have crossed the nuclear Rubicon. Besides, financial strength and armed prowess are linked—the proceeds of economic growth when invested in creating military technology can generate a mutually reinforcing cycle of innovation, productivity gains and capacity creation of hard power. With the creation of a chief of defence staff post and the restructuring of the ministry of defence by the government, India has finally taken the first step not only towards operational effectiveness[164] (better coordination between the navy, air and land forces through theatre commands). Such a step also facilitates defence indigenization[165] led by private industry, as a more holistic procurement view can now be undertaken. Between 2020 and 2022, India took a calibrated approach of winding down imports of several hundred defence products, subsystems and components[166]—items such as assault rifles, sniper rifles, light combat aircraft, mine-protected vehicles, rocket launchers, naval helicopters, artillery gun systems, anti-ship missiles—that would henceforth be sourced exclusively from Indian manufacturers. Indian defence manufacturers are not just substituting for arms and equipment imports—they are sprucing up foreign policy options by enabling the government to offer such arms and equipment to India's friends. Additionally, in June 2021, India took the step of corporatizing the British-era Ordnance Factory Boards (OFBs) into seven public sector units. As corporate entities, the public sector defence manufacturers would now have to operate with better standards and enhanced transparency—and now that they are corporatized, a public listing or even complete privatization of these companies is also possible in the future.

In today's world, direct military aggression has been increasingly supplemented by indirect economic aggression. New frontiers such as cyber and space warfare will become flashpoints as well. These frontiers alongside the emergence of unmanned aerial vehicles, especially low-cost drones, are transforming warfare. India was at the receiving end after the Pokhran nuclear tests in 1998, when it attracted the ire of the international community and economic sanctions were imposed. The national response was to accelerate economic reforms. The tests, along with faster growth, paved the way for the US–India nuclear deal a decade later that recognized India as a legitimate nuclear power.

In the aftermath of the Pokhran tests, Congress President Sonia Gandhi had said that 'real strength lies in restraint, not in the display of shakti'.[167] Amartya Sen asserted that 'moral resentment cannot justify a prudential blunder'.[168] Perhaps they forgot that Pakistan already had nuclear weapons, so the Vajpayee government's decision to go overtly nuclear did not result in India losing any conventional advantage, but signalled India's emergence as a 'great power', as persuasively argued by the doyen of strategic affairs K. Subrahmanyam.[169] As Prime Minister Modi's Balakot decision in 2019 to launch air strikes in Balakot demonstrated, India has a range of viable responses to Pakistani terrorism.

Harvard University cognitive psychologist Steven Pinker expounds in his book *The Better Angels of Our Nature* on how, relative to the past centuries, war and political violence have declined dramatically in the second half of the twentieth century, a phenomenon he characterizes as the 'New Peace'.[170] He suggests that the maturing of the idea of nation-states has contributed to bringing this about. Governments can step in to restore law and order when violence erupts. Religious, nationalist and racial hyper-chauvinism that caused many wars seem to have been tempered with a near-universal enunciation, if not full internalization, of basic human rights. The rise of global commerce, too, deserves credit for curbing wars. With nations being tied together economically, destructive military entanglement is not in anybody's interest.

It is true that some of these assumptions seem to buy into a teleology of the world moving towards a liberal order in a near-linear fashion—something brought into question by the unprecedented violence in the first half of the twentieth century despite a rise in trade and peace in the nineteenth century. The counter-strain to such Kantian optimism or 'liberal internationalism' has its roots in Kautilyan and Machiavellian pessimism, updated and packaged for modern times as the important framework of realism.

Realism says that nation-states are by far the most important actors in geopolitics, not supranational organizations or even global and local civil society actors. This description of foreign affairs is largely valid. But realism does not come with any specific prescriptions except the anodyne, indeed tautological, dictum of 'following the national interest'. The question then is, what is national interest?

A country prioritizing its interests presupposes a world view inherent in its decision making. This is where constructivism comes in—the third theory in modern foreign policy studies (after realism and liberal internationalism), and a theory that has completely different axioms from the other two. Instead of having a neo-Hegelian liberal view or a neo-Hobbesian realist view about the world, constructivism asks that one first specify one's preferences as well as time frames for the desired results and only then would a foreign policy answer emerge.

One version of a constructivist foreign policy would be the controversial but much misunderstood neo-conservative world view which gives a high priority to the interventionist promotion of so-called liberal values abroad. America's Iraq invasion has somewhat discredited this school of thought, yet many would agree today that America should have intervened to defeat Hitler even if Imperial Japan (which attacked Pearl Harbour) was not the ally of the Nationalist Socialist state of Germany. This evangelism of 'liberal values' once again gathered momentum in the aftermath of Russia's invasion of Ukraine in 2022. Wisely enough, India once again declined to join the Western bloc—as it had done during the mobilization against Iraq in 2002—and decisively 'took its own side' to quote External Affairs Minister S. Jaishankar.[171] India, in fact, ramped up purchases of discounted oil offered by Russia as the world experienced a severe energy price shock, and defended its position in doing so by stating that the Indian people are the government's first priority.[172]

So, while one should be opportunistic there must be some philosophical framework that guides decision-making in foreign policy and this framework should be part of a holistic larger vision that encompasses domestic policymaking as well—in India's case, that is a civilizational world view. Being just a realist, therefore, as is increasingly fashionable on the so-called Right wing of the political spectrum after the collapse of the Soviet Union, is akin to simply stating that India must become a rich and powerful nation, and doesn't answer the 'how' or 'what to do' when that influence is secured.

Independent India's foreign policy has focused on keeping the country united and physically secure, and also maintained a largely accommodating posture in international relations, though this has been evolving. There is a tendency to ignore the important and focus on just the urgent, and India sometimes seems to have no explicit grand strategy. Moreover, sometimes India's preferences have been influenced by internal political vote banks, not just when it comes to Sri Lanka and Israel, but in trade talks too. This partially negates the realist idea of nation-states as black boxes whose internal considerations do not influence foreign policy.

Foreign policy design, then, requires that we think about our priorities—how important are individual rights abroad? How important are India's civilizational and republican values? Should India have asked the Dalai Lama to take asylum somewhere else to keep better ties with undemocratic China? After all, the cold-blooded realist argument could be that given India has no direct territorial interest in Tibet, so why not exchange the Tibetan leader for some concessions? Should PSUs go on a mercantilist overdrive in Africa, Americas and Australia in a clear imitation of China?

Similarly, should arms imports be encouraged as a way of keeping relations warm with Russia and France? Empirical evidence suggests that domestically developed military technology has spinoff benefits and can be a feeder for civilian sector innovations,[173] but what about urgent import requirements? What about the middle ground of foreign investment in defence, where FDI limit has recently been raised to 74 per cent? These are some questions that require a discussion because the eventual strategy is dictated by the priorities that emerge from the fundamental belief system underlying that philosophy.

Economic size expands the scope for a nation's diplomacy and defence. In an age when full-fledged wars are becoming rare, economic strength also makes funds available for the deployment of strategic international aid to win friends and influence people. Trade can and is being used as a strategic instrument. Money talks a bit more, now that muscle walks a bit less.

Political leaders must understand the importance of higher sustainable economic growth rates not just for domestic prosperity but for international influence. The American economy is about seven times bigger than India's, and the Chinese economy is around five times larger. India needs higher sustained growth rates because that is what will strengthen the nation with Dinkar's shakti. Knowledge, wealth and power together will complete the *tridevi* of Saraswati, Lakshmi and Durga.

India's Moment

India's intellectual and political landscape, long the preserve of a powerful consociationalist- and socialist-leaning cartel, faces a singularity.[1] The collapse of the old dispensation—as evidenced by not just the ignominious defeat of the Congress party in 2014 and 2019 general elections but also the spectacular decimation of the doctrinaire communist parties—has only followed their intellectual implosion. Similarly, after the pandemic is over and clashes with China end for now, India's economy in 2021 could be at a unique inflection point with strong demographic, technological, policy and geopolitical tailwinds. But all this did not come easy.

The first proactively reformist (that is, driving reforms without the exigency of a crisis) government India had was the BJP-led NDA headed by Atal Bihari Vajpayee. On 28 April 1998, in his first speech to an industry chamber as Prime Minister, Vajpayee unequivocally said,[2] 'We must grow faster. We can grow faster. We simply have no other alternative.' He assured that his government would 'broaden, deepen and speed up' liberalization:

> I come from a political tradition that does not look upon commerce and industry with suspicion. When it was conventional political expediency to decry entrepreneurship, we championed their cause ... we aim to enable Indian entrepreneurs—small, medium or big—to create more wealth for themselves and for the nation ... Draw up big plans. When the big become bigger, the small and medium players would grow up to occupy their places.

Vajpayee reinforced his strong pro-market message by saying, 'Many industrialists want competition—but in other industries. In their own industry, they want protection.' Vajpayee was referring to the anti-liberalization mindset prevalent in industry with respect to domestic policy in particular, where incumbents—rusty from decades of command-and-control cronyism that handed them captive customers in the domestic market—were resisting reform in their sectors lest carefully laid apple carts with practically guaranteed profit streams were disrupted.

The political-intellectual cartel jumped to interpret BJP-NDA government's defeat in the 2004 election as the rejection of reforms. But there were several voices that differed. Columbia University's Arvind Panagariya wrote in July 2004, 'The demonization of reforms not only distorts facts, it also endangers growth that is essential for poverty alleviation.'[3] With remarkable prescience, Panagariya observed that 'the real danger lurking behind the rhetoric that the reforms ignored the poor or agriculture is that the government may simply end up substituting higher expenditures for the reforms'.

This is exactly where India found itself a decade later. In an echo of the manner in which the Communist parties helped Indira Gandhi stay in power after the Congress split in 1969,[4] India's Communist parties won a record number of seats in the 2004 elections and gave support to the Congress party, which formed the UPA government led by Prime Minister Manmohan Singh. A bacchanalia of spending ensued, as Manmohan Singh rode the growth wave seeded by Atal Bihari Vajpayee. Just a few years into Manmohan Singh's second term, the abdication of liberalization came home to roost, with persistent inflation and plummeting growth.

It is not just their endorsement of failed economic ideas, but their duplicity on secularism that is a searing indictment of the entrenched intelligentsia. The 2004 elections results, besides being bandied about as a rejection of reforms that did not have a 'human face', were also proffered as a defeat of 'communal forces' and the victory of 'secular' forces. The UPA government tied education, housing and poverty alleviation schemes to a citizen's religion. The most bizarre manifestation of this identity-centric approach was the creation of a women's only bank[5] after the ghastly 2012 gang rape in Delhi, as if such puerile tokenism would make Indian women secure and empowered.

The *ancien regime*—memorably christened the Khan Market gang by Prime Minister Modi—lapped up all of this and there was no protest. Those opposing these ideas were, ironically, from the 'sectarian' and 'communal' forces. In 2010, historian Ramachandra Guha said the alternative to Congress party's idea of India 'is either Naxalism or balkanization'.[6]

Political scientist Christophe Jaffrelot upbraided the BJP for not putting up more Muslim candidates.[7] It didn't seem to strike Jaffrelot that the position that only Muslims could represent Muslims in a democratic republic was no different from Muhammad Ali Jinnah's demagoguery.

Notably, Mohammadali Carim Chagla, who served as the first chief justice of the Bombay High Court from 1947 to 1958 observed:[8]

> The Congress Government has also followed what I can only call the old British policy of communalism. In my view, if it is communalism to pass over and ignore a man with merit simply because he happens to be a Muslim or a Christian or a Parsi, it is also communalism to appoint a person merely because he happens to be a Muslim or member of some other minority community. It is injurious to the interests of minorities themselves to have posts and offices filled by men who have no merit, merely because they want representation in high offices . . . When I am told there is no minority representation in a particular post, I often ask the question: is there any deserving person who has been passed over?

As Jawaharlal Nehru University political scientist Ajay Gudavarthy observed,[9] 'The Hindutva brand of politics seems to be a step ahead in articulating the idea of justice for all, which should have ideally come from those championing secularism and more so from the religious minorities themselves.'

Even beyond debates on how the republic should evolve, the very notion that India is civilizational entity has surprisingly come to be contested. Hearing a petition against the use of Sanskrit *shloka* '*Asato ma sadgamaya*', which means 'lead me from darkness to light' in the Kendriya Vidyalayas, the Supreme Court of India said that the petition raised 'questions of seminal importance as to the correct interpretation of Article 28(1)' of the Constitution, which says that 'no religious instruction shall be provided in any education institution wholly maintained out of State funds'.[10] To this, Solicitor General of India Tushar Mehta pointed out that the shloka from the Upanishads is not necessarily religious in nature, and that the Supreme Court's own motto, '*Yato dharmastato jayah*', or 'where is there is Dharma there is victory', is from the Mahabharata.

In contrast, the Congress-led Union government in 1968 saw fit to give the motto of '*Dharmo rakshati rakshitah*' (Dharma protects its protectors) to India's external intelligence agency, the Research and Analysis Wing. When the galaxy of leaders who fought for freedom from colonial rule decided that the Constitution of India should carry illustrations of episodes from India's great epics, the Ramayana and Mahabharata (a version of the Mahabharata illustration that comes in the directive principles section of original Constitution graces the front cover of this book), they similarly bowed to that civilizational history. The modern Indian State is the inheritor and flagbearer of this heritage.

The combination of pseudo-secularism and socialist economics exacerbated social divisions. The former creates the basis for power sharing and guaranteed group representation even as the latter suppresses supply and slows down the expansion of the pie for everybody.

The 'progressives' confront an intellectual singularity because they have little moral and intellectual room to manoeuvre to a space that's not occupied already—the so-called 'Right' is taking ownership of the idea of justice and development for all, and the Modi government's Jan Dhan–Aadhaar–Mobile foundation is writing the epitaph for inefficient doles. With infrastructure coming up across the country, from the remotest corners of the North-East region to the northernmost and southernmost regions, India is getting physically connected like never before. Along with the explosion of telecommunications and digital services, physical connectivity will raise aspirations of all Indians and dissolve divisions, helping expand the middle class and further forge a common national identity built on the civilizational bedrock.

Citizens of all backgrounds are seeing through the pernicious effects of spurious liberalism. The only way out for those opposed to the idea of India as a civilizational republic is to make ideological and political concessions. On the sociocultural side, these opponents need to reconsider their views on a uniform civil code, CAA and Article 370. On the economic side, while being true to an egalitarian ethos, they need to accept the benefits of choice in welfare and competition in the economy.

Narendra Modi set a national aspiration that no Indian Prime Minister ever articulated when he proclaimed in 2015 that India should aim to be a $20 trillion economy.[11] In moments of crisis and despondency, such talk may seem facetious, but for too long India has been a nation of 'unfulfilled greatness',[12] and a 'super power of the future', which never quite arrives. Over three decades ago in 1989, *Time* magazine commented on India's military capabilities and contemporary examples of the country's power projection in Sri Lanka, Maldives and against Pakistan in the treacherous Siachen region, worrying that 'India's new stature has profound implications for the strategic and diplomatic balance of the area and raises a host of foreign policy challenges for the US'.[13]

But frequently, India has brushed away extant economic failures by harking back to past glory. It should be remembered, though, that economic rejuvenation is not an end in itself. Just as socialist economics and spurious secularism feed off each other in a destructive cycle, in the same way a liberalized economy and individual freedom reinforce each other. Moving forward on the path of more economic and personal freedoms is necessary if India is to fulfil its potential for greatness.

This is the politico-economic context in India as we complete seventy-five years of independence. The Modi government has made substantial efforts to bring in important, long-overdue reforms detailed through this book. On the economic side, these include the implementation of a bankruptcy code, the creation of a common national market through indirect tax reforms, the liberalization of agriculture, the formalization of the real estate sector, the reorganization of the Indian Railways bureaucracy, opening up FDI across industries, an unprecedented push to universalize sanitation and electrification, digitalization in governance and an incipient market-driven universal health access programme.

In the area of internal cohesion and national security, some of the steps taken are the barring the practice of triple talaq, introducing a need-based criteria for reservations, peace accords[14] to address long-pending regional grievances in North-East India, closing a land border agreement with Bangladesh to address long-festering boundary issues,[15] removing the special status derived from Article 370 to integrate Jammu, Kashmir and Ladakh with India, defence administrative reforms culminating in the creation of the chief of defence staff post, the indigenization of defence production led by private industry and administrative reforms in the ministry of external affairs.

Much remains to be done, and the Modi government has seen withering criticism from several quarters, but to borrow the illustrious political scientist Samuel Huntington's quip on America,[16] Narendra Modi is a disappointment only because he is also a hope.

With India having experienced a semblance of prosperity since the liberalization of the 1990s, there is an endogenous momentum for more freedom in economic and social life. India's young population is a generation that has tasted the alternative to the monochromatic world that their parents and grandparents inhabited, and they will not settle for less. In this sense, a new way that is a clean break from the socialistic, feudal past is not just the correct policy prescription for India, but also makes for good politics. For reasons of dynastic politics and inertia, as discussed earlier, most of India's opposition parties have so far been slow to respond to the changed context.

The glaring deficiency confronting India has been the absence of bipartisan political consensus on the reform path. In his 1998 speech, Vajpayee had said:

> It is high time all sections of our society, including those in business, industry and politics, sank their partisan obsessions and focused their attention on the all-important national imperative: Growth. Let the common patriotic mantra for one and all be: Growth, More Growth and Still More Growth.[17]

India today is attempting to achieve economic growth with individual freedom—expanding social change in a grand undertaking to re-architecture the republic. This India will be more secure, equal, and prosperous, seeking a greater sway in world affairs. There is an intellectual contest underway between those who are striving to build this New India, and those who are invested in perpetuating its antithesis—indeed, a section of the Indian intelligentsia has gone so far as to proclaim that 'India must not become a superpower.'[18] Such absurd, even comical, self-emasculation may win plaudits in academic seminars—especially those held on foreign soil—but mercifully, the sentiment doesn't have much salience in India itself.

As home to a sixth of all humanity, India can and should stake claim to be a world power. For India to succeed and all Indians to thrive and prosper, it falls upon our leaders to both recognize that there is an intense desire for a better tomorrow among India's billion-plus people, and to draw lessons from the mistakes made in the past.

The tide of heightened aspiration has created a singularity exerting insurmountable forces that are crushing and inescapable. Without deep introspection, the cynics long accustomed to shaping India's self-image and direction will be unable to emerge from the singularity they find themselves in. India would in fact be best served if there was an intellectual and political consensus on the criticality of economic growth and individual rights, along with the recognition that India is a Civilizational State which can lead to a new universalism without homogenizing humanity. As a well-known prayer in India goes:[19]

ॐ सर्वे भवन्तु सुखिनः सर्वे सन्तु निरामयाः ।
सर्वे भद्राणि पश्यन्तु मा कश्चिद्दुःखभाग्भवेत् ।
ॐ शान्तिः शान्तिः शान्तिः ॥

Om, may all become happy,
May all be healthy
May all see what is auspicious,
May no one suffer in any way.
Om Peace, Peace, Peace.[20]

Notes

Introduction

1. Vikas Bajaj, 'Opinion | In India, a Dangerous and Divisive Technocrat.' *New York Times*, 22 December 2012. https://www.nytimes.com/2012/12/23/opinion/sunday/indias-divisive-technocrat.html.

2. Rajeev Mantri and Harsh Gupta, 'Let Us Debate the Idea of India', Livemint, 23 January 2013, https://www.livemint.com/Opinion/V7b5nL25jmtHFatG3tS2UN/Let-us-debate-the-idea-of-India.html.

3. Mathew Idiculla, 'Resurrection of the Oped Space', Newslaundry, https://www.newslaundry.com/2013/04/03/resurrection-of-the-oped-space. Accessed 20 April 2020.

4. Rajeev Mantri and Harsh Gupta, 'A New Idea of India', *Swarajya*, 18 September 2014, https://swarajyamag.com/books/a-new-idea-of-india. Accessed 13 April 2020.

5. Ramachandra Guha, 'Remembering Rajaji: The Men and Women of Character Who Once Ruled and Guided Us', *Telegraph*, 25 December 2002, https://www.telegraphindia.com/opinion/remembering-rajaji-the-men-and-women-of-character-who-once-ruled-and-guided-us/cid/1015814. Accessed 31 May 2020.

6. 'Seven Shackles', http://savarkar.org/en/Encyc/2017/5/22/Seven-shackles.html. Accessed 24 Aug. 2022.

7. Vikram Sampath, 'Savarkar Wanted to Smash Caste System, Cooked Prawns and Didn't Worship the Cow,' ThePrint, 10 December

2018, https://theprint.in/opinion/savarkar-wanted-to-smash-caste-system-cooked-prawns-and-didnt-worship-the-cow/161016/.

8.   Niranjan Rajadhyaksha, 'Savarkar Unplugged: From Film and Science to Caste and Hindutva' Livemint, 19 March 2016, https://www.livemint.com/Sundayapp/10jRCglrp6H3ZHp0PiXIwL/Savarkar-unplugged-From-film-and-science-to-caste-and-Hindu.html.

9.   Ernest Renan, 'What is a Nation?', text of a conference presentation delivered at the Sorbonne on 11 March 1882, in Ernest Renan, *Qu'est-ce qu'une nation?* trans. Ethan Rundell (Paris, Presses-Pocket, 1992).

10. V.S. Naipaul, 'Fourth Walter B. Wriston Lecture in Public Policy: Our Universal Civilization', *City Journal*, 30 October 1990, https://www.city-journal.org/html/our-universal-civilization-12753.html.

11. Ingmar Oldberg, 'Huntington's "Clash of Civilizations" and Russia', https://www.ui.se/globalassets/butiken/ui-brief/2014/huntingtons-clash-of-civilizations-and-russia.pdf. Accessed 31 May 2020.

12. B.R. Ambedkar, 'Pakistan, or, The Partition of India', http://www.columbia.edu/itc/mealac/pritchett/00ambedkar/ambedkar_partition/. Accessed 2 June 2020.

13. Diana L. Eck, *India: A Sacred Geography* (Harmony Books: New York, 2012).

14. Klaus K. Klostermaier, *A Survey of Hinduism*, 3rd ed. (SUNY Press: Albany, 2010).

15. Pandurang Vaman Kane, *History of The Dharma Shastra*, Vol. 2 (Bhandarkar Oriental Research Institute: Pune, 1941).

16. Ram Swarup, *Hinduism and Monotheistic Religions*. 2nd ed. (Voice of India: New Delhi, 2015).

17. Nani Ardeshir Palkhivala, *Our Constitution Defaced and Defiled* (Macmillan: New Delhi, 1974).

18. Wei-Wei Zhang, *The China Wave: Rise of a Civilizational State* (World Scientific: 2012).

Chapter 1: India, That Is Bharat

1.   Arthur Llewellyn Basham, *The Wonder That Was India: A Survey of the History and Culture of the Indian Sub-Continent Before the Coming of the Muslims* (Sidgwick & Jackson: London, 1967).

2. Rajeev Mantri and Harsh Gupta, 'A New Idea of India', *Swarajya*, 18 September 2014, https://swarajyamag.com/books/a-new-idea-of-india. Accessed 13 April 2020.

3. Erwin Schrodinger, *What Is Life? With Mind and Matter and Autobiographical Sketches*, reprint ed. (Cambridge University Press: Cambridge, 2012).

4. Nassim Nicholas Taleb, *Skin in the Game: Hidden Asymmetries in Daily Life* (Penguin Random House India: Gurgaon, 2018).

5. Richard Feynman, 'What Is Science?', http://www.feynman.com/science/what-is-science/. Accessed 14 April 2020.

6. 'The Pathology of Partition', *Friday Times: Naya Daur*, 6 November 2015, https://www.thefridaytimes.com/2015/11/06/the-pathology-of-partition/.

7. S.P. Agrawal and J. C. Aggarwal, *Nehru on Social Issues* (Concept Publishing Company: New Delhi, 1989).

8. Swapan Dasgupta, *Awakening Bharat Mata: The Political Beliefs of the Indian Right* (Penguin Random House: Gurgaon, 2019).

9. Kumar Anshuman, 'Congress Leaders Supported Abrogation of Article 370 in 1964', *Economic Times*, 12 August 2019, https://economictimes.indiatimes.com/news/politics-and-nation/congress-leaders-supported-abrogation-of-article-370-in-1964/articleshow/70637139.cms?from=mdr.

10. Achyut Mishra, 'Dissent in Congress over Article 370 Isn't New: Its MPs Supported Bill to Scrap It in 1964.' ThePrint, 12 August 2019, https://theprint.in/india/dissent-in-congress-over-article-370-isnt-new-its-mps-supported-bill-to-scrap-it-in-1964/275764/.

11. Thomas Paine, *Common Sense,* https://www.ushistory.org/paine/commonsense/sense2.htm. Accessed 28 May 2020.

12. 'Hindu Rashtra Is No Political Philosophy: Advani', *Times of India*, 10 February 2003, https://timesofindia.indiatimes.com/india/Hindu-rashtra-is-no-political-philosophy-Advani/articleshow/37003397.cms. Accessed 3 June 2020.

13. Friedrich Nietzsche, *Beyond Good and Evil by Friedrich Nietzsche* (BookRix, 2014).

14. Chandra Bhan Prasad et al., *Defying the Odds: The Rise of Dalit Entrepreneurs* (Penguin Random House India: Gurgaon, 2014).

15. 'Australia "Too Scared" to Sledge Virat Kohli's India Because of IPL Deals - Michael Clarke', *ESPNcricinfo*, 7 April 2020, https://www.espncricinfo.com/story/_/id/29005698/australia-too-scared-sledge-virat-kohli-india-ipl-deals-michael-clarke.

16. 'The Holocaust', *History*, https://www.history.com/topics/world-war-ii/the-holocaust. Accessed 1 June 2020.

17. Lalit K. Jha, 'Pakistani Army Triggered 1971 "Genocide": Sheikh Hasina', *Mint*, 22 September 2017, https://www.livemint.com/Politics/xhktMmtpFTrCM92hfMaHSI/Pakistani-army-triggered-1971-genocide-Sheikh-Hasina.html.

18. Rana Mitter, *Forgotten Ally: China's World War II, 1937–1945* (Houghton Mifflin Harcourt: New York, 2013).

19. Soutik Biswas, 'How Churchill "Starved" India', BBC Soutik Biswas's India, https://www.bbc.co.uk/blogs/thereporters/soutikbiswas/2010/10/how_churchill_starved_india.html. Accessed 17 April 2020.

20. 'Population Control, Marauder's Style', *New York Times*, https://archive.nytimes.com/www.nytimes.com/imagepages/2011/11/06/opinion/06atrocities_timeline.html?pagewanted=all. Accessed 17 April 2020.

21. Nayantara Sahgal, *Jawaharlal Nehru: Civilizing a Savage World* (Penguin India: New Delhi, 2010).

22. Guy Sorman, *The Genius of India* (Macmillan: 2001).

23. Mohammadali Carim Chagla, *Roses in December: An Autobiography* (Bharatiya Vidya Bhavan: Bombay, 1974).

24. Guy Sorman, *The Genius of India* (Macmillan India: 2001).

25. Stockholm International Peace Research Institute, Sipri.org. 2020. *SIPRI Military Expenditure Database | SIPRI*. https://www.sipri.org/databases/milex. Accessed 29 May 2020.

26. *2020 Military Strength Ranking*. https://www.globalfirepower.com/countries-listing.asp. Accessed 29 May 2020.

27. Sri Aurobindo, *Uttarpara Speech* (Sri Aurobindo Ashram Publication Department: 1999).

28. 'Great Awakening | Definition, Key Figures, & Facts', *Encyclopedia Britannica*, https://www.britannica.com/event/Great-Awakening. Accessed 10 June 2020.

29. 'Counter-Counterculture', *The American Conservative*, https://www.theamericanconservative.com/articles/counter-counterculture/. Accessed 18 April 2020.

30. Rajeev Mantri and Harsh Gupta, 'India's Cocooned Intellectual Elite', *Mint*, 24 July 2013, https://www.livemint.com/Opinion/zRcdXsCfiTQRL9eHY9iU8H/Indias-cocooned-intellectual-elite.html.

31. Ashok Malik, 'Problem with Indian intellectual discourse is the so-called opinion shapers, in media and academia, have no stake in the real economy', Twitter, 12 December 2012, https://twitter.com/malikashok/status/278794951825969153. Accessed 18 February 2020.

32. D.D. Guttenplan, 'How Much Is a Professor Worth?' *New York Times*, 2 April 2012, https://www.nytimes.com/2012/04/02/world/europe/02iht-educlede02.html. Accessed 17 April 2020.

33. Scott Jaschik, 'Faculty Pay, Around the World', *Inside Higher Ed*, 22 March 2012, https://www.insidehighered.com/news/2012/03/22/new-study-analyzes-how-faculty-pay-compares-worldwide. Accessed 17 April 2020.

34. Thomas Sowell, *Intellectuals and Society* (Basic Books: New York, 2011).

35. Vishnu Som, 'Yes it does. It represents a fundamental threat to millions of Muslims in our country', Twitter, https://twitter.com/vishnundtv/status/6265784755. Accessed 17 April 2020.

36. Beck Sullivan and Kristin Gourlay, 'Here's Where Abortions Are Now Banned or Strictly Limited, and Where They May Be Soon.' NPR, 24 June 2022. NPR, https://www.npr.org/sections/health-shots/2022/06/24/1107126432/abortion-bans-supreme-court-roe-v-wade.

37. *India's Amended Law Makes Abortion Safer and More Accessible*, World Health Organisation, 12 April 2021, https://www.who.int/india/news/detail/13-04-2021-india-s-amended-law-makes-abortion-safer-and-more-accessible. Accessed 29 June 2022.

38. Pujya Gurudev Swami Chinmayananda's Birth Centenary: The Release of Commemorative Coins, www.youtube.com, https://www.youtube.com/watch?v=zXM_sok_R7I. Accessed 1 October 2022.

39. A Quote by Matshona Dhliwayo. https://www.goodreads.com/quotes/7657000-if-you-wear-a-mask-for-too-long-there-will. Accessed 18 April 2020.

Chapter 2: From Civilization to Nation

1. B.R. Ambedkar, 'Is It Really Necessary to Divide What Has Long Been a Single Whole?' *Pakistan or the Partition of India*, ed. Fran Pritchett, online version sourced from *Dr. Babasaheb Ambedkar: Writings and Speeches*, Vol. 8 (Education Department, Government of Maharashtra: Bombay, 1990), first published by Thacker and Co., Bombay, December 1940, http://www.columbia.edu/itc/mealac/pritchett/00ambedkar/ambedkar_partition/513.html. Accessed 17 April 2020.

2. Vinayak Damodar Savarkar, *Hindu Rashtra Darshan* (Veer Savarkar Prakashan: 1984).

3. 'Thatcher Urges Western Nations to Stand Firm in Union University Speech', https://www.uu.edu/events/scholarshipbanquet/1998/. Accessed 10 June 2020.

4. 'Remarks by President Trump to the People of Poland', The White House, https://www.whitehouse.gov/briefings-statements/remarks-president-trump-people-poland/. Accessed 30 May 2020.

5. 'Not His Finest Hour: The Dark Side of Winston Churchill', *The Independent*, 28 October 2010, http://www.independent.co.uk/news/uk/politics/not-his-finest-hour-the-dark-side-of-winston-churchill-2118317.html.

6. 'Is India a Country or a Continent?', *Economist*, February 2017, https://www.economist.com/asia/2017/02/09/is-india-a-country-or-a-continent. Accessed 17 April 2020.

7. 'EU Gets Nobel Peace Prize in Oslo', *BBC News*, 10 December 2012, https://www.bbc.com/news/world-europe-20664167. Accessed 17 April 2020.

8. Sunil Khilnani, *The Idea of India* (Penguin India: New Delhi, 2004).

9. Samuel P. Huntington, *The Clash of Civilizations and the Remaking of World Order* (Simon and Schuster: New York, 2007).

10. Francis Fukuyama, *The End of History and the Last Man* (Penguin Adult: London, 1992).

11. Francis Fukuyama, *The Origins of Political Order: From Prehuman Times to the French Revolution* (Profile Books: 2011).

12. Pandurang Vaman Kane, *History of The Dharma Shastra*, Vol. 2 (Bhandarkar Oriental Research Institute: Pune, 1941).

13. Strobe Talbott, *Engaging India: Diplomacy, Democracy, and the Bomb* (Brookings Institution Press: Washington DC, 2004).

14. 'Vajpayee at Home in Pune; Didn't Want to Be Called 'Guest' in City', *Hindustan Times*, 16 August 2018, https://www.hindustantimes.com/pune-news/vajpayee-at-home-in-pune-didn-t-want-to-be-called-guest-in-city/story-eKhdBokOKdOnTgTWQuQB1J.html.

15. 'Atal Bihari bajpai bhashan savarkar', YouTube, 24 May 2013, accessed 18 April 2020, https://www.youtube.com/watch?v=U0S9179jgRc. Translated from the Hindi language by the authors.

16. Gavin D. Flood, *An Introduction to Hinduism* (Cambridge: Cambridge University Press, 1996).

17. Rotilă, V. 'Is Religion a Necessary Condition for the Emergence of Knowledge? Some Explanatory Hypotheses', *Postmodern Openings*, vol. 10, no. 3 (2019), pp. 202–228, doi:10.18662/po/89

18. Dhananjay Keer, *Dr. Ambedkar: Life and Mission* (Popular Prakashan: Mumbai, 1971).

19. Ambedkar, *Pakistan or Partition of India*, http://www.columbia.edu/itc/mealac/pritchett/00ambedkar/ambedkar_partition/412d.html. Accessed 29 June 2022.

20. Tathagata Roy, *Syama Prasad Mookerjee: Life and Times* (Penguin Random House India: Gurgaon, 2018).

21. 'Explained: Amid China Head Start, Modi Push to Claim India's Place in Nepal's Buddhist Heritage.' *Indian Express*, 16 May 2022, https://indianexpress.com/article/explained/explained-pm-narendra-modi-nepal-visit-sher-bahadur-deuba-7919433/.

22. Vinayak Damodar Savarkar, *Hindutva: Who Is a Hindu?* (Hindi Sahitya Sadan: New Delhi, 2003).

23. Mohit M. Rao, 'Caste System Has Left Imprints on Genes: Study', *The Hindu*, 27 January 2016, https://www.thehindu.com/sci-tech/science/Caste-system-has-left-imprints-on-genes-study/article14022623.ece. Accessed 18 April 2020.

24. Analabha Basu, Neeta Sarkar–Roy and Partha P. Majumder, 'Genomic Reconstruction of the History of Extant Populations of India Reveals Five Distinct Ancestral Components and a Complex Structure', *Proceedings of the National Academy of Sciences*, vol. 113, no. 6 (2016), pp. 1594–99, accessed 18 April 2020, https://doi.org/10.1073/pnas.1513197113.

25. *Constituent Assembly Debates: Vol. 7: 4 November 1948 to 8 January 1949* (Lok Sabha Secretariat: New Delhi, 1999).

26. Rajeev Mantri and Harsh Gupta, 'One versus Group', *Indian Express*, 13 February 2013, accessed 19 April 2020, http://archive. indianexpress.com/news/one-versus-group/1073208/0;

27. Harsh Gupta, 'Against Entrenched Identities', *Indian Express*, 8 March 2013, accessed 19 April 2020, https://indianexpress.com/ article/opinion/columns/against-entrenched-identities/.
    Will Kymlicka, *Multicultural Citizenship: A Liberal Theory of Minority Rights* (Clarendon Press: 1996).

28. Vrinda Narain, *Gender and Community: Muslim Women's Rights in India* (University of Toronto Press: Toronto, 2001).

29. Steven Ian Wilkinson, 'India, Consociational Theory, and Ethnic Violence, *Asian Survey* 40, no. 5 (2000), 767–91, accessed 19 April 2020, https://doi.org/10.2307/3021176.

30. Ibid.

31. Moushumi Das Gupta, 'Less than 1% of OBC Castes Corner 50% Reservation Benefits, 20% Get None, Govt Panel Finds', ThePrint, 11 July 2020, https://theprint.in/india/governance/less-than-1-of-obc-castes-corner-50-reservation-benefits-20-get-none-govt-panel-finds/458860/.

32. Sunetra Choudhury 'Panel May Recommend Splitting 27% OBC Quota into Three Bands', *Hindustan Times*, 12 June 2019, accessed 19 April 2020, https://www.hindustantimes.com/india-news/panel-may-recommend-splitting-27-obc-quota-into-three-bands/story-9XUA9UWxL9qE6vVABUeINN.html.

33. Gary S.S. Becker, *The Economics of Discrimination* (University of Chicago Press: Chicago, 1971).

34. Mary Ann Tétreault and Robert Allen Denemark, *Gods, Guns, and Globalization: Religious Radicalism and International Political Economy* (Lynne Rienner: Colorado, 2004).

35. Herbert Marcuse, *Towards a Critical Theory of Society: Collected Papers of Herbert Marcuse,* Vol. 2 (Routledge: London, 2013).

36. Jan Narveson, *Respecting Persons in Theory and Practice: Essays on Moral and Political Philosophy* (Rowman & Littlefield: Maryland, 2002).

37. 'What Is Uniform Civil Code', *Business Standard*, https://www. business-standard.com/about/what-is-uniform-civil-code. Accessed 30 May 2020.

38. Adam Liptak, 'Muslim Woman Denied Job Over Head Scarf Wins in Supreme Court', *New York Times*, 1 June 2015, https://www.nytimes.com/2015/06/02/us/supreme-court-rules-in-samantha-elauf-abercrombie-fitch-case.html.

39. 'India's Plural and Diverse Identity Is Under Threat', The Wire, https://thewire.in/culture/indias-plural-diverse-identity-threat. Accessed 15 June 2020.

40. 'Hamid Ansari Backs Sharia Court Proposal, Says Each Community Has Right to Practice Own Personal Law', *Financial Express*, 12 July 2018, https://www.financialexpress.com/india-news/hamid-ansari-backs-sharia-court-proposal-says-each-community-has-right-to-practice-own-personal-law/1242014/.

41. Mahesh Rangarajan, 'Indira: The Print Ages by A Century', *Outlook India Magazine,* 6 November 2017, https://www.outlookindia.com/magazine/story/indira-the-print-ages-by-a-century/299463.

42. Markandey Katju, 'Taking Firm Steps to Emancipation', *The Hindu*, 27 June 2019. *www.thehindu.com*, https://www.thehindu.com/opinion/op-ed/taking-firm-steps-to-emancipation/article28159385.ece.

43. Vinayak Damodar Savarkar, *Hindu Rashtra Darshan: A Collection of the Presidential Speeches Delivered from the Hindu Mahasabha Platform* (L.G. Khare: Mumbai, 1949).

44. Harsh Gupta, 'Against Entrenched Identities', *Indian Express*, 8 March 2013, http://archive.indianexpress.com/news/against-entrenched-identities/1084736/0. Accessed 20 April 2020.

45. 'Sachar Committee Report', Ministry of Minority Affairs, Government of India, accessed 20 April 2020, http://www.minorityaffairs.gov.in/reports/sachar-committee-report.

46. 'I do not support child marriage but I do say that it's not for us the majority to dictate to minorities how to live their lives' Twitter, https://twitter.com/malinip/status/349882475125809155. Accessed 30 May 2020.

47. Rajeev Mantri and Harsh Gupta. 'Views | Making Lemonade from Lemons – The RTE Edition.' Livemint, 2 May 2012, https://www.livemint.com/Opinion/rwyGB5FZmFlcQg7FgpMpYN/Views--Making-lemonade-from-lemons--The-RTE-edition.html.

48. 'Muslims Should Shed Attitude of Minorityism, Says M.J. Akbar', *The Hindu*, 19 February 2013, https://www.thehindu.com/news/national/muslims-should-shed-attitude-of-minorityism-says-mj-akbar/article4429030.ece. Accessed 20 April 2020.

49. Anoo Bhuyan, 'At Supreme Court, All Three Religious Groups Backing Section 377 Are Christian', The Wire, 18 July 2018, https://thewire.in/lgbtqia/at-supreme-court-all-three-religious-groups-backing-section-377-are-christian. Accessed 20 April 2020.

50. 'Erode District: Pastor Flays Supreme Court for Gay Sex Ruling, Arrested', *Times of India*, 11 September 2018, https://timesofindia.indiatimes.com/city/coimbatore/pastor-flays-supreme-court-for-gay-sex-ruling-arrested/articleshow/65761044.cms. Accessed 20 April 2020.

51. Milli Gazette, 'A step towards self-destruction', Twitter, 6 September 2018, accessed 20 April 2020, https://twitter.com/milligazette/status/1037596450052562944?s=20.

52. All India Muslim Personal Law Board, 'Legalizing homosexuality is against Indian values and culture. No religion allows immorality. The government must pass a bill to protect the rights of women as they are the major victims of legalised homosexuality', Twitter, 7 September 2018, accessed 20 April 2020, https://twitter.com/AIMPLB_Official/status/1038083943629824002?s=20.

53. DNA Web Ream, 'Homosexuality is against nature, religion: Jamiat Ulema-e-Hind', DNA, 7 September 2018, accessed 20 April 2020, https://www.dnaindia.com/india/report-homosexuality-is-against-nature-religion-jamiat-ulema-e-hind-2660096/amp.

54. Ravish Tiwari, 'Government Walked BJP Tightrope on Section 377: Said Yes—and a No as Well', *Indian Express*, 12 July 2018, accessed 20 April 2020, https://indianexpress.com/article/india/government-walked-bjp-tightrope-on-section-377-said-yes-and-a-no-as-well-5255849/.

55. Nidhi Sethi, ed., '"LGBTQ Community Part of Society": Mohan Bhagwat Keeps Up with Times', NDTV, 20 September 2018, accessed 20 April 2020, https://www.ndtv.com/india-news/lgbtq-community-part-of-society-mohan-bhagwat-keeps-up-with-times-1919153.

56. 'Government Walked BJP Tightrope on Section 377: Said Yes — and a No as Well', *Indian Express,* 12 July 2018, https://indianexpress.

com/article/india/government-walked-bjp-tightrope-on-section-377-said-yes-and-a-no-as-well-5255849/.

57. *Made in Heaven*, Excel Entertainment, Tiger Baby Films, 2019.

58. 'Kerala Muslim Groups Intensify Campaign against Gender Politics, Homosexuality', *New Indian Express*, 23 June 2022, https://www.newindianexpress.com/states/kerala/2022/jun/23/kerala-muslim-groups-intensifycampaign-against-gender-politics-homosexuality-2468582.html. Accessed 29 June 2022.

59. 'IUML Works Closely with SDPI, Radical Islamist Organisations in Kerala: CPM', *New Indian Express*, 27 April 2022, https://www.newindianexpress.com/states/kerala/2022/apr/27/iuml-works-closely-with-sdpi-radical-islamist-organisations-in-kerala-cpm-2447158.html. Accessed 29 June 2022.

60. PIB India, 'In a significant move ensuring reproductive rights to women, government increases limit on termination of pregnancy from 20 to 24 weeks; move aimed at discouraging informal termination of pregnancies and reducing maternal mortality rate', Twitter, 29 January 2020, accessed 20 April 2020, https://twitter.com/pib_india/status/1222435055793950720?s=21.

61. Richard Howard Stafford Crossman, *The God That Failed* (Columbia University Press: New York, 2001).

62. 'Lucknow Pact | India [1916],' *Encyclopedia Britannica*, https://www.britannica.com/event/Lucknow-Pact. Accessed 30 May 2020.

63. 'Poona Pact | India [1932],' *Encyclopedia Britannica*, https://www.britannica.com/event/Poona-Pact. Accessed 30 May 2020.

64. Ramachandra Guha, *India After Gandhi: The History of the World's Largest Democracy* (Pan Macmillan: New Delhi, 2011).

65. George Orwell, *Politics and the English Language* (Penguin Books: London, 2013).

66. Jairam Ramesh, *Kautilya Today: Jairam Ramesh on a Globalizing India* (India Research Press: New Delhi, 2002).

67. Rajeev Mantri, 'Hindus Don't Always Have Equality with Minorities', Livemint, 19 March 2015, https://www.livemint.com/Opinion/HG2cMf1rqwdJe2a3M5ANcM/Hindus-dont-always-have-equality-with-minorities.html.

68. Julio Ribeiro, 'As a Christian, Suddenly I Am a Stranger in My Own Country, Writes Julio Ribeiro', *Indian Express*, 17 March 2015.

Accessed 21 April 2020, https://indianexpress.com/article/opinion/columns/i-feel-i-am-on-a-hit-list/.

69. Vaiju Naravane, 'Pope Takes up Christians Issue with Vajpayee', *The Hindu*, 27 June 2000, accessed 21 April 2020, https://www.thehindu.com/todays-paper/tp-miscellaneous/tp-others/pope-takes-up-christians-issue-with-vajpayee/article28029304.ece.

70. Swati Goel Sharma, 'Selective Data on Communal Violence in India: IndiaSpend, English Media Have a Lot To Answer For', 14 November 2018, accessed 4 June 2020, https://swarajyamag.com/ideas/selective-data-on-communal-violence-in-india-indiaspend-english-media-has-a-lot-to-answer-for.

71. Anand Vardhan, 'The Missing Mewat in Haryana's Dalit Story,' Newslaundry, 26 January 2018, accessed 4 June 2020, https://www.newslaundry.com/2018/01/26/nuh-haryana-jind-rape-media-selective-news.

72. Aarti Dhar, 'Mother Teresa's Aim Was Conversion, Says Bhagwat', *The Hindu*, 24 February 2015, https://www.thehindu.com/news/national/mother-teresas-aim-was-conversion-says-bhagwat/article6926462.ece.

73. Rajeev Mantri, '*Why Mother Teresa's Success Is a Reflection of The Wounded Civilization That Is India*, https://swarajyamag.com/culture/why-mother-teresas-success-is-a-reflection-of-the-wounded-civilization-that-is-india. Accessed 4 June 2020.

74. Aroup Chatterjee, *Mother Teresa: The Untold Story* (Fingerprint: 2016).

75. 'Mother Teresa addresses the Scripps Clinic staff, January 14 1992', https://www.youtube.com/watch?v=DMwBBgTkAdg. Accessed 15 June 2020.

76. Christopher Hitchens, 'The Pope Beatifies Mother Teresa, a Fanatic, a Fundamentalist and a Fraud', *Slate Magazine*, 20 October 2003, accessed 21 April 2020, https://slate.com/news-and-politics/2003/10/the-fanatic-fraudulent-mother-teresa.html.

77. Ram Swarup, *Proselytisation as It Is Practised*, 23 May 1988, accessed 7 June 2020 http://voiceofdharma.org/books/ca/app5.htm.

78. Christian Medical College, Vellore, Admissions Prospectus 2019–20, accessed 31 May 2020, https://www.cmch-vellore.edu/SITES/Education/prospectus.pdf,

79. PTI, 'Conversion Claim: St Stephen's Principal Dragged to Court', *Financial Express*, 1 February 2015, https://www.financialexpress. com/india-news/conversion-claim-st-stephens-principal-dragged-to-court/37630/.

80. Ramachandra Guha, 'St Stephen's: Murder in the Cathedral?' *Outlook*, 25 June 2007, accessed 21 April 2020, https://www. outlookindia.com/magazine/story/st-stephens-murder-in-the-cathedral/234958.

81. 'Press Release of the Conference on "Charter of Hindu Demands"', Charter of Hindu Demands, 24 September 2018, http:// hinducharter.org/2018/09/24/press-release-of-the-conference-on-charter-of-hindu-demands/.

82. 'What Is Shah Bano Case?' *Indian Express*, 23 August 2017, https://indianexpress.com/article/what-is/what-is-shah-bano-case-4809632/.

83. Rajeev Mantri and Harsh Gupta, 'EWS Quota: Narendra Modi's Move to Curb the Ills of Identity Politics', *Hindustan Times*, 11 February 2019, https://www.hindustantimes.com/analysis/ews-quota-narendra-modi-s-move-to-curb-the-ills-of-identity-politics/ story-mfINvycMswHMiIA6AyyGzO.html.

84. 'Only 3 Votes against, Lok Sabha Clears Quota Bill; Rajya Sabha Test Today', *Indian Express*, 9 January 2019, https://indianexpress. com/article/india/only-3-votes-against-lok-sabha-clears-quota-bill-rajya-sabha-test-today-5529444/.

85. 'Owaisi Opposes Reservation Bill for "Economically Weaker" General Category', *Indian Express*, 8 January 2019, https://indianexpress. com/article/india/owaisi-opposes-reservation-bill-for-economically-weaker-general-category-5529198/.

86. Karl R. Popper, E.H. Gombrich and Alan Ryan, *The Open Society and Its Enemies,* New One-Volume Ed. (Princeton University Press: Princeton, 2013).

87. '"Tolerant" Qureshi back in the day comparing himself to Mahmud of Ghaznavi out to demolish Somnath mandir' Twitter, https://twitter.com/nailainayat/status/13121153802869 39136, October 3 2021. Accessed 1 October 2022.

88. 'Uttarpara Speech [Spiritual Experiences]', in *Cosmic Consciousness, Sri Aurobindo (1906–1910)*, accessed 21 April 2020, http://

www.sriaurobindoinstitute.org/saioc/Sri_Aurobindo/uttarpara_
speech#uttarpara_speech.

89. Roger Scruton, ed., *Liberty and Civilization: The Western Heritage*
     (Encounter Books: New York, 2010).

90. 'Irish Unification Is Becoming Likelier', *The Economist*, 13 February
     2020, accessed 21 April 2020, https://www.economist.com/
     leaders/2020/02/13/irish-unification-is-becoming-likelier.

91. Hamdani, Yasser Latif, 'A Short History of Ahmadi Persecution',
     Friday Times—Naya Daur, 13 August 2022, https://www.
     thefridaytimes.com/2022/08/14/a-short-history-of-ahmadi-
     persecution/.

92. 'Pulwama & Kashmir's Ancient Heart', https://www.livehistoryindia.
     com/amazing-india/2019/03/03/pulwama-kashmirs-ancient-heart.
     Accessed 8 June 2020.

93. Srijan Shukla, 'Kashmir Was Never Just a 1947 Problem, It Is a
     5,000-Year-Old Battle of Histories', ThePrint, 11 August 2019, accessed
     22 April 2020, https://theprint.in/opinion/kashmir-was-never-just-a-
     1947-problem-it-is-a-5000-year-old-battle-of-histories/275418/.

94. Ramachandra Guha, *India After Gandhi: The History of the World's
     Largest Democracy* (Pan Macmillan: New Delhi, 2011).

95. Naziha Syed Ali, 'The Truth about Forced Conversions in Thar',
     Dawn, 17 July 2017, https://www.dawn.com/news/1345304.

96. Amish, 'Time to Understand the CAA, with Reason', *Hindustan
     Times*, 29 December 2020, https://www.hindustantimes.
     com/analysis/time-to-understand-the-caa-with-reason/story-
     amSa0PNuZHqAT29xELuqgJ.html.

97. Kartikeya Tanna, 'West's Ill-Informed Criticism of CAA Ignores
     Similarities to US' Lautenberg Amendment, Overlooks India's
     Refugee Policy', Firstpost, https://www.firstpost.com/india/wests-
     ill-informed-criticism-of-caa-ignores-similarities-to-us-lautenberg-
     amendment-overlooks-indias-refugee-policy-7890181.html.
     Accessed 2 June 2020.

98. Anthony Read and David Fisher, *The Proudest Day: India's Long
     Road to Independence* (W.W. Norton: New York, 1998).

99. Nadeem F. Paracha, 'The Election That Created Pakistan', *Dawn*,
     11 May 2014, accessed 22 April 2020, http://www.dawn.com/
     news/1105473.

100. Venkat Dhulipala, *Creating a New Medina: State Power, Islam and the Quest for Pakistan in Late Colonial North India* (Cambridge University Press: New Delhi, 2015), review by Ian Talbot in *The Journal of Asian Studies*, vol. 74, no. 4 (2015), pp. 1054–55, accessed 22 April 2020, https://www.jstor.org/stable/24738595.

101. Sreeparna Banerjee, Anasua Basu Ray Chaudhury and Ambalika Guha, 'The 2015 India–Bangladesh Land Boundary Agreement: Identifying Constraints and Exploring Possibilities in Cooch Behar', ORF, July 2017, accessed 22 April 2020, https://www.orfonline.org/research/the-2015-india-bangladesh-land-boundary-agreement-identifying-constraints-and-exploring-possibilities-in-cooch-behar/.

102. Kenneth J. Cooper, 'India, Pakistan Kindle Hope for Peace', *Washington Post*, 21 February 1999, accessed 22 April 2020, https://www.washingtonpost.com/archive/politics/1999/02/21/india-pakistan-kindle-hope-for-peace/a0b3a8d7-3fda-4168-aa48-f66b5e741564/.

103. 'A Kashmir Look at Partition: Girilal Jain', *Girilal Jain Archive*, 19 February 1990, accessed 22 April 2020, http://www.girilaljainarchive.net/1990/02/a-kashmir-look-at-partition-girilal-jain/.

104. C. Christine Fair, *Fighting to the End: The Pakistan Army's Way of War* (Oxford University Press: New York, 2014).

105. 'Pakistan's Strategic Culture: Implications for How Pakistan Perceives and Counters Threats', *The National Bureau of Asian Research (NBR)*, https://www.nbr.org/publication/pakistans-strategic-culture-implications-for-how-pakistan-perceives-and-counters-threats/. Accessed 3 August 2022.

106. Ritu Rathi, 'Opinion | How Abrogation of Article 370 Has Changed the Lives of Women in Kashmir.' News18, 5 August 2022, https://www.news18.com/news/opinion/opinion-how-abrogation-of-article-370-has-changed-the-lives-of-women-in-kashmir-5694811.html.

107. Ram Kumar Pahan, 'How Article 370 Deprived ST/SC of Their Rights', *The Pioneer*, 2 November 2019, https://www.dailypioneer.com/2019/state-editions/how-article-370-deprived-st-sc-of-their-rights.html. Accessed 24 August 2022.

Chapter 3: Saving Secularism from the Secularists

1. 'Secular Word Is the Biggest Lie, Says Uttar Pradesh CM Yogi Adityanath', *Indian Express*, 14 November 2017, https://indianexpress.com/article/india/secular-word-is-the-biggest-lie-says-yogi-adityanath-uttar-pradesh-cm-raipur-4936367/.

2. Rajeev Mantri and Harsh Gupta, 'The Nehruvian Condescension towards Minorities', *Mint*, 4 June 2013, accessed 22 April 2020, https://www.livemint.com/Opinion/h953KJCyrVIMah1Cp8OTwO/The-Nehruvian-condescension-towards-minorities.html.

3. Dhananjay Mahapatra, 'Is Govt Ready for Uniform Civil Code after 63 Yrs?', 16 August 2010, *Times of India*, accessed 22 April 2020, https://timesofindia.indiatimes.com/india/Is-govt-ready-for-uniform-civil-code-after-63-yrs/articleshow/6316723.cms.,

4. 'I think we must take the concept of group rights seriously if we want the world to believe that we are a genuine democracy!' Twitter, https://twitter.com/malinip/status/323358401117687809. Accessed 2 June 2020.

5. Shanoor Seervai, 'Why Muslims Still Can't Adopt in India.' *WSJ*, 19 Mar. 2014, https://blogs.wsj.com/indiarealtime/2014/03/19/why-muslims-still-cant-adopt-in-india/.

6. N.R. Narayana Murthy, *Better India: A Better World* (Penguin Books India: New Delhi, 2010).

7. Jagdish N. Bhagwati and Arvind Panagariya, *Why Growth Matters: How Economic Growth in India Reduced Poverty and the Lessons for Other Developing Countries* (Public Affairs: New York, 2013).

8. Hamid Umar Dalwai, *Muslim Politics in Secular India*, (Hind Pocket Books: Delhi, 1968).

9. Abhiram Ghadyalpatil and Shreya Agarwal, 'Hamid Dalwai, the Man Who Led Triple Talaq Stir in 1967', Livemint, 23 August 2017, https://www.livemint.com/Politics/LsHfiKKArFEALIqF2HKBgP/Hamid-Dalwai-the-man-who-led-triple-talaq-stir-in-1967.html.

10. Kiran Deshta, *Uniform Civil Code: In Retrospect and Prospect* (Deep & Deep Publications: New Delhi, 1995).

11. Ibid.

12. Ibid.

13. Shoumojit Banerjee, 'Noted Social Activist, Author Mehrunnisa Dalwai No More', *The Hindu*, 9 June 2017, *www.thehindu.com*, https://www.thehindu.com/news/national/other-states/noted-social-activist-author-mehrunnisa-dalwai-no-more/article18869181. ece.

14. Ramachandra Guha, 'India's Dangerous Divide', *Wall Street Journal*, 6 December 2008, accessed 22 April 2020, https://www.wsj.com/articles/SB122852093316784075.

15. Partha Chatterjee, 'Secularism and Toleration', *Economic and Political Weekly*, vol. 29, no. 28 (1994), pp. 1768–77, accessed 22 April 2020, http://cscs.res.in/dataarchive/textfiles/textfile.2008-07-22.5413891426/file.

16. Dr J.K. Bajaj, 'Religion Data of Census 2011: I Numbers Matter', 24 October 2015, accessed 22 April 2020, https://blog.cpsindia.org/2015/10/religion-data-of-census-2011-i-numbers.html.

17. Dr J.K. Bajaj, 'Religion Data of Census 2011: II Worsening Imbalance', 26 October 2015, accessed 22 April 2020, https://blog.cpsindia.org/2015/10/religion-data-of-census-2011.html.

18. Ibid.

19. 'I accept that large scale conversion happens in Andhra Pradesh, but it happens in other states too: Raghu Ramakrishna Raju, MP, YSRCP, tells Padmaja Joshi on @thenewshour' Twitter, https://twitter.com/timesnow/status/1264962176902500355. Accessed 2 June 2020.

20. Koenraad Elst, 'Appendix 1. Girilal Jain on Hindu Rashtra', in *Ayodhya and After: Issues before Hindu Society* (Voice of India: New Delhi, 1991), accessed 22 April 2020, https://archive.org/stream/AyodhyaAndAfterKoenraadElst_201709/Ayodhya%20And%20After%20-%20Koenraad%20Elst_djvu.txt .

21. Rajeev Mantri, 'Saving Secularism from the "Secularists" ', *Mint*, 24 March 2014, accessed 22 April 2020, https://www.livemint.com/Opinion/NjnmAZDTjUMUyZjhETSzIL/Saving-secularism-from-the-secularists.html.

22. Krishnadas Rajagopal, 'Supreme Court Rules NCMEI Has Wide Powers', *The Hindu*, 18 April 2018, accessed 22 April 2020, https://www.thehindu.com/news/national/supreme-court-rules-ncmei-has-wide-powers/article23590265.ece.

23. Vidya Subrahmaniam, 'Muslim Deprivation Widespread: Sachar Committee', *The Hindu*, 1 December 2006, accessed 22 April 2020, https://www.thehindu.com/todays-paper/muslim-deprivation-widespread-sachar-committee/article18496766.ece.

24. 'PM's 15 Point Programme', http://www.minorityaffairs.gov.in/prime-ministers-15points. Accessed 31 May 2020.

25. PTI, 'Post-Sachar: Centre Carries out Survey Based on Religion', *Times of India*, 28 January 2007, accessed 22 April 2020, https://timesofindia.indiatimes.com/india/Post-Sachar-Centre-carries-out-survey-based-on-religion/articleshow/1498531.cms.

26. Aman Sharma, 'There Aren't Enough Muslim Policemen in Country, Says Home Ministry Report', *India Today*, 21 July 2012, accessed 22 April 2020, https://www.indiatoday.in/india/north/story/muslim-policemen-in-india-home-hinistry-sachar-committee-110479-2012-07-21.

27. PTI, 'Muslims Must Have First Claim on Resources: PM', *Times of India*, 9 December 2006, accessed 22 April 2020, https://timesofindia.indiatimes.com/india/Muslims-must-have-first-claim-on-resources-PM/articleshow/754937.cms.

28. IANS, 'Army Chief against Recruitment by Religion', *Hindustan Times*, 13 February 2006, accessed 22 April 2020, https://www.hindustantimes.com/india/army-chief-against-recruitment-by-religion/story-4Drf6k54LnDj46Q6AUgX3M.html.

29. Mukesh Ranjan, 'NAC tells govt: give jobs scheme minority focus', *Asian Age*, 13 May 2013, accessed 22 April 2020, https://www.pressreader.com/india/the-asian-age/20130512/281479273931044. Accessed 20 January 2020.

30. Sandeep Joshi and Gargi Parsai, 'Government Forced to Defer Communal Violence Bill', *The Hindu*, 5 February 2014, accessed 22 April 2020, https://www.thehindu.com/news/national/government-forced-to-defer-communal-violence-bill/article5656766.ece.

31. 'BJP, RSS Conducting "Terror Training Camps: Shinde"', *The Hindu Business Lline*, 12 March 2018, accessed 22 April 2020, https://www.thehindubusinessline.com/news/national/bjp-rss-conducting-terror-training-camps-shinde/article20566633.ece.

32. IANS, 'Shinde Wants Fast-Track Courts for Jailed Muslim Youths', *India Today*, 11 May 2013, accessed 22 April 2020, https://www.

indiatoday.in/india/north/story/sushilkumar-shinde-for-fasttrack-courts-for-jailed-muslim-youths-163176-2013-05-11.

33. PTI, 'Shinde to Write to CMs on Jailed Minority Youths', *The Hindu Business Line*, 10 January 2014, accessed 22 April 2020, https://www.thehindubusinessline.com/news/national/shinde-to-write-to-cms-on-jailed-minority-youths/article23124354.ece.

34. 'Jains Granted Minority Status', *The Hindu*, 21 January 2014, accessed 22 April 2020, https://www.thehindu.com/news/national/jains-granted-minority-status/article5598368.ece.

35. Sanjeev Nayyar, 'Why Did the Ramakrishna Mission Say They Are Not Hindus?' eSamskriti, August 2002, accessed 22 April 2020, https://www.esamskriti.com/essay-chapters.aspx?sectionname=National-Affairs&subsectionname=For-The-Followers-Of-Dharma&topicname=Why-Did-The-Ramakrishna-Mission-Say-They-Are-Not-Hindus&chapter=1.

36. Girish Pattanashetti, 'The Lingayat Gamble Fails', *The Hindu*, 15 May 2018, accessed 21 April 2020, https://www.thehindu.com/elections/karnataka-2018/karnataka-assembly-poll-results-the-lingayat-gamble-failed/article23896190.ece.

37. 'Akhilesh Govt Lines up yet Another Muslim Vote-Catcher: Waqf Tribunals', *Indian Express*, 18 February 2014, accessed 23 April 2020, https://indianexpress.com/article/cities/lucknow/akhilesh-govt-lines-up-yet-another-muslim-vote-catcher-waqf-tribunals/.

38. Biswajeet Banerjee, 'Anything for Muslim Vote', *Pioneer*, 27 December 2013, accessed 23 April 2020, https://www.dailypioneer.com/2013/columnists/anything-for-muslim-vote.html.

39. 'Allahabad High Court Slams Akhilesh Yadav Government's Move to Drop Cases against Varanasi Serial Blasts Suspects.' NDTV, 23 November 2012, accessed 29 June 2022, https://www.ndtv.com/india-news/allahabad-high-court-slams-akhilesh-yadav-governments-move-to-drop-cases-against-varanasi-serial-bla-505361.

40. 'Muzaffarnagar: Tales of Death and Despair in India's Riot-Hit Town', BBC News, 25 September 2013, accessed 23 April 2020, https://www.bbc.com/news/world-asia-india-24172537.

41. Pervez Siddiqui, 'Holi: UP Witnesses Record Dip in Clashes on Holi This Year', *Times of India*, 4 March 2018, accessed 23 April 2020,

https://timesofindia.indiatimes.com/city/lucknow/up-witnesses-record-dip-in-clashes-on-holi-this-year/articleshow/63153868.cms.

42. 'Yogi Adityanath's Education Overhaul: English Starts at Nursery Level in UP', *Hindustan Times*, 7 April 2017, accessed 23 April 2020, https://www.hindustantimes.com/india-news/yogi-adityanath-s-education-overhaul-english-starts-at-nursery-level-in-up/story-dldnabbP01JmaEii1nARwN.html.

43. PTI, 'TTD Cash Deposits in Banks Crosses Rs 12,000 Cr Mark', *Business Line*, 24 April 2019, accessed 23 April 2020, https://www.thehindubusinessline.com/news/variety/ttd-cash-deposits-in-banks-crosses-rs-12000-cr-mark/article26932228.ece.

44. Amarnath K. Menon, 'AP Govt Ask Tirumala Tirupati Devasthanams to Transfer Surplus Funds to the Treasury', *India Today*, 22 July 2013, accessed 23 April 2020, https://www.indiatoday.in/magazine/indiascope/story/19830331-ap-govt-ask-tirumala-tirupati-devasthanams-to-transfer-surplus-funds-to-the-treasury-770538-2013-07-22.

45. 'Andhra Asks Temples to Break FDs and Pay Dues, Consequence of Govt Lethargy.' *News Minute*, 21 July 2022, https://www.thenewsminute.com/article/andhra-asks-temples-break-fds-and-pay-dues-consequence-govt-lethargy-166064.

46. Amarnath K. Menon, 'Discount on Religion', *India Today*, 16 February 2008, accessed 23 April 2020, https://www.indiatoday.in/magazine/states/story/20080225-discount-on-religion-735446-2008-02-15.

47. Arun Shourie, *Falling over Backwards: An Essay on Reservations and on Judicial Populism* (HarperCollins: New Delhi, 2012).

48. Ramesh Kandula, 'AP Announces Benefits for Minorities', *Tribune*, 18 February 2008, accessed 23 April 2020, https://www.tribuneindia.com/2008/20080219/nation.htm#4.

49. Sushil Rao, 'Son-in-Law Also Rises under YSR Tutelage', *Times of India*, 25 November 2008, accessed 23 April 2020, https://timesofindia.indiatimes.com/city/hyderabad/Son-in-law-also-rises-under-YSR-tutelage/articleshow/3757616.cms.

50. Sulogna Mehta, 'Temple Calves End up in Slaughter Houses', *Times of India*, 28 April 2013, accessed 23 April 2020, https://timesofindia.indiatimes.com/city/hyderabad/Temple-calves-end-up-in-slaughter-houses/articleshow/19761922.cms.

51. 'Tirumala Tirupati Devasthanams Staffers Held for Conversions', *Times of India*, 25 July 2012, accessed 23 April 2020, https://timesofindia.indiatimes.com/city/hyderabad/Tirumala-Tirupati-Devasthanams-staffers-held-for-conversions/articleshow/15129733.cms.

52. Srinivasa Rao Apparasu, '44 Non-Hindus Working in Tirupati Temple to Be Shifted to Other Departments', *Hindustan Times*, 6 January 2018, accessed 23 April 2020, https://www.hindustantimes.com/india-news/44-non-hindu-employees-working-in-tirumala-temple-to-be-shifted-to-other-departments/story-FyU77dUOnTfhyQaDiBFF4L.html.

53. ANI, 'TDP is the only party that constructed Haj houses in Hyderabad, Vijayawada & Kadapa. We promoted Urdu & built thousands of mosques across the state: Andhra Pradesh CM N Chandrababu Naidu at foundation laying event of Haj House in Vijayawada', Twitter, 12 May 2018, accessed 23 April 2020, https://twitter.com/ANI/status/995342478063497216.

54. 'Furore Over Tirupati Tirumala Temple Board's Decision to Sell 23 Land Assets In TN, TTD Chief Says 129 Properties Sold Since 1974', https://swarajyamag.com/news-brief/furore-over-tirupati-tirumala-temple-boards-decision-to-sell-23-land-assets-in-tn-ttd-chief-says-129-properties-sold-since-1974. Accessed 1 June 2020.

55. Prasad Nichenametla, 'Jagan Reddy's Christian Politics Is under Fire for "Burdening Exchequer" & Conversions', ThePrint, 24 November 2019, https://theprint.in/politics/jagan-reddys-christian-politics-is-under-fire-for-burdening-exchequer-conversions/325407/.

56. Srinivasa Rap Apparasu, 'Telangana Raises Muslim Quota to 12% Taking State's Total Quota above SC Limit', *Hindustan Times*, 16 April 2017, accessed 23 April 2020, https://www.hindustantimes.com/india-news/telangana-assembly-passes-bill-increasing-quota-for-muslims-scs-and-sts-to-12-state-s-total-quota-goes-above-sc-limit-of-50/story-ZCArBKggR7f5nqnRQ3jVnI.html.

57. Arihant Pawariya, 'Hiking Quota, Judicial Powers to Wakf Board: Dangerous Turn To KCR's Muslim Appeasement Politics', *Swarajya*, 20 January 2017, accessed 23 April 2020, https://swarajyamag.com/politics/hiking-quota-judicial-powers-to-wakf-board-dangerous-turn-to-kcrs-muslim-appeasement-politics.

58. Srinivasa Rao Apparasu, 'KCR's Christmas Gift Scheme for Poor to Cost Telangana Govt around Rs 15 Crore', *Hindustan Times*, 9 December 2017, accessed 23 April 2020, https://www. hindustantimes.com/india-news/kcr-s-christmas-gift-scheme-for-poor-to-cost-telangana-govt-around-rs-15-crore/story-ejrdGvuzFmdVgjvdNFB3BP.html.

59. 'CM KCR Promises Rs 10 Cr for Churches', *Telangana Today*, 23 December 2017, accessed 23 April 2020, https://telanganatoday. com/cm-kcr-promises-rs-10-cr-churches.

60. Asif Yar Khan, '70 Minority Residential Schools to Come up in State', *The Hindu*, 16 February 2016, accessed 23 April 2020, https://www.thehindu.com/news/cities/Hyderabad/70-minority-residential-schools-to-come-up-in-state/article8242783.ece.

61. 'KCR Gives Nod for Separate Board for Recruitment of Teachers in Residential Schools', *Siasat Daily*, 20 April 2018, accessed 23 April 2020, https://archive.siasat.com/news/kcr-gives-nod-separate-board-recruitment-teachers-residential-schools-1345015/.

62. 'Urdu Is Second Official Language Now', *The Hindu*, 17 November 2017, accessed 23 April 2020, https://www.thehindu.com/news/cities/Hyderabad/urdu-is-second-official-language-now/article20493655.ece.

63. Yunus Y. Lasania, 'Telangana to Set up IT Corridor, Industrial Estate for Muslims', *Mint*, 23 October 2017, accessed 23 April 2020, https://www.livemint.com/Politics/rccGOqIMrGVhjZr2Xw9uBL/Telangana-to-set-up-IT-corridor-industrial-estate-for-Musli.html.

64. Supreme Court of India, K.P. Manu, Malabar Cements Ltd vs Chairman, Scrutiny, 26 February 2015.

65. Universal Religious Freedom, 'Reservation Matrix. Telangana Social Welfare Residential Educational Institutions Admissions (Intermediate/HSC program with integrated coaching for JEE etc.). Conversion to X alone is recognized', Twitter, 11 December 2017, accessed 23 April 2020, https://twitter.com/by2kaafi/status/940232435836395520.

66. PTI, 'Mamata's Allowance for Imams, Muezzins Unconstitutional: High Court', *The Hindu*, 2 September 2013, accessed 23 April 2020, https://www.thehindu.com/news/national/other-states/mamatas-allowance-for-imams-muezzins-unconstitutional-high-court/article5085896.ece.

67. 'Mamata Govt to Donate Bicycles to Girls from Minority Section', *Times of India*, December 26 2012, accessed 31 May 2020. https://timesofindia.indiatimes.com/city/kolkata/Mamata-govt-to-donate-bicycles-to-girls-from-minority-section/articleshow/17770400.cms.

68. Arshad Ali, 'West Bengal: 10,000 Muslim Clerics to Hit the Streets against Mamata Banerjee', *Indian Express*, 31 October 2016, accessed 23 April 2020, https://indianexpress.com/article/india/india-news-india/mamata-banerjee-muslims-clerics-protest-november-8-unfulfilled-promises-3730075/.

69. 'Bengal to set up medical college, 500-bed hospital for minorities', 18 September 2012, accessed 2 June 2020, http://twocircles.net/2012sep18/bengal_set_medical_college_500bed_hospital_minorities.html

70. 'Aliah University No Longer Under Minority Affairs Department, Muslims Fear This Will Impact Minority Enrollment', TwoCircles.net, 27 September 2017, accessed 23 April 2020, http://twocircles.net/2017sep27/417154.html.

71. 'I Have Not Let Down Minorities, Says Mamata', *The Hindu*, 19 January 2013. accessed 23 April 2020, https://www.thehindu.com/todays-paper/tp-national/tp-otherstates/i-have-not-let-down-minorities-says-mamata/article4322132.ece.

72. NewsX, 'Taslima's Attackers Freed for Vote: Mamata Banerjee Ignores Law for Minority', *YouTube*, 23 September 2013, accessed 23 April 2020, https://www.youtube.com/watch?v=XYB3GczeNW8.

73. 'Taslima Expulsion Case Revoked to Woo Muslims', *Aamar Kolkata*, 25 September 2013, accessed 23 April 2020, http://aamaarkolkata.blogspot.com/2013/09/taslima-expulsion-case-revoked-to-woo_24.html.

74. PTI, 'Another Controversy over Taslima Nasreen, TV Serial Postponed', *Indian Express*, 9 January 2014, accessed 23 April 2020, https://indianexpress.com/article/india/india-others/another-controversy-over-taslima-nasreen-tv-serial-postponed/.

75. Madhuparna Das and Subrata Nagchoudury, 'Mamata Banerjee Doesn't Meet US Envoy over Muslim 'Disapproval', *Financial Express*, 23 February 2014, accessed 23 April 2020, https://www.financialexpress.com/archive/mamata-banerjee-doesnt-meet-us-envoy-over-muslim-disapproval/1228299/.

76. 'Wary of Muslim 'Disapproval', Mamata Doesn't Meet US Envoy', *Indian Express*, 5 March 2014, accessed 23 April 2020, https://indianexpress.com/article/india/politics/wary-of-muslim-disapproval-mamata-doesnt-meet-us-envoy/.

77. 'Mamata Assured Me She Would Never Support BJP', *The Hindu*, 21 March 2014, accessed 23 April 2020, https://www.thehindu.com/news/national/mamata-assured-me-she-would-never-support-bjp/article5811388.ece.

78. 'FIR against Kolkata Shahi Imam Maulana Barkati for Refusing to Give up Lal Batti, Says It Is His 'Right' ', *India Today*, 12 May 2017, accessed 23 April 2020, https://www.indiatoday.in/india/story/kolkata-shahi-imam-maulana-noor-ur-rehman-barkati-lal-batti-red-beacon-vip-culture-fir-976611-2017-05-12.

79. Arkamoy Dutta Majumdar, 'Triple Talaq Bill Only Intended at Inciting Muslim Community: Mamata Banerjee', Livemint, 3 January 2018, accessed 23 April 2020, https://www.livemint.com/Politics/dllrCuDKFFvqx4gw9TjpjK/Triple-talaq-bill-only-intended-at-inciting-Muslim-community.html.

80. PTI, 'Congress Says Will Scrap Triple Talaq Law after Winning Lok Sabha Polls', *India Today*, 7 February 2019, accessed 23 April 2020, https://www.indiatoday.in/elections/lok-sabha-2019/story/congress-backs-triple-talaq-says-will-scrap-law-after-winning-lok-sabha-polls-1450507-2019-02-07.

81. 'New Scheme for the Homeless Minorities', *The Hindu*, 13 July 2013, accessed 23 April 2020, https://www.thehindu.com/news/national/karnataka/new-scheme-for-the-homeless-minorities/article4911555.ece.

82. Anil Budur Lulla, 'Karnataka's Bridal Brouhaha', *Open*, 7 November 2013, accessed 23 April 2020, https://openthemagazine.com/features/india/karnatakas-bridal-brouhaha/.

83. Vanu Dev, 'Karnataka Congress Chief Sparks Minorities Row', Mail Online, 7 October 2013, accessed 23 April 2020, https://www.dailymail.co.uk/indiahome/indianews/article-2447218/Karnataka-Congress-chief-G-Parameshwara-sparks-minorities-row.html.

84. BJP Karnataka, 'In this letter marked 'extremely urgent' & addressed to police chiefs of major districts, DG of Police asks opinion on dropping cases of communal violence registered against members

of minority community in the last 5 yrs. In 2015 @Siddaramaiah had dropped 175+ cases against PFI', Twitter, 25 January 2018, accessed 23 April 2020, https://twitter.com/BJP4Karnataka/status/956586334373625856.

85. 'Muzrai Circular on Mutts Rankles BJP', *The Hindu*, 8 February 2018, accessed 23 April 2020, https://www.thehindu.com/news/national/karnataka/muzrai-circular-on-mutts-rankles-bjp/article22686079.ece.

86. 'Mutts and Gurudwaras across Karnataka Likely to Come under Muzrai Department', *New Indian Express*, 24 January 2018, accessed 23 April 2020, https://www.newindianexpress.com/states/karnataka/2018/jan/24/mutts-and-gurudwaras-across-karnataka-likely-to-come-under-muzrai-department-1762525.html.

87. PTI, 'Karnataka Polls Will Be 'Secularism vs Communalism' Contest: Siddaramaiah', *Indian Express*, 17 March 2018, accessed 23 April 2020, https://indianexpress.com/article/india/karnataka-polls-secularism-communalism-contest-siddaramaiah-rahul-gandhi-5101191/.

88. Vijaya Karnataka, 'Karnataka to Reward Minority Students Getting First Class in First Attempt', *Times of India*, 3 September 2018, accessed 23 April 2020, https://timesofindia.indiatimes.com/city/bengaluru/karnataka-to-reward-minority-students-getting-first-class-in-first-attempt/articleshow/65659847.cms.

89. 'Kerala Government Launches Housing Scheme for Widows, Divorcees from Minority Communities', TwoCircles.net, 30 June 2017, accessed 23 April 2020, http://twocircles.net/2017jun30/412262.html.

90. PTI, 'Beef Fests across Kerala to Protest Ban on Sale of Cattle for Slaughter', *The Hindu Business Line*, 27 May 2017, accessed 23 April 2020, https://www.thehindubusinessline.com/news/national/beef-fests-across-kerala-to-protest-ban-on-sale-of-cattle-for-slaughter/article9714132.ece.

91. 'CPI(M) Controlled Temple Board Closed Veda Classes, Runs Non-Veg Restaurant That Serves Beef', *SatyaVijayi*, 19 March 2018, accessed 23 April 2020, https://satyavijayi.com/cpim-controlled-temple-board-removes-vedic-school-runs-non-veg-restaurant-serves-beef-items/.

92. 'Underage Marriage among Muslims in Kerala Ignites Debate', *Indian Express*, http://archive.indianexpress.com/news/underage-marriage-among-muslims-in-kerala-ignites-debate/1177466/0. Accessed 1= June 2020.

93. 'Hadiya Court Case: Supreme Court to Study If Under-18 Muslim Girl Can Marry on Attaining Puberty', *Times of India*, https://timesofindia.indiatimes.com/india/sc-to-study-if-under-18-muslim-girl-can-marry-on-attaining-puberty/articleshow/71072845.cms. Accessed 15 June 2020.

94. Priya Jaiswal, 'Government Mulls to Revise Women's Legal Age for Marriage from 18 to 21', 14 June 2020, https://www.indiatvnews.com/news/india/women-legal-age-for-marriage-india-2020-revise-sharda-act-women-and-child-development-626094.

95. 'Row over Hamid Ansari Attending PFI Conference', *The Hindu*, 23 September 2017, accessed 23 April 2020, https://www.thehindu.com/news/national/kerala/row-over-hamid-ansari-attending-pfi-conference/article19744617.ece.

96. Shaju Philip, '13 Guilty of Chopping Kerala Professor's Hand', *Indian Express*, 1 May 2015, accessed 23 April 2020, https://indianexpress.com/article/india/india-others/13-guilty-of-chopping-kerala-professors-hand/.

97. 'SC Dismisses Plea Filed by PFI Leader Azim Sharief for Relief against UAPA Charges for Allegedly Murdering RSS Activist', Firstpost, https://www.firstpost.com/india/sc-dismisses-plea-filed-by-pfi-leader-azim-sharief-for-relief-against-uapa-charges-for-allegedly-murdering-rss-activist-6910211.html. Accessed 15 June 2020.

98. ANI, 'I want to tell you that if you want to keep secularism alive then fight for your rights, became a political power, vote for your (Muslim) candidates. If Muslims become a political power, secularism and democracy will be strengthened: AIMIM Chief Aasaduddin Owaisi', Twitter, 24 June 2018, accessed 23 April 2020, https://twitter.com/ANI/status/1011108597890191368.

99. Dean Nelson, 'India General Election: Sonia Gandhi Appeals to Muslims to Reject Narendra Modi', *Telegraph*, 2 April 2014, accessed 23 April 2020, https://www.telegraph.co.uk/news/worldnews/asia/india/10739877/India-general-election-Sonia-Gandhi-appeals-to-Muslims-to-reject-Narendra-Modi.html.

100. Sita Ram Goel, *Freedom of Expression: Secular Theocracy Versus Liberal Democracy* (Voice of India: New Delhi, 1998).

101. Prasanta Mazumdar, 'No Yoga Day in Mizoram on International Yoga Day', *New Indian Express*, 21 June 2018, accessed 23 April 2020, https://www.newindianexpress.com/nation/2018/jun/21/no-yoga-day-in-mizoram-on-international-yoga-day-1831542.html.

102. Esha Roy, 'Tripura: After We Joined BJP, Mosque Turned Us Out, Says Group of Villagers', *The Indian Express*, 13 February 2018, accessed 23 April 2020, https://indianexpress.com/article/north-east-india/tripura/tripura-after-we-joined-bjp-mosque-turned-us-out-says-group-of-villagers-5061500/.

103. 'Choose Between Trishul and Cross: Nagaland Baptist Church to Political Parties', News18, 3 March 2018, accessed 23 April 2020, https://www.news18.com/news/politics/choose-between-trishul-and-cross-nagaland-baptist-church-to-political-parties-1657635.html.

104. 'Immersion of Vajpayee Ashes: BJP Criticised for Imposing "Alien Culture" on Nagaland', *The Hindu*, 25 August 2018, accessed 23 April 2020, https://www.thehindu.com/news/national/other-states/immersion-of-vajpayee-ashes-bjp-criticised-for-imposing-alien-culture-on-nagaland/article24781410.ece.

105. ANI, 'Congress Questions Arrest of 2002 Akshardham Attacker Ahead of Gujarat Polls', *Business Standard*, 5 November 2017, accessed 23 April 2020, https://www.business-standard.com/article/news-ani/congress-questions-arrest-of-2002-akshardham-attacker-ahead-of-gujarat-polls-117110500276_1.html.

106. 'Now, Church Politics in Gujarat: Gandhinagar Archbishop Thomas Macwan Urges Christians to Save India from Nationalist Forces', *Financial Express*, 24 November 2017, accessed 23 April 2020, https://www.financialexpress.com/elections/gujarat-assembly-elections-2017/gujarat-election-church-letter-by-archbishop-thomas-macwan-bjp-congress/944927/.

107. 'Delhi Archbishop Asks Christians to Pray Ahead of 2019 Polls, RSS Says It's a Direct Attack on Indian Secularism', 22 May 2018, accessed 23 April 2020, https://www.outlookindia.com/website/story/delhi-archbishop-asks-christians-to-pray-ahead-of-2019-polls-rss-says-its-a-dire/312068.

108. 'Rajasthan CM Ashok Gehlot Sanctions Rs 188 Lakh for Madrasas after Centre Stops Giving Grants', https://www.timesnownews.com/india/article/rajasthan-cm-ashok-gehlot-sanctions-rs-188-crore-for-madrasas-after-centre-stops-giving-grants/515965. Accessed 1 June 2020.

109. 'Government to Connect Madrasas to Mainstream Education', *Hindustan Times*, 12 June 2019, *Hindustan Times*, https://www.hindustantimes.com/education/government-to-connect-madrasas-to-mainstream-education/story-bA77I2WETG2N4LbVEqa NLO.html.

110. 'Arvind Kejriwal Announces Salary Hike for Imams of All Mosques in Delhi', Zee News, 23 Jan. 2019, https://zeenews.india.com/india/arvind-kejriwal-announces-salary-hike-for-imams-of-all-mosques-in-delhi-2173451.html.

111. 'Madhya Pradesh to Increase Salaries of Imams, Muezzins', *Outlook India*, https://www.outlookindia.com/newsscroll/madhya-pradesh-to-increase-salaries-of-imams-muezzins/1744110. Accessed 1 June 2020.

112. IANS, 'Badruddin Ajmal Applauds India's Vote at UN against US' Jerusalem Decision; Sushma Swaraj Says "Now You Vote for Us"', Firstpost, 13 December 2017, accessed 23 April 2020, https://www.firstpost.com/india/badruddin-ajmal-applauds-indias-vote-at-un-against-us-jerusalem-decision-sushma-swaraj-says-now-you-vote-for-us-4272389.html.

113. Subramanian Swamy, 'Freeing Temples from State Control', *The Hindu*, 20 January 2014, accessed 23 April 2020, https://www.thehindu.com/opinion/lead/freeing-temples-from-state-control/article5594132.ece.

114. 'Govts of 5 southern states control 90,700 temples: @ARanganafthan72, Author tells Navika Kumar on @thenewshour.' Twitter, https://twitter.com/timesnow/status/1197903744643432449. Accessed 1 June 2020.

115. 'Supreme Council to have its say in St. Stephen's interview panel', *The Hindu*, 23 May 2019, https://www.thehindu.com/news/cities/Delhi/supreme-council-to-have-its-say-in-st-stephens-interview-panel/article27222332.ece.

116. A. Srivathsan, 'Reforms in the House of God', *The Hindu*, 13 January 2014, accessed 23 April 2020, https://www.thehindu.com/opinion/op-ed/reforms-in-the-house-of-god/article5570711.ece.

117. Mohammad Ali, 'Cleric Backs Modi's Refusal to Wear Skullcap', *The Hindu*, 22 April 2014, accessed 23 April 2020, https://www.thehindu.com/news/national/cleric-backs-modis-refusal-to-wear-skullcap/article5934979.ece.

118. 'Kejriwal and Sibal Hug Each Other at Eid', *Times of India*, 14 January 2014, accessed 4 June 2020, https://timesofindia.indiatimes.com/videos/news/Kejriwal-and-Sibal-hug-each-other-at-Eid-function/videoshow/28796965.cms.

119. Rajeev Mantri and Harsh Gupta, 'Saving Rationalism from the Rationalists', Livemint, 19 November 2013, accessed 23 April 2020, https://www.livemint.com/Opinion/HuIlxXDgWh7C18k249AYQI/Saving-rationalism-from-the-rationalists.html.

120. Kumar Ketkar, 'Narendra Dabholkar: The Relentless Rationalist', Dilip Simeon's Blog, 23 August 2013, accessed 24 April 2020, https://dilipsimeon.blogspot.com/2013/08/kumar-ketkar-narendra-dabholkar.html.

121. PTI, 'The Anti-Black Magic and Superstition Ordinance Has Been Promulgated in Maharashtra', DNA, 24 August 2013, accessed 24 April 2020, https://www.dnaindia.com/india/report-the-anti-black-magic-and-superstition-ordinance-has-been-promulgated-in-maharashtra-1879444.

122. 'Finally, Karnataka Assembly Passes Anti-Superstition Bill', *News Minute*, 17 November 2017, accessed 24 April 2020, https://www.thenewsminute.com/article/finally-karnataka-assembly-passes-anti-superstition-bill-71748.

123. PTI, 'National Anti-Black Magic Bill Required: Dabholkar's Daughter', *The Hindu*, 16 September 2013, accessed 24 April 2020, https://www.thehindu.com/news/national/other-states/national-antiblack-magic-bill-required-dabholkars-daughter/article5134507.ece.

124. Krishna Kumar, 'Narendra Dabholkar's Murder: Pune Police Release Sketch of One of the Suspects', *India Today*, 22 August 2013, accessed 24 April 2020, https://www.indiatoday.in/india/west/story/

narendra-dabholkar-killing-maharashtra-government-approves-anti-superstition-ordinance-174534-2013-08-22.

125. Matthew Inman, 'How to Suck at Your Religion', The Oatmeal, accessed 24 April 2020, https://theoatmeal.com/comics/religion.

126. Nassim Nicholas Taleb, 'How to Be Rational about Rationality', Medium, 22 August 2017, accessed 24 April 2020, https://medium.com/incerto/how-to-be-rational-about-rationality-432e96dd4d1a.

127. Jim Davies, 'Explaining the Unexplainable', Nautilus, 22 August 2013, accessed 24 April 2020, http://nautil.us/issue/4/the-unlikely/explaining-the-unexplainable.

128. B.F. Skinner, 'Superstition' in the Pigeon', *Journal of Experimental Psychology*, Vol. 38, no. 2 (1948), 168–172, accessed 24 April 2020, https://doi.org/10.1037/h0055873

129. 'Cricketers and Their Superstitions', *Times of India*, 16 May 2012, accessed 24 April 2020, https://timesofindia.indiatimes.com/life-style/spotlight/Cricketers-and-their-superstitions/articleshow/13150829.cms.

130. Nassim Nicholas Taleb, *Skin in the Game: Hidden Asymmetries in Daily Life*. (Penguin Random House India: Gurgaon, 2018).

131. Jordan Peterson's comprehensive analysis of totalitarianism & individual sovereignty, https://www.youtube.com/watch?v=aBoqkGtbEQQ. Accessed 2 June 2020.

132. Advertising Atheism, https://www.youtube.com/watch?v=48V0m2lia5U. Accessed 2 June 2020.

133. Johannes Quack, *Disenchanting India: Organized Rationalism and Criticism of Religion in India* (Oxford University Press: New York, 2011).

134. 'Warkaris Set to Protest Anti-Superstition Bill', *Pune Mirror*, 7 November 2013, https://punemirror.indiatimes.com/pune/cover-story/Warkaris-set-to-protest-anti-superstition-bill/articleshow/31149135.cms. Accessed 2 June 2020.

135. Rajeev Mantri and Harsh Gupta, 'The Importance of Free Speech Absolutism', *Mint*, 15 February 2012, accessed 24 April 2020, https://www.livemint.com/Opinion/rejf94piLwZdGS7YY9cOVJ/Views--The-importance-of-free-speech-absolutism.html.

136. Tabassum Barnagarwala, 'Editor Once, Now Shirin Has to Sell Her Jewellery, Borrow to Make Ends Meet', *Indian Express*, 17 July 2015, accessed 1 May 2020, https://indianexpress.com/article/cities/

mumbai/editor-once-now-shirin-has-to-sell-her-jewellery-borrow-to-make-ends-meet/.

137. 'Where Executed Blasphemy Killer Is Revered as a Saint', *New Indian Express*, 22 October 2016, access 29 June 2022, https://www.newindianexpress.com/thesundaystandard/2016/oct/22/where-executed-blasphemy-killer-is-revered-as-a-saint-1530804.html.

138. 'Udaipur: Citing Prophet "Insult", 2 Kill Man on Video, Threaten PM Modi', *Indian Express*, 29 June 2022, https://indianexpress.com/article/india/udaipur-tailor-killed-allegedly-for-social-media-post-backing-nupur-sharma-7996860/.

139. 'Columnist Sentenced to Six Months' Imprisonment for Casteist Article', *Indian Express*, 29 January 2011, accessed 24 April 2020, http://archive.indianexpress.com/news/columnist-sentenced-to-six-months-imprisonm/743511.

140. Dwaipayan Ghosh, 'Tibetans Shocked at Rockstar Diktat', *Times of India*, 9 November 2011, accessed 24 April 2020, https://timesofindia.indiatimes.com/city/delhi/Tibetans-shocked-at-Rockstar-diktat/articleshow/10660419.cms.

141. 'Full Transcript: I'm Returning to India, Deal with It - Salman Rushdie to NDTV', https://www.ndtv.com/india-news/full-transcript-im-returning-to-india-deal-with-it-salman-rushdie-to-ndtv-568445. Accessed 1 June 2020.

142. Ravi Shanker Kapoor, *There Is No Such Thing As Hate Speech: A Case For Absolute Freedom Of Expression* (Bloomsbury Publishing: London, 2017).

143. Shrijeet Phadke, 'History of the First Amendment—Intolerance Towards Freedom of Speech', MyIndMakers, 17 December 2019, accessed 24 April 2020, https://www.myind.net/Home/viewArticle/history-of-the-first-amendment-intolerance-towards-freedom-of-speech.

144. *Jawaharlal Nehru Selected Speeches: Volume 2: 1949–1953* (Publications Division, Ministry of Information & Broadcasting: New Delhi, 2017).

145. Ramachandra Guha, 'Verdicts on Nehru: Rise and Fall of a Reputation', *Economic and Political Weekly*, vol. 40, no. 19 (2005), 1958–62. JSTOR.

146. 'Sec 66A: Curbs on Free Speech Are Part of Nehru Family Legacy.' Firstpost, 4 December 2012, https://www.firstpost.com/india/sec-66a-curbs-on-free-speech-are-part-of-nehru-family-legacy-544470. html. Accessed 2 June 2020.

147. Madhavi Pothukuchi, 'Jailed for Anti-Nehru Poem & Celebrated for Bollywood Songs, Majrooh Sultanpuri Had It All.', ThePrint, 1 October 2019, https://theprint.in/theprint-profile/jailed-for-anti-nehru-poem-celebrated-for-bollywood-songs-majrooh-sultanpuri-had-it-all/299167/.

148. 'Brandenburg Test.' *LII / Legal Information Institute*, https://www. law.cornell.edu/wex/brandenburg_test. Accessed 1 June 2020.

149. 'India: World Prison Brief', accessed 24 April 2020, https://www. prisonstudies.org/country/india.

150. 'Don't Just Look at Defence Budget. India's Intelligence Services, Police Desperately Need Funds.' ThePrint, 30 Jan. 2022, https:// theprint.in/opinion/security-code/india-intelligence-bureau-police-desperately-need-funds-budget/815409/.

151. Saeed Shah, 'Mainstream Pakistan Religious Organisations Applaud Killing of Salmaan Taseer', *Guardian*, 5 January 2011. *www. theguardian.com*, https://www.theguardian.com/world/2011/jan/05/ pakistan-religious-organisations-salman-taseer.

152. 'TMC's Derek O'Brien Slams Right-Wing Blogger, Twitter Demands Apology for Slander.' *Hindustan Times*, 3 Feruary 2017, https://www.hindustantimes.com/india-news/tmc-s-derek-o-brien-slams-right-wing-blogger-twitter-demands-apology-for-slander/ story-F7fOWdrsHDHL3N7qWC9liP.html.

153. Arunkumar Bhatt, 'Vajpayee Frowns on Banning of Books, *The Hindu*, 17 January 2004, accessed 24 April 2020, https://www. thehindu.com/todays-paper/vajpayee-frowns-on-banning-of-books/ article27552086.ece.

154. Lala Lajpat Rai, 'The Hindu–Muslim Problem (1924), Pt. 2: The Unity Conference and the Relativity of Rights', compiled by Frances W. Pritchett, accessed 24 April 2020, http://www.columbia.edu/itc/ mealac/pritchett/00islamlinks/txt_lajpatrai_1924/02part.html.

155. Rajeev Mantri and Harsh Gupta, 'Nellie and Delhi: "Secular" Riots versus "Communal" Riots ', Firstpost, 12 February 2014, accessed 24 April 2020, https://www.firstpost.com/india/nellie-and-delhi-secular-riots-versus-communal-riots-1384231.html.

156. John Elliott, 'India's Lethargy', *Financial Times*, 14 October 2009, accessed 24 April 2020, https://www.ft.com/content/a51ba57a-b89a-11de-809b-00144feab49a.

157. PTI, 'PM Manmohan Singh Takes Oath as Rajya Sabha Member', Livemint, 17 June 2013, accessed 24 April 2020, https://www.livemint.com/Politics/xr2cCdCzI3tlahsds3x4TI/PM-Manmohan-Singh-takes-oath-as-Rajya-Sabha-member.html.

158. Harsh Mander, 'Nellie: India's Forgotten Massacre', *The Hindu*, 14 December 2008, accessed 24 April 2020, https://www.thehindu.com/todays-paper/tp-features/tp-sundaymagazine/Nellie-Indiarsquos-forgotten-massacre/article15402276.ece.

159. 'H.S. Phoolka Releases Video of Rajiv Gandhi's Speech Justifying 1984 Riots', *Indian Express*, 19 November 2015, accessed 24 April 2020, https://indianexpress.com/article/india/india-news-india/video-of-rajiv-gandhis-infamous-tree-falls-comment-released-by-aap-bjp-leaders/.

160. Tavleen Singh, *Durbar* (Hachette India: 2017).

161. 'Budget 1991–92: Speech of Shri Manmohan Singh, Minister of Finance', 24 July 1991, accessed 24 April 2020, https://www.indiabudget.gov.in/doc/bspeech/bs199192.pdf.

162. UNI, 'Manmohan Blames RSS for Anti-Sikh Riots', Rediff on the NeT, 2 September 1999, accessed 24 April 2020, https://www.rediff.com/election/1999/sep/02man.htm.

163. PTI, 'Congress Not Involved in 1984 Anti-Sikh Riots, Says Rahul Gandhi', *The Hindu*, 25 August 2018, https://www.thehindu.com/news/national/congress-not-involved-in-1984-anti-sikh-riots-says-rahul-gandhi/article24778475.ece.

164. Times Now, 'Former Prime Minister Manmohan Singh stirs a fresh row by sharing stage with 1984 riots accused Sajjan Kumar', Twitter, 7 October 2017, accessed 24 April 2020, https://twitter.com/TimesNow/status/916584821287092224.

165. UNI, 'Sonia Says Sorry to Sikhs for 'June 6' Army Action and 1984 Riots', Rediff on The NeT, 27 January 1998, accessed 25 April 2020, https://www.rediff.com/news/1998/jan/27sorry.htm.

166. PTI, '1984 Riots Not Comparable with Post-Godhra Violence: Amartya Sen', *Indian Express*, 18 December 2013, accessed 25 April 2020, http://archive.indianexpress.com/news/1984-riots-not-comparable-with-postgodhra-violence-amartya-sen/1209088.

167. D. Bandyopadhyay, 'Census of Political Murders in West Bengal during CPI-M Rule: 1977–2009', *Mainstream Weekly*, 22 August 2010, accessed 1 May 2020, http://www.mainstreamweekly.net/article2234.html.

168. S.K. Sharma and Usha Sharma, *Encyclopaedia of Higher Education: Convocation Address* (Mittal Publications: New Delhi, 2005).

169. 'Jawaharlal Nehru's last TV Interview: May 1964', Prasar Bharti Archives, accessed 6 June 2020, https://www.youtube.com/watch?v=zlTfXWFQYGQ

170. 'The Mostly South Asian Origins of Indian Muslims', *Discover Magazine*, 11 October 2009, https://www.discovermagazine.com/mind/the-mostly-south-asian-origins-of-indian-muslims.

171. Eaaswarkhanth Muthukrishnan, et al. 'Diverse Genetic Origin of Indian Muslims: Evidence from Autosomal STR Loci.' *Journal of Human Genetics*, vol. 54, no. 6 (June 2009), 340–48. *www.nature.com*, doi:10.1038/jhg.2009.38.

172. Rajeev Mantri and Harsh Gupta, 'Narendra Modi as the Anti-Nehru', Livemint, 2 September 2013, accessed 25 April 2020, https://www.livemint.com/Opinion/DCrr6B9v1MvR6QTEMGDcJM/Narendra-Modi-as-the-antiNehru.html.

173. 'Jurists Stress Need to Retain Article 356', Rediff on The NeT, 31 October 1998, accessed 25 April 2020, https://www.rediff.com/news/1998/oct/31art.htm.

174. Sanjaya Baru, *The Accidental Prime Minister: The Making and Unmaking of Manmohan Singh* (Penguin Random House India: Gurgaon, 2015).

175. 'The Movement of Freedom: C. Rajagopalachari', Spontaneous Order, https://spontaneousorder.in/the-movement-of-freedom-c-rajagopalachari/. Accessed 2 June 2020.

176. H.L. Erdman, *The Swatantra Party and Indian Conservatism* (Cambridge University Press: New York, 2007).

177. Shuchi Bansal, 'Rajagopalachari's "Swarajya" to Be Relaunched Soon', Livemint, 17 September 2014, accessed 25 August 2020, https://www.livemint.com/Consumer/DwmLpRVJAHcanTLOrwtN2J/Rajagopalacharis-Swarajya-to-be-relaunched-soon.html.

178. Balaji Sadasivan, *The Dancing Girl: A History of Early India* (Institute of Southeast Asian Studies: Singapore, 2011).

179. 'Mosques Built after Demolishing Temples Are a Sign of Slavery: Mahatma Gandhi in 1937.' *India Today*, 28 May 2022, accessed 20 June 2022, https://www.indiatoday.in/india/story/mosques-built-demolishing-temples-sign-slavery-mahatma-gandhi-1955356-2022-05-28.

180. P.N. Chopra and Prabha Chopra, eds., *Inside Story of Sardar Patel: The Diary of Maniben Patel, 1936–50* (Vision Books: New Delhi, 2002).

181. Mahendra Prasad Singh and Subhendu Ranjan Raj, eds., *The Indian Political System* (Pearson: New Delhi, 2011).

182. Hindol Sengupta, *The Man Who Saved India* (Penguin Random House India: Gurgaon, 2018).

183. 'The 1955 Avadi Congress Session Set India on the Path of a Socialist Society', *The Week*, https://www.theweek.in/theweek/cover/2021/08/12/the-1955-avadi-congress-session-set-india-on-the-path-of-a-socialist-society.html. Accessed 24 August 2022.

184. 'Report to the All India Congress Committee, By Jawaharlal Nehru: Avadi: January 1955', http://indianculture.gov.in/reports-proceedings/report-all-india-congress-committee-avadi-january-1955-0. Accessed 24 August 2022.

185. 'The 1955 Avadi Congress Session Set India on the Path of a Socialist Society', *Week*, https://www.theweek.in/theweek/cover/2021/08/12/the-1955-avadi-congress-session-set-india-on-the-path-of-a-socialist-society.html. Accessed 24 August 2022.

186. Makkhan Lal, 'On KM Munshi's Birth Anniversary, Remembering His Fight to Rebuild Somnath Temple', ThePrint, 30 December 2018, https://theprint.in/opinion/on-km-munshis-birth-anniversary-remembering-his-fight-to-rebuild-somnath-temple/25283/.

187. 'Biography to Explore Personal, Unheard Episodes of V.P. Menon's Life.' *The Hindu*, 20 January 2020, https://www.thehindu.com/books/biography-to-explore-personal-unheard-episodes-of-vp-menons-life/article30606065.ece.

188. 'Khurshid Says Sonia Cried over Batla Pics; Cong Red-Faced', *Times of India*, 11 February 2012, accessed 25 April 2020, https://timesofindia.indiatimes.com/india/Khurshid-says-Sonia-cried-over-Batla-pics-red-faced-Cong-denies-claim/articleshow/11843860.cms.

189. B.R. Ambedkar, 'The Annihilation of Caste', accessed 6 June 2020, https://ccnmtl.columbia.edu/projects/mmt/ambedkar/web/readings/aoc_print_2004.pdf

190. Abhinav Prakash Singh, 'Subaltern Hindutva', *Seminar,* http://www.india-seminar.com/2019/720/702_abhinav_prakash_singh.htm. Accessed 7 June 2020.

191. Lion M.G. Agrawal, *Freedom Fighters of India* (Gyan Books: New Delhi, 2008).

192. Ravindra Kumar, *Life and Work of Sardar Vallabhbhai Patel* (Atlantic Publishers & Distributors: New Delhi, 1991).

Chapter 4: Profit Is Not a Dirty Word

1. Gita Piramal, *Business Legends* (Penguin Books India: New Delhi, 1999).

2. Rajeev Mantri and Harsh Gupta, 'The Duplicitous Language of the Economic Left', Livemint, 5 July 2012, accessed 25 August 2020, https://www.livemint.com/Opinion/z0em2v0rZq2lQKNYeNsKCK/Views--The-duplicitous-language-of-the-economic-left.html.

3. 'Two Concepts of Liberty', *Isaiah Berlin Virtual Library*, accessed 25 April 2020, http://berlin.wolf.ox.ac.uk/published_works/tcl/.

4. Amartya Sen, *Development as Freedom* (Oxford University Press: New York, 2001).

5. Amartya Sen, 'Karl Marx 2.00', *Indian Express*, 5 May 2018, accessed 25 April 2020, https://indianexpress.com/article/opinion/columns/karl-marx-philosophy-200th-birth-anniversary-5163799/.

6. Massimo Livi-Bacci, 'On the Human Costs of Collectivization in the Soviet Union', *Population and Development Review*, vol. 19, no. 4 (1993), 743–66, accessed 25 April 2020, https://doi.org/10.2307/2938412.

7. 'What There Is to Learn from the Soviet Economic Model', *The Economist*, 9 November 2017, accessed 25 April 2020, https://www.economist.com/finance-and-economics/2017/11/09/what-there-is-to-learn-from-the-soviet-economic-model.

8. Mahendra Prasad Singh and Subhendu Ranjan Raj, eds., *The Indian Political System* (Pearson: New Delhi, 2011).

9. Walter Crocker, *Nehru: A Contemporary's Estimate* (Random House: New Delhi, 2011).

10. M.S. Swaminathan, 'Jawaharlal Nehru and Agriculture in Independent India', *Current Science*, vol. 59, no. 6 (1990) 303–07, accessed 25 April 2020, https://www.jstor.org/stable/24092753.

11. Prabhu Ghate, 'Book Review: review of *An Indian Political Life: Charan Singh and Congress Politics,* by Paul R. Brass, *Sage Journals*, 17 April 2008, accessed 25 April 2020, https://doi.org/10.1177/2321023018762830.

12. Madhusree Mukerjee, *Churchill's Secret War: The British Empire and the Ravaging of India during World War II* (Penguin Random House India: Gurgaon, 2018).

13. Vimal Mishra et al., 'Drought and Famine in India, 1870–2016', *Geophysical Research Letters*, vol. 46, no. 4 (2019), 2075–83, *Wiley Online Library*, accessed 25 April 2020, https://doi.org/10.1029/2018GL081477.

14. Jagdish Bhagwati, *In Defense of Globalization* (Oxford University Press: New York, 2007).

15. Rajeev Mantri and Harsh Gupta, 'The Morality of Markets', Livemint, 24 February 2014, accessed 26 April 2020, https://www.livemint.com/Opinion/bQY5SN4kfB9abHDPnXnJ4I/The-morality-of-markets.html.

16. 'Rahul Gandhi Tears into Modi's 'Suit-Boot Ki Sarkar', 21 April 2015, accessed 26 April 2020, *Times of India*, https://timesofindia.indiatimes.com/india/Rahul-Gandhi-tears-into-Modis-suit-boot-ki-sarkar/articleshow/46993611.cms.

17. IANS, 'UPA Has Changed Development Paradigm: Rahul Gandhi', *New Indian Express*, 10 September 2013, accessed 26 April 2020, https://www.newindianexpress.com/nation/2013/sep/10/UPA-has-changed-development-paradigm-Rahul-Gandhi-515395.html.

18. 'Nyay Scheme 2019: Everything You Need to Know about Rahul Gandhi's Income Guarantee Scheme', *Financial Express*, 9 April 2019, accessed 26 April 2020, https://www.financialexpress.com/economy/nyay-scheme-2019-everything-you-need-to-know-about-rahul-gandhis-income-guarantee-scheme/1542454/.

19. NDTV, 'We are empowering India by giving the common man all kinds of rights: Rahul Gandhi in Jammu rally', Twitter,

6 November 2013, accessed 26 April 2020, https://twitter.com/ndtv/status/397988009536004097.

20. 'Rahul Trashes BJP's 'Capitalist Politics', Visits Dalit Colony', *Hindustan Times*, 24 October 2013, accessed 26 April 2020, https://www.hindustantimes.com/india/rahul-trashes-bjp-s-capitalist-politics-visits-dalit-colony/story-UTGObkAFIBpaTupgAHI76O.html.

21. 'Cabinet Amends Essential Commodities Act, Approves Ordinance to Ease Barrier-Free Trade.' *Indian Express*, 3 June 2020, https://indianexpress.com/article/india/cabinet-amends-essential-commodities-act-farmers-6440842/.

22. Sanjeeb Mukherjee, 'Our Goal Is to Make Farmer Prosperous, Boost Income: Agriculture Minister.' *Business Standard India*, 17 May 2020, https://www.business-standard.com/article/economy-policy/central-law-on-inter-state-trade-won-t-encroach-on-state-s-domain-tomar-120051700693_1.html.

23. 'From Plate to Plough: A 1991 Moment for Agriculture', *Indian Express*, 18 May 2020, https://indianexpress.com/article/opinion/columns/economic-package-agriculture-relief-fund-farmers-nirmala-sitharaman-ashok-gulati-6414759/.

24. 'Rich Farmers Dominate Farm Protests in India. It's Happening since Charan Singh Days.' ThePrint, 30 Sept. 2020, https://theprint.in/opinion/rich-farmers-dominate-farm-protests-in-india-its-happening-since-charan-singh-days/513027/.

25. Salvatore Babones, 'India's Rich Farmers Are Holding Up Reforms Designed to Help the Poor.' *Foreign Policy*, https://foreignpolicy.com/2021/03/30/modi-india-farmers-protests-agriculture-reforms-rich-versus-poor/. Accessed 28 June 2022.

26. Sheela Bhatt, 'Modi's Retreat Will Haunt Indian Politics for A Long, Long Time', Rediff, https://www.rediff.com/news/column/sheela-bhatt-modis-retreat-will-haunt-indian-politics-for-a-long-long-time/20211119.htm. Accessed 28 June 2022.

27. 'Farmers' Protest | Foreign Funds Received by Bharatiya Kisan Union Faction under FCRA Scanner', Moneycontrol, https://www.moneycontrol.com/news/india/farmers-protest-foreign-funds-received-by-bharatiya-kisan-union-faction-under-fcra-scanner-6253961.html. Accessed 28 June 2022.

28. A. Narayanamoorthy, 'Why India's Lopsided Farm Procurement Benefits Punjab', 14 May 2021, https://www.thehindubusinessline.com/opinion/the-crop-procurement-scheme-is-lopsided/article34560177.ece.

29. 'One Nation, One Ration Card' Scheme: 5 More States Join the Initiative', Livemint, 1 May 2020, https://www.livemint.com/news/india/-one-nation-one-ration-card-scheme-5-more-states-join-the-initiative-11588331166781.html.

30. Kumar Anand, 'B. R. Shenoy: A Forgotten Economist and What Modi Can Learn from Him.' Swarajyamag, https://swarajyamag.com/economy/b-r-shenoy-a-forgotten-economist-and-what-modi-can-learn-from-him. Accessed 8 June 2020.

31. 'Free Enterprise and Democracy by A. D. Shroff (February 11, 1956)', Indian Liberals, https://indianliberals.in/bn/content/free-enterprise-and-democracy-by-a-d-shroff-feb-11-1956/. Accessed 3 Aug. 2022.

32. Nandini Saraf, *The Life and Times of Lokmanya Tilak* (Prabhat Prakashan: New Delhi, 2012).

33. 'PM Modi's exclusive interview to News24', *YouTube*, 17 May 2019, accessed 4 June 2020, https://www.youtube.com/watch?v=UgEgqfy1hl0.

34. Charles Wheelan, *Naked Economics: Undressing the Dismal Science* (W.W. Norton & Company: New York, 2010).

35. Rajeev Mantri Harish Gupta, 'Winning the Intellectual Battle for Economic Liberalization', Livemint, 21 March 2013, accessed 26 April 2020, https://www.livemint.com/Opinion/hjUdBaLNgjwdQiqpdUp7bO/Winning-the-intellectual-battle-for-economic-liberalization.html.

36. David McCandless et al., '20th Century Death', Information Is Beautiful, accessed 26 April 2020, https://informationisbeautiful.net/visualizations/20th-century-death/.

37. Richard D. Heffner, 'Living within Our Means: Milton Friedman Interview', *The Open Mind*, 7 December 1975, accessed 26 April 2020, http://www.thirteen.org/openmind-archive/public-affairs/living-within-our-means.

38. Swaminathan S. Anklesaria Aiyar, 'Socialism Kills: The Human Cost of Delayed Economic Reform in India', Cato Institute, 21 October

2009, accessed 26 April 2020, https://www.cato.org/publications/ development-briefing-paper/socialism-kills-human-cost-delayed-economic-reform-india.

39. Nani Ardeshir Palkhivala, *Our Constitution Defaced and Defiled* (Macmillan India: Bombay, 1974).

40. Ashish Sharma and Pragya Singh, 'Everyone's a Socialist in One of the World's Fastest Growing Economies', *Mint*, 28 June 2007, https:// www.livemint.com/Home-Page/b23B1KQsSv0tSkdvC4UWKO/ Everyones-a-socialist-in-one-of-the-worlds-fastest-growing.html.

41. Rajeev Mantri and Harsh Gupta, 'The Story of India's Telecom Revolution', *Mint*, 8 January 2013, accessed 28 April 2020, https:// www.livemint.com/Opinion/biNfQImaeobXxOPV6pFxqI/The-story-of-Indias-telecom-revolution.html.

42. Firstpost, 'Rahul: You got mobile phones because Rajiv Gandhi heard you. You could express your demands', Twitter, 11 December 2012, accessed 28 April 2020, https://twitter.com/firstpost/ status/278441797326360576.

43. Nistula Hebbar, 'Sam, Son of a Carpenter', *Financial Express*, 7 February 2012, accessed 28 April 2020, https://www.financialexpress. com/archive/sam-son-of-a-carpenter/908677/.

44. Sam Pitroda and Mehul Desai, *The March of Mobile Money: The Future of Lifestyle Management* (HarperCollins: Noida, 2010).

45. 'New Telecom Policy, 1999', Department of Telecommunications, Ministry of Communications, Government of India, accessed 28 April 2020, https://dot.gov.in/new-telecom-policy-1999.

46. Rashmi Pratap, 'Idea Cellular Is Emerging Company of the Year', *Economic Times*, 30 December 2009, accessed 28 April 2020, https://economictimes.indiatimes.com/news/company/corporate-trends/idea-cellular-is-emerging-company-of-the-year/ articleshow/5393837.cms.

47. Arvind Panagariya, *India: The Emerging Giant* (Oxford University Press: New York, 2010).

48. Sukumar Muralidharan, 'The Telecom Tangle', *Frontline*, 14 August 1999, accessed 28 April 2020, https://frontline.thehindu.com/cover-story/article30257823.ece.

49. Ajith Pillai and Murali Krishnan, 'A Bailout That Could Kick Back', *Outlook*, 9 August 1999, accessed 28 April 2020, https://

www.outlookindia.com/magazine/story/a-bailout-that-could-kick-back/207913.

50. Arvind Panagariya, *India: The Emerging Giant* (Oxford University Press: New York, 2010).

51. 'Wilful Defaulters Beneficiaries of "Phone Banking" under UPA Regime: Nirmala Sitharaman.' *The Hindu*, 29 April 2020. *www.thehindu.com*, https://www.thehindu.com/business/wilful-defaulters-beneficiaries-of-phone-banking-under-upa-regime-nirmala-sitharaman/article31460008.ece.

52. PTI, 'India Reaping Benefits of Bank Nationalization: Mukherjee', Livemint, 19 July 2009, accessed 27 April 2020, https://www.livemint.com/Politics/OkIUDQ5x0nIbZN85FFcV0N/India-reaping-benefits-of-bank-nationalization-Mukherjee.html.

53. 'Sonia Bats for the Aam Aadmi, Praises Bank Nationalisation', *Business Standard India*, 22 November 2008, 29 January 2013, accessed 27 April 2020, https://www.business-standard.com/article/economy-policy/sonia-bats-for-the-aam-aadmi-praises-bank-nationalisation-108112201020_1.html.

54. Amiya Kumar Mohapatra and Srirang Jha, 'Bank Recapitalization in India: A Critique of Public Policy Concerns', *Sage Journals: FIIB Business Review*, vol. 7, no. 1 (March 2018), 10–15, 16 April 2018, accessed 27 April 2020, https://doi.org/10.1177/2319714518766113.

55. 'ArcelorMittal Says It Has Completed Acquisition of Essar Steel', *Mint*, 16 Dec. 2019, https://www.livemint.com/companies/news/arcelormittal-says-it-has-completed-acquisition-of-essar-steel-11576499405991.html.

56. James C. Scott, *Seeing Like a State: How Certain Schemes to Improve the Human Condition Have Failed* (Yale University Press: New Haven, 1998).

57. Ibid.

58. 'UPI, CoWIN, ONDC: Public Digital Infrastructure Has Put India on the Fast Lane of Tech-Led Growth.' News18, 28 May 2022, https://www.news18.com/news/opinion/upi-cowin-ondc-public-digital-infrastructure-has-put-india-on-the-fast-lane-of-tech-led-growth-5263255.html.

59. 'UID Isn't Just a Number, It Is an Identity: Nandan Nilekani.' *Economic Times*, 12 September 2010, https://economictimes.

indiatimes.com/opinion/interviews/uid-isnt-just-a-number-it-is-an-identity-nandan-nilekani/articleshow/6537880.cms.

60. 'Economic Survey Moots Central Welfare Database of Citizens.' *The Hindu*, 4 July 2019. www.thehindu.com, https://www.thehindu.com/business/economic-survey-moots-central-welfare-database-of-citizens/article28287057.ece.

61. Lee Kuan Yew, et al., *Lee Kuan Yew: The Grand Master's Insights on China, the United States, and the World* (MIT Press: 2012).

62. 'Full Text: Prime Minister Narendra Modi's Speech on 68th Independence Day.' *Indian Express*, 16 Aug. 2014, https://indianexpress.com/article/india/india-others/full-text-prime-minister-narendra-modis-speech-on-68th-independence-day/.

63. Asli Demirgüç-Kunt, Leora Klapper, Dorothe Singer, Saniya Ansar, and Jake Hess. 2018. The Global Findex Database 2017: Measuring Financial Inclusion and the Fintech Revolution. Washington, DC: World Bank. doi:10.1596/978-1-4648-1259-0. License: Creative Commons Attribution CC BY 3.0 IGO

64. Asli Demirgüç-Kunt, Leora Klapper, Dorothe Singer, and Saniya Ansar. 2022. Global Findex Database 2021: Financial Inclusion, Digital Payments, and Resilience in the Age of COVID-19. Washington, DC: World Bank. doi:10.1596/978-1-4648-1897-4.

65. McKinsey Global Institute, 'Digital India: Technology to transform a connected nation', 27 March 2019, accessed 4 June 2020, https://www.mckinsey.com/business-functions/mckinsey-digital/our-insights/digital-india-technology-to-transform-a-connected-nation

66. 'Record in the Grand Schemes of Things: Direct Benefit Transfers Cross Rs 25 Tn, 56% Achieved Amid Pandemic', News18, 18 Sept. 2022, https://www.news18.com/news/india/record-in-the-grand-schemes-of-things-direct-benefit-transfers-cross-rs-25-tn-56-achieved-amid-pandemic-5983525.html.

67. Omidyar Network-Boston Consulting Group, 'Credit Disrupted – Digital MSME Lending in India,' 21 November 2018, accessed 4 June 2020, https://www.omidyar.com/insights/credit-disrupted.

68. Morgan Stanley, 'UPI – The Indian Payments Juggernaut', 4 September 2019

69. Ibid.

70. 'UPI Usage at All-Time High, February Records 132 Crore Transactions.' Moneycontrol, 3 March 2020, accessed 4 June 2020, https://www.moneycontrol.com/news/business/economy/upi-usage-at-all-time-high-february-records-132-crore-transactions-4996061.html.

71. Reserve Bank of India, Press Releases. https://www.rbi.org.in/Scripts/BS_PressReleaseDisplay.aspx?prid=53886. Accessed 6 July 2022.

72. Priyanka Pani, 'RuPay Makes a Quantum Leap in 4 Years.' *The Hindu Business Line*, https://www.thehindubusinessline.com/money-and-banking/rupay-makes-a-quantum-leap-in-4-years/article27164842.ece. Accessed 4 June 2020.

73. Ishaan Gera, 'RuPay Cards Are Expanding Footprint but Domestic Performance Remains Muted', 16 May 2022, *Business Standard*, https://www.business-standard.com/article/finance/rupay-cards-are-expanding-footprint-but-domestic-performance-remains-muted-122051600547_1.html.

74. 'Exclusive: Mastercard Lodged U.S. Protest over Modi's Promotion of Indian Card Network RuPay.' *Reuters*, 2 Nov. 2018. in.reuters.com, https://in.reuters.com/article/india-mastercard-idINKCN1N65IS.

75. 'UAE Will Be First Middle East Country to Issue RuPay Card.' *Mint*, 22 August 2019, https://www.livemint.com/companies/news/uae-will-be-first-middle-east-country-to-issue-rupay-card-1566466476882.html.

76. 'India Proposes Use of RuPay Card to Oman', WION, https://www.wionews.com/india-news/india-proposes-use-of-rupay-card-to-oman-478161. Accessed 6 July 2022.

77. 'UPI, Rupay Services Will Be Available in France Soon.' *Mint*, 17 June 2022, https://www.livemint.com/news/india/upi-rupay-cards-brace-for-european-entry-npci-to-launch-digital-payment-services-in-france-soon-11655423247576.html.

78. Hemant Mohapatra, '6 Months Later: Return to India after 15yrs in the US', *Medium*, 6 January 2019, https://medium.com/swlh/6-months-later-return-to-india-after-15yrs-in-the-us-c33b76f95c47.

79. Hindol Sengupta, 'How to Make a Billion People Rich', 5 April 2017, accessed 5 June 2020, https://www.linkedin.com/pulse/how-make-billion-people-rich-hindol-sengupta.

80. '"This Can Be as Big as UPI" — Understanding the Big New Thing in India', *Medium*, 20 August 2019, https://blog.usejournal.com/this-can-be-as-big-as-upi-understanding-the-big-new-thing-in-india-76465995997f.

81. 'Sahay, India's Fintech Disruption Sequel', The Ken, 8 May 2020, https://the-ken.com/story/sahay-indias-fintech-disruption-sequel/.

82. ONDC Project, https://pib.gov.in/Pressreleaseshare.aspx?PRID=1814143. Accessed 28 June 2022.

83. Derryl D'Silva, et al., 'The Design of Digital Financial Infrastructure: Lessons from India', December 2019, Bank for International Settlements, https://www.bis.org/publ/bppdf/bispap106.htm.

84. https://www1.undp.org/content/digital/en/home/stories/building-digital-public-goods--takeaways-from-indias-covid-19-va.html

85. Rajeev Mantri, 'India's Opportunity to Lead the World in 5G', *Mint*, 24 April 2018, accessed 28 April 2020, https://www.livemint.com/Opinion/gw3osisaAbZVOm5ve3jP2N/Indias-opportunity-to-lead-the-world-in-5G.html.

86. *IT & ITeS Industry in India: Market Size, Opportunities, Growth, IBEF.* https://www.ibef.org/industry/information-technology-india.aspx. Accessed 5 June 2020.

87. 'Explained: How New Rules for Other Service Providers Could Ease Working of BPO, ITeS Players.' *Indian Express*, 9 Nov. 2020, https://indianexpress.com/article/explained/explained-how-new-rules-for-other-service-providers-could-ease-working-of-bpo-ites-players-7018322/.

88. Rajeev Mantri, 'Reassessing Received Wisdom and Addressing Policy Challenges of the New Technology Age', *Digital Debates - CyFy Journal 2018*, GP-ORF Series, Observer Research Foundation and Global Policy Journal, October 2018, accessed June 2 2020, https://www.orfonline.org/wp-content/uploads/2018/10/Digital-Debates-Journal_v13.pdf

89. Rajeev Mantri, 'Aamir Khan and the Pursuit of Excellence', *Wall Street Journal*, 12 January 2010, accessed 27 April 2020, https://www.wsj.com/articles/SB126335730113227507.

90. Federal Reserve Bank of St. Louis, 'Constant GDP per Capita for India', *FRED*, 20 December 2019, accessed 27 April 2020, https://fred.stlouisfed.org/series/NYGDPPCAPKDIND.

91. S. L. Kirloskar, Cactus and Roses (Macmillan India: New Delhi, 2003).

92. T. N. Ninan, et al., 'Both Nehru and Mrs Gandhi Developed Polite Ways of Telling Me to Shut up: J.R.D. Tata', *India Today*, 15 August 1986, accessed 4 June 2020, https://www.indiatoday.in/magazine/interview/story/19860815-both-nehru-and-mrs-gandhi-developed-polite-ways-of-telling-me-to-shut-up-j.r.d.-tata-801137-1986-08-15.

93. 'HT Archives| Policy of Controls Takes Away Creative Genius of People: GD Birla', *Hindustan Times*, 26 January 2020, https://www.hindustantimes.com/india-news/republic-at-70-policy-of-controls-takes-away-creative-genius-of-people-writes-gd-birla/story-BoTNGRwS69heYMrhXqDd2J.html.

94. Nasreen Munni Kabir, *Talking Films and Songs: Javed Akhtar in Conversation with Nasreen Munni Kabir* (Oxford University Press: New Delhi, 2018).

95. Niranjan Sahoo, 'Half a Century of India's Maoist Insurgency: An Appraisal of State Response', Observer Research Foundation, 12 June 2019, accessed 27 April 2020, https://www.orfonline.org/research/half-a-century-of-indias-maoist-insurgency-an-appraisal-of-state-response-51933/.

96. 'This Indian TikTok Star Wants You to Know His Name', *The Economist*. 13 September 2019, https://www.economist.com/news/2019/09/13/this-indian-tiktok-star-wants-you-to-know-his-name. Accessed 3 June 2020.

97. Andy Warhol, *The Philosophy of Andy Warhol* (Penguin: London, 2007).

98. Rajeev Mantri, 'The Jugaad Myth', *Pragati*, 31 May 2010, http://pragati.nationalinterest.in/2010/06/the-jugaad-myth/.

99. Karl Marx and Frederick Engels, *The Communist* Manifesto (International Publishers: New York, 2014).

100. Rajeev Mantri and Harsh Gupta, 'India Must Promote Market Competition to Eradicate Social Discrimination', *Mint*, 4 June 2014, accessed 27 April 2020, https://www.livemint.com/Opinion/hxfvT5IeW1OmhkfgNdWy5O/India-must-promote-market-competition-to-eradicate-social-di.html.

101. 'UP Colleges Ban Jeans to Check Eve-Teasing!' *Ahmedabad Mirror*, 10 June 2009, accessed 5 June 2020, https://ahmedabadmirror. indiatimes.com/news/india/UP-colleges-ban-jeans-to-check-eve-teasing/articleshow/37475376.cms.

102. Gary S. Becker, *The Economics of Discrimination* (University of Chicago Press: Chicago, 2010).

103. Gary Becker and Richard Posner, 'Competitive Markets and Discrimination Against Minorities', The Becker–Posner Blog, 7 September 2008, accessed 28 April 2020, https://www.becker-posner-blog.com/2008/09/competitive-markets-and-discrimination-against-minorities-becker.html.

104. Abhijit Banerjee et al., 'Labor Market Discrimination in Delhi: Evidence from a Field Experiment', *Journal of Comparative Economics*, vol. 37, no. 1 (2009), 14–27, accessed 28 April 2020, https:// EconPapers.repec.org/RePEc:eee:jcecon:v:37:y:2009:i:1:p:14-27.

105. Aarefa Johari, 'Liberal 'Hindu' Newspaper Reiterates No-Meat Policy in Office, Sparks Debate on Vegetarian Fundamentalism', Scroll.In, 18 April 2014, accessed 28 April 2020, http://scroll.in/ article/662132/liberal-hindu-newspaper-reiterates-no-meat-policy-in-office-sparks-debate-on-vegetarian-fundamentalism.

106. Kumar Mangalam Birla, 'Butter Chicken at Birla', *McKinsey & Company*, December 2013, accessed 28 April 2020, https://www. mckinsey.com/featured-insights/asia-pacific/butter-chicken-at-birla.

107. Chandra Bhan Prasad, 'Shades of Mobility | Outlook India Magazine', *Outlook,* 31 October 2011, https://www.outlookindia. com/magazine/story/shades-of-mobility/278702.

108. Chandra Bhan Prasad, 'Markets and Manu: Economic Reforms and Its Impact on Caste in India', Center for the Advanced Study of India (CASI), January 2008, accessed 28 April 2020, https://casi.sas. upenn.edu/content/markets-and-manu-economic-reforms-and-its-impact-caste-india-chandra-bhan-prasad.

109. 'Zoroastrian Co-Operative . . . vs District Registrar Co-Operative . . . on 15 April, 2005', *Indian Kanoon*, accessed 28 April 2020, https:// indiankanoon.org/doc/713373/.

110. Milton Friedman and Rose D. Friedman, *Capitalism and Freedom,* Fortieth Anniversary Edn, (University of Chicago Press: Chicago, 2002).

111. Rajeev Mantri and Harsh Gupta, 'Economic Development as Political Strategy', Livemint, 10 October 2012, accessed 28 April 2020, https://www.livemint.com/Opinion/rcOPYHBPNZAg1Imp9hYiYL/Economic-development-as-political-strategy.html.

112. Shantanu Gupta, 'Indira Gandhi vs Morarji Desai: How JNU Was at the Centre of Battle to Capture Academia', ThePrint, 17 January 2020, https://theprint.in/pageturner/excerpt/indira-gandhi-vs-morarji-desai-how-jnu-was-at-the-centre-of-battle-to-capture-academia/350831/.

113. The Dharma Dispatch, 'The Sinister Communist Slaughter of Indian History in Five Phases', https://thedharmadispatch.substack.com/p/the-sinister-communist-slaughter. Accessed 2 August 2022.

114. Surajit Dasgupta, 'A History of 'Tolerance', Swarajyamag, https://swarajyamag.com/magazine/a-history-of-tolerance. Accessed 2 August 2022.

115. 'Top Scientists Unhappy over Appointment of Professor Nurul Hasan as CSIR Vice-President.' *India Today*, 29 February 1980, https://www.indiatoday.in/magazine/indiascope/story/19800229-top-scientists-unhappy-over-appointment-of-professor-nurul-hasan-as-csir-vice-president-806468-2014-02-05. Accessed 2 Aug. 2022.

116. 'Speech of India's greatest lawyer Nani Palkhivala on Emergency: Nani Palkhivala on 24th–26th Constitutional Amendments, YouTube, 14 February 2017, accessed 29 April 2020, https://www.youtube.com/watch?v=G9PqkitIUsQ.

117. 'Soniaji, Mungeri Lal Will Have the Last Laugh: Venkaiah', *Economic Times*, 7 January 2004, accessed 29 April 2020, https://economictimes.indiatimes.com/elections-2004/soniaji-mungeri-lal-will-have-the-last-laugh-venkaiah/articleshow/408891.cms.

118. 'Agriculture, Forestry, and Fishing, Value Added (% of GDP)—India, 1960–2021', *The World Bank Data*, 2019, accessed 2 August April 2022, https://data.worldbank.org/indicator/NV.AGR.TOTL.ZS?locations=IN.

119. 'Manufacturing, Value Added (% of GDP)—India, 1960–2021', *The World Bank Data*, accessed 2 August 2022, https://data.worldbank.org/indicator/NV.IND.MANF.ZS?locations=IN.

120. Arvind Panagariya, *India Unlimited: Reclaiming the Lost Glory* (HarperCollins India: 2020).

121. 'Return of Protectionism: Panagariya Sounds Alarm over Modi's New Trade Template for India', *Economic Times*, 12 February 2018, accessed 29 April 2020, https://economictimes.indiatimes.com/news/economy/policy/budget-2018-has-ensured-the-return-of-protectionism/articleshow/62876012.cms.

122. Lillian Goldman Law Library, Yale Law School, 'The Avalon Project: First Annual Message of George Washington', *A Compilation of the Messages and Papers of the Presidents* (Bureau of National Literature Inc.: New York, 1897), accessed 29 April 2020, https://avalon.law.yale.edu/18th_century/washs01.asp. Accessed 30 January 2020.

123. 'Founders Online: Alexander Hamilton's Final Version of the Report, 5 December 1791', National Archives, accessed 29 April 2020, http://founders.archives.gov/documents/Hamilton/01-10-02-0001-0007.

124. Douglas A. Irwin, 'The Aftermath of Hamilton's Report on Manufactures', National Bureau of Economic Research, https://doi.org/10.3386/w9943.

125. 'India Now Has 268 Mobile Handset and Component Manufacturing Units, 6.7 Lakh Jobs Created: ICEA', *Indian Express*, 22 November 2018, https://indianexpress.com/article/technology/tech-news-technology/india-now-has-268-mobile-handset-and-component-units-6-7-lakh-jobs-created-icea-5457529/.

126. 'Cabinet approves Production Linked Incentive Scheme for Large Scale Electronics Manufacturing', Press Information Bureau, 21 March 2020, accessed 4 June 2020 https://pib.gov.in/PressReleseDetail.aspx?PRID=1607487.

127. ANI, 'India Now the Second-Largest Mobile Phone Manufacturer in the World: Ravi Shankar Prasad', ThePrint, 2 June 2020, https://theprint.in/india/india-now-the-second-largest-mobile-phone-manufacturer-in-the-world-ravi-shankar-prasad/433982/.

128. Prasid Banerjee, 'India Calls on Firms to Help Them Be World Champs in Electronic Manufacturing.' Livemint, 2 June 2020, https://www.livemint.com/industry/manufacturing/india-calls-on-firms-to-help-them-be-world-champs-in-electronic-manufacturing-11591082765781.html.

129. 'Mobile Phone Exports Jump 75% in 2021–22', *Financial Express*, 25 March 2022, https://www.financialexpress.com/industry/mobile-phone-exports-jump-75-in-2021-22/2471199/. Accessed 28 June 2022.

130. 'India Market Strategy – Export boost to manufacturing', Credit Suisse, 11 January 2022, PDF document available with authors. YouTube video discussion: 'India's Manufacturing Sector Turning a Corner - Neelkanth Mishra, Co-Head of Asia Pacific Strategy & India Equity Strategist for Credit Suisse', ThePrint, 24 January 2022, accessed 29 June 2022, https://www.youtube.com/watch?v=2TvTV5TCuRw

131. 'Make-in-India: Need a Brand-New Policy to Curb Imports', *Financial Express*, 12 August 2019, https://www.financialexpress.com/opinion/made-for-india-vs-make-in-india/1672881/.

132. Tirumala Venkatesh, 'Xiaomi Is Only Assembling Phones in India but This Is How Manufacturing Ecosystems Are Built', *Swarajya*, 11 April 2018, accessed 4 June 2020, https://swarajyamag.com/economy/building-a-manufacturing-ecosystem-screwdriver-technology-will-show-the-way.

133. 'Government Eyes $17 Billion Investment Proposals to Boost Local Manufacturing', *Times of India*, 3 June 2020, accessed 4 June 2020 https://timesofindia.indiatimes.com/business/india-business/govt-eyes-17bn-investment-proposals-to-boost-local-manufacturing/articleshow/76166375.cms.

134. Yogima Seth Sharma, 'PLI Scheme Draws Investment of ₹2.34 Lakh Crore in 14 Sectors.' *Economic Times*, 21 April 2022, https://economictimes.indiatimes.com/news/economy/policy/pli-scheme-draws-investment-of-2-34-lakh-crore-in-14-sectors/articleshow/90968836.cms.

135. 'The End of Car Production in Australia—What Went Wrong', *Autocar*, 16 October 2017, accessed 29 April 2020, https://www.autocar.co.uk/car-news/industry/end-car-production-australia-what-went-wrong.

136. 'Information Technology Agreement', World Trade Organization, accessed 29 April 2020, https://www.wto.org/english/tratop_e/inftec_e/inftec_e.htm.

137. Tirumala Venkatesh, 'Xiaomi Is Only Assembling Phones in India but This Is How Manufacturing Ecosystems Are Built', *Swarajya*, 11 April 2018, accessed 29 April 2020, https://swarajyamag.com/economy/building-a-manufacturing-ecosystem-screwdriver-technology-will-show-the-way.

138. Prasannan Parthasarathi, *Why Europe Grew Rich and Asia Did Not: Global Economic Divergence, 1600–1850* (Cambridge: Cambridge University Press, 2011).

139. '"Made in China" Electric Vehicles Could Turn Sino-EU Trade on Its Head' | Merics, 30 May 2022, accessed 28 June 2022. https://merics.org/en/short-analysis/made-china-electric-vehicles-could-turn-sino-eu-trade-its-head.

140. 'Piyush Goyal Plans for 'future Ready' Commerce Ministry to Get USD 2 Trillion Exports by 2027.' ThePrint, 20 Feb. 2022, https://theprint.in/economy/piyush-goyal-plans-for-future-ready-commerce-ministry-to-get-usd-2-trillion-exports-by-2027/839832/.

Chapter 5: Decolonizing the Indian State

1.   Daron Acemoglu and James A. Robinson, *Why Nations Fail: The Origins of Power, Prosperity and Poverty* (Profile: 2012).

2.   Thomas Hobbes, *Leviathan* (Penguin Classics: New York, 2017).

3.   'Maddison Historical Statistics', University of Groningen, 10 November 2017, https://www.rug.nl/ggdc/historicaldevelopment/maddison/releases/maddison-project-database-2018

4.   'Ahilya Bai Holkar: The Feisty Queen of Maheshwar', Indic Today, 31 May 2020, https://www.indictoday.com/quick-reads/ahilya-bai-the-feisty-queen-of-maheshwar/.

5.   Anil A. Athale, *Struggle for Empire: Anglo-Maratha Wars, 1679–1818* (Reliance: 2001).

6.   'Premature Imitation and India's Flailing State', *Marginal Revolution*, 23 September 2019, https://marginalrevolution.com/marginalrevolution/2019/09/premature-imitation-and-indias-flailing-state.html.

7.   Utpal Bhaskar, 'Nine from Outside the IAS Set to Become Joint Secretaries in Government', Livemint, 13 Apr. 2019, https://www.livemint.com/politics/policy/nine-from-outside-the-ias-set-to-become-joint-secretaries-in-government-1555133560315.html.

8.   'A Chronology of Income Tax since 1950s', *India Today*, 15 February 2010, accessed 6 May 2020, https://www.indiatoday.in/business/budget/story/a-chronology-of-income-tax-since-1950s-67424-2010-02-15.

9. *Seventh CPC Pay Commission, Department of Expenditure, Ministry of Finance, Government of India* https://doe.gov.in/seventh-cpc-pay-commission. Accessed 7 June 2020.

10. Iain Marlow, 'India Has 1.3 Billion People, but Fewer Than 1,000 Diplomats', *Bloomberg*, 31 August 2018, accessed 30 April 2020, https://www.bloomberg.com/news/articles/2018-08-30/india-s-diplomat-shortage-leaves-it-far-behind-asian-rival-china.

11. Bharat Karnad, 'Restructuring of MEA Misses out on Basics', Security Wise, 2 February 2020, accessed 30 April 2020, https://bharatkarnad.com/2020/02/02/restructuring-of-mea-misses-out-on-basics/.

12. 'If Shashi Tharoor's Panel Has Its Way, India's Diplomatic Corps Could Grow in Quantity and Quality', Firstpost, 4 August 2016, accessed 30 April 2020, https://www.firstpost.com/world/india-is-strapped-for-diplomats-but-if-shashi-tharoors-panel-has-its-way-you-could-become-one-2931362.html.

13. Huma Siddiqui, 'In the Biggest Reform Ever MEA Gets Overhauled', *Financial Express*, 2 February 2020, accessed 30 April 2020, https://www.financialexpress.com/defence/in-the-biggest-reform-ever-mea-gets-overhauled/1852299/.

14. PTI, 'Over 2,400 IAS, IPS Posts Vacant: Government', *Economic Times*, 19 July 2018, accessed 30 April 2020, https://economictimes.indiatimes.com/news/politics-and-nation/over-2400-ias-ips-posts-vacant-government/articleshow/65056607.cms.

15. Anand Vardhan, 'Why the Drop in Civil Services Vacancies Is Neither New nor Alarming', Newslaundry, 15 February 2018, accessed 30 April 2020, https://www.newslaundry.com/2018/02/15/indian-civil-services-vacancies-reform-ravish-kumar-ias-modi.

16. PTI, '5 Lakh Posts Vacant in Police Forces', *Economic Times*, 13 July 2018, accessed 30 April 2020, https://economictimes.indiatimes.com/news/defence/5-lakh-posts-vacant-in-police-forces/articleshow/56562943.cms.

17. 'IAS, IPS, IFS, IRS Should Have Specific Civil Service Entrance Exams. At Least Discuss It', ThePrint, 15 March 2022, https://theprint.in/opinion/ias-ips-ifs-irs-should-have-specific-civil-service-entrance-exams/872584/.

18. 'Why Agnipath Scheme Needs to Be Extended to All India Services', *Indian Express*, 24 July 2022, https://indianexpress.com/article/

opinion/columns/why-agnipath-scheme-needs-to-be-extended-to-all-india-services-8048997/.

19. Atul Thakur, '68% of IAS Officers Have Average Tenures of 18 Months or Less', 8 January 2014, *Times of India*, accessed 30 April 2020, https://timesofindia.indiatimes.com/india/68-of-IAS-officers-have-average-tenures-of-18-months-or-less/articleshow/28203370.cms.

20. Aashish Chandorkar, 'The Railways Is Finally Out of the Shadow of the British', *Hindustan Times*, 14 January 2020, accessed 30 April 2020, https://www.hindustantimes.com/analysis/the-railways-is-finally-out-of-the-shadow-of-the-british/story-HCD3WRNznoZanE6roxqkOK.html.

21. *Seventh CPC Pay Commission, Department of Expenditure, Ministry of Finance, Government of India* https://doe.gov.in/seventh-cpc-pay-commission. Accessed 7 June 2020

22. 'PhD Holders among 23 Lakh Applicants for Peon Jobs in UP,' *Hindustan Times*, 16 September 2015, https://www.hindustantimes.com/india/phd-holders-among-23-lakh-applicants-for-peon-jobs-in-up/story-OqHzHbvo16gUN2DfTkfYlI.html.

23. Manjari Singh et al., 'A Study for Comparing Salaries/ Emoluments in the Government Sector vis-à-vis Central Public Sector Undertakings/ Private Sector in India', Indian Institute of Management Ahmedabad, October 2015, accessed 30 April 2020, https://www.academia.edu/27462260/A_Study_for_Comparing_Salaries_Emoluments_in_the_Government_Sector_vis-%C3%A0-vis_Central_Public_Sector_Undertakings_Private_Sector_in_India_Indian_Institute_of_Management_Ahmedabad.

24. Mayank Jain, 'Government Employees Earn (Much) More than Private Sector Ones—but Only at the Entry-Level', Scroll.In, 30 June 2016, accessed 30 April 2020, http://scroll.in/article/810922/government-employees-earn-much-more-than-private-sector-ones-but-only-at-the-entry-level.

25. 'Article 311 in the Constitution of India 1949', Indian Kanoon, accessed 30 April 2020, https://indiankanoon.org/doc/47623/.

26. T.C.A. Srinivasa Raghavan, '2017 Wishlist: Mr Modi, Start an Intellectual Assault on Victorian Underpinnings of Bureaucracy', *Swarajya*, 6 January 2017, accessed 30 April 2020, https://

swarajyamag.com/magazine/2017-wishlist-mr-modi-start-an-intellectual-assault-on-victorian-underpinnings-of-bureaucracy.

27. Rajeev Mantri and Harsh Gupta, 'Towards a Transparent State', Livemint, 2 July 2013, accessed 3 May 2020, https://www.livemint.com/Opinion/1lqE0XadOCvobSKiY4OMLO/Towards-a-transparent-state.html.

28. Sanjeev Sanyal, 'Why We Need a "Transparency of Rules" Act', Business Standard, 27 April 2013, accessed 3 May 2020, https://www.business-standard.com/article/opinion/why-we-need-a-transparency-of-rules-act-113042700527_1.html.

29. Jaideep A. Prabhu, 'India's Allodoxaphobia', Swarajya, 30 January 2013, accessed 3 May 2020, https://swarajyamag.com/commentary/indias-allodoxaphobia.

30. 'A New Goldmine', The Economist, 18 May 2013, accessed 3 May 2020, https://www.economist.com/business/2013/05/18/a-new-goldmine.

31. 'UPI, CoWIN, ONDC: Public Digital Infrastructure Has Put India on the Fast Lane of Tech-Led Growth', News18, 28 May 2022, https://www.news18.com/news/opinion/upi-cowin-ondc-public-digital-infrastructure-has-put-india-on-the-fast-lane-of-tech-led-growth-5263255.html.

32. Harsh Gupta, 'Dual, Differentiated GST', Mint, 4 August 2009, accessed 30 April 2020, https://www.livemint.com/Opinion/QlE8YWbvLBsuTPHTeFcrMK/Dual-differentiated-GST.html.

33. sadna_gupta@yahoo.com, 'Nehru Press Conference 10 July 1946', India's Constitutional Question—The Cabinet Mission Plan 1946, July 2009, accessed 30 April 2020, https://sites.google.com/site/cabinetmissionplan/nehrupressconference10july1946.

34. John Firth and Ernest Liu, 'Manufacturing Underdevelopment: India's Freight Equalization Scheme, and the Long-run Effects of Distortions on the Geography of Production', July 18, accessed 6 June 2020, http://barrett.dyson.cornell.edu/NEUDC/paper_316.pdf

35. Harsh Gupta, 'Dual, Differentiated GST', Mint, 4 August 2009, accessed 30 April 2020, https://www.livemint.com/Opinion/QlE8YWbvLBsuTPHTeFcrMK/Dual-differentiated-GST.html.

36. Samir Saran, 'Why India Should Sign a Free-Trade Deal with Itself', World Economic Forum, 3 October 2016, accessed 30 April 2020,

https://www.weforum.org/agenda/2016/10/india-free-trade-deal-economic-growth/.

37. PTI, 'Over 1.03 Crore Businesses Registered under GST: Government', *Economic Times*, 9 March 2018, accessed 30 April 2020, https://economictimes.indiatimes.com/news/economy/policy/over-1-03-crore-businesses-registered-under-gst-government/articleshow/63232433.cms.

38. Gireesh Chandra Prasad, 'GST Rate Cuts Now Benefitting Consumers More than before: Survey', *Mint*, 23 April 2019, https://www.livemint.com/politics/policy/gst-rate-cuts-now-benefitting-consumers-ore-than-before-survey-1555993654594.html.

39. Harsh Gupta, 'Dual, Differentiated GST', Livemint, 4 August 2009, accessed 30 April 2020, https://www.livemint.com/Opinion/QlE8YWbvLBsuTPHTeFcrMK/Dual-differentiated-GST.html.

40. D.P. Sengupta and R. Kavita Rao, 'Direct Taxes Code and Taxation of Agricultural Income', *Economic and Political Weekly*, Vol. 47, no. 15 (April 2012), 7–8.

41. Rajeev Mantri and Harsh Gupta, 'The Conclusive Case for School Choice', Livemint, 22 October 2013, accessed 1 May 2020, https://www.livemint.com/Opinion/LI8HU3WD2LsgNO8lPVyhgK/The-conclusive-case-for-school-choice.html.

42. Karthik Muralidharan and Venkatesh Sundararaman, 'The Aggregate Effect of School Choice: Evidence from a Two-Stage Experiment in India', National Bureau of Economic Research, September 2013, accessed 1 May 2020, https://doi.org/10.3386/w19441.

43. Bibek Debroy, 'Haq Centre, Budget for Children and SSA', *Indian Express*, 23 November 2010, accessed 1 May 2020, https://indianexpress.com/article/opinion/web-edits/haq-centre-budget-for-children-and-ssa/.

44. James Tooley, *The Beautiful Tree: A Personal Journey into How the World's Poorest People Are Educating Themselves* (Cato Institute: 2013).

45. 'Review: The Beautiful Tree', *Maxim Institute*, 31 July 2009, https://www.maxim.org.nz/review_the_beautiful_tree/.

46. Greg Forster, 'A Win-Win Solution: The Empirical Evidence on School Choice', Friedman Foundation for Choice, May 2016, accessed 1 May 2020, https://www.edchoice.org/wp-content/uploads/2016/05/2016-5-Win-Win-Solution-WEB.pdf.

47. Parth J. Shah and Corinna Braun-Munzinger, 'Education Vouchers: Global Experience and India's Promise', *Policy Review No. 1,* Centre for Civil Society, February 2006, accessed 1 May 2020, https://ccs. in/education-vouchers-global-experience-and-india-s-promise.

48. Geeta Gandhi Kingdon, 'The Private Schooling Phenomenon in India: A Review', *SSRN*, 26 March 2017, accessed 1 May 2020, https://papers.ssrn.com/abstract=2940602.

49. Tushar Gupta, 'Why Are Government Schools in India Losing Millions of Students Each Year?' *Swarajya*, 29 April 2018, accessed 1 May 2020, https://swarajyamag.com/ideas/why-are-government-schools-in-india-losing-millions-of-students-each-year.

50. Pranab Bardhan, 'Nature of Opposition to Economic Reforms in India', *Economic and Political Weekly*, vol. 40, no. 48 (2005), 4995–98, 26 November 2005, accessed 1 May 2020, https://www.epw.in/journal/2005/48/perspectives/nature-opposition-economic-reforms-india.html.

51. Rajeev Mantri and Shiladitya Sengupta, 'Liberate Higher Education to Compete in the Knowledge Economy', *Mint*, 2 September 2014, accessed 1 May 2020, https://www.livemint.com/Opinion/ZhBn3kjzrDS5wFAUSDhigK/Liberate-higher-education-to-compete-in-the-knowledge-econom.html.

52. 'QS World University Rankings 2020', Top Universities, 5 June 2019, https://www.topuniversities.com/university-rankings/world-university-rankings/2020.

53. Shailendra Mehta, 'Why Is Harvard #1? Governance and the Dominance of US Universities', *SSRN*, 5 April 2012, accessed 1 May 2020, https://papers.ssrn.com/abstract=2039675.

54. Henry Rosovsky, *The University: An Owner's Manual* (W. W. Norton & Company: 1990).

55. Shailendra Mehta, 'Why Is Harvard #1? Governance and the Dominance of US Universities', *SSRN*, 5 April 2012, accessed 1 May 2020, https://papers.ssrn.com/abstract=2039675.

56. 'Bill to Replace UGC, AICTE with Higher Education Commission of India to Be Introduced before Cabinet in October', Firstpost, 25 September 2019, accessed 1 May 2020, https://www.firstpost.com/india/bill-to-replace-ugc-aicte-with-higher-education-commission-of-india-to-be-introduced-before-cabinet-in-october-7400901.html.

57. Achyut Mishra, 'What Is National Medical Commission Bill and Why Doctors Are against It' ThePrint, 1 August 2019, https://theprint. in/theprint-essential/what-is-national-medical-commission-bill-and-why-doctors-are-against-it/270981/.

58. '12% Increase in Indians Studying in the U.S. in 2017', *U.S. Embassy & Consulates in India*, 13 November 2017, https://in.usembassy.gov/u-s-hosts-million-international-students-second-consecutive-year/.

59. 'World University Rankings.' *Times Higher Education (THE)*, 20 August 2019, https://www.timeshighereducation.com/world-university-rankings/2020/world-ranking.

60. 'Innovation's Golden Goose.' *The Economist*. 14 December 2002, accessed 8 June 2020, https://www.economist.com/technology-quarterly/2002/12/14/innovations-golden-goose.

61. 'The Protection and Utilisation of Public Funded Intellectual Property Bill, 2008', *PRSIndia*, 23 January 2009, https://www.prsindia.org/billtrack/the-protection-and-utilisation-of-public-funded-intellectual-property-bill-2008-83.

62. Rajeev Mantri, 'How to Break the Back of India's Left-Wing Ecosystem', Livemint, 22 February 2016, https://www.livemint.com/Opinion/K7BtzvPYmyO0KlDn21iixH/How-to-break-the-back-of-Indias-Leftwing-ecosystem.html.

63. 'Tribute to Santosh Bhattacharyya', *Mainstream Weekly*, http://www.mainstreamweekly.net/article2694.html. Accessed 3 August 2022.

64. Surojit Gupta, 'Intolerance Has Always Existed: Niti Aayog's Bibek Debroy', *Times of India*, 5 November 2015, accessed 1 May 2020, https://timesofindia.indiatimes.com/india/Intolerance-has-always-existed-Niti-Aayogs-Bibek-Debroy/articleshow/49666174.cms.

65. Sanjeev Sanyal, 'The Left Paralysis', *Week*, 21 February 2016, accessed 1 May 2020, https://www.theweek.in/columns/guest-columns/the-left-paralysis.html.

66. Priscilla Jebaraj, 'Higher Education Bill in Winter Session', *The Hindu*, 26 September 2019. *www.thehindu.com*, https://www.thehindu.com/education/higher-education-bill-in-winter-session/article29512512.ece.

67. 'Explained: India's National Education Policy, 2020', *Indian Express*, 31 July 2020, https://indianexpress.com/article/explained/reading-new-education-policy-india-schools-colleges-6531603/.

68. 'How National Education Policy 2020 Is Transforming the Vision for Education in India', *Indian Express*, 29 July 2021, https://indianexpress.com/article/opinion/columns/national-education-policy-nep-2020-transforming-india-7429011/.

69. https://www1.undp.org/content/digital/en/home/stories/building-digital-public-goods--takeaways-from-indias-covid-19-va.html

70. Surjit Bhalla, Karan Bhasin, and Arvind Virmani, 'Pandemic, Poverty, and Inequality: Evidence from India' (April 1, 2022). IMF Working Paper No. 2022/069

71. Gaurav Dalmia, 'Indian Economic Policy: Stimulus, Deficits and Privatisation.' Institute for New Economic Thinking, https://www.ineteconomics.org/perspectives/blog/indian-economic-policy-stimulus-deficits-and-privatization. Accessed 24 August 2022.

72. 'Wait, Watch and Then Respond to COVID-19's Economic Impact: Sanjeev Sanyal, Principal Economic Adviser', *Economic Times*, 7 July 2021, https://economictimes.indiatimes.com/news/economy/policy/wait-watch-and-then-respond-to-covid-19s-economic-impact-sanjeev-sanyal-principal-economic-adviser/articleshow/84196241.cms?from=mdr.

73. Krishna Kant, 'A First in 3 Decades, Retail Inflation in US Higher than India for 4 Months', *Business Standard India*, 15 February 2022, https://www.business-standard.com/article/economy-policy/a-first-in-3-decades-retail-inflation-in-us-higher-than-india-for-4-months-122021500034_1.html

74. Arpit Gupta et al. 'Inequality in India Declined During COVID | NBER.' *NBER*, www.nber.org, 22 December 2021, https://www.nber.org/papers/w29597.

75. 'India's Forex Reserves Remain Fourth Largest Globally, Says RBI Governor', *New Indian Express*, https://www.newindianexpress.com/business/2022/aug/05/indias-forex-reserves-remain-fourth-largest-globally-says-rbi-governor-2484398.html

76. 'RS Sharma Writes: The CoWIN Story Started with the Pandemic, but It Won't End with It', *Indian Express*, 7 June 2022, https://indianexpress.com/article/opinion/columns/the-cowin-story-started-with-the-pandemic-but-it-wont-end-with-it-7956262/.

77. 'Healthcare's Digital Transformation Will Democratise It', *Economic Times*, https://timesofindia.indiatimes.com/india/healthcares-digital-

transformation-will-democratise-it/articleshow/86684331.cms.
Accessed 6 July 2022.

78.   'Toilets Built Under Swachh Bharat Mission' https://pib.gov.in/
pib.gov.in/Pressreleaseshare.aspx?PRID=1797158. Accessed 2 Aug.
2022.

79.   Samyak Pandey, 'In Rural Punjab, Nal Se Jal Has Brought Not Just
Water but Also a Luxury Few Had: "Free Time"', ThePrint, 26 Feb.
2021,   https://theprint.in/india/governance/in-rural-punjab-nal-
se-jal-has-brought-not-just-water-but-also-a-luxury-few-had-free-
time/611647/.

80.   Eric French, et al. 'End-of-Life Medical Expenses.' VoxEU.Org, 22
September 2019, https://voxeu.org/article/end-life-medical-expenses.

81.   Rajeev Mantri and Harsh Gupta, 'Dissolving India's Medical
Guild', *Mint*, 8 October 2016, https://www.livemint.com/Opinion/
sGo3mUKhmXdBMjjtXCu6IM/Dissolving-Indias-medical-guild.
html.

82.   PTI, 'India to Increase Public Health Spending to 2.5% of GDP: PM
Modi', *Economic Times*, 12 December 2018, accessed 2 May 2020,
https://economictimes.indiatimes.com/articleshow/67055735.cms.

83.   'National Medical Commission to Be Set up by February: Health
Ministry', 12 January 2020, https://www.businesstoday.in/current/
economy-politics/national-medical-commission-to-be-set-up-by-
february-health-ministry/story/393659.html. Accessed 9 June 2020.

84.   India Moves from 130 to 129 in Human Development Index:
UNDP Report', *Economic Times*, 9 December 2019, https://
economictimes.indiatimes.com/news/politics-and-nation/india-
moves-from-130-to-129-in-human-development-index-undp-
report/articleshow/72439419.cms

85.   Swagata Yadavar, 'India's Infant Mortality Down 42% in 11 Years
yet Higher Than Global Average', IndiaSpend, 2 June 2019, accessed
2 May 2020, https://www.indiaspend.com/indias-infant-mortality-
down-42-in-11-years-yet-higher-than-global-average/.

86.   *Mortality Rate, under-5 (per 1,000 Live Births) - India | Data*. https://
data.worldbank.org/indicator/SH.DYN.MORT?locations=IN.
Accessed 9 June 2020.

87.   PTI, 'India's Population Grew at 1.2% Average Annual Rate
between 2010 and 2019: UN', *BusinessLine*, 11 April 2019, accessed

2 May 2020, https://www.thehindubusinessline.com/news/indias-population-grew-at-12-average-annual-rate-between-2010-and-2019-un/article26803237.ece.

88. PMJAY Dashboard, accessed 9 June 2020, https://dashboard.pmjay.gov.in/publicdashboard/

89. Hao Yu, 'China's Medical Savings Accounts: An Analysis of the Price Elasticity of Demand for Health Care', *The European Journal of Health Economics*, Vol. 18, no. 6 (July 2017), 773–85. *Springer Link*, doi:10.1007/s10198-016-0827-9.

90. 'If We Must Build a Surveillance State, Let's Do It Properly.' *Bloomberg*, 22 April 2020, https://www.bloomberg.com/opinion/articles/2020-04-22/taiwan-offers-the-best-model-for-coronavirus-data-tracking.

91. Asit Ranjan Mishra and Shreya Nandi, 'Non-Strategic-Sector PSEs to Be Privatized', Livemint, 18 May 2020, https://www.livemint.com/news/india/non-strategic-sector-pses-to-be-privatized-11589743303798.html.

92. 'Yadav Secures Support Against Air India Sell Off', *Telegraph*, 22 August 2000, accessed 9 June 2020 https://www.telegraphindia.com/business/yadav-secures-support-against-air-india-selloff/cid/889484.

93. R. Jagannathan, 'PM Modi Interview 4: On India Inc, Air India Sale and PSU Banks—Why the Government Is Not Coy on Privatisation at All', *Swarajya*, 2 July 2018, accessed 2 May 2020, https://swarajyamag.com/business/modi-on-india-inc-air-india-sale-and-psu-banks-not-coy-on-privatisation-at-all.

94. 'Explained: What Air India Deal Means for the Govt, Tata Group', *Indian Express*, 13 Oct. 2021, https://indianexpress.com/article/explained/explained-what-the-deal-means-for-govt-tatas-7561333/.

95. Shankkar Aiyar, 'State PSUs . . . Zombieland of Taxpayer Monies', BQ Prime, 30 July 2019, accessed 30 June 2022, https://www.bqprime.com/opinion/state-psus-zombieland-of-taxpayer-monies.

96. Rajeev Mantri and Harsh Gupta, 'Why Does India Have 77 Union Ministers?' *Mint*, 12 September 2011, accessed 2 May 2020, https://www.livemint.com/Opinion/rWTfY0rDt3bHdSxevlQ4qK/Views--Why-does-India-have-77-Union-ministers.html.

97. Harsh Gupta, 'Defecting from Anti-Defection.' *Mint*, 7 June 2009, https://www.livemint.com/Opinion/wtY0yGwCtxQ7URWxrlfXpL/Defecting-from-antidefection.html.

98. Sreenivas Janyala, 'Why KCR Wants Concurrent List out: Regional Issues, National Ambitions', *Indian Express*, 17 December 2018, accessed 2 May 2020, https://indianexpress.com/article/explained/why-kcr-wants-concurrent-list-out-regional-issues-national-ambitions-5496560/.

99. 'Economic Survey 2018–19', *IBEF*, accessed 4 May 2020, https://www.ibef.org/economy/economic-survey-2018-19.

100. 'Economic Survey Flags Ballooning Pile of Pending Cases, Says 8,500+ Judges Needed to Clear Backlog', News18, 4 July 2019, https://www.news18.com/news/india/economic-survey-flags-ballooning-pile-of-pending-cases-says-8500-judges-needed-to-clear-backlog-2216877.html.

101. IndiaSpend, 'Story in Numbers: 3 in 4 Prisoners in Indian Jails Await Trial, Shows Data', 4 September 2022, https://www.business-standard.com/article/current-affairs/story-in-numbers-3-in-4-prisoners-in-indian-jails-await-trial-shows-data-122090400914_1.html.

102. CBGA, 'Memorandum to the Fifteenth Finance Commission on Budgeting for the Judiciary in India', IndiaSpend, 24 January 2019, accessed 31 May 2020, http://www.cbgaindia.org/wp-content/uploads/2019/01/Memorandum-on-Budgeting-for-Judiciary-in-India.pdf

103. Mudit Kapoor and Shamika Ravi. 'Performance of the Supreme Court and Tenure of Chief Justices of India: An Observational Analysis (1950 to 2019).' Brookings, 22 October 2019, https://www.brookings.edu/blog/up-front/2019/10/22/performance-of-the-supreme-court-and-tenure-of-chief-justice-of-india-an-observational-analysis-1950-to-2019/.

104. Niranjan Sahoo and Jibran A. Khan, 'Improving India's Justice Delivery System: Why Infrastructure Matters,' *ORF Issue Brief No. 562, July 2022*, Observer Research Foundation.

105. Surya Prakash B.S., 'Examining the Funding Deficit of the Judiciary', *Mint*, 15 December 2016, https://www.livemint.com/Opinion/b1DNafTIUNGtzY3IR8gtbI/Examining-the-funding-deficit-of-the-judiciary.html.

106. Manish Sabharwal, 'Problem Is Wages, Not Jobs; Answer Lies in Formalisation, Financialisation', *Indian Express*, 22 March 2018,

https://indianexpress.com/article/explained/manish-sabharwal-problem-is-wages-not-jobs-minimum-salary-unemployment-indian-gdp-5106348/.

107. 'Vacancy Positions', Department of Justice, Ministry of Law & Justice, Government of India, accessed 4 May 2020, https://doj.gov.in/appointment-of-judges/vacancy-positions.

108. Japnam Bindra, 'With 4 New Judges, SC to Function at Full Strength', *Mint*, 23 September 2019, accessed 5 May 2020, https://www.livemint.com/news/india/four-supreme-court-judges-take-oath-of-office-taking-total-strength-to-34-1569241745278.html.

109. 'Explained | Over 47 Million Cases Pending in Courts: Clogged State of Indian Judiciary.' *The Hindu*, 10 May 2022, https://www.thehindu.com/news/national/indian-judiciary-pendency-data-courts-statistics-explain-judges-ramana-chief-justiceundertrials/article65378182.ece.

110. PTI, 'India Needs over 70,000 Judges to Clear Pending Cases: CJI T.S. Thakur.' *Mint*, 8 May 2016, https://www.livemint.com/Politics/UK7YukMWA4OjoiQw32h1bN/India-needs-over-70000-judges-to-clear-pending-cases-CJI-T.html.

111. Alok Prasanna Kumar, 'How Many Judges Does India Really Need?' *Mint*, 12 July 2016, accessed 5 May 2020, https://www.livemint.com/Politics/3B97SMGhseobYhZ6qpAYoN/How-many-judges-does-India-really-need.html.

112. Gautam Chikermane, 'Supreme Court Embraces AI to Deliver 21st Century Process Reforms.' ORF, https://www.orfonline.org/expert-speak/supreme-court-embraces-ai-to-deliver-21st-century-process-reforms-66417/. Accessed 10 June 2020.

113. Harish Narasappa, 'Capacity in the Judiciary', Daksh, 2 May 2017, accessed 5 May 2020, http://dakshindia.org/capacity-in-the-judiciary/.

114. 'Doing Business 2020: Reforms Boost India's Business Climate Rankings; Among Top Ten Improvers for Third Straight Year', World Bank, 24 October 2019, accessed 6 June 2020, doi:https://www.worldbank.org/en/news/press-release/2019/10/24/doing-business-india-top-10-improver-business-climate-ranking. Accessed 10 June 2020.

115. 'Misallocation in the Market for Inputs: Enforcement and the Organization of Production', *The Quarterly Journal of Economics*, Vol.

135, no. 4 (November 2020), 2007–58, https://doi.org/10.1093/qje/qjaa020

116. Gautam Chikermane and Rishi Agrawal, *Jailed for Doing Business: The 26,134 Imprisonment Clauses in India's Business Laws*, February 2022, Observer Research Foundation.

117. *Action Plan to Reduce Government Litigation | Department of Justice | Ministry of Law & Justice | GoI*, 13 June 2017, accessed 9 June 2020, https://doj.gov.in/page/action-plan-reduce-government-litigation

118. 'Hire Better Public Prosecutors through Exam, Tackle India's Abysmal Conviction Rates', ThePrint, 1 February 2022, https://theprint.in/opinion/hire-better-public-prosecutors-through-exam-tackle-indias-abysmal-conviction-rates/817384/.

119. Sayan Ghosal, 'Why India's Courts Are Struggling to Find Judges', *Business Standard India*, 16 June 2016, https://www.business-standard.com/article/specials/why-india-s-courts-are-struggling-to-find-judges-116061600898_1.html.

120. Aditi Singh, 'Justice Jasti Chelameswar's Lasting Legacy: Striking a Note of Dissent', *Mint*, 18 May 2018, accessed 3 May 2020, https://www.livemint.com/Politics/DsUXbu4j6FweYzZMnD7SAM/Justice-Jasti-Chelameswars-lasting-legacy-striking-a-note.html.

121. 'All You Need to Know about NJAC.' *Mint*, 11 August 2015, https://www.livemint.com/Politics/rcsu24yGQ0frdanyQ9fVVL/All-you-need-to-know-about-NJAC.html.

122. Krishnadas Rajagopal, 'SC Bench Strikes down NJAC Act as "Unconstitutional and Void"', *The Hindu*, 17 Oct. 2015, https://www.thehindu.com/news/national/supreme-court-verdict-on-njac-and-collegium-system/article7769266.ece.

123. Samanwaya Rautray, 'SC Refuses to Reopen Verdicts Which Created Collegium System', *Economic Times*, 7 November 2019, accessed 3 May 2020, https://economictimes.indiatimes.com/news/politics-and-nation/sc-refuses-to-reopen-verdicts-which-created-collegium-system/articleshow/71948708.cms.

124. Makkhan Lal, 'Constitution, Judiciary and the Memories of Congress Rule', 9 July 2018, https://www.vifindia.org/article/2018/july/09/constitution-judiciary-and-the-memories-of-congress-rule

125. Dushyant Dave, 'Chief Justice Is a Man with All the Failings—Dr. Ambedkar on May 24, 1949', *Bar and Bench*, 23 April 2019, accessed

3 May 2020, https://www.barandbench.com/columns/chief-justice-is-a-man-with-all-the-failings-dr-ambedkar.

126. Pradeep Thakur, 'Allahabad HC Judgeship List: It's All in the Family', *Times of India*, 12 March 2018, accessed 3 May 2020, https://timesofindia.indiatimes.com/india/allahabad-hc-judgeship-list-its-all-in-the-family/articleshow/63261443.cms.

127. Pradeep Thakur, 'Government Gives Collegium "Proof" of Nepotism in Picks for Allahabad HC Judges', *Economic Times*, 1 August 2018, https://economictimes.indiatimes.com/news/politics-and-nation/government-gives-collegium-proof-of-nepotism-in-picks-for-allahabad-hc-judges/articleshow/65223203.cms.

128. 'Why Was Lawyer Kin of Then CJI Made High Court Judge, Government Asks Supreme Court', *Indian Express*, 7 May 2015, https://indianexpress.com/article/india/india-others/why-was-lawyer-kin-of-then-cji-made-high-court-judge-government-asks-supreme-court/.

129. 'All in the Family', *Outlook*, 19 September 2016, accessed 3 May 2020, https://www.outlookindia.com/magazine/story/all-in-the-family/297828.

130. 'Every Third HC Judge Is "Uncle"', *Hindustan Times*, 3 May 2014, https://www.hindustantimes.com/punjab/every-third-hc-judge-is-uncle/story-emvLdM8SlnlknyCQ4A7uLM.html.

131. 'Read All That Happened When Supreme Court Heard PIL to Ban "Sardar Jokes"', 30 October 2015, accessed 6 June 2020, https://www.legallyindia.com/views/entry/read-all-that-happened-when-supreme-court-heard-pil-to-ban-sardar-jokes.

132. 'Supreme Court Rejects Kohinoor PIL; States Can't Pass Order on Reclaiming Diamond from Britain', Firstpost, https://www.firstpost.com/india/supreme-court-rejects-kohinoor-pil-states-cant-pass-order-on-reclaiming-diamond-from-britain-3396470.html. Accessed 10 June 2020.

133. 'Do Images on Condom Packets Violate Law? SC Wants to Know', *Indian Express*, 27 April 2016, https://indianexpress.com/article/india/india-news-india/do-images-on-condom-packets-violate-law-supreme-court-wants-to-know-2771955/.

134. 'Bombay High Court Questions Hosting IPL Matches in Drought-Hit State.' Cricinfo, 6 April 2016, http://www.espncricinfo.com/indian-premier-league-2016/content/story/995409.html.

135. 'SC Orders Ban on Sale of Liquor at Shops within 500 Metres of Highways.' *Hindustan Times*, 15 December 2016, https://www.hindustantimes.com/india-news/supreme-court-orders-closure-of-liquor-shops-on-national-state-highways/story-7z6sMkQukzBsfHC2uDLa5J.html.

136. 'River Rafting, Other Water Sports Banned in Uttarakhand, HC Cites Environment, Safety.' *Hindustan Times*, 21 June 2018, https://www.hindustantimes.com/india-news/hc-bans-river-rafting-paragliding-other-water-sports-in-all-uttarakhand-rivers/story-SH027zKqyDAMEmoZGOUwFP.html.

137. Dinsa Sachan, 'Supreme Court Ruling Brings Clinical Trials to a Halt in India', Chemistry World, 15 October 2013, last accessed 2 July 2020, https://www.chemistryworld.com/news/supreme-court-ruling-brings-clinical-trials-to-a-halt-in-india/6690.article.

138. Apoorva Mandhani, 'Supreme Court Squarely to Blame for Economic Slowdown, Says Senior Advocate Harish Salve', ThePrint, 16 September 2019, accessed 3 May 2020, https://theprint.in/india/governance/judiciary/supreme-court-squarely-to-blame-for-economic-slowdown-says-senior-advocate-harish-salve/292115/.

139. M.J. Antony, 'Crowded Corridors of Justice', *Business Standard*, 18 February 2020, accessed 3 May 2020, https://www.business-standard.com/article/opinion/crowded-corridors-of-justice-120021801466_1.html.

140. Ananthakrishnan G., 'National Law Day: Judicial Activism Based on Flawed Premise, Says Arun Jaitley', *Indian Express*, 26 November 2017, accessed 4 May 2020, https://indianexpress.com/article/india/national-law-day-judicial-activism-based-on-flawed-premise-says-arun-jaitley-4954840/.

141. Ashok K.M., '"Step by Step, Brick by Brick, the Edifice of India's Legislature Is Being Destroyed by Judiciary": Finance Minister', 12 May 2016, Livelaw, accessed 4 May 2020, https://www.livelaw.in/step-step-brick-brick-edifice-indias-legislature-destroyed-judiciary-finance-minister/.

142. PTI, 'Unelected People Think They Can Impose Will on Govt through Courts: Harish Salve', 30 May 2020, *Times of India*, https://timesofindia.indiatimes.com/india/unelected-people-

think-they-can-impose-will-on-govt-through-courts-harish-salve/
articleshow/76102563.cms. Accessed 9 June 2020.

143. Krishnadas Rajagopal. 'SC Modifies Order, Says Playing of National Anthem in Cinema Halls Is Not Mandatory.' *The Hindu*, 9 Jan. 2018. *www.thehindu.com*, https://www.thehindu.com/news/national/sc-modifies-order-says-national-anthem-not-mandatory/article22403095.ece.

144. Tribune News Service, 'SC: Should We Wear Patriotism on Sleeves?' *Tribune*, 24 October 2017, accessed 7 June 2020 https://www.tribuneindia.com/news/nation/archive/sc-should-we-wear-patriotism-on-sleeves-486383.

145. 'Section 377 Ruling: What the Judges Said', *New Indian Express*, 7 September 2018, accessed 7 June 2020, https://www.newindianexpress.com/nation/2018/sep/07/section-377-ruling-what-the-judges-said-1868657.html.

146. Rajeev Mantri and Harsh Gupta, 'How Hinduism Got Distorted in the Sabarimala Debate', ThePrint, 10 January 2019, accessed 3 May 2020,

147. PTI, 'Women Activists Express Concern over Acceptance of Supreme Court's Sabarimala Verdict', ThePrint, 28 September 2018, 4 May 2020, https://theprint.in/india/governance/women-activists-express-concern-over-acceptance-of-supreme-courts-sabarimala-verdict/126202/.

148. Kuldeep Kumar, 'Ravan's Fiddle Lives On ...' *The Hindu*, 22 July 2016, accessed 4 May 2020, https://www.thehindu.com/features/metroplus/Ravan%E2%80%99s-fiddle-lives-on%E2%80%A6/article14503093.ece.

149. S, Lekshmi Priya, 'The Legend of Kamakhya: How the Bleeding Goddess Celebrates the "Shakti" Every Woman Has', *Better India*, 2 Sept. 2017, https://www.thebetterindia.com/114044/the-legend-of-kamakhya-temple-assam-bleeding-goddess-assam/.

150. '5 Temples in India Where Men Are Not Allowed', *Times of India*, https://timesofindia.indiatimes.com/travel/destinations/5-temples-in-india-where-men-are-not-allowed/photostory/83956698.cms?picid=83956704. Accessed 1 Oct. 2022.

151. Japnam Kaur Bindra, 'SC Issues Notice on Plea for Entry of Muslim Women into Mosques', Livemint, 17 April 2019, https://www.

livemint.com/politics/news/sc-issues-notice-on-plea-for-entry-of-muslim-women-into-mosques-1555441362136.html.

152. Sanya Dhingra, 'Leprosy No Longer Grounds for Divorce, but a Long Way to Go before Stigma Is Removed', ThePrint, 8 January 2019, accessed 4 May 2020, https://theprint.in/india/governance/leprosy-no-longer-grounds-for-divorce-but-a-long-way-to-go-before-stigma-is-removed/174806/.

153. 'Lok Sabha Clears Bill to Remove Leprosy as Ground for Divorce, Owaisi Says Interference', *Indian Express*, 8 January 2019, accessed 4 May 2020, https://indianexpress.com/article/india/lok-sabha-clears-bill-to-remove-leprosy-as-ground-for-divorce-owaisi-says-interference-5527628/.

154. Dhananjay Mahapatra, 'Can't Interfere in Animal Sacrifice Tradition: Supreme Court', *Times of India*, 28 September 2015, accessed 4 May 2020, https://timesofindia.indiatimes.com/india/Cant-interfere-in-animal-sacrifice-tradition-Supreme-Court/articleshow/49144192.cms.

155. Arihant Pawariya, 'Dahi Handi & Jallikattu: SC's Meddling in Hindu Rituals Is Direct Attack on Freedom of Religion', *Swarajya*, 25 August 2016, accessed 4 May 2020, https://swarajyamag.com/culture/dahi-handi-and-jallikattu-scs-meddling-in-hindu-rituals-is-direct-attack-on-freedom-of-religion.

156. Krishnadas Rajagopal, 'No Jallikattu in Tamil Nadu This Year', *The Hindu*, 12 January 2016, accessed 4 May 2020, https://www.thehindu.com/news/national/No-Jallikattu-in-Tamil-Nadu-this-year/article13995898.ece.

157. Aankhi Ghosh, 'Kesavananda Bharati Judgment: The Major Minority', *Bar and Bench - Indian Legal News*, 29 December 2017, accessed 10 June 2020 https://www.barandbench.com/columns/kesavananda-bharati-basic-structure.

158. Hindol Sengupta, *Recasting India: How Entrepreneurship Is Revolutionizing the World's Largest Democracy* (Palgrave Macmillan: London, 2014).

159. G. G. Mirchandani, *Subverting the Constitution* (Abhinav Publications: New Delhi, 1977).

160. H. M. Seervai, *Constitutional Law of India: A Critical Commentary* (Universal Law Publishing: New Delhi, 2013).

161. 'Shrines to knowledge and wealth', *Financial Times*, 6 September 2004, accessed 9 June 2020, https://www.ft.com/content/2a43a024-002f-11d9-ad31-00000e2511c8.

162. Rajeev Mantri and Harsh Gupta, 'The Kelkar Doctrine: Economic Development as Foreign Policy', *Mint*, 31 December 2012, accessed 2 May 2020, https://www.livemint.com/Opinion/xFNf11XqIob1Spu7CfBBFO/The-Kelkar-Doctrine-Economic-development-as-foreign-policy.html.

163. 'Vajpayee's Biting Criticism, At Age 36, Of Nehru During a Time of War', NDTV, https://www.ndtv.com/opinion/vajpayees-biting-criticism-at-age-36-of-nehru-during-a-time-of-war-1473003. Accessed 2 June 2020.

164. Elizabeth Roche, 'India Could Have Upto Five Theatre Commands: CDS Bipin Rawat', Livemint, 17 February 2020, accessed 3 May 2020, https://www.livemint.com/news/india/india-could-have-upto-five-theatre-commands-cds-bipin-rawat-11581952322682.html.

165. Elizabeth Roche, 'Govt Working to Ensure Funds to Purchase Weapons from Domestic Vendors: Nirmala Sitharaman', Livemint, 9 April 2018, accessed 3 May 2020, https://www.livemint.com/Politics/ZkusN61fbNjP6WqCYHfR7M/Govt-working-to-ensure-funds-to-purchase-weapons-from-domest.html.

166. Ajai Shukla, 'Rajnath Singh Releases Third List of Defence Items Banned for Import', *Business Standard India*, 8 April 2022, https://www.business-standard.com/article/economy-policy/rajnath-singh-releases-third-list-of-defence-items-banned-for-import-122040800032_1.html.

167. Saba Naqvi Bhaumik and Harish Gupta, 'Pokhran Nuclear Tests: BJP Euphoric, Opposition Responds with Stunned Confusion', *India Today*, 1 June 1998, accessed 2 May 2020, https://www.indiatoday.in/magazine/nation/story/19980601-pokhran-nuclear-tests-bjp-euphoric-opposition-responds-with-stunned-confusion-826491-1998-06-01.

168. 'India and the Bomb1', *Frontline*, 16 September 2000, https://frontline.thehindu.com/th-nation/article30255005.ece.

169. Amitav Ghosh, 'Countdown', *New Yorker*, 19 October 1998, accessed 6 June 2020, https://www.newyorker.com/magazine/1998/10/26/countdown-2.

170. Steven Pinker, 'Violence Vanquished', *Wall Street Journal*, 24 September 2011, accessed 2 May 2020, https://www.wsj.com/articles/SB10001424053111904106704576583203589408180.

171. '"No, India Not Sitting on Fence": Jaishankar Says Europe Has to Change Mindset', *Hindustan Times*, 3 June 2022, https://www.hindustantimes.com/india-news/no-india-not-sitting-on-fence-jaishankar-says-europe-has-to-change-mindset-1016542455499431.html.

172. ANI, 'Jaishankar Defends India's Russian Oil Imports, Says Moral Duty to Ensure Best Deal', ThePrint, 17 Aug. 2022, https://theprint.in/world/best-deal-jaishankar-defends-indias-crude-oil-imports-from-russia-2/1085763/.

173. Enrico Moretti, et al., 'The Intellectual Spoils of War: How Government Spending on Defence Research Benefits the Private Sector', VoxEU, 18 December 2019, https://voxeu.org/article/how-government-spending-defence-research-benefits-private-sector.

India's Moment

1.   Rajeev Mantri and Harsh Gupta, 'A Singularity Moment in Indian Politics', *Mint*, 27 May 2014, accessed 5 May 2020, https://www.livemint.com/Opinion/zMOyxiYzBKrf7BpgAqgk2H/A-singularity-moment-in-Indian-politics.html.

2.   Sujata K. Dass, *Atal Bihari Vajpayee* (Kalpaz Publications: New Delhi, 2004).

3.   'It is the human face, not scar face - The Economic Times', 28 July 2004, listed at https://www.ap2231.indianeconomy.columbia.edu/pagee. (text available with the authors).

4.   Arvind Panagariya, 'March to Socialism under Prime Minister Indira Gandhi Offers an Interesting Parallel', *Economic Times*, 24 August 2011, https://economictimes.indiatimes.com/opinion/et-commentary/march-to-socialism-under-prime-minister-indira-gandhi-offers-an-interesting-parallel/articleshow/9715049.cms

5.   'Bharatiya Mahila Bank Launched by Prime Minister of India', Jagranjosh.com, 20 Nov. 2013, https://www.jagranjosh.com/current-affairs/bharatiya-mahila-bank-launched-by-prime-minister-of-india-1384930669-1.

6.   'If The Family Loses This Hand', *Outlook India Magazine*, 28 April 2014, https://www.outlookindia.com/magazine/story/if-the-family-loses-this-hand/290344. Accessed 1 May 2020.

7. Christophe Jaffrelot, 'Silence Speaks More', Carnegie Endowment for International Peace, https://carnegieendowment.org/2013/11/07/silence-speaks-more-pub-53555. Accessed 1 May 2020.

8. Mohammadali Carim Chagla, *Roses in December: An Autobiography* (Bharatiya Vidya Bhavan: Bombay, 1974).

9. Ajay Gudavarthy, 'Debating the Secular-Communal Divide', *The Hindu*, 25 March 2014, https://www.thehindu.com/opinion/lead/debating-the-secularcommunal-divide/article5827168.ece.

10. 'Supreme Court Refers Petition against Sanskrit Prayer in KVs to 5-Judge Bench', *Hindustan Times*, 28 January 2019, https://www.hindustantimes.com/india-news/supreme-court-refers-petition-against-sanskrit-prayer-in-kvs-to-5-judge-bench/story-6OfSl9xi52pT1lfJzDOoOI.html.

11. 'Need to Dream of an India with a $20 Trillion Economy, says PM Modi', *Economic Times*, 17 January 2015. https://economictimes.indiatimes.com/news/economy/policy/economic-times-global-business-summit-need-to-dream-of-an-india-with-a-20-trillion-economy-says-pm-modi/articleshow/45917600.cms.

12. 'India Is a Nation of Unfulfilled Greatness – Lee Kuan Yew', Belfer Center for Science and International Affairs, https://www.belfercenter.org/publication/india-nation-unfulfilled-greatness. Accessed 1 May 2020.

13. Munro, Ross H. 'India: The Awakening of An Asian Power,' *Time*, 3 April 1989, content.time.com, https://content.time.com/time/subscriber/article/0,33009,957371,00.html.

14. 'Naga Accord Is Nearly Final: No Change in State Boundary, Removal of AFSPA, Flag Last Hurdle', *Indian Express*, 26 April 2018, https://indianexpress.com/article/india/naga-accord-is-nearly-final-no-change-in-state-boundary-removal-of-afspa-flag-last-hurdle-pm-modi-5152058/.

15. Sushanto Talukdar, 'The Third Bodo Accord: A New Deal', *Frontline*, 28 February 2020, https://frontline.thehindu.com/the-nation/article30800941.ece. Accessed 8 June 2020.

16. 'India, Bangladesh Sign Historic Land Boundary Agreement', *Reuters*, 6 June 2015, https://in.reuters.com/article/bangladesh-india-land-treaty-idINKBN0OM0IV20150606.

17. Samuel Phillips Huntington, *American Politics: The Promise of Disharmony* (Belknap Press: Cambridge, US, 1982).

18. 'Vajpayee's Pep Pill.' *Outlook India Magazine*, 11 May 1998.

19. Ramachandra Guha, 'Ten Reasons Why India Will Not and Must Not Become a Superpower', Irving K. Barber Learning Centre, 30 April 2010. https://ikblc.ubc.ca/ramachandra-guha-ten-reasons-why-india-will-not-and-must-not-become-a-superpower/. Accessed 1 May 2020.

20. 'The Source of सर्वे भवन्तु सुखनि:—sarve bhavantu sukhinaḥ by @Sampadananda https://j.mp/2UpngdX', Twitter, https://twitter.com/bibekdebroy/status/1246626285964521473. Accessed 8 June 2020; Sarve Bhavantu Sukhinah, Sarve Santu Niramayah ॐ सर्वे भवन्तु सुखनि:सर्वे सन्तु निरामयाः।. https://www.speakingtree.in/blog/sarve-bhavantu-sukhinah-sarve-santu-niramayah. Accessed 8 June 2020.

Index